COMMON GROUND

David M. Sofian

January 28, 1998

COMMON GROUND

THE WEEKLY TORAH PORTION THROUGH THE EYES OF A CONSERVATIVE, ORTHODOX, AND REFORM RABBI

SHAMMAI ENGELMAYER, JOSEPH S. OZAROWSKI, AND DAVID M. SOFIAN

edited and with an introduction by
STEVE LIPMAN

JASON ARONSON INC.
Northvale, New Jersey
Jerusalem

This book was set in 11 pt. Stempel Garamond by Alabama Book Composition of Deatsville, Alabama.

Library of Congress Cataloging-in-Publication Data

Engelmayer, Shammai.
    Common ground : the weekly Torah portion through the eyes of a
Conservative, Orthodox, and Reform rabbi / by Steve Lipman, ed. ;
Shammai Engelmayer, Joseph Ozarowski, David Sofian.
        p.   cm.
    ISBN 0-7657-5992-6 (alk. paper)
    1. Bible.   O.T.   Pentateuch—Commentaries.   I. Lipman, Steve.
II. Ozarowski, Joseph S.   III. Sofian, David.   IV. Title.
BS1225.3.E56 1997
222'.107—dc21   97–13609

Manufactured in the United States of America. Jason Aronson Inc. offers books and cassettes. For information and catalog write to Jason Aronson Inc., 230 Livingston Street, Northvale, New Jersey 07647.

Contents

Introduction vii

B'REISHIT/GENESIS 1
B'reishit: Genesis 1:1–6:8 3
Noah: Genesis 6:9–11:32 9
Lech Lecha: Genesis 12:1–17:27 14
VaYera: Genesis 18:1–22:24 20
Chaye Sarah: Genesis 23:1–25:18 26
Toldot: Genesis 25:19–28:9 31
Va'Yetze: Genesis 28:10–32:3 40
Va'Yishlach: Genesis 32:4–36:43 46
Va'Yeshev: Genesis 37:1–40:23 52
Miketz: Genesis 41:1–44:17 59
Va'Yigash: Genesis 44:18–47:27 67
Va'Yechi: Genesis 47:28–50:26 75

SHMOT/EXODUS 81
Shmot: Exodus 1:1–6:1 83
Va'Era: Exodus 6:2–9:35 89
Bo: Exodus 10:1–13:16 98
Beshalach: Exodus 13:17–17:16 106
Yitro: Exodus 18:1–20:23 114
Mishpatim: Exodus 21:1–24:18 121
Trumah: Exodus 25:1–27:19 130
Tetzaveh: Exodus 27:20–30:10 137
Ki Tisa: Exodus 30:11–34:35 145
VaYakhel: Exodus 35:1–38:20 154
Pekudei: Exodus 38:21–40:38 161

VAYIKRA/LEVITICUS 169
Vayikra: Leviticus 1:1–5:26 171
Tzav: Leviticus 6:1–8:36 178
Shmini: Leviticus 9:1–11:47 184
Tazria: Leviticus 12:1–13:59 191
Mtzora: Leviticus 14:1–15:33 196
Acherei Mot: Leviticus 16:1–18:30 202
Kedoshim: Leviticus 19:1–20:27 209
Emor: Leviticus 21:1–24:23 215
B'Har: Leviticus 25:1–26:2 221
B'Chukotai: Leviticus 26:3–27:34 227

BAMIDBAR/NUMBERS 233
Bamidbar: Numbers 1:1–4:20 235
Naso: Numbers 4:21–7:89 240
Beha'alotecha: Numbers 8:1–12:16 247
Shelach Lecha: Numbers 13:1–15:41 255
Korach: Numbers 16:1–18:32 262
Chukat: Numbers 19:1–22:1 268
Balak: Numbers 22:2–25:9 278
Pinchas: Numbers 25:10–30:1 287
Matot: Numbers 30:2–32:42 296
Masei: Numbers 33:1–36:13 305

D'VARIM/DEUTERONOMY 313
D'varim: Deuteronomy 1:1–3:22 315
Va'etchanan: Deuteronomy 3:23–7:11 321
Ekev: Deuteronomy 7:12–11:25 330
R'eih: Deuteronomy 11:26–16:17 337
Shoftim: Deuteronomy 16:18–21:9 343
Ki Tetze: Deuteronomy 21:10–25:19 351
Ki Tavo: Deuteronomy 26:1–29:8 358
Netzavim: Deuteronomy 29:9–30:20 364
Va'yelech: Deuteronomy 31:1–30 371
Ha'azinu: Deuteronomy 32:1–52 376
V'zot Ha'beracha: Deuteronomy 33:1–34:12 383

Introduction

Steve Lipman

This book is the result of an ancient principle and modern technology.

First, the ancient principle—a statement in the Midrash, the collection of millennia-old supra-biblical tales and rabbinic interpretations—that there are "seventy faces to the Torah." In other words, each word and verse in the Hebrew Bible can be viewed in a myriad of ways that differ completely from, and often contradict, each other and are all equally valid. Seventy is an allegorical figure, not strictly limited to that amount, which had significance in the Bible, including the traditional number of the ancient world's nations and world views.

This multi-faceted outlook—that the Torah, like a sparkling diamond, reflects and refracts light in an infinite number of illuminating ways—is the foundation of countless scholarly commentaries that have been written about Torah, our spiritual source of light, in every generation from ancient Mount Sinai until today. According to one authority, a certain act or statement in the Torah has one meaning, while another knowledgeable scholar may offer exactly the opposite meaning.

Torah, not bound by our finite powers of understanding, can accept both as valid. There is more than one spiritual path to Judaism's truth, more than one physical path of correct conduct.

These paths are united by the "Common Ground" they share—recognition of the central role Torah plays in a Jew's life. That common ground unites the authors of this book, who represent the major denominational divisions of Judaism.

Nearly two decades ago, when I began a personal quest to study and understand *Chumash*, The Five Books of Moses, I became intrigued by the seemingly infinite number of commentators who offered explanations that were internally consistent yet diametrically at odds with colleagues' equally well-reasoned explanations. On a practical level, I realized that this apparent dissonance epitomized how observant Jews, absolutely committed to Jewish tradition and practice, could respectfully expound laws and philosophies that appeared to contradict those put forward by their partners-in-*Yiddishkeit*.

For example, classical scholars disagree over the opening word in the Ten Commandments. Does the word "I"—*anochi* in Hebrew—constitute a commandment of belief or simply a declaration of identity?

Maimonides considers the phrase introduced by *anochi*, "I am the Lord your God, who brought you out of the land of Egypt, out of the house of bondage," to be a positive mitzvah: The first *mitzvah* is that He commanded us to believe in the Deity, that is, that we believe that there is a cause and motive force behind all existing things. This idea is expressed in the statement, "I am the Lord your God."

However, Don Isaac Abarbenel, a fifteenth-century philosopher and community leader in Spain, disagrees. He states that the Decalogue's introductory phrase

> . . . constitutes no commandment, either dogmatic or practical, but is merely a preface to the subsequent commandments and injunctions, a declaration making known to the Children of Israel, Who was addressing them.

Similarly, there are conflicting interpretations of the Israelites' construction of the golden calf in the wilderness. While in one place the Talmud declares that, "by worshipping the calf the Israelites indicated that they accepted idolatry," many commentators view the act differently. They say that the newly freed slaves, longing for the return of Moses from the heights of Mount Sinai, built the calf as an intermediary to the Lord, in Whom they had never lost faith.

Rabbi Samson Raphael Hirsch, a leader of nineteenth-century German Jewry, writes that the Israelites' desire for "gods that shall go before us" shows "clearly that here it is not a case of idolatry in the usual sense, not a turning away from God. That which Aaron was to make was not to take the place of God, but of Moses."

The Torah's philosophic and halakhic works are packed with such apparent contradictions. This realization gave my fledgling studies added incentive; my simple explanations, apparently at variance with those of the masters, might have some worth. Guided by rabbis who pointed out where my—or others'—interpretations clashed with established norms of Jewish belief or behavior, I pressed forward with my individual quest, which eventually expanded.

This is where modern technology—the fax—came in.

In my ongoing program of trying to understand the Torah's mystical and linguistic mysteries, I shared my questions about the week's Torah portion with some like-minded journalistic colleagues at my office. In time, I began to send a printout of the questions to a select circle of rabbinic advisors and interested friends. We traded opinions and insights through the mail, in person, or by phone. But it was the fax—and more recently, electronic mail—that turned a trickle of comments into a weekly flood of exchanged messages, replete with tentative answers, respectful critiques, and appreciated suggestions for further research.

Given enough time, we can modify and fine tune a theory, electronically sending each other copies of original rabbinic sources, until it assumes a credible shape.

While I am an Orthodox Jew, I am open to the insights of my friends—all more learned than I in the homiletic skills—from every so-called branch of Judaism. I say so-called, because the Torah does not divide the Jewish people into branches, denominations, or camps, other than the 12 tribes descended from Jacob's sons. For 2,000 years, since the destruction of the Second Temple in Jerusalem and the dispersion of the tribes to the four corners of the world, the distinction among Kohen, Levi, and Yisrael, descendants of whose tribes are the only ones universally recognized by Judaism, is the only Jewish division still intact.

I take to heart the philosophy of ben Zoma in *Ethics of the Fathers*: "Who is wise? The one who learns from every person." I am wise enough to realize how much I have left to learn—from everyone.

While disagreeing respectfully with some fundamental interpretations of basic Jewish thought held by friends who identify themselves as Reform, Conservative, Reconstructionist, or other labels on the ideological spectrum, I can legitimately gain insight from their teachings. While finding their positions on Jewish observance inconsistent with traditional Jewish belief, I can respect their sincerity and commitment to Jewish peoplehood.

In short, I can maintain my allegiance to traditional interpretation of scriptures, disagreement over which has caused a lamentable schism between the Orthodox and non-Orthodox, while civilly discussing that which we share—a belief in the Torah's centrality to Jewish life. Hence this book. Hence this title. The "Common Ground" we share is holy ground. It has been my good fortune over the years to find men and women whose interest in Torah study transcended their respective denominational labels.

My network of Orthodox friends, which started with Rabbi Joseph Ozarowski, spiritual leader of a synagogue in a New York suburb, quickly grew to include such non-Orthodox friends as Shammai Engelmayer, who had earlier served as editor of the newspaper where I have worked as a reporter for 13 years. He now heads a growing Conservative congregation in New Jersey.

Interested in further expanding my ideological circle of scholars, it was natural for me to seek out someone in the Reform movement, who turned out to be Rabbi David Sofian, a pulpit rabbi in Chicago. My communication with Rabbi Sofian has been, so far, limited to fax and phone. I have looked forward to his weekly faxed answers, and I find them to be as clear and trenchant as those offered by the Orthodox rabbis in whose company I usually find myself.

A published collection of our questions and answers seemed a logical step.

None of the rabbis in these pages write continuously from a strictly doctrinaire point of view. The only perspective they share is that there is no purely Reform, Conservative, or Orthodox perspective. Rabbi Sofian rarely turns to Reform or non-Jewish scholars to buttress his interpretations, and Rabbi Ozarowski's answers are not limited only to sources that reflect "Orthodox" thinking.

In offering this book to the public, I do not suggest that any answers, let alone questions, are necessarily exhaustive or definitive. Torah is too deep and too complex to be limited to any single set of interpretations, no matter how novel we may believe them to be. Every year, as I begin my cycle of studying the weekly Torah portion after Simchat Torah, I find many questions and possible answers that totally escaped my notice in previous years. I also find that interpretations, which I once considered particularly deep and analytically watertight, seem, in the light of another year's study, superficial and waterlogged.

But, my interest never wanes.

As a *ba'al teshuvah*, a veteran newcomer to an observant lifestyle, my greatest religious joy comes from opening up my shelves full of commentaries on parshah—the 54 portions into which The Five Books of Moses, from Genesis to Deuteronomy, the creation of the world to the death of Moses, are divided. One word—missing, repeated, or out of context—or a single letter may yield a profound foundation about God or human nature that a casual reading of the text would not suggest.

I initiate my own study during the week before a particular parshah is to be read during Saturday morning services in synagogue. This practice of reading, or chanting—*leining* in Yiddish—a section of the Torah from a handwritten scroll in public, in *shul*, each week has ancient roots. From the biblical command to assemble the people at the end of every 7 years and read the Law "in their hearing" grew the tradition, dating back at least to the first half of the third century B.C.E., of a reading on the Sabbath, festivals, and new moons. Smaller excerpts are read on Mondays and Thursdays.

According to the Babylonian Talmud, the entire Torah was read—often taught and translated in the vernacular—in one year's Sabbaths in Babylonia and other diaspora communities, while an annual 3-year cycle of 153, 155, or 167 divisions was followed in Palestine. In time, the former practice was universally accepted. This is the case today, despite unsuccessful attempts by some Reform congregations in the United States and Germany to reintroduce the triennial cycle in the 1800s.

The reading of each parshah—referred to as a *sidrah* in Sephardic circles—is supplemented by the *Haftarah* (literally, the "addition"), a related selection from one of the prophetical books. This practice is suggested by the Mishnah, the original compilation of Oral Law.

Ashkenazic and Sephardic congregations sometimes have different *Haftarot*. In both communities, the year's cycle ends and begins on Simchat Torah, following the Succot holiday.

Each parshah is commonly identified by the first—or one of the first—key word or words. For instance, *Parshat VaYera*, the fourth parshah in Genesis, which begins, *VaYera HaShem*, "And God appeared (*era*) to Avraham. . . ." Although Ashkenazim and Sephardim have different pronunciations for many Hebrew words, including the name of *parashiot* (*B'reishis* or *B'reishit*, *Yisro* or *Yitro*), I have chosen here the latter Sephardic variation, which is prevalent in contemporary Israel. For the sake of readers who lack a comprehensive Jewish background, I have included the Hebrew (*B'reishit*, *Shmot*, etc.) and English (Genesis, Exodus, etc.) names for the individual names of The Five Books of Torah.

Because the number of weeks in a year usually exceeds the total of *parshiot*—except for leap years, when an extra month is added to the Hebrew calendar and the number of Sabbaths is 55—some portions are normally doubled, read together on the Sabbath, dependent on the occurrence of holidays that fall on the seventh day and whose own biblical readings supersede the Sabbath's.

For me, a Saturday morning on which I have not worked out a satisfactory answer to the week's main question is an incomplete Sabbath.

My advice—to fully appreciate each question and its answers, first read the question posed for each week's parshah, then close the book. Try to answer the question yourself, or with friends, before turning to the three contributors' answers. If you have a *Chumash* available, preferably with commentaries, in English, Hebrew, or any other preferred language, look up the cited passages—see if the question makes sense to you. Then open the book again; compare your answer with the rabbis'. Save your notes to refer to in future years.

I learned in *yeshiva* that one of the most effective ways to study the Torah is to examine the commentaries of Rashi (an acronym for Rabbi Shlomo ben Yitzchak), the eleventh-century French scholar whose interpretations of the Written Law and Oral Law are considered the clearest, most fundamental, and most ubiquitous learning tools. His Torah commentaries are readily available in English.

You can understand the Torah by understanding "what bothered Rashi." What unanswered question was he trying to answer? Why did he make a comment on an apparently self-understood word or phrase? What did he read between the lines that we don't?

Rashi made a comment on the Torah only if he deemed something missing or murky; his comments are deceptively profound—comprehensive commentaries are available on his commentaries. Simply understanding Rashi's reason—or other commentators', if your interest in advanced knowledge grows—is a good first step toward understanding the Torah itself.

Look for your own questions. Any question, no matter how primary you may consider it, is worthwhile. Your ability to ask questions will inevitably aid your skill in answering them. You needn't be an expert to attempt an answer. God tells Moses that "*lo b'shamayim he*"—"the Torah is not in the Heavens"; its sphere is the Earth, accessible and available to anyone who seeks his or her share in it. The tools are also down here, in our probing minds.

The Torah is an open book. It is written cryptically, with historical lacunas and unclear allusions, to encourage our intellectual involvement. If you're stumped, don't despair. Even the greatest commentators, scholars of unquestionable erudition, sometimes confessed that the meaning of a phrase or passage was inexplicable.

I am not a scholar. My Hebrew and Aramaic skills are quite primitive. Most of my reference books are in English, translations from the original—usually—Semitic languages. But that handicap has not prevented me from finding questions—and sometimes answers—that I think can withstand critical analysis.

If you are a newcomer to Torah study, don't strive for complicated answers—or for any answer. I repeat: Just look for questions. In the *Haggadah*'s story of the four sons, who represent spiritual levels of the Jewish people, the lowest rung is the *aino yodai'ah*—"the one who is not able to ask"—the one who is farthest removed from Jewish tradition.

Rabbi Simcha Bunim of Pshischa, an early Chasidic leader, led his disciples on a walk one day. He pointed to a group of Jews engaged in conversation and stated, "Do you see those Jews over there? They are dead." He explained to his puzzled chasidim, "They are dead because they have stopped asking questions and searching for answers."

One chasid was particularly upset by his rebbe's answer. Finally, he approached Rabbi Bunim and asked, "Rebbe, how do I know that I am not dead?"

The rabbi turned to his disciple and smiled. "Because," he said, "you asked."

The Torah teaches that a good question is as valuable as an answer. That ancient principle is still contemporary today. As contemporary as the fax.

Shammai Engelmayer

Many years ago, while I was managing editor of *The New York Jewish Week*, a troubling thought occurred to me regarding the weekly Torah commentary we published. It was written by a modern Orthodox rabbi and represented his views and those of his brand of Orthodoxy. Yet Orthodoxy is not monolithic. It is not a "movement," as is Conservative or Reform, but a rubric under which are found many movements, each with its unique approach to "Torah Judaism" and each laying claim to authenticity. How, I wondered, could we continue to publish this column as representative of Orthodoxy as a whole?

Clearly, we could not, but we also could not do two other things: We could neither drop the column (Torah study belongs in a Jewish newspaper), nor open it up to the myriad of opinions and views of Orthodox Judaism (there simply was not enough room).

I was stymied and decided to leave things the way they were for a while, hoping for a flash of inspiration that would solve the "problem," if indeed that was the problem.

As it turned out, it was not the real problem. I discovered this when a representative of the Reform movement came to visit our offices with a complaint. The *Jewish Week*, he said, was an Orthodox newspaper and presented the Orthodox view. The rest of the community was ill-served, he said.

It was a startling comment, especially considering that both the publisher and I were Conservative, not Orthodox, and we thought we were producing a newspaper that addressed the entire community, not just one segment of it. We could even point to the articles we had published and the issues we had addressed as proof.

Our visitor, however, was not buying our defense. The real proof of our orientation, he said, was in the Torah column. It represented only one point of view—the "Orthodox." Non-Orthodox opinion need not apply. That colored the rest of the newspaper, he insisted.

My eyes opened. Suddenly, I realized why I had not been able to solve my own problem with the column. It was not that the column failed to reflect all of Orthodoxy, but all of religious Judaism. There were other approaches to Torah; other lessons to be learned; other messages to be heard. What was needed was a column that alternated between the streams, allowing different voices to speak and enabling the reader to see that Torah is not the exclusive domain of any one brand of religious philosophy.

It was so obvious, I had to wonder why I failed to see it until then. Thinking about it, I understood why: I was Conservative by orientation and traditional by philosophy (best summed up as religious Judaism that is allowed to evolve from within the halakhic system), but Orthodox in training and, admittedly, inclination. Unconsciously or otherwise, I personally believed that the Conservative and Reform approaches to the Torah were not authentic because they viewed the Torah not as the legitimate revealed word of God, but as the product of man's imagination, albeit perhaps inspired by God.

On the other hand, to me, the Torah was nothing less than God's word, even if it was not dictated to *Moshe Rabbeinu* (Moses, our Teacher) in the exact form we have it today. (Obviously, my approach was not Orthodox, either. To the Orthodox, there is no question but that every word was dictated to Moshe by God. Not even many of the rabbis of the Talmud or the commentators who followed them believed that. Also, I believe that the truths in the Torah are different for each generation; as understanding of the world deepens, so does our understanding of what the Torah has to say.)

The more I thought about what the man had said, the more I realized that I was so conceited and arrogant in my own beliefs, that I missed the whole point. God had crafted the Torah the way He had crafted His entire message at Sinai. Tradition tells us that God spoke to each person at Sinai in his or her own language, meaning that He spoke to each person in a way that she or he could best understand Him.

Not only does the Torah contain different truths for each generation, but for each person within each generation. Merely because the Conservative and Reform approaches differed from mine, as much as mine differed from the Orthodox, did not mean that what they had to say was less valid, or less authentic.

Thus was born a new Torah column in *The Jewish Week*—"A Sabbath Week" (the name was given to it by one of its three contributors, Rabbi Gershon Cohen z"l [*zichrono livracha*, may his memory be for a blessing], at the time the chancellor of The Jewish Theological Seminary of America). Our readers would be exposed to different truths each week, coming from uniquely different perspectives. The message of the Torah would finally be heard in a variety of its voices.

When Steve Lipman approached me about doing this volume, I jumped at the opportunity. This book would go that column one better and do what space considerations would not permit in a newspaper setting. Three voices would be heard at the same time, addressing the same issues. Three truths about the Torah would be revealed side by side, rather than one alternating truth each week.

I could only hope that what I had to say was as relevant, as cogent, and as inspired by God as my Orthodox and Reform co-authors.

I have not read what my co-authors have written. That was part of the plan for this volume; we did not want to be influenced in any way by the other's opinions to the point where we would be responding to what we thought each other might say rather than to the questions of the week. Thus, I cannot speak to their approach to the text, only of mine. I can only say that their approaches are as legitimate as mine and as valid.

My answers are based on an assumption: What the Torah says is what the Torah means (although the meaning, at times, may be metaphorical). If God says He made a mistake in creating the human race, as He does in *parshat Noach*, I accept God at His word (although I do not begin to pretend to know what that means in the context of God other than to know that it is light years away from what it means in the context of human error; to assert that God can make a mistake as humans do is to impose yet another unwarranted anthropomorphism on Him). When we are told that Ya'akov (the patriarch Jacob) did nasty things as a youth and a young adult, I believe that Ya'akov did those nasty things (part of what the Torah is trying to tell us, as I see it, is that each of us has the capacity to rise above our baser natures).

My approach will surely anger some and amuse others. If, in the process, I help the reader to come nearer to the Torah and its truths, if I help give the reader a deeper appreciation for and commitment to a "Torah way of life," as each stream defines that term, my contributions will have achieved their purpose.

If, at the same time, the three of us by our contributions help to bring greater understanding and tolerance among Judaism's fractious religious streams, then we will have done God's work.

Finally, there are six more personal reasons why I agreed to contribute to this book, and an unknown number of reasons equally personal. The six known reasons are Shifra Cohen, Arielle Engelmayer, Zachary Cohen, Talia Engelmayer, Nurit Engelmayer, and Zvi Hirsch Cohen, the six grandchildren God has blessed me with to date. Being only 51 years old, I hope to have the *zechut* to meet my grandchildren and great-grandchildren yet unborn (hence my unknown number of personal reasons). I wrote my entries as much with them in mind as with the reader. I wanted to convey to them my love of Torah, the people to whom it was given and, above all, the God whose words these are. I wanted to pass on to them what I hope is my genuine commitment to *klal Yisrael* and to our continued evolution into His nation of priests, His holy nation.

Most important, I wanted to inspire them to study, to learn, and to pass on their love of Torah, of their people, and of their God to their children, grandchildren, and great-grandchildren.

It is to them—Shifra, Arielle, Zachary, Talia, Nurit, and Zvi, and to their siblings, cousins, children, grandchildren, and great-grandchildren yet to come—that I dedicate my contributions to this volume. May they live Torah-true lives (however each eventually defines the term) and may they live those lives under the guiding hand of a *Mashiach* (Messiah) who has tarried long enough.

Joseph Ozarowski

It has been my joy to share Torah by fax with Steve Lipman over the years. His incisive questions have stimulated much discussion in our family and congregation and provided a wonderful basis for many a deep and animated conversation. They also gave me the opportunity to research and study Torah issues through the eyes of the great commentators, including early rabbinic, medieval, and modern ones.

I am delighted that his format, through this book, will see a wider audience and hopefully help a diverse Jewish people find meaning and stimulation in the pleasure, enrichment, and spiritual inspiration of our eternal Torah.

We often used the faxed *sidrah* questions as the foundations for *Divrei Torah* over our Shabbat table. I especially want to thank my dear family—my wife Ashira, and my children Eli, Shalom, Chani, and little Raphi—for their insight and sharing. Their thoughts are frequently reflected through my portion of this work.

We also used Steve's questions as the basis for my weekly Shabbat afternoon *Chumash Shiur* (Torah Study class), at the Elmont Jewish Center in Elmont, N.Y., during the year of 5755/1994–95. I want to thank the regulars and semi-regulars of this group for their participation: Israel Halpert, Dr. Leslie (Henech) Weinstein, Phil Neiman, Leo Karpfen, Harry Azriel Pasternak, Milt Reitzfeld, Willie Reitzfeld, Seymour Daiches, Seymour Kaye, Arnie Bolnick, Sam Goldman, and Al Rosenberg. Their responses, opinions, and ideas are included throughout this work. They have enriched me as well.

Finally, I offer my thanks to the *Ribbono Shel Olam*, the Almighty, who has given our people the gift of the Torah, granted me the personal strength of mind and body to study it myself, and allowed me to teach it to others.

David Sofian

A fortunate day occurred nearly 17 years ago, when I met Rabbi Joseph Ozarowski. I was soon to become the rabbi of Congregation Shaarai Shomayim in Lancaster, Pa., and Joe was the rabbi of Congregation Degel Israel in the same town.

Due to similar interests and to our children being the same age, we began a precious friendship. Our paths later diverged as our careers took us to different locations. As I understand it, it was Joe who suggested to Steve Lipman that I be included in this project.

Even though Joe and I represent different streams within the contemporary American Jewish scene, and often have different points of view, I treasure our relationship and have always been stimulated to additional learning as a result of it. I am grateful to him and to Steve for this opportunity to learn still further by participating in this project.

I am also grateful to Steve Lipman's study format used in this book. His challenging questions caused me to think in new ways as I discovered fresh insights in the traditional materials I turned to. Discovering the sources and learning about the history of the Torah's development is interesting. However, I have always felt that the most fruitful Jewish approach to Torah study begins by learning to see the Torah through the eyes of the rabbis and their works. This is why in virtually every one of my answers, traditional rabbinic material is discussed extensively.

This form of learning went beyond me in that the parshah questions often served as the basis for discussion in my weekly adult Torah study class, which is part of our religious school at Emanuel Congregation of Chicago. If the questions asked and the answers given stimulate others as they already have here, I believe the project will have accomplished its goal.

My assumption, based on the nature of the questions asked, has been that this book is aimed at Jews who are prepared to study the Torah above the beginning level. In my answers, while striving to be brief, I tried to offer something relevant to this audience and at the same time not be too technical for readers earlier in the process of serious Torah study. I must thank my wife, Dr. Simone L. Sofian, who was very helpful in this regard. Her broad knowledge of Judaism, Hebrew, and commitment to Jewish life made her a perfect test case for my responses.

Working on this project has demonstrated to me once again the wisdom of this passage from the Siddur. *Ash-rey-nu, mah tov khel-kei-nu, u-mah na-eem go-ra-lei-nu, u-mah ya-fah y'ru-sha-tei-nu.* Indeed, how greatly we are blessed, how good is our portion, how pleasant our lot, and how beautiful our heritage!

B'reishit/Genesis

B'reishit: Genesis 1:1–6:8

Prophetical Reading
Isaiah 42:5–43:10

Overview of Torah Portion

God creates heaven and earth in six days and rests on the seventh. Influenced by the serpent, Eve eats from the forbidden Tree of the Knowledge of Good and Evil and convinces Adam to do the same. They are expelled from the Garden of Eden. Their first son, Cain, kills his younger brother, Abel, and is condemned to exile from God's presence. Disgusted by mankind's wickedness, God considers destroying all living creatures.

Key Verses

"And the Lord God planted a garden eastward, in Eden; and there He put the man whom He had formed. And out of the ground the Lord God made to grow every tree that is pleasant to the sight and good for food" (Genesis 2:8–9).

Discussion Question

MAN AND NATURE: A basic principle of Judaism is that we don't rely on miracles; our human efforts are our obligation, and the predictable laws of nature our guide. Yet Adam begins his life in a fully developed garden. Why was he not given some seeds and a shovel? If he needed to eat, would a minimal amount of trees and vegetation not suffice? What does a full garden imply about man's relation to God and the world?

Shammai Engelmayer

In the beginning, God created a completely different world than the one in which we live. It was a perfect world, in which humankind would want for nothing. It was also an unreal world because it was so perfect that humankind had virtually nothing to do; thus, the only thing that could not grow in the Garden of Eden was the human spirit.

Adam was born with a shovel; the question errs on this point. It was his job (and the job of those who would follow him, meaning us) to tend the garden, to be the steward of creation, and to care for the property of the landlord. But only minimal effort was needed. The garden could practically take care of itself. Food was abundant; the relationship between humankind and the lesser creatures was friendly, nurturing, and cooperative; and the climate was regulated. If necessity is the mother of invention, nothing was needed in the garden that could spark the creative spirit in humans.

God knew that; after all, it was He who created the human being. He also understood human nature. If He hadn't created the perfect world, and then taken it away, He would have given humankind nothing for which to strive. The garden was thus a necessary prelude to real life.

But what was it that was taken away? Not the garden itself, but what it represented: perfection. It is that for which we strive in our lives, yet it always remains just out of reach. If things are bad, they can be improved. If they are good, they can be bettered. Perfection is the carrot at the end of the stick; no matter how close we get to it, it's always just a little farther away.

On the other hand, God knew that He could not simply put humanity on this earth and expect it to fend for itself. Human nature is selfish in the extreme. The human being would do just enough to satisfy immediate, personal needs. The broader world would be on its own. The human would have God as the example: If God had wanted the broader world included in the picture, he would have created a different kind of existence for humanity, one in which everyone's needs were cared for. Because He did not do so, individual humans need not do so, either.

So God created the perfect world, both as an answer to those who would engage in selfish rationalizations and to provide humanity with the ultimate goal: To recreate the Garden of Eden in the real world.

Sadly, too many humans spend less time seeking the perfection of the Garden of Eden than in making excuses for why they cannot, or should not, be involved in assisting the less fortunate. We have created a whole system of such excuses, from "survival of the fittest," to "look out for number one" and "me first." The more money we make, the more we want to make and the less interested we are in sharing. As for the rest of God's Creation— animal, vegetable, or mineral—they are there to be used and abused by us because we are the superior species; if they get in the way of our pursuit of wealth or our progress, they are to be shoved aside or destroyed.

We have concluded that the Garden of Eden is a piece of fiction (and, perhaps, God is, too) and, therefore, we have no need to strive for something that never was. That, of course, misses the point: Whether the garden ever physically existed is irrelevant to whether it could exist, if only we would create it by creating the perfect world.

Joseph Ozarowski

One of the great aspects of the Torah in general and *B'reishit* in particular is that this material can be studied and seen on so many different levels. I took the liberty of asking my congregants your question last Shabbat morning instead of a sermon. Many of them suggested that the fully completed garden was simply an illustration of *Hashem*'s creative abilities, an example of the Divine work described in the first chapter of Genesis. On the other hand, one of my children, in an extremely animated discussion of this question over Shabbat dinner, pointed out that the *Hizkuni* commentary (thirteenth-century France), mentioned in the Artscroll *Chumash* (1994), on page 12, hypothesized that God actually formed the first human outside the garden, and led the human around the outside before entering in. This was so that the alternatives could be seen before the first commandment regarding the forbidden fruit was given. Others of my congregants opined that the garden was an experiment, a sort of "biosphere," to see whether the first human could live properly.

I tend toward to the last answer, but with a twist. For years, I have understood Adam and Eve as adolescents growing up. This is not the only approach to the early parts of *B'reishit*, but it does answer many questions and also has some support in the text and commentaries. The first humans are placed in the garden and given a simple commandment by God restricting their food. They may not eat from a specific tree. They do not follow this and must reap the consequences of their actions. Their response begins in a childish fashion, pointing the finger ("She made me do it. . . . The snake made me do it"). All the issues of growing up come into play here: Sexuality (see Rashi-Rabbi Shlomo ben Yitzhaki, eleventh-century France—who describes the snake seeing the humans innocently making love and becoming jealous); issues of free choice, good and evil, and morality (see the commentaries of Ramban, thirteenth-century Spain, and

Abarbenel, fifteenth-century Spain); and awareness of mortality (the snake's taunt that they will not die and their eventual realization that they will). Like children growing up, they try to deny their misdeed and hide, but in the end they must confront their action.

Following this approach, the aftermath of the man being forced to work the Earth and the woman in pain as she bears children do not have to be seen as punishments, but simply the normal but difficult aspects of life that all adults must learn to face. This is certainly not "Original Sin" as Christianity derives it from the chapter. Finally, at the end of chapter 3 and the story, the first man and woman are referred to by names—Adam and Eve—implying an attainment of self-identity. They are also clothed by God as they are ejected from the garden. Like any good parent, God must throw them out of the house so they can live normal lives on their own, but *Hashem* nonetheless provides for them even as they are forced to provide for themselves.

Thus, the story truly had to emerge the way it did. If Adam and Eve would have begun their lives with seeds, a shovel, and minimal vegetation, they would not have learned the lessons about life that they did. And we too would not have learned as much.

(Please note that in this essay, as well as throughout my portion of the entire text, I interchangeably use the various Names of the Deity, including God, Hashem, Lord, etc.)

David Sofian

First let's ask if you are correct that we are not to rely on miracles? The support we need is found in *Mishnah Avot* 5:6. "Ten things were created on the eve of Sabbath between the suns at nightfall; the mouth of the earth, the mouth of the well, the mouth of the she-ass, the rainbow, the manna and the rod and the *Shamir*, and the letters and the writing and the Tables of stone. Some say also: The evil spirits and the sepulchre of Moses and the ram of Abraham our father. Some say also: The tongs made with tongs." (The Mishnah, Herbert Danby: Oxford University Press, 1933).

Avot is teaching that the Torah's miracles were all preprogrammed into creation. They happen only once and at the right time. Consequently, we are not to rely on their reoccurrence or on additional miracles. Now, since this is the case, what are we to make of Adam in a garden where all his needs are taken care of? And what does that state of affairs say about his relationship with God?

One way to answer the question, following a straightforward reading of the Torah text itself, is to say the original plan for human beings was to live within the opulence of Eden with all their needs taken care of. Although the Torah does say that the man was placed there to tend and protect the garden, the setting indicates that within this divine plan the man and woman would simply rely on God's benevolence expressed by the garden. God only requires that they obey the commandment not to eat the fruit.

The story suggests that their relationship with God is intended to be much the same as a small child's relationship with his or her parents. Parents provide the supportive environment for small children and expect obedience. God provides the supportive environment for the man and woman and expects obedience.

However, this plan for our relationship with God is destroyed by human disobedience. Human life as it now prevails is the consequent. This, then, would be the point of the narrative. It is human disobedience, sin, that leads to the situation where bread results from the sweat of our brow and tilling the soil is hard work.

Thus, we would have to say the Jewish value that focuses on human self-reliance results from life after the garden. Judaism sees and accepts that the relationship with God has changed. Man's and woman's punishment is that they are no longer allowed to be dependent.

God made it so that we must plant the seeds and work the shovel. Yet, quite meaningfully, Judaism does not stop here but goes on to teach us about the positive value of human behavior. Our Judaism doesn't just leave us focused on that human behavior that removed us from the garden, but it directs us to that human behavior that can hasten a return. Our behavior makes a difference and our behavior is ours to decide. Looked at this way, we see that the responsibility is ours to do whatever we can to improve the world, and recreate the garden.

Another way to answer the question is not to deal with the whole of the narrative but to center on why God tempts the man and woman with the fruit in the first place. Why did God create them so that they could be tempted at all? Their freedom to choose whether to obey the commandment or not calls into question the straightforward interpretation discussed above.

Perhaps the original plan was not that human beings would live forever in the garden. Perhaps the divine plan for humans was something other than continuous dependence upon God for a supportive environment. Perhaps the man and woman were intended all along to grow out of their childlike state and mature into self-reliant adults. If this is the case, the temptation of the fruit would be to facilitate this process. In this view, God is not just the supportive parent providing for the child, but is supportive by creating the conditions wherein the child can and must grow and mature.

This is hinted at in the story itself when God calls out to the man after he has eaten the fruit, "Where are you?" As Rashi points out, God certainly knows the answer to this question. The question can only be for the man's benefit. God is calling out, "Where are you going? Are you capable of fulfilling your own needs? Does your new awareness of self mean you have matured enough to leave the garden and take responsibility for yourself?"

Here God relates to us as the benevolent parent of an adolescent instead of as the parent of a small child. God intends and wants us to express our freedom of choice, even if it is negatively expressed at first, so that we will grow and mature. Leaving the garden is not a result of punishment for sin *per se*, but a result of our inherent nature, which God created. The "punishment" is intended to prod us into growing into what we are supposed to be: Beings who can determine right from wrong and who have the freedom to choose. God requires us to see that we are not children but are free to choose and be held responsible for working the soil, judging good from bad, and improving God's creation, inspired by the memory of the garden.

Noah: Genesis: 6:9–11:32

Prophetical Reading
Isaiah 54:1–55:5

Overview of Torah Portion

Angered by mankind's corruption, God orders Noah to build an ark and stock it with every member of the animal kingdom. A flood destroys the earth's human and animal inhabitants. Upon leaving the ark, Noah builds an altar on which he offers sacrifices of thanks to God. God promises not to destroy the world again with a flood. The descendants of Noah spread east, starting to build a tower with its top in heaven. God scatters the people and introduces a multiplicity of languages. Terah takes his son Abram and other members of the family from Ur toward Canaan.

Key Verses

"And God said, 'This is the sign of the covenant that I am giving between Me and you and every living creature that is with you for perpetual generations. I have set my bow in the clouds and it will be a sign of the covenant between Me and the earth. And it will be, when I bring clouds over the earth and the bow is seen in the cloud, that I will remember My covenant . . . and the waters will no more become a flood to destroy all flesh'" (Genesis 9:12–15).

Discussion Question

GOD'S REMINDER: That God needs a reminder is baffling enough; that the reminder is somehow dependent on it being seen by humans is even more perplexing. If the rainbow is God's guarantee that He will not bring another cataclysmic flood upon the earth, what is our role as observer? Is God's awareness of the rainbow not sufficient? Is the bow made visible for our sake or for His?

Shammai Engelmayer

There is an assumption in this question: God is perfect. Yet one of the lessons of *Noach* is that God is *not* perfect. In fact, so far, He has made two serious errors and is about to make a third.

The first one was creating humankind, giving it free will, *and then leaving it to find its own way to morality and righteousness.* (It's the italicized part that was the mistake.) That left the human with the task of learning how to live from his or her surroundings—in other words, to learn how to be human beings by watching the animals.

Nowhere do we see God having a heart-to-heart, say, with Adam and Chava (Eve), explaining to them the right and wrong way. He had to know that they needed a talking-to. After all, He gave them only two commandments—to procreate and to keep their hands off that tree. Since He didn't need to command them to engage in sexual relations (that is a natural process, after all), that means that they violated the only real commandment He gave them.

Tossing them out of the Garden was not really that big of a deal, either. They hadn't been around long enough to know what they were losing and, besides, as soon as He gave them those clothes to wear, He was already well on His way to seeing that they make it through to the end of their lives in relative peace and comfort.

If moving them from the Garden of Eden was anything but a location change, the text does not reflect it. We are not offered any scenes of Adam and Chava paying for their sin by working hard in the fields, finding it tough to make ends meet, or any such thing.

Then comes Kayin (Cain). Clearly, no one has bothered to tell him or Hevel (Abel) the consequences of violence. When he killed his brother, he learned that lesson the hard way. God recognizes that, and it is reflected in Kayin's so-called punishment. But the punishment for murder is death, not appointment to the post of Builder of Cities (although there is a suggestion in the text that it was his son who built the cities). Even now, God is neglecting to send any kind of moral message to humankind.

Finally, when the situation gets so out of hand that He needs to do something, what He does is destroy the world, leaving just one family to restock humanity. The Flood was God's admission that He had made a mistake the first time around, one which now needs correcting.

Only now, He goes too far. His second mistake is letting His anger get the best of Him. So He sets the bow in the heavens—for Him and for us. It calms us. We know the storms will not last; the world will be here tomorrow. For Him, it serves as a reminder that, no matter what we do, He has given us free will. We must find our own course. If we destroy the world, so be it; but He must never again destroy it for us.

Unfortunately, this leads to His third and most serious mistake: Destroying all life except for those on the ark did nothing to end evil and immorality in the world. They still continued. Indeed, that is the point of the strange incident regarding the nakedness of Noach and Cham's (Ham's) apparently disgraceful conduct. Unless He was prepared to wipe the slate clean and start Creation all over again, killing all but those on the ark failed to achieve its purpose as God had stated it to Noach; namely, to cleanse the evil from humankind.

There will be a full discussion of this aspect in the answer to the next question.

Joseph Ozarowski

For whom is the rainbow meant? The commentaries differ in their responses to this question. Ramban, for example, explicitly states that it serves to remind God of the covenant, that *Hashem* will never again destroy the Earth. On the other hand, Samson Raphael Hirsch (nineteenth-century Germany) suggests that because the Torah terms the rainbow an *ot*, a tangible reminder of the covenant, it is similar to other such items such as Shabbat, *milah* (circumcision), and *tefillin*.

All of these are termed *ot* by the Torah and remind us of God's teachings. So, too, this rainbow is also meant for us. However, even the most cursory reading of the actual text of the rainbow covenant in verses 8–17 clearly yields the notion that the covenant and the rainbow that symbolizes it is between and for both God and humankind. One can discern this idea of mutuality at least a half-dozen times in the verses.

What this rainbow symbolizes for us is discussed by many homileticians, both medieval and modern. I like the idea (first suggested to me by Rabbi Aaron Rine of Chicago) that ancient civilizations would symbolize peace-making by breaking their weapons, similar to the way the United States and Russia today destroy their missiles when making peace. Thus, the rainbow is a broken bow, or the bow without the string. Further, the bow is pointed heavenward, reminding us that any divine arrows of destruction cannot be pointed at us. Finally, the rainbow can only occur when there is both light and water. Being part rain and part sun, the rainbow thus reminds us that there will never again be a flood where total rain obscures the light.

Another significant explanation is the one offered by Rashi who writes, "Between God and all living things" (vs. 16), between the heavenly attribute of *din*—"judgment"—and between you. For the text should have been written, "Between Me and between all living things. . . ." But, it means that when the attribute of *din* comes to accuse you, I will see the above-mentioned sign (of the rainbow).

Din refers to God's organizational and judgmental aspects in Creation. Nature has its rules created by God, and these are not often to our liking. The world inexorably goes on, and it is often filled with death, destruction, and pain. I believe Rashi is suggesting that the rainbow reminds God, as well as us, that there is *din* in the world—and the flood was its most extreme example. But the rainbow also reminds both sides of the divine-human covenant that there is a compassionate side to God—that of *rahamim* (mercy). Though there will never again be a flood of the magnitude of Noah's, the forces that caused the flood—both Divine and natural—still exist. The rainbow reminds both God and us that in spite of the pain and sorrow in the world, *Hashem*'s love and care can still give us strength and heal our wounds.

David Sofian

Ramban offers us an interesting comment in his exposition to our passage. He wants to know why the sign (*ot*) is a rainbow? Let's begin with that question. In reference to the phrase, "this is a sign" (*zot ot*), he proposes that perhaps the significance is to be found in the shape of the bow in the sky. Likening the rainbow to an archer's bow, he notes that it is not threateningly directed towards earth but is turned the other way. It also is stringless. Hence, maybe its very shape communicates God's intent.

Continuing his comment, he explains that the true nature of an *ot* cannot be discerned from its physical nature. Ramban wants us to understand that an *ot* acts as a reminder solely because God sets it up to do so. Ramban points out that circumcision is also an *ot* in the same way. Thus, the rainbow's significance is not in its shape or direction, but merely that God fixed it as a sign, as a mark, of the agreement made with humankind never to send another flood.

Following Ramban, we will not find an answer to the question posed in the physical nature of the rainbow. There is nothing intrinsic about the rainbow that would tell us if the bow was made visible for our sake or for

God's. Ramban's point teaches us that the sign, the bow, is significant only because God singled it out to act as a reminder.

Keeping Ramban's point in mind, I do not find it perplexing that an *ot* is set up as a reminder for human beings. Following the cataclysm of the flood, human beings would crave something that could be seen as an ongoing physical reminder of God's promise not to destroy the earth. The rainbow, which would follow any threatening storm accomplishes this reassurance wonderfully, and I do not find it perplexing that the sign only has its effect if it is observed. That is the very nature of an *ot*. Its *otness* is only fulfilled if it is a reminder, and it can only be a reminder if it is observed by those it intends to remind.

It is baffling to think that God somehow needs the *ot* as a reminder. Clearly, God does not need to be reminded of anything. Having noted that, let's suppose, *keev-ya-khol* (as if it could be), that God does need to be reminded of something. What would that be?

The beginning of the parshah tells us that God brought the flood because the earth was filled with violence. Simply wiping the earth clean is not a guarantee that violence will not reappear. The earth always stands in need of judgment. God, sitting on the seat of judgment (*midat ha-din*), could invariably conclude that the earth deserves destruction.

Yet, God promised not to destroy the earth again. Therefore, the rainbow acts as an ongoing "reminder," not just for humankind, but for God also, reminding God to address the earth from the seat of mercy (*midat ha-rakamim*). We might say metaphorically that God needs the *ot* to bring the *midat ha-rakamim* to fore, guaranteeing the fulfillment of God's promise.

Lech Lecha:
Genesis 12:1–17:27

Prophetical Reading
Isaiah 40:27–41:16

Overview of Torah Portion

Avram, at God's command, travels to Canaan. Because of a famine in Canaan, he journeys with his wife, Sarai, to Egypt. Fearing harm if he is found to be married to Sarai, he requests that she claim they are brother and sister. Their plot uncovered, they are expelled. Back in Canaan, Avram separates from Lot, his nephew, who settles in Sodom. Avram rescues Lot, a kidnap victim. Avram has a son, Ishmael, with Hagar, Sarai's handmaid. God promises that Avram and Sarai will have their own son, Yitzchak. God commands the circumcison of all Jewish males.

Key Verses

"In that day the Lord made a covenant with Avram, saying 'Unto your seed I have given this land, from the river of Egypt . . .'" (Genesis 15:18).

"And when Avram was 90 years old, the Lord appeared to Avram, and said to him, 'I am God Almighty. Walk before me and be whole hearted. And I will make my covenant between Me and you. . . . And you shall be the father of a multitude of nations'" (Genesis 17:1–4).

"And I will establish My covenant between Me and your seed after you throughout their generations. . . .'" (Genesis 17:7).

"And God said to Avraham, 'You shall keep My covenant, you and your seed after you throughout their generations'" (Genesis 17:9).

Discussion Question

ANCIENT CONTRACTS: A covenant, or *brit*, is a contract that binds both parties to perform a particular action. God will give the Promised Land to the Jewish people. But what is their responsibility? God establishes the covenant with Avram (Avraham after his name is changed) hundreds of years before Mount Sinai, before the Ten Commandments, before the Torah. If the covenant implies more than Avraham's personal piety or the performance of circumcision, a single *mitzvah*, what is the Jews' part of the bargain? How can the covenant be established before all of their responsibilities, given later in the Torah, are clearly defined?

Shammai Engelmayer

Did you ever wonder why the Torah does not start with Avraham? After all, this is the book of *our* laws, the history of *our* birth and development, the record of *our* covenantal relationship with God. And yet, we start off by telling stories about people who are not a part of us. Adam was not an *Ivri*—a Hebrew; Kayin and Noach certainly were not; those folks on the Tower of Babel had nothing to do with us. So why do we take up so much space on things that are of no consequence? Tell us that God created the world and that, twenty generations later, He told Avram (as our first patriarch is known when he is first introduced to us) to pick himself up and head for Canaan.

The reason is simple: When God created the world, we weren't even a gleam in His eye. He put humankind on the planet and expected great things. Instead, He saw only horrible things. And so, ten generations after He created the world, He brought the Great Flood and started over again. But when He did, He made a promise: He would never again destroy the world in a single act of devastation.

I said before that God had made two mistakes—giving humankind free will but leaving it to find its own way to morality and righteousness, and letting His anger get the best of Him—and that these led to a third mistake that was the most serious: Destroying all life except for those on the ark did nothing to end evil and immorality in the world. They still continued. The flood thus failed to achieve its goal, as explained by God to Noach.

Ten generations later, God is again confronted with the sort of moral corruption that led to the global holocaust. Only now, no flood was possible, for God promised humankind after the last deluge not to send another one. A new answer was needed. That answer was Israel.

We are the alternative to the flood. Destroying humankind did nothing to reform humankind. Perhaps a "kingdom of priests, a holy nation" could.

And so, God turned to Avram and said, "Pick yourself up and go where I tell you to go, say what I tell you to say, teach what I tell you to teach, and do what I tell you to do. For this, I will reward you with this wonderful land I'm sending you to."

In other words, God decided that, finally, it was time to demonstrate to humankind the proper way to live. He chose Avram and his family to do the showing.

This was not a complicated task. All that was required of the family of Avram was to act nobly and unselfishly, caring for others at least as much as for themselves, and spreading the idea that one God ruled the world and that He required neither child sacrifice nor any other abominable practice.

Only, the task would prove too difficult even for Avram, who would soon be renamed Avraham in recognition of his fealty to God. The patriarch would have his own moral lapses (such as the two times he jeopardized his wife's chastity to save his own skin). Yitzchak's lapses were even greater, and Ya'akov, well, here was a very troubled young man who took so long to grow up that his children picked up a lot of bad habits and practically abandoned any divine mission to further their own aims.

God, however, could not give up now. He had made two covenants— with humanity (no more global destruction) and with Israel. So, after Egypt, He modified His deal with the latter. Israel's mission remained, but now He heaped on a whole series of laws and regulations to constantly remind Israel of its obligations as His "kingdom of priests."

Looked at in this way, the fact that the Torah begins as it does is not strange, at all. This isn't "our" story, but the story of God's efforts to reform humanity. We follow those efforts, step by step. Along the way, we learn what our role is in those efforts. Each time we fall short, God refines His covenant with us to set us back on track and keep us there. So, there is nothing unusual in a covenant with Avram that includes the Land of Promise but not the ritual laws of Sinai. The need for those laws had not yet manifested itself.

We must remember that those laws are not what concern God. He really could not care whether or not we followed any of them (although we should care), so long as we keep to the program: Demonstrating, through the way we live our lives, how God wants all people to live. Ritual laws are there only as reminders and as a means of keeping us sufficiently apart from those whom we influence so that they will not influence us.

One final note: I have referred here to *ritual* laws, not all the laws contained in the Torah. The non-ritual laws, in truth, existed before Sinai. These are the laws that define Israel's mission, not the ritual laws. And these laws all boil down to one category: They regulate behavior. Frankly, we did not need a *Moshe Rabbenu* (Moses, our Teacher) to tell us that we have to worry about the widows and orphans, that our weights and measures must be honest, that lost property must be returned. These laws existed from the beginning of human existence and are automatically included in Israel's from the moment Avram begins the long walk to Canaan. That they eventually had to be enunciated only shows how little we truly understood our mission.

Joseph Ozarowski

The question goes to the very heart of the Covenant concept. My recently Bar-Mitzvahed son, Shalom, offered one possible answer. If we accept the rabbinic tradition that the patriarchs kept the mitzvot on their own while they were living in *Eretz Yisrael*, then we can understand this observance as their side of the covenant, just as their descendants kept the mitzvot following the covenant God made with them at Mount Sinai.

However, it is also possible to see the *brit*/covenant as an unfolding experience. Thus, it may not be neccessary for both sides to fully keep their parts of the bargain immediately. *Brit* is referred to at least a dozen times in this week's *sidrah*. The first reference in Chapter 15 is the *brit bein hab'tarim*—the "Covenant between the pieces." It is primarily a promise and an assurance. Abraham's descendants would multiply, be enslaved, and subsequently be freed. They would leave their slavery with great possession, and eventually be repatriated to the Homeland promised to Abraham. The extensive references to the Covenant in Chapter 17 begin with the assurance that Abraham's progeny would multiply and survive (17:2–9), the confirmation of Abraham's side of the *brit* via circumcision (17:10–14), and the continuation of this *brit* via the son Abraham and Sarah would have, to be named Isaac. So at this early stage of the *brit*, most of the Covenant is a promise.

In Exodus and Deuteronomy, the *brit* is expanded to encompass the agreement between God and Abraham's descendants—the Jewish People. In his monumental *Kol Dodi Dofek,* Rabbi Dr. Joseph B. Soloveitchik, of blessed memory, understands *brit* as having two parts. The first is *brit goral,* the covenant of fate that all Jews receive. This collective *brit* comes from shared historical circumstances, shared suffering, shared responsibility and liability, and shared activity. This covenant is not voluntary—each Jew is a part by virtue of the above.

The later covenant is *brit yiud*—the covenant of destiny—a voluntary relationship into which a Jew enters by imitating Hashem, by observing mitzvot, and doing acts of *hesed* (kindness), thus encountering the God of Israel.

The *brit* promised to Abraham is still unfolding for us, his descendants and heirs. Rabbi Soloveitchik's understanding of the dual nature of the *brit* still challenges us today. We still have the shared past of the *brit goral*. Will we have the shared future of the *brit yiud*?

David Sofian

The question posed essentially asks why the Sinaitic covenant, embodied in the Torah with all its mitzvot and responsibilities, isn't presented in the original covenantal statement to Abraham. Why does God not begin the relationship by just giving Abraham the Torah?

Asking this question is like asking, "Why must a story begin at the beginning?" The answer is that the covenantal relationship must begin with the simplest and most basic agreement, and then with time, grow into its full form. Simply put, it is too soon for Torah to be introduced.

At the beginning of the parshah, God commands Abram to leave home and go to a land God will show him. God's promise at this point is to make of Abram a great nation. The promise of the land comes only after Abram acts on God's original command and sets out for Canaan.

The beginning point of the covenant is with Abram's willingness to respond to God's initial commandment. Telling the story this way emphasizes the importance of the individual person within the covenant. The covenant begins with God's contact and Abram's response. Anything more than this, let alone the complexity of the entire Torah, would have been too much for him, too soon.

This is evidenced in the second time God promises Abram that he will be a great nation. In *B'reishit*, Chapter 15, Abram questions God's introductory promise by drawing attention to his lack of offspring. Abram wants to make Dammesek Eliezer, head of his household, his heir. God responds by assuring him that he will have biological offspring of his own, and then has Abram look at the numerous stars and reiterates that his offspring will be equally numerous. Abram, already elderly, begins to wonder and begins to question.

It is clear, even from the beginning, that Abram's faith is special. He hears

Lech Lecha, and he goes. Yet, in Chapter 15, Abram has questions, if not doubts. His relationship with God is still new and, perhaps, in his own mind, still tentative. Certainly, he was not ready for the entirety of the Torah. How overwhelming that would have been.

The covenantal story must begin as it does. The agreement must begin simply and clearly. Step by step, the relationship grows even as Abraham's family grows.

This question can also be answered by recognizing the community context of Torah. I indicated above how the importance of the individual is emphasized by the narrative of a single person, Abraham. Nevertheless, Torah, in its full expression, presupposes a full-blown Jewish community to be meaningful. It assumes peoplehood. That community will grow from Abraham just as God promised.

Only when a whole people comes forth from Egypt and arrives at Sinai can Torah be received. We need to see how all that happened. We need to learn the story as it develops. This then is another answer. We, the current Jewish community, and for that matter every generation of Jewish community that was and will be, need to know the story of how our community came about so that we can understand its significance. In order to do that, the story must begin at the very beginning, with Abraham, the individual, the progenitor of our people.

All this calls to mind the famous Rashi, who explains why the Torah begins as it does rather than in Chapter 12 of *Shmot* with the first command. There, Rashi answers the question, If the Torah is about commandments, why not begin with the first commandment?

In essence, the answer he gives is that, first, we must have the proper context for what comes later. Parshah *Lech Lecha* begins teaching us the context we first need to know, before the rest can unfold.

VaYera: Genesis 18:1–22:24

Prophetical Reading
2 Kings 4:1–37

Overview of Torah Portion

Three men/angels visit Abraham, repeating God's promise that Sarah will bear a son in a year. Told of Sodom's impending destruction, Abraham pleads on the city's behalf that a certain number of righteous people can be found living there. Two of the angels rescue Lot from Sodom's demise. Abraham and Sarah travel to Gerar, where again he identifies her as his sister and again the truth is uncovered. The king of Gerar invites the pair to settle in his land. Yitzchak is born. Abraham expels Hagar and Ishmael. Abraham makes a pact with the king of Gerar. God tells Abraham to offer Yitzchak as a sacrifice; an angel stops the sacrifice in the nick of time.

Key Verses

"And the two angels came to Sodom. . . . And Lot saw them. . . . And he said, 'Behold, my lords, please turn aside into your servant's house and stay all night.' And he made them a feast" (Genesis 19:1–3).

"The men of the city . . . surrounded the house . . . and they called to Lot, 'Where are the men who came to you tonight? Bring them out to us that we may know them.' And he said, 'Please do not do so wickedly. Behold, I have two daughters who have not known a man. Please let me bring them out to you and you shall do to them as is good in your eyes'" (Genesis 19:4–8).

Discussion Question

PARADOXICAL PEOPLE: Noah, the ark builder, and Lot, Abraham's nephew, are two of the most morally ambiguous figures in the Torah. Noah is described as "righteous . . . in his generations," which many commentators call relative praise. Lot heroically opened his home to strangers but cowardly offered his virgin daughters to appease the hostile Sodomites.

Noah and Lot lived amidst corruption. Neither tried to rebuke the doers of evil. But both play key roles as genealogical links. Noah, after the flood, becomes the father of mankind. Lot, through the son Moab born to his daughter, becomes a forebear of King David and ultimately the Messiah. Why do these men, not entirely righteous, earn such vital roles? Is God settling for second best? Abraham would seem a better choice in King David's direct lineage. What is the contemporary lesson for us?

Shammai Engelmayer

Noach and Lot are "morally ambiguous figures," according to the question, which then wonders whether God is settling for "second best" in choosing "the father of mankind" and David's ancestor.

Well, Noach was not second best. Whatever the Torah meant by "righteous . . . in his generations," the fact is, he was the best there was *at the time*. Noach was a product of his age and his environment. If he had faults and foibles that would qualify his righteousness in a later time, *in his own time they were neither faults nor foibles*. Should we say that Avraham was less righteous because he brought to his mysterious visitors dishes made of meat and of milk? Of course not; in his time, that was not an issue.

Noach, for his part, showed his innate sense of righteousness by rising above his environment. One can only assume, therefore, that he would have done so in any environment. The way he lived his life in the period before the Great Flood, therefore, cannot be used as proof that he would have been less righteous, say, during Avraham's time, or David's. The assumption must be made that he would have lived a righteous life as is defined in any period in which he might have found himself.

As for Lot (by far the best there was in Sodom), the question assumes that he remained silent amid the corruption around him, but the text suggests he did not. Two strangers appear out of nowhere and Lot is right at the gate, waiting to greet them and spirit them to safety. This suggests a man who, by his actions, is saying a great deal to the residents of Sodom. He did not just arrive at the gate haphazardly; the text makes clear he was there, in full view of the city's elders, waiting for any strangers who might show up (thereby emulating his Uncle Avraham, which shows that the young man who earlier had selfishlesly chosen greener pastures had grown up). This took a lot more courage than someone who talks about morality, but does nothing about it.

As for his daughters, what we think morally repugnant does not count. What does count is the environment in which Lot existed. Women in general had the status of dishrags in those days. Whatever the father or husband wanted to do with them could be done. Lot was not doing anything more than saying, "Here, I have some property of value; take that instead."

But why his daughters? For one thing, he may already have considered them lost. After all, they were engaged to be married to men of Sodom. That says something about their character and moral station, not Lot's (just as their seduction of Lot later says something about them). That he was willing to give them in marriage to Sodomites would suggest that he considered them little more than Sodomites themselves.

For another, maybe Lot was taking a calculated risk. These men at the door did not want women, they wanted men—and the men they wanted were the two strangers. Perhaps Lot was banking on impressing the Sodomites with how serious he took his obligation to protect the guests in his home, but not having his offer accepted. Clearly, Lot is not a strong figure, but he has morals and is willing to stand up and be counted.

As far as his being David's ancestor, however, rather than Avraham, here we have a problem with the question. Lot is the ancestor of Moab—all of it, not any specific line beyond the immediate eponymous one. Nations do not flow from people's loins; only national founders do. Not even infant Israel is pure: Caleb is a Kenite; a "mixed multitude" joined the Exodus (and their is no record that they ever separated from Israel); Moshe's children are as much Midianites as they are Israelites (or more so, since they were raised as Midianites). So, while Lot may have been ancestor to Moab, it's a stretch to absolutely claim that he was the ancestor of Ruth.

Avraham, on the other hand, is the direct ancestor of David. Avraham is Yehudah's (Judah's) great-grandfather, after all. That makes David as much "of the line of Avraham" as it does "of the line of Yehudah." And, in a patriarchal age, patrilineal descent is all that matters. If it were otherwise, we would know him as David of the line of Tamar, not David of the line of Yehudah.

Now, if you want to discuss morally ambiguous people whom God chooses, suggesting that He settles for "second best," how about discussing a man who would sacrifice his wife's honor to save his neck at the drop of a stranger's leer? How about a man who will argue with God to save Sodomites, but utters not even a whisper when God tells him it is okay to toss one son into the desert and slit the throat of the other?

Now, there is a character worthy of the title "morally ambiguous." Yet

Avraham is a man much esteemed by us precisely because of his character. We ignore the ambiguities and magnify the traits we hold dear.

Why are we not equally willing to give Noach similar latitude? Could it stem from the fact that he was a non-Jew, and that non-Jews, no matter when they lived (including the age before there were Jews), are somehow incapable of being completely moral?

I wonder what Iyuv (Job), who himself was a non-Jew, would say to that?

Joseph Ozarowski

Noah and Lot are both paragons of imperfection. Both maintain some strands of monotheistic morals amidst a corrupt society. Yet, both somehow give up important moral characteristics in their lives. Noah's relative righteousness could be seen as credit or criticism. As Rashi so succinctly puts it, "There are those of our Rabbis who explain this to his praise, and there are those who explain it to his disgrace." The late Rabbi Menachem Sacks of Chicago, in his delightful homiletical work *Menachem Tzion* (Jerusalem: Machon Harav Frank, 1978), tries to see the redeeming qualities by emphasizing Rashi's wording as follows: If you want to count yourself among the followers of the rabbis, judge Noah favorably, in spite of the fact that there are others who may be quick to criticize.

Lot, while seemingly hospitable, was ready to offer his daughters to the crowd for abuse. Further, his acts of incest with his daughters resulted in the genealogy, which eventually leads to the nation of Moab, Ruth, King David, and the Messiah. Again, the rabbis differ on the purity of the family's motives. But, it is possible to argue for the need to do what they did. The daughters getting their father drunk and raping him can be considered an act of desperation in a world that they thought had come to an end.

Thus, they realized that only by having sex with Lot would they be able to preserve the species and pave the way for eventual redemption via the promised Messiah (see Midrash B'reishit Rabba 51:8). A further argument can be based on Psalm's 89:3, which states, "The world is built on *hesed*," usually translated as kindness. But in Leviticus 20:17, the Torah bans incest and refers to it as *hesed*! Thus, there are moments when the world is indeed built on incest, at times when everything and everyone else is destroyed! (See *Sanhedrin* 58b, where it is suggested that Cain married his sister based on this very verse.) After all, if any of us survived a nuclear holocaust, in a situation such as the well-known movie *On the Beach*, how would we behave?

By the way, the Messiah's other *yichus* are not so pristine. The ancestors of David's Jewish side were Judah and Tamar (see *B'reishit* 38), protagonists of another steamy, sexy, not-so-pure story. It is so interesting to compare the Christian understanding of a Messiah born through "Immaculate Conception," with that of the Jewish Messiah born through a rather *schmutzedik* ancestry. But our notion of the world's redemption suggests that it will come through dealing with real life, which is often packed with dirt. The Torah's stories of real people teach us that we can affirm sanctity, holiness, and a way to live amidst the *schmutz*, eventually leading to the world's redemption.

David Sofian

The kind of moral ambiguity brought up here is the norm rather than the exception in biblical materials. The question refers to Noah and Lot, but could equally refer to Aaron's involvement with the golden calf, Miriam's and Aaron's rebellion against Moses, David's behavior regarding Bathsheba, or Solomon's wives and his idolatry. We can even point to Moses' killing of the Egyptian, breaking the tablets, and striking the rock.

Surely, all of these people play key roles in the development of future generations and are only some of the possible examples. *Tanakh*, the Hebrew Bible, does not give us idealized heroes who are perfect people. Instead, *Tanakh* depicts our ancestors as real, multi-faceted people who possess admirable and deplorable traits.

The goal of this narrative is not to show how the Jewish people are descended from entirely righteous antecedents. Our task, as the inheritors of the tradition, is to begin with the story as told and try to learn from it.

Lot's importance is in his contrast to Abraham. Lot is certainly a secondary character, but his presence helps us appreciate Abraham better. The contrast begins in *Lech Lecha*, when we learn of the quarreling between Abram's herdsmen and Lot's. Abram's great desire for peace, his magnanimous, generous character is brought out in contrast to Lot's selfishness. Lot chooses the lush plain where Sodom is located.

Still within that parshah, another aspect of Abram's character is evidenced when we see his reaction to his kinsman, Lot, being taken captive. He spares no effort to defeat the abductors. Lot helps us see Abram's generosity, family commitment, and courage.

In *VaYera* the comparison continues. The parshah opens by showing us Abraham's version of hospitality. Upon looking up and seeing the three strangers, Abraham disparages his efforts, saying he will only bring a morsel of bread and a little water. Yet, both he and Sarah spare no effort, bringing curds, milk, and meat and waiting on them as they rest. We saw before, a clear contrast of Abraham's generosity and Lot's selfishness.

In this case, Abraham's luster is brought into focus by Lot trying to be like Abraham but failing. Lot also insists on the angels accepting his hospitality. Yet, his earlier choice returns to haunt him. Whereas Abraham is in control of his environment and consequently the hospitality he shows his guests, Lot is in Sodom and must contend with the Sodomites. The Sodomites interfere in Lot's attempt to welcome the strangers. Only the blinding light produced by the angels keeps a disaster from happening. As the story proceeds, Lot continues to be ineffectual. We see Abraham's strength in Lot's weakness.

The midrashic tradition, however, does not want us to see Lot in a totally unsympathetic light. The midrash is aware that Lot is pivotal for future developments, so it asks why God saw to it that Lot was saved? Midrash B'reishit Rabbah 51:6 answers this question by referring us back to *Lech Lecha* and the episode of Abram and Sarai in Egypt.

Making the point again, this particular section of the story shows us that Abram also was not wholly righteous. Every biblical personality has flaws. Fearing for his own life, Abram passes Sarai off as his sister. The midrash points out that Abram would not have been able to do that without Lot's silence. In other words, Lot's family loyalty, his connection to Abram, is demonstrated in that instance. For this, he is saved.

The answer to the question then is that God is not settling for second best. God is dealing with real human beings, made of flesh and blood, all of whom are, to a greater or lesser extent, paradoxical people.

Chaye Sarah:
Genesis 23:1–25:18

Prophetical Reading
1 Kings 1:1–31

Overview of Torah Portion

The matriarch Sarah dies in Hebron at the age of 127. Abraham buries her in the cave of the Machpelah, which he buys from Ephron for 400 silver shekels. Abraham dispatches his servant to his homeland to find a wife for Isaac. The servant returns with Rivka, whom Isaac marries. Abraham marries Keturah and has six more children. Abraham dies at 175 and is buried in the cave of the Machpelah by Isaac and Ishmael.

Key Verses

"Abram dwelled in the land of Canaan. . . . And the Lord said to Abram . . . 'Please lift up your eyes and look . . . to the north and to the south and to the east and to the west. For all the land that you see, I will give to you and to your seed forever'" (Genesis 13:12–15).

"And when Abram was ninety years old and nine, the Lord appeared to Abram and said to him . . . 'I will give to you and to your seed after you the land of your sojournings, all the land of Canaan, for an everlasting possession'" (Genesis 17:1–8).

"And Abraham bowed down before the people of the land [the children of Heth]. And he spoke unto Ephron . . . saying, 'I will give the price of the field' . . . and Abraham weighed to Ephron the silver . . . 400 shekels of silver" (Genesis 23:12–16).

26

Discussion Question

AN EXPENSIVE GIFT: Abraham, the first monotheist, the man who teaches the world about God, is promised repeatedly that he and his descendants will inherit all of Canaan, the Promised Land—with God as the ultimate guarantor. It is Abraham's land. So why is a purchase of the burial place, in the middle of Canaan, necessary? Why could Abraham—or God—not claim the land as Jewish property, based on the heavenly deed? Is it a matter of legality or morality? What precedent does this transaction—and Jacob's later purchase of land in Shechem—set for the twentieth-century purchase of land in Palestine/Israel from Arab landowners?

Shammai Engelmayer

First, the easy answer: When Avraham was offered the land as a gift from Ephron, he had no choice but to pay for it—and top shekel, too—precisely because the land was his by divine right. God gave him the land as an inheritance forever, but who would have believed that when, in black ink on white parchment, it said that Ephron was the one who made to Avraham a gift of the land, or a portion of it? The moment Ephron made the offer, therefore, any chance of claiming that piece of land was gone. Avraham had to pay for it in order to protect God's interests. In this case, that meant avoiding any possibility that someone other than God could lay claim to being the one with the right to decide the fate of the land.

There is a problem with that answer, however, and it exists in the question, too. It assumes that God was giving Avraham and his family a "free" gift; that Avraham's descendants through the Yitzchak-Ya'akov line merely have to claim the land to have it in perpetuity. This was not the case. God gives nothing for nothing. Israel must earn its inheritance, not just once but in every generation. Failure to live up to the bargain results in losing the inheritance temporarily (just how temporarily is for God to decide).

Now, in the desert, God presented a whole set of obligations Israel must have undertaken as its "rental fee" for the land. "But," said the Israelites, "there were no such preconditions when you first made the promise to *Avraham Avinu* (Father Abraham)? How can you change the deal now?"

Across the Jordan, as they were given their marching orders for the conquest of Canaan, again they cried out: "Whoa, there! What do you mean 'fight?' God said the land was ours. That's what He told Avraham. It's our inheritance, no questions asked. So let God evict the present tenants and we'll move in. We don't need to fight; we have His word."

Of course, Israel made no such arguments. It couldn't. Even though Avraham inherited the land, he still had to "earn" it, in the present case by paying for it. From the very beginning, it was clear there were no freebies being offered. The inheritance comes with a catch.

The bottom line of that catch is that we must now be a "kingdom of priests, a holy nation," meaning that we are to teach by example how God wants all of His children to live. Just as Avraham had to pay a fair market price for "his own" land, so must we pay a fair market price for "our" land. Just as Avraham would have had to look for another tract if Ephron said no deal, so must we be prepared to accept no for an answer. The land is ours, but only if we play fair with those to whose land it also belongs.

Today, we are back in the land because God brought us back to the land. His hand is everywhere, from the fortuitous circumstance that put Theodor Herzl in front of the *Ecole Militaire* on the day Captain Alfred Dreyfus was humiliated, to General Edmund H. H. Allenby's breaking through to "the gates of Palestine" at the very same time the British were issuing the Balfour Declaration, to the creation of a United Nations so that Isaiah's prophecy could be fulfilled (that *the nations of the world* shall restore Israel to Zion), even to our survival of the *Shoah*. He brought us back.

Our inheritance is ours again, and now, like Avraham, we must pay for it—and pay fairly—*dunam* by *dunam*.

Let no one make a mistake about this. God has given us a tremendous opportunity. He has brought *Mashiach* to our gate, but withholds permission to enter. First He must see whether we are worthy to receive *Mashiach*. He is testing us, to see whether we have learned how to be "a kingdom of priests, a holy nation," and whether, after nearly 4,000 years, we are finally willing to assume that role.

Like Avraham, if we truly trust in God, then we must also trust in His word, so that the land for which we pay fair price today—or trade away in the name of preserving life and establishing peace—will be ours tomorrow in any case. We will have given up nothing, but we will have brought glory to the Name of God.

As Avraham did in closing his deal with Ephron, in so doing we will be protecting God's interest.

Joseph Ozarowski

The *Radak* (R. David Kimche, thirteenth-century Provence) points out that the *M'arat Hamakhpela*, the Cave of the Patriarchs, was the first piece of Holy Land purchased by our ancestors. God had already promised the land to Abraham. Ephron was willing to give Abraham the Cave for free. But Abraham, knowing that he was an instrument of God's plan and his descendants' destiny, understood that there had to be more. His progeny had to have a stake in the land wrought by normal, human means, one that would last through the generations. Thus, a purchase.

There is a wonderful midrash (*B'reshit Rabba* 79:7) that explains this idea.

> Rabbi Yuden ben Simon says "[there were] three places that the nations of the world cannot oppress Israel, this is stolen property in your hands." These are the *M'arat Hamakhpela*, (as purchased for a high price by Abraham in our *sidrah*), the [place of] the Temple (as purchased by King David and noted in 1 Chronicles 21) and the [future] burial spot of Joseph in Shekhem [as purchased by Jacob in Genesis 33].

The Torah is not only a book of rules and instruction. It is also a book of history—the history of our people. Thus, these three incidents of purchase reinforce our people's connection to our land—not only via a God-given inheritance, but also by an enduring, accepted, legal means.

Is it not ironic that these three places, symbolic of our people's bond to *Eretz Yisrael*, are the three most hotly disputed places in Israel today? On any given week, open up a newspaper and see some incident, dispute, or violence regarding Shekhem (Nablus), the Temple Mount in Jerusalem, or the Cave of the Patriarchs. And is it not also ironic that Hevron, site of the Cave, has as its Hebrew root *haver*, meaning "friendship" or "connection?" Or that Jerusalem's name means "City of Peace?"

Regardless of how the Mideast Peace Process turns out, and irrespective of whatever pragmatic concessions Israel may make to Palestinian rule for its own security and peace, we have a right to this land. Every Jew should remember that we share a bond with our land. This bond began with Abraham's high-priced purchase of a cave in which to bury his wife, as recorded in this *sidrah*.

(I thank my dear father-in-law, Rabbi Dr. Shlomo Rapoport of Chicago, for pointing out the above-mentioned sources to me).

David Sofian

Rashi quotes an *aggadic* tradition in reference to verse 4 of Chapter 23 that anticipates your question. That verse is where Abraham says to the children of Heth, "A stranger (*ger*) and a sojourner (*Toshav*) am I among you." The *aggadah* Rashi refers to interprets the words *ger* and *Toshav* this way. If you want, I am a stranger, but if not, I will be a settler and will take it by judgment, for the Holy One who is blessed said to me, "to your seed shall I give this land."

In other words, it would be better for me to accomplish my goal, aware that you see me as a stranger without standing. Only if that does not work will I assert my claim as a settler, an owner. Abraham chooses to accept the reality of the situation as it is.

The answer to your question lay in Abraham's perceptiveness and in his sensitive character. Yes, he had the right to the land secured by God's promise to him. And yes, we saw in Abraham's rescue of Lot that he understood the use of force if necessary. However, Abraham's most basic proclivity is peaceful conflict resolution, as we saw in the case of the dispute between his herdsmen and Lot's.

There he chose peace even if it was to his financial detriment. That same character trait also is evident here as he prefers to buy the land from the people he lives among, even at an outrageous price, in order to foster peaceful relations. *Midrash B'reishit Rabbah* tells us that the shekels referred to in this story were actually each worth twenty-five regular shekels.

Buying the land fosters peaceful relations because transfer of ownership is universally recognized in this way. Rashi also wants us to know that, if that did not work, Abraham was prepared to go further and claim his God given right.

We reach the same conclusion when we consider the teaching in *Mishnah Avot*, which tells us Abraham was tested ten times. Surely, the most significant test was the binding of Isaac in Parshah *VaYera*. Yet, it was not the only test. Abraham is being tested here, as well. God has promised him the land. The test is about what means Abraham will use to begin to realize possession of it? As we said, Abraham chose a universally recognized approach, which minimized potential conflict. It is clear to me that Abraham passed this test.

As with so many stories in the Torah, this one is about our ancestors' role in the covenant. As God's partner, Abraham had an active role to play. Although God promised him the land, he could not simply wait for God to bring the promise to fruition. Abraham, like his descendants after him, has to determine how he will endeavor to make God's promise real. It is Abraham's choice to do so in a way that will encourage peace with his neighbors.

You ask what precedent this sets for today. I think the answer is clear. Abraham's choice continues to be a momentous model. Even though Abraham may have had other means at his disposal, he chose the path that encouraged harmonious relations with his neighbors.

Toldot: Genesis 25:19–28:9

Prophetical Reading
Malachi 1:1–2:7

Overview of Torah Portion

Rivke gives birth to Jacob and Esau. Esau sells his birthright to his brother for a bowl of pottage. Because of famine, Isaac and Rivke travel to Gerar, then return to Beersheva. Rivke helps Jacob trick Isaac into giving him the blessing intended for Esau, the couple's first-born son. Jacob flees to Haran.

Key Verses

"And the first came out, red all over like a hairy mantle, and they called his name Esau. And after that his brother came out, and his hand had hold on Esau's heel, and his name was called Jacob" (Genesis 25:25–26).

"And God appeared to Jacob again . . . and blessed him. And God said to him, 'Your name is Jacob. Your name shall not be called Jacob any more, rather Israel shall be your name.' And He called his name Israel" (Genesis 35:9–10).

Discussion Question

WHAT'S IN A NAME?: A person's name—whether bestowed directly by God or by parents with Divine inspiration—reflects the individual's essential character and mission. This is particularly true of the biblical patriarchs; God assigned names to Abraham, Isaac, and Jacob.

Commentators disagree whether Jacob's original name was given by his father, or by God. Whatever the case, Jacob's name had holy roots. But, it was based on an incident at Jacob's birth; he grasped Esau's heel (akeiv). Is it accurate to name someone based on a trait exhibited barely out of the womb? Does a heavenly given name determine the recipient's destiny? Can a person not change the character that the name reflects? Does the subsequent changing of Jacob's name to Israel indicate that he had changed his essence, or that God changed His mind?

Shammai Engelmayer

What's in a name? In June 1967, Israeli forces won a miraculous victory on three separate fronts in just six days. Included in that victory was the impossible dream come true: The so-called "Old City" of Jerusalem, the Jerusalem of the Bible, the seat of Israel's kings and home of the Holy Temple, was back in Jewish hands. It was the first time Jews fully controlled the city since Roman troops surrounded it exactly 1,900 years earlier, in the siege that would lead to Jerusalem's destruction in 70 C.E. It was clear to me that the period known as the *atchalta di'geula*, the beginning of redemption, was surely underway.

My daughter was born in November 1967, just five months after that miraculous victory. I named her Malka Geula (meaning "queen of redemption"). My grandmother's name was Malka, which accounted for my daughter's first name. The year she was born and its portent for the Jewish future determined her middle name.

People name children for all sorts of reasons, some serious (as in my daughter's case), some frivolous (witness how many Elvises there are). In patriarchal times, Hebrew and non-Hebrew alike often named children as memorial for an event (i.e., Ya'akov, meaning "held by the heel"), or as a prayer (i.e., Yechiel, meaning "may God live"). Actually, this practice continued long after the age of the patriarchs. Elvis, for example, is probably a corruption of the ancient Germanic name Elvin, which means "godly friend."

The people of the ancient world believed that names had power. It is not unusual, therefore, for people to assume new names as a way of memorializing an enhanced status (and, sometimes, a diminished one). Thus, Avram's name is expanded; Ya'akov's is changed.

But are these as significant in the Torah as we are led to believe? Yitzchak, rather than Ya'akov, would suggest that the answer is, "probably not."

Yitzchak's name means "he will laugh," and implies laughter, light-heartedness, joy—inappropriate for someone whose life seems to have been one long tragedy. He grows up being taunted by an older brother, Yishmael; his father, Avraham, tries to kill him; his mother, Sarah—the only person he can truly trust and fully love—dies too soon; his twin sons, Esau and

Ya'akov, are enemies of each other; the former is a neer-do-well boor and the latter a con man and a thief.

About the only good thing that happens to Yitzchak is that he goes blind, so he cannot see what a mess exists all around him.

His name gave Yitzchak no protection against his fate. It merely memorialized an event—in this case, the laughter that ensued when it was suggested that 90-year-old Sarah would have a baby in twelve months' time.

There are even suggestions in the text, beginning with *Toldot*, that there was nothing laughable about the character of Yitzchak. From the text, we see that:

- Yitzchak was influenced by material things and his love could be bought with sensory pleasures: "Yitzchak favored Esau because he (Yitzchak) had a taste for game" (Genesis 25:28).
- He was willing to profit by the misery of others. When famine struck the land, he traveled to Gerar, where he was so successful at agriculture that he built a small fortune within a single year and angered the local natives. There was only one way he could have done so—by selling the local population the food it desperately needed (Genesis 26). While making a profit is not evil in and of itself, there is no evidence in the text that Yitzchak showed any concern for the welfare of the community around him. This is significant, as well, for what it shows about his care for pacts of friendship.
- Yitzchak viewed friendship pacts as one-sided in his favor alone. He went to Gerar because he felt he could be safe there. After all, his father and Avimelech had made a pact. When he prospered while everyone else starved, the existence of that pact alone should have made him want to share the wealth with the native population that had befriended his father (especially since he expected it to honor the pact by protecting him). Yet his actions cause him to be expelled from the region (Genesis 26:16).
- Only after he is gone did Avimelech re-establish the pact (Genesis 26:28), but only because it was apparent that God was with Yitzchak and his family (about who more will be said later). Contrast this to the way Avraham treats strangers, laying out a big feast for the weary traveler and expecting nothing in return.
- Like Esau, Yitzchak viewed such matters as birthrights and blessings as commodities to be traded. Thus, he said to Esau, "Take your gear, your quiver and your bow, and go out into the field and hunt me some game. Then prepare a dish for me as I like it . . . that I may give you my innermost blessing . . ." (Genesis 27:3). The blessing, of course, was not really his to give so freely, for it was tied in with God's

promise and he must have known God's intentions. It is inconceivable, for example, that Rivka (the matriarch Rebecca) had not told her husband what God had told her during her pregnancy — "And the older shall serve the younger" (Genesis 25:23).

It is also inconceivable that Yitzchak did not know that Esau had been willing to trade his birthright for a bowl of lentil stew. Considering how detailed are the scenes in which Ya'akov tricks Yitzchak into blessing him and Yitzchak realized his error, had the patriarch not known of the lentil stew incident until then, we would have expected to hear him howl with rage when Esau mentioned it. Yet, the otherwise involved scene offers us nothing like that.

Finally, we know for certainty that Yitzchak was disgusted with Esau's choices of wives (Genesis 26:35). There is at least the suggestion, then, that:

- Yitzchak was arrogant enough to attempt to thwart God's will.
- Yitzchak was not an original thinker. (Why else would he resort to the same ploy that twice put his mother in jeopardy, namely claiming that Rivka was his sister?)

The way his ruse was discovered also points up two other traits:

- Yitzchak was crude and immodest in his behavior (much as his son Esau appears to be); and,
- Yitzchak was not too bright.
  How else can we explain that he was seen fondling his "sister" in public in a manner that made it plain that she was really his wife?

That he was not too bright is also evident from the success of Rivka's plan. Ya'akov wore the skin of kids on his arms and neck. This undoubtedly made the mild-mannered twin hairier than his brother could possibly have been. At the same time, it did nothing to provide Ya'akov with the kind of muscular arms one associates with "a hunter, an outdoorsman" (Genesis 25:27). Yet, despite the fact that he is obviously suspicious, Yitzchak falls for the ruse and blesses Ya'akov in Esau's place.

We also cannot ignore the fact that, not until he was alone with his father on Mount Moriah did it occur to Yitzchak that there was no sacrificial animal to be seen; or that his anger at Esau's choice of wives was unfounded, since Genesis 28:6–9 makes it obvious that he never told his favorite son not to marry local women.

Yitzchak, then, answers one part of the question: It is not always wise to name someone based on a trait exhibited at birth (or, in his case, an event that occurs beforehand). Eventually, the name itself will engender laughter when it is compared to the person who bears it. (I believe it is significant that, unlike Avram and Ya'akov, God does not see fit to either amend Yitzchak's name or give him a new one.)

On the other hand, Ya'akov was appropriately named: He *was* a heel. Who else denies his famished twin brother a bowl of soup? Who else would steal from his brother or deceive his father? Worse, who in his right mind would do such stupid things when they were unnecessary since his future was guaranteed by God? Only a heel.

Did his name make him that? No, his character did (and, very likely, his environment). When he finally wrestles with his dark side and defeats it, it is appropriate for him to get a new name because his character has changed.

This leaves us with a new question that must be addressed: If Yitzchak is as I have portrayed him, why, as Avimelech believed, was God still with him and his family?

For one thing, He could not abandon Yitzchak because Ya'akov would become Yisrael (Israel) and, through him, God's covenant would be on its way to fulfillment. So he needed Yitzchak. For another, He is very likely responsible for many of Yitzchak's flaws; after all, it was He who had Yitzchak put on the altar in the first place, an unsettling experience in any circumstance.

Finally, there is the fact that God, as the God of history, would not be denied. Yitzchak was one of His chosen. Yet Yitzchak, if my reading of the text is correct, chose to run away from his responsibilities. Whether in revenge for the *Akedah* (the "binding" of him on a sacrificial altar, done by his father at the behest of God), or for whatever reason, Yitzchak would appear to have wanted nothing to do with any mission from God. God, however, would not let Yitzchak escape.

This is important for us to emphasize. Knowing that God will not be denied means knowing that there is light at the end of the tunnel. Regardless of how terrible things get for Jews over the millennia, regardless of how poorly we represent God's will, God's promise will be fulfilled. We have a reason to go on. We will survive. We will be redeemed. Indeed, we *are* being redeemed; hence, my daughter's name.

The rabbis of old, of course, sought to make Yitzchak into a great man, just as they tried to defend Ya'akov's actions. They would not—or could not—accept the Torah at its word. They would not—or could not—accept that their forebears, having been God's chosen, could have been flawed in any way because this suggested to them that God is less than perfect (something that God Himself admits, but they deny).

In so doing, however, they ignored one of the essential beauties of the Torah: It tells it like it is, warts and all. People are people, not gods and not saints. They operate on the same level as we do. They make mistakes; they do rotten things; and, like us, they have the capacity to change; to do *teshuvah*. That is what happened to Ya'akov.

By denying the character flaws, we also lose an important message the Torah is trying to give us. There is a price to pay for trying to thwart God's will, even if it's not immediately apparent.

Both Yitzchak and Ya'akov prosper and, through them, God's promise is fulfilled. Yet, for turning a blind eye to God's will, Yitzchak goes blind (although not totally, perhaps; the text is unclear). For deceiving Esau, Ya'akov is deceived by Lavan; for deceiving his father, Ya'akov is deceived by his sons; for taking advantage of his father's sightlessness, his own sight wanes; for seeking to drive a wedge between Yitzchak and his beloved son, Ya'akov's sons take his beloved son away from him; for taking Esau's birthright by cunning and deception, Ya'akov sees his son Reuven attempt to seize the birthright by sleeping with one of Ya'akov's wives; for treating Leah with such disdain, he loses Rachel much too soon.

Recognizing that our forebears were just people and that they had flaws does not diminish the Torah or Judaism. Rather, it enhances them because it imbues them with reality. The Torah is the book of life in the real world, not in utopia (which is why it ends *before* Israel crosses into Canaan, not after). Judaism is not a system of blind faith and instant salvation, but of living in the real world.

As for God, He emerges as the God of real people living in a real world, and He makes allowances for that. He does not expect perfection; He only expects that we try.

Joseph Ozarowski

Throughout the Torah, many children were named based on incidents that occurred as they were born. The examples are simply too numerous to mention, but even a cursory look at Genesis and the first part of Exodus will bear out this idea. Yet other biblical figures, such as Noah (see Genesis 5:29), had names based on their parents' hopes and aspirations. Whether the child grows to live out these hopes and aspirations are, of course, up to that child as he or she grows to adulthood.

In cases where names in the Torah were changed—Abram and Sarai to Abraham and Sarah (Genesis 17:5, 15), Jacob to Israel (Genesis 32:29, 35:10), and Hoshea to Joshua (Numbers 13:16)—the changes reflected the growth of the individual. In these cases, the people in question had exhibited the attributes of spiritual strength and leadership and had moved their lives in those directions. God confirmed the change via their names. (In Joshua's case, it is Moses who renames him, invoking God as part of the name change.)

Name changing is still used to reflect a person's changed destiny. Rabbinic literature (Rosh Hashana 16b and *Genesis Rabba* 44:12) suggests changing the name as a way of "tearing up the Evil Decree" and refers to Abraham and Sarah as proof. To this day, there is a tradition to change the Hebrew name of a desperately ill individual, hoping that this will change that person's fate and allow him or her to recover. (For more on name changing for an ill person, see the end of Chapter 5 in my book *To Walk in God's Ways—Jewish Pastoral Perspectives on Illness and Bereavement* [Northvale NJ: Jason Aronson, 1995.])

Rabbi David Hoffman's commentary (early twentieth-century Germany) suggests that even after Ya'akov/Jacob received his new name of Yisrael/ Israel, he retained the name Ya'akov. These names are both used in the remainder of the Book of Genesis. Rabbi Hoffman points out that Jacob is referred to as such in the context of subsequent events that affect him as an individual. But in the context of his being the founder of the Jewish People, he is referred to as Israel. This certainly fits into our thesis of a changed name reflecting the fact that the person, with the help of Hashem, can indeed change his or her destiny. It is noteworthy that Israel still maintains his original name of Jacob, with all of its original negative connotations. Even when one has in effect changed his or her fate, one cannot fully divorce him- or herself from the past.

Today's naming traditions point to both the past and future. Many Jews will name children after relatives. Ashkenazic tradition encourages naming after deceased relatives while Sephardic tradition honors living grandparents. However, some people will still name children after events connected with birth. Our oldest son was named after my wife's two grandfathers. Our second son was named after my *chavruta* (Torah study partner) and closest friend, and after my father's brother, who was killed in the Holocaust. But our daughter was named after my wife's grandmothers and also given a second middle name of *Orah*—light. You see, she was born at one minute before midnight on *Tisha B'av*, the anniversary of the Temple's destruction. So, on the darkest day of Jewish history and of our calandar, a ray of light shone.

Our fourth child was not named after any person but in an odd way after my doctoral dissertation, which later became my first book. We had already been considering Raphael Simcha as a name, but it turned out that I finished my dissertation the week Raphi was born. My topic was illness and bereavement. Raphael means "God heals," the antidote for illness, and Simcha means "joy," the antidote for bereavment! What better hope can parents share than for their baby to grow up offering healing and joy to a world filled with pain and sorrow. May it be God's will that this is so!

David Sofian

As you point out, there can be no doubt that our third patriarch's name change is significant in this narrative. The commentators suggest to us several ways of understanding this change. For example, *B'reishit* 39:10 says, "your name is Jacob," before the name Israel is given. Several commentators suggest that this indicates that "Israel" would not replace the name Jacob, but be an addition to it.

S'forno tells us that the name change points to Israel eventually ruling over the Canaanites. *Or Ha-Khaim* (referenced in the Stone Edition of the *Chumash*, p. 188) sees an enhancement of Jacob's original soul in the adding of the name Israel. Benno Jacob ("Genesis," referenced in The Torah: A Modern Commentary, U.A.H.C. [Schocken: Berlin, 1934], p. 233) analyzed the forty-five times the name Jacob is used and the thirty-four times the name Israel is used from Chapter 35 to the end of *B'reishit*. He concludes that "Jacob" is used whenever material or physical matters are concerned and "Israel" whenever spiritual considerations are being featured.

My own starting point is to look at the Hebrew root of the name Jacob. The Hebrew root *ayin-koof-vet* has several meanings. One possible definition is, "crooked." I am unable to know for sure whether this meaning preexisted its use in Jacob's name, or if the meaning came about as a result of its use in the Jacob narrative. However, given that we find the root with this meaning in Jeremiah 17:9 (the heart is deceitful [*akov ha-lev*] above all things), we can assume that this name reflects Jacob's later deceit.

Even the text's own explanation that his name derived from his holding onto Esau's heel at birth hints at this meaning. The heel is curved, not straight. Jacob's hold on the heel insinuates Jacob's hold on crookedness rather than honesty. The point is that we learn about Jacob's initial character from his original name.

Later, in Chapter 32:27–29, we are introduced to his new name. There, the emissary he wrestles with says to him, "Your name shall no more be called Jacob, but Israel: For you have striven with God and with men, and have prevailed." Rashi's comment here supports the above interpretation of "Jacob" by indicating that with the new name, Israel, the earlier character stain of supplanting his brother with deceit could be removed.

The emissary's comment about "Israel" signifying striving with God and men can mean that Jacob had struggled to grow and change. What he needs to do is admit what he had done so he would be ready to grow into the next stage of his life. That is how Jacob would be ready to become Israel—and that is precisely what happens.

We see this in the narrative when Jacob encounters Esau and they reconcile. After struggling with the emissary (God, man, himself), he admits his deceit by offering Esau a present in Chapter 33:11. It is the word used here for "present" that is significant. Jacob offered Esau his blessing (*birkhati*). I do not think this word choice is an accident. It draws us back to the deceit that Jacob used in acquiring blessing from Isaac in the first place. Only after Esau accepts do we read the key verse to which you point. After Esau accepts, God appears to Jacob again and actually changes his name as the emissary had said would happen. God is confirming here that Jacob had indeed changed as a result of his struggles with the granting of the new name.

Then the answer to your question is, yes, a person can change the character that one's name reflects. Doing so requires self-evaluation, growth, and change.

Va'Yetze: Genesis 28:10–32:3

Prophetical Reading
Hosea 12:13–14:10

Overview of Torah Portion

On the way to Haran, Jacob dreams of angels going up and down a ladder to heaven. God promises to guard Jacob's steps. In Haran, he works seven years for Laban to secure Rachel as a wife. Laban substitutes Leah, Rachel's older sister, for Rachel on the wedding night. Jacob agrees to work another seven years to acquire Rachel. Leah, Rachel, and their handmaids give birth to 11 sons, progenitors of the Hebrew tribes, and one daughter, Dinah. At the end of twenty years, despite Laban's trickery, Jacob leaves with his wives, children, and great riches.

Key Verses

"And the servant . . . said, 'Oh Lord, the God of my master Abraham . . ., show kindness to my master Abraham. . . . Let it be that the girl to whom I shall say, 'Please let down your pitcher, that I may drink,' and she shall say 'Drink, and I will give your camels drink also,' she shall be the one you have appointed for your servant, for Isaac. And in that I shall know that you have done kindness to my master'" (Genesis 24:9, 12, 14).

"And it came to pass, when Jacob saw Rachel the daughter of Laban, his mother's brother, and the sheep of Laban, his mother's brother, that Jacob went near and rolled the stone from the well's mouth and watered the flock of Laban, his mother's brother. And Jacob kissed Rachel and lifted up his voice and wept. . . . And Jacob loved Rachel" (Genesis 29:10–11, 18).

Discussion Question

Of wives and wells: When Eliezer, Abraham's servant, was dispatched to Abraham's homeland years earlier to find a wife for Isaac, he prayed to God and established a condition for determining a fitting spouse for his master's son—Isaac's future wife would offer water to Eliezer and his camels. In a similar scenario, however, the Torah does not record Jacob offering a prayer or setting criteria for determining his own wife. Instead, he rolls the stone off the well and he waters the flocks. Why the difference between the behavior of Eliezer and Jacob? Why does Jacob not demand some action, the performance of kindness or some other trait, before choosing Rachel? What do the two approaches teach us about finding a mate?

Shammai Engelmayer

There is a big difference between the arrival of Avraham's servant in Haran (it is not certain that he was Eliezer, by the way) and Ya'akov's arrival: The servant was there to find a woman suitable for the role God ordained for the woman who would marry Yitzchak; Ya'akov was there to find a wife.

For the servant, the task was a daunting one. He was Avraham's agent, not Yitzchak's, and so he had to follow Avraham's guidelines, not Yitzchak's. Thus, he had to choose someone who could fill the role of matriarch of a clan that had been promised greatness. This woman would have to help move that promise along to fulfillment.

Yitzchak would have had other concerns, such as whether his wife-to-be was nice to look at; whether she appealed to his passionate side; whether she would be someone he would enjoy spending time with doing nothing in particular; and whether she would be a friend, as well as a mate.

These were not the servant's concerns, but he knew he was as human as Yitzchak. Left to his own devices, he would choose a wife the way Yitzchak (or almost anyone else) would, albeit from his perspective rather than Yitzchak's, since he is doing the choosing (for example, maybe he was more attracted to tall, lanky brunettes, while Yitzchak may have preferred short redheads; whatever Yitzchak's preferences, there is no evidence the servant ever asked him what he wanted in a wife). That would not do in this case. So, the servant appeals to God for help, and God helps. He leads the servant to Rivka (Rebecca). She is the "right" choice—from God's perspective and Avraham's.

On the other hand, there are suggestions in the text that she was not "right" from Yitzchak's point of view, at least not for the life of their marriage. She obviously appealed to him physically, because he is publicly seen "sporting" with her the way a husband and wife might play with each other—but that was early in their marriage.

Later on, we see that Rivka has little faith in his judgment, and he obviously cares nothing about hers. That is why she sets up this elaborate deception that led to Ya'akov's taking the blessing Yitzchak would have given to Esau. It is only after that incident that Yitzchak heeds Rivka's advice and sends Ya'akov to Haran, but that may have had less to do with caring about Rivka and more with not wanting his devious little boy around anymore. (Or, more likely, he did not want his favorite son, Esau, to be guilty of fratricide.)

Ya'akov, of course, would operate on the same wavelength as his father, or the servant, would have, had he been left to his own devices. He chooses his wife the way most of us choose ours: hormonally. Rachel appealed to him; Leah did not. He chose Rachel, but got Leah anyway. He made it clear through their marriage that, while he would have sex with Leah in order to have children, he would never *make love* to Leah. That was reserved only for Rachel.

What do we learn from all this? Not much, really. The servant's actions show us the importance of faithfully carrying out an "agency" (acting on behalf of someone else), but it shows us little about how to choose a wife. His commission was not from Yitzchak, but Avraham, and it had less to do with choosing a wife for Yitzchak than a mother for Israel.

We also do not know who Rivka's competition was, so we can only judge how good a choice she turned out to be, not whether she was the best choice overall. As far as the kind of choice she was from our perspective, she was perfect—but we were not married to her; Yitzchak was.

As for Ya'akov's way, well, Ya'akov rejected Leah, but she was faithful to her role—and to him—nonetheless. And she was the mother of Yehudah and Levi. Thus, Rachel is far less anyone's matriarch than she is their *tante*arch. So, from our perspective, not only did Ya'akov choose poorly, but he acted reprehensibly toward Leah afterwards.

The Torah recognizes that in two important laws: Prohibiting marriage to one sister while the other yet lives, and insisting that the son of the "hated" wife, if he is the chronological first-born, be granted the title and rights of the first-born son. (First-born, in the Torah, is not a chronological designation, but a gratuitous title. It could go to the physical first-born, or to whomever of his children the father designates. Thus, Reuven loses the title to Yehudah when he sleeps with one of his father's other wives. And Yoseph, the son of the "loved" wife, inherits the traditional double-share of the first-born.)

One possible lesson may have to do with who chooses the wife: Of all the principal figures in the Torah, only Yitzchak has a wife chosen for him, and Ya'akov has one foisted on him; everyone else, including Ya'akov, chooses their own. (Chava does not count; God did not choose her from among a collection, but created her from scratch.) So, perhaps the Torah is trying to tell us that the choice is ours to make, not someone else's.

Joseph Ozarowski

Eliezer's agenda was well-planned and thought-out. His stated mission was to find a proper wife for his master's son, and he had the time and wherewith to work out logical criteria. He looked for a woman who would fit into the Abrahamic ideal of hospitality and kindness. He waited for the right person to show these qualities and found them in Rivka. Jacob, on the other hand, fled his brother's anger and was lucky to have escaped with his life. He had no specific agenda of finding a "*shiddukh*," (a match). Thus, his actions were spontaneous acts of kindness when he found both refuge with family and also a woman for whom he fell. This act of moving the stone could not have been easy. Yet, as Rashi comments, this was like "a person taking a stopper out of a bottle, showing you his great strength." When overcome by emotion—the energy of escape, the joy at finding refuge—one is capable of unexpected things. Perhaps, as the *Saba* from Slabodka (nineteenth-century Russia) suggests, this is why we refer to Jacob's act when praying for rain on *Shmini Atzeret*: "He unified his heart and rolled a stone off the mouth of the well of water. . . . For his sake (O God), do not hold water back."

There is a third case of a *shiddukh* made near a well of water and thirsty animals. Moses, in Exodus 2:16–19, not only helped water the flock of Jethro's daughters, but protected them while they were attacked by the other shepherds. We may be able to discern a progression: Eliezer, friend of the Patriarchs but not one himself, allows Rivka to do the work in watering the flock. Jacob, ancestor of the tribes, waters the flock himself. Moses, prophet of God and teacher of Torah, also gives water to the animals, but he goes further by standing up for justice on behalf of the injured. Perhaps *shiddukh*, a symbol of Jewish survival and endurance, along with water, a symbol of life, can teach us about the need for acts of kindness and justice as the basis for Judaism.

David Sofian

It is possible that the two situations you draw to our attention are more similar than you indicate. Of course, they are alike in that both are about the general subject of determining a spouse. However, it is possible to see an even more significant parallel.

In the first case, Abraham's servant, who tradition tells us was Eliezer, seeks a divine sign in order to make the choice required of him. The sign occurs and he proceeds accordingly. You point out the key difference that Jacob didn't seek a similar sign.

However, perhaps Jacob didn't seek a sign because he already had the divine guidance he needed. This is suggested in Rashi's quote of *Midrash B'reishit Rabbah* in his commentary to *B'reishit* 29:1. He tells us that "so Jacob lifted his feet" means that Jacob's journey became easier after he learned the good tidings of God's protection. His feet were light, and so the travelling was easier.

In other words, Jacob understood from his encounter with God at Beth El that God was with him; therefore, he knew his choices would be the correct ones. If so, the two episodes are significantly similar in that Abraham's servant and Jacob both look to God for confirmation of the choice each needs to make.

However, that said, the situations do not strike me as at all similar. To see how key the disparity is, we need to look at the personalities involved. Let's begin with Isaac.

The Torah does not tell us much about Isaac. Indeed, there are no Isaac stories in and of themselves. Isaac always serves as a supporting character in either the Abraham narratives or the Jacob narratives. This is the case in the key verses you give. Of all the classic Torah characters, only Isaac needs his father to arrange a marriage for him. Isaac is passive, he tends to acquiesce in the stronger personalities around him.

In other words, the situation in *Chaye Sarah* is of a father who has so much reason in his old age to be concerned with his son's future that he take steps to ensure his son marries properly.

So, Abraham sent a servant to do the finding. Assigning him this amount of responsibility puts the servant in a very difficult position. Given what we've said about Isaac, we can assume he would have felt the weight of securing Isaac a good match. Since the covenant is to be carried on through Isaac, it would be necessary to find exactly the right woman for him, a strong person who would complement him suitably. The servant had to find a woman who would not only please Isaac but please Abraham and further God's covenantal plans.

Given this situation, as we might expect, the servant was reluctant to accept the task. Abraham had to coerce him into swearing out an oath to guarantee that he would do it. It is not surprising that the servant wanted help in making this selection. This help came in the form of a divine sign. The difficulty of making an impossible decision was taken off the servant in this way.

The circumstance in our current parshah is very different. Jacob acts in his own behalf. The decision became his to make. He saw Rachel for himself and determined what to do. Many things can be said about the decisions Jacob made, but as we have come to understand him throughout his stories, we see now he cannot be accused of being indecisive. He was not a mere servant, being asked to find a spouse for the subservient son of his master. Therefore, he didn't need God's intervention with a sign.

From my point of view, these episodes are not about different approaches to finding mates. Rather, these stories are about emphasizing the different personalities of the two men involved.

Va'Yishlach:
Genesis 32:4–36:43

Prophetical Reading
Hosea 11:7–12:12

Overview of Torah Portion

Jacob, returning to Canaan and fearful of his brother Esau's wrath, offers some of his animals and servants to appease Esau's anger. Alone on the far side of the Jordan, Jacob wrestles one night with a man/angel who changes Jacob's name to Israel. Jacob and Esau reunite peacefully. Esau returns to Seir and Jacob travels to the city of Shechem. In revenge for the rape of their sister, Dinah, by a member of Shechem's ruling family, Shimon and Levi persuade all the city's men to undergo circumcisions; they then kill all the males, who were weakened by the surgery. Jacob, on God's command, travels to Beth-El, where God confirm's Jacob's name change. Rachel dies giving birth to Benjamin and is buried in Bethlehem. Isaac dies in Hebron and is buried by Jacob and Esau. Esau leaves Canaan.

Key Verses

"And Jacob was left alone, and a man wrestled with him until dawn broke. And he [the man] said, 'Let me go, because the dawn is breaking.' And he [Jacob] said, 'I will not let you go unless you bless me'" (Genesis 32: 25–27).

Discussion Question

ANOTHER BLESSING: Jacob has already received his father's blessing—the one intended for Esau, and another one when he flees from Beersheva. God

46

re-establishes the Patriarchs' covenant with Jacob and promises to bring him back safely to Canaan. Why does Jacob ask the person with whom he wrestles—man or angel—for another blessing? What else does Jacob need? Is God's pledge not sufficient?

Shammai Engelmayer

Why, indeed, did Ya'akov ask "the man" for a blessing? Being able to answer that question will allow us to answer the bigger questions: Who was that man and what really happened at the *Yabbok*?

Clearly, "the man" is more than that. Ya'akov's nocturnal wrestling partner is called a man in the text, but his desire to be gone by daybreak, the fact that Ya'akov asked him for a blessing, the wording of the blessing given to him by the man, and the whole scene would suggest that this "man" was something else.

There are a number of explanations. One I like in particular is that Ya'akov confronted his own self that night. He had not been a particularly nice individual, thus far. In fact, he was a liar and a cheat, among other things. But once he crossed back over the Yabbok, he was the father of a new nation, one chosen by God for a unique mission. Even he must have understood that the Ya'akov who had lived until then must give way to a new Ya'akov, one better suited for the role he must then henceforth play. So, "the man" is actually Ya'akov's dark side and the "battle" is metaphorical.

As I said, I like the explanation, but it is not wholly satisfying. What this scenario fails to account for is the blessing. It becomes an anomaly. Why would Ya'akov have asked himself for a blessing? And how does the blessing—including a name change that suggests he wrestled with both gods (so "*Elohim*" should be translated here) and men, and won—fit into such an explanation? Clearly we need to seek on.

The second possibility is that "the man" is a messenger of God. Again, it represents a battle for Ya'akov's soul. God could not allow the old Ya'akov to cross the *Yabbok*. Somehow, that Ya'akov must be replaced by a kinder, gentler patriarch.

This version would explain the blessing. Ya'akov is really asking, "Who am I?" The answer is that he is no longer Ya'akov, but Yisrael (Israel). He is a new man, one whose faults caused him to be repudiated by God, but whose inner strength allowed him to overcome those faults and overturn the evil decree.

"You are a person who has done *teshuvah*," comes the response, according to this understanding. "You are a new person, as if reborn. And just as you fought with yourself and overturned your life, so you have managed to overturn My decree against you. Your new self deserves a new name. That name shall be Yisrael."

This solution, too, offers many possibilities for lessons. The problem with it is that God did not change Ya'akov's name to Israel until Beth-El. If "the man" had been God's agent, there would have been no need for God to have done so later on.

This leaves us with an answer that is much simpler and perfectly logical.

The Ya'akov who escaped from his father-in-law Lavan (Laban) is already a reformed man who has overcome his character flaws. By now, he has come to realize: Bad things keep happening to him (his brother Esau's desire for vengeance, Lavan's deceitfulness, Lavan's possible attempts to kill him). Eventually, he had to ask himself, "why?" The answer is obvious: It's because of the kind of person he is. Esau wanted vengeance because of what Ya'akov did to him, not once but twice. Lavan deceived him about whom he was marrying because Ya'akov showed disdain for local custom; he wanted Rachel then, not after Leah found a husband for herself. Lavan wanted to kill him because Ya'akov, in whom he bestowed so much trust, used his position with Lavan to make himself richer—something that suggested a violation of that trust.

By the time Ya'akov reached the Yabbok, he knew he was a changed man—but Esau did not. He needed to know who Ya'akov was. Is the man who crossed the river into Canaan the same one who crossed the river out of Canaan? Was he still a threat to Esau, or was he finally prepared to be a brother?

So, Esau met Ya'akov in the middle of the night, challenged him to prove himself worthy of coming home. There would be no deceptions this time; the battle would be on Esau's terms. Esau was the stronger by far and the more experienced in combat. If Ya'akov had truly changed, the God of Avraham and Yitzchak would show Himself to be the God of Ya'akov, as well. He would give him the strength to overcome Esau. It is trial by combat.

Why at night? Because Esau was honorable. If Ya'akov won, meaning that he was a changed man, then Esau wanted the world to know that this was his brother, not his enemy. At the same time, he did not want his reputation as a fighter marred by losing a battle with a simple shepherd. The battle had to take place away from anyone's view, in total secrecy.

Ya'akov, meanwhile, needed to know that Esau would no longer be a threat to him. Was this the first battle of many—or the one and only? He asked for a blessing because blessings were thought to have a power of their own. Once given, as Esau had learned so bitterly from Yitzchak, they could not be retrieved. Ya'akov needed to hear what Esau's response would be. He needed to hear Esau's heart.

The words Esau used to bless Ya'akov made it clear to him that Esau was no longer his enemy, but his brother. As for the blessing, Esau undoubtedly ascribed Ya'akov's earlier behavior to the influence of alien gods—gods in whom he himself may have believed. That Ya'akov could overcome his character flaws is, to Esau, a sign that he had overcome the influence of these gods; in other words, that he had "wrestled" with these gods and defeated them.

So the twin brothers return to their respective camps and prepare to stage their "reunion."

Just because Esau gave his brother a new name, however, means nothing. Only God can change Ya'akov's name, which He does at Beth-El. Interestingly, when God calls him Yisrael, He gives no reason for the change. He is merely confirming what Esau already concluded: Ya'akov had confronted his demons and had overcome them.

Joseph Ozarowski

I believe that the meaning of the extra blessing stemming from Jacob's fight with the mysterious stranger depends on the stranger's identity. The Torah refers to him as *ish*, (a man). If the plain sense of the text is correct, that he was simply human, then I can find no profound teaching from the additional blessing. Indeed, this approach raises more questions, such as how did this mysterious human stranger know Jacob's name? What was he doing there in the middle of the night?

Many commentators accept the idea that the stranger was an angelic or heavenly figure. The angel could have been a direct representative of God, or, as the midrash puts it, the *saro shel Esav*, Esau's guardian angel. If either of these is so, Rashi then offers us the best answer to our question. Rashi suggests that the grammar of the word *berakhtani* does not mean, "You bless me," but rather, Jacob asking the angel to confirm the blessings he (Jacob) had already received from his father and that Esau would still want.

My favorite approach is a third one that suggests this battle actually took place inside of Jacob's head. Maimonides (twelfth-century Spain/Egypt) in *Guide for the Perplexed*, concludes that the entire incident was part of a prophetic vision. Ralbag (Gersonides—fourteenth-century Provence) also follows this approach. Abarbenel goes even further, tying the dream and struggle to Jacob's anxious state, the anticipation of meeting his brother the next day.

We might summarize this school of thought by saying that, ultimately, Jacob is wrestling with himself and is engaged in a great psychic battle with his inner soul rather than with an outsider. Perhaps the Torah is attempting to teach us that, to find the ultimate source of blessing, we have to look deep within ourselves. We have to find our inner strengths and weaknesses before we face the dawn of an unknown day, just as Jacob did.

(I highly recommend to the interested reader two fine essays: "On Jacob's Struggle With the Angel" in *Meditations on the Torah* by B.S. Jacobson. Tel-Aviv:Sinai, 1977, and Nechama Leibowitz's "And A Man Struggled With Him" in *Studies in the Weekly Torah Portion* (Genesis). Jerusalem: WZO, 1973.)

David Sofian

Rashi offers an answer to your question in his comment to chapter 32:27 and the Hebrew word, *berakhtani,* "bless me." As I alluded to in my comment to *Parashat Toldot,* Rashi tells us Jacob wanted confirmation of his father's blessings because he believed Esau was contesting them. This confirmation comes when his opponent tells him that his name will be changed from Jacob to Israel.

B'reishit itself tells us that the name change refers to the patriarch striving with God and with men and prevailing. Rashi adds that the opponent meant that it will no longer be said Jacob's blessings came to him through insinuation and deceit. Rather the current blessing, as expressed in his new name, indicates how the earlier blessings resulted from his superiority.

Another approach to your question is to ask about the nature of the being with whom Jacob wrestled. If we can determine who this being is, perhaps we will know why Jacob is seeking a blessing from that being. *Midrash B'reishit Rabbah* 78:3 tells us Jacob was wrestling with Esau's guardian angel. We know from the context of the narrative that Jacob is full of trepidation regarding his reunion with his brother Esau. Then, in seeking the angel's blessing, Jacob is seeking resolution of the specific problem at hand. Jacob wants an assurance that he no longer need fear Esau's continued anger.

As I said above, the Torah text itself explains that the name "Israel" means that Jacob was wrestling with God (Elohim). Then, Jacob's opponent was not an angel or an agent. In order to understand why Jacob wants a blessing now, we need to focus on the nature of the struggling. Possibly, the struggling is about Jacob recognizing how his relationship with God is moving to a new plain.

Back when Jacob left his home and encountered God at Beth El, he made his relationship with God conditional on God being his protector. Now his relationship with God results from a struggle that ends in unconditional faith. Therefore, Jacob sought confirmation of his growth with a blessing. Jacob only becomes Israel if he first wrestles with God.

One more possibility is that Jacob's wrestling opponent in this fascinating part of the patriarchal narrative was not an angel nor God, but Jacob himself. Chapter 32:25 says, "Jacob was left alone. And a man (*ish*) wrestled with him until the break of dawn." The being here is clearly called a man. This presents the possibility that Jacob is struggling with himself since he is the man present already.

Jacob is about to be reunited with his brother. He is not only unsure of what to expect from Esau, but also from himself, as he is about to return home. Perhaps he is worried that he could revert to the person he was. He must have been filled with questions, with self doubts. He needed to confirm his own growth and development. Therefore, he wrestles with himself, with his self-doubts, in a moment of personal crisis. If so, his own expression of blessing was a statement of self-approval for the person he had become. Now that he realized he was no longer Jacob the immature trickster, but the responsible Israel, he is ready to face his long estranged brother.

Even as his name change suggested his struggles were with God, the text's explanation of the name change also suggests that, at the same time, the struggles were with himself. It says the name "Israel" means he wrestled with God and with men. If the men here are a reference to Jacob's self, even as the man (*ish*) earlier in the story may have been a reference to Jacob's self, then perhaps the Torah is implying that, when we wrestle with God, we wrestle with our own soul, and that, when we wrestle with our own soul, we wrestle with God. If so, when Jacob receives the blessing and new name, he not only receives God's validation but his own validation for growth and development.

Va'Yeshev:
Genesis 37:1–40:23

Prophetical Reading
Amos 2:6–3:8

Overview of Torah Portion

Joseph's dreams of his eventual ascendancy evoke his brothers' jealousy. Away watching their flocks, they throw him into a pit, then sell him to an Egyptian-bound caravan, dipping his prized coat of many colors into goat's blood and presenting it to Jacob as proof of Joseph's demise. Judah has an illicit liaison with his daughter-in-law, Tamar. Joseph, sold into servitude in Egypt, attracts the attention of his master's amorous wife. Spurned, she accuses Joseph of attacking her. Joseph is put into prison, where he correctly interprets the dreams of the king's imprisoned butler and baker.

Key Verses

"And Laban said to him [Jacob] . . . 'I observed that the Lord blessed me for your sake'" (Genesis 30:27).

"And his [Joseph's] master saw that the Lord was with him and the Lord made all that he did prosper in his hand" (Genesis 39:3).

Discussion Question

RECOGNIZING GOD'S HAND: Both Laban, Jacob's uncle and employer, and Potiphar, Joseph's master, acknowledge that their prosperity results from the blessed status of their Hebrew worker. Yet, Laban attempts to cheat Jacob out of his deserved wages, and the nearly cuckolded Potiphar puts accused Joseph into prison. If Laban and Potiphar see the hand of an all-powerful God, why do they deal harshly with the mortal source of their blessings? Are both cases similar? Even if Laban and Potiphar are not pious, why do they act against their own self-interest?

Shammai Engelmayer

The question presupposes that Lavan and Potiphar both recognized the Lord as God. They did not. All they were admitting to, respectively, is that Ya'akov's God is Ya'akov's God and that Yoseph's God was Yoseph's God.

They also had gods, however, and believed their gods to be more powerful than any other deity or pantheon of deities. That is why they believed in their gods. When things went well for them, through the aid of Ya'akov and Yoseph, they were then willing to admit that God had something to do with it; after all, their gods had something to do with their fortunes. But when things went awry, they had no fear of God, nor paid Him any mind, for their gods were greater and more powerful.

Your question also presupposes that a gift from God was a license to live outside the law and the standards of society. Lavan and Potiphar recognized that God had given special gifts to Ya'akov and Yoseph. But his gift did not give Ya'akov the right to abuse his father-in-law's trust by lining his own pockets at Lavan's expense (which he did do, irrespective of his motives). And his gift did not give Yoseph the right to rape Potiphar's wife (a crime with which he was charged, but which he did not do, although Potiphar could not know that). Yet your question, at least the way it is phrased, implies such license. Lavan and Potiphar should have dismissed the infractions, the question suggests; they were getting rich off of Ya'akov and Yoseph; it was in their best interests to look the other way.

It is in no one's interest to look the other way, nor is that what God wants us to do. God never said, "Behold, I give you My Law. It is the Law for all of you—except those in whom I show special favor. They can do as they please and none shall have cause for complaint, for I am the Lord."

None was more beloved by God than Moshe Rabbeinu, yet Moshe had to pay for his wrongdoing. David was a special favorite of the Lord's, yet the sword never departed from his house after Uriah was killed. If God does not look the other way, we who are created in His image should not, either.

On the other hand, neither Lavan nor Potiphar had cause for too much complaint. What Ya'akov did was wrong, but Lavan had it coming to him for the way he had tricked Ya'akov and used the gift God gave his son-in-law to line his own pockets. Potiphar should have investigated the rape charge because he clearly had his suspicions. Otherwise, he either would have had Yoseph put to death (the way slaves would be treated for attacking the master's "property"), or would have exacted a heavy fine out of him (the way free men would be treated when found guilty of rape, which in the ancient world was seen as a financial loss for father or husband, not as a crime against the violated woman).

In a sense, then, they did go against their own interests, something we humans have been doing since the very beginning. Belief in God has no relevance here. Adam and Chava not only knew God and believed in Him, they knew the extent of His power better than anyone after them could. Yet, they ate of the forbidden fruit and actually thought they could hide the truth from God. That was acting against their own interests.

Kayin knew God's might; he certainly must have been told about the Garden of Eden and what happened there. That did not stop him from trying to deny he killed Hevel.

The generation of the Exodus saw at least nine of the ten plagues God brought on Egypt, as well as the splitting of the sea. It "heard" His "voice" at Sinai. Egypt meant slavery and death for Israel. God clearly meant freedom and life. Yet, how often did it rebel in the desert, saying each time "would we had stayed in Egypt?"

Look at the Serbs and Croats. Long ago, they must have concluded that the only things they gained by their fighting were endless death, destruction, and despair. Yet, look how long it too for them to stop the guns.

Why do we humans act like this? Because we spend so much time looking out for number one that we cannot see that acting for the greater good is the only true way to guarantee better lives for ourselves. When everyone is healthy, wealthy, and wise, there is nothing we cannot accomplish. But, if we each seek to gain advantage over the other and at his or her expense, if from birth to death we see ourselves in a rat race rather than a human race, all we can build is a future filled with jealousies, petty hatreds, murders, and ever-bigger mega-bombs.

With all due deference to the late Lubavitcher Rebbe, z"l, (may his memory be for a blessing), the key to bringing Mashiach is not through the celebration of two *Shabbatot* in a row by all Jews. Rather, it is by all people spending two weeks loving their neighbors as they would love themselves. Before those two weeks were up, we would all realize that the Messiah has been here all along—kept buried deep inside each of us by the weight of our egocentricity.

Joseph Ozarowski

While the cases of Lavan and Potiphar bear some similarities, there are also some crucial differences, especially in the area raised about their faith in Hashem. According to many commentaries, Potiphar only reluctantly committed Joseph to prison. This was because of his great respect and fondness for the young Hebrew, and perhaps because he knew how well Joseph managed household affairs.

However, Potiphar was afraid that, without some action here, people would have suspected his wife's infidelity to him and their children's paternal *yichus*. (For more on this, see the commentary in the Artscroll *Chumash*, p. 217.) Thus, Potiphar was indeed acting in his own self-interest, but not necessarily his material self-interest.

Lavan saw the God of Jacob as "just another one of the gods" and was willing to acknowledge Hashem in this way. The textual proof is from the quoted verse, "I observed that the Lord blessed me for your sake. . . ." The Hebrew *nihashti* has a connotation of magic or witchcraft. Thus, Hertz's *The Pentateuch* (London: Soncino, 1962) translates this as "I have seen the signs . . ." and Artscroll, "I have learned by divination that Hashem has blessed me. . . ." Lavan's faith was rather imperfect, second-rate. Later, in the final agreement with Jacob, Lavan invoked both Jacob's God and his own. (Jacob, of course, only invoked Hashem.) So, in a sense, Lavan was also acting in his own self-interest. I suppose it is in his own self-interest to hedge his bets, but not to get too chummy with Jacob's God.

We might ask where these two pagans even got the idea of monotheism, a single God who blesses those who keep His faith. One answer may be derived from the fact that both Jacob and Joseph frequently referred to God in their talk. One of the major characteristics of all the major patriarchal figures is their planting monotheism into the world around them. (For more on this and further proofs from the text, see Nechama Leibowitz's "Joseph Brings God into Pharoah's Life" in *Studies in the Weekly Torah Portion* (Genesis). Jerusalem: WZO, 1973.)

When one constantly hears talk of faith in God, it cannot help but rub off. I remember, as a teen in 1967, when my father received a phone call from Israel just after the Six-Day War. My dad, while Jewishly committed, well-educated in Torah, and deeply immersed in Yiddish culture, was at the time not particularly religious in the theological sense. All of a sudden, my father started repeating, almost chanting, "*Baruch Hashem, Baruch Hashem!*" ("Blessed be God, blessed be God!") I had never heard him say this, and I could not understand what was going on until after the call. You see, we had a long-lost cousin in Israel, married to a *Rosh Yeshiva*, the only religious end of my father's family. When telling my father how she was doing, she kept saying, "*Baruch Hashem, Baruch Hashem!*" My father was simply repeating this with her! Words do have an effect.

Halvai, there should be people around whose faith and trust in the Almighty can influence others in the world to acknowledge the goodness, richness, and love in Hashem's world, rather than constantly seeking material gain.

David Sofian

Perhaps Laban was being less than completely honest when he said God blessed him for Jacob's sake. This approach becomes more plausible when we recognize Laban's willingness to use words dishonestly if they furthered his purpose.

In *Parashat Va'Yetze* (Chapter 29:15), Laban magnanimously indicated that Jacob shouldn't have to work for nothing just because he was kin and then asks Jacob what his wages should have been. Jacob suggested that he work seven years for Rachel and Laban immediately agrees saying, "Better that I give her to you than that I should give her to an outsider." What could be clearer than this arrangement? Nevertheless, showing just how insincere his earlier words were, without hesitation, he substituted Leah when the times came. When Jacob confronted him, he simply responded by saying, "It is not the practice in our place to marry off the younger before the older." How easily Laban lies.

Midrash B'reishit Rabbah Chapter 70:19 goes even further in revealing Laban's deceitful character. In reference to *B'reishit* 29:22, "And Laban gathered all the people of the place and made a feast," the midrash tells us how Laban reminded the people about Jacob's positive influence on their lives. He pointed out to them how their water shortage came to an end as soon as Jacob came into their midsts. He used this reminder to convince them that keeping Jacob with them for as long as possible was to their advantage.

To do this, Laban needed them to agree not to let on to the planned substitution of Leah for Rachel. However, their promise of cooperation is not sufficient. Laban wants each of them to give him a material pledge to demonstrate concrete commitment to his plan. They do this, as well. Yet deceiving Jacob is not enough for Laban. He also deceived all those he gathered by inappropriately using their pledges to pay for the wedding feast he had arranged. Given the Torah text itself and this midrash, we should have no trouble imputing other motivations to Laban than the ones he officially states.

Laban's true motivations come out by looking at the context of his remark in *B'reishit* 30:27. Just prior to this verse, Jacob expressed to Laban his desire to return home. Clearly, Laban did not want this to happen, given all the work he had received from Jacob and the good fortune that has coincided with his presence. So, the verse in question is really about Laban trying to convince Jacob to stay. We know, given his character, that he would be willing to say anything to achieve his goal. Laban's reference to God blessing him on Jacob's account is just part of that attempt.

Verse 27 begins with Laban saying to Jacob, "If I have found favor in your eyes. . . ." This could be merely a polite opening. However, S'forno tells us that it really means, "if you love me." Laban's initial strategy is to try drawing on Jacob's sense of family connection and loyalty. When that is not enough, Laban then goes on to say, "I have observed the signs and the Eternal has blessed me for your sake."

Now Laban is appealing to Jacob's piety. Once we adopt this point of view, even the words Laban uses in his appeal are revealing of his true intent. He says, *nihashti* (I have read the signs), which Rashi tells us means Laban divined that he had been blessed for Jacob's sake. Laban could have made his point without this word. Using it hints at his disingenuousness, for Laban is pointing to the occult (*nihashti*) even as he is invoking God's name. Laban is trying to deceive Jacob again, this time into staying.

In short, as always, Laban believed he was acting in his own interest. His interest was in keeping Jacob with him and he was using his usual tactic of dishonesty and trickery with words in the hopes of keeping him.

This brings us now to the question of Potiphar. Perhaps, as with Laban, we should not simply take what he said at face value. After all, the midrash also brings Potiphar's character into question. *Midrash B'reishit Rabbah* 86:3 informs us how even Potiphar's name refers to his involvement with idolatrous practice. The midrash advises us that Potiphar and Potephera were the same person and that both these names are connected with idolatrous practice.

Furthermore, *B'reishit* 39:1 refers to Potiphar as a *S'rees Paroh*, which is usually translated as an officer of Pharaoh. In the same *B'reishit Rabbah* section (86:3), an entirely different slant on this designation is given. The word *S'rees* can also be related to castration. From this, the midrash infers Potiphar purchased Joseph for the purpose of sodomy and for this reason God emasculated him. Hence, he became a *S'rees Paroh*. His inclinations and practices must have colored all his perceptions. Additionally, his later willingness to believe his wife's accusations against Joseph and his throwing

Joseph in prison entitles us to doubt whether his recognition of the Eternal was genuine.

On the other hand, we could follow Ramban, who suggested that Potiphar did indeed feel real affection for Joseph, shown in the very fact that after the incident with his wife, he had Joseph imprisoned rather than killed. Perhaps Potiphar doubted his wife's story and perhaps Potiphar did truly recognize that God was with Joseph. This point of view is bolstered by the midrashic connection of Potiphar and Potephera. Joseph later married Asnat, daughter of Potephera. Potiphar's willingness to make this match may then reveal his true affection for and appreciation of Joseph. From this point of view, Potiphar was not dealing harshly with Joseph by placing him in prison, but was actually acting out of kindness and love. Potiphar would then be very different from Laban, whose deceitful character goes uncontested.

Miketz: Genesis 41:1–44:17

Prophetical Reading
Zechariah 2:14–4:7

Overview of Torah Portion

Joseph, in prison for "two full years" after interpreting the butler's and baker's dreams, is called upon to interpret Pharaoh's. After predicting the imminent start of seven bountiful years to be followed by seven years of famine, he is appointed Pharaoh's second in command. Jacob sends ten of his sons to Egypt, where Joseph has instituted a successful rationing program, to buy provisions. Accusing them of being spies, he demands that his brothers return with his remaining sibling, Benjamin. When they return to Egypt and set out again for Canaan, Joseph has a silver goblet placed in Benjamin's sack. Joseph threatens to enslave Benjamin, while releasing the other brothers.

Key Verses

"And Joseph said to Pharaoh, 'the dream of Pharaoh is one . . . Behold, seven years of great plenty are coming to the whole land of Egypt'" (Genesis 31:25, 29).

"And the seven years of famine began to come . . . and there was famine in all the lands. . . . And the famine was over all the face of the earth" (Genesis 31:54, 56).

Discussion Question

GLOBAL FAMINE: First, Joseph prophesied that a major famine would strike Egypt. Then, seven years later, all of Egypt's neighboring lands, including Canaan, were also stricken with famine. Finally, according to Jewish tradition, Jacob's family had sufficient food despite the famine, but he sent his sons to Egypt to avoid arousing his neighbors' jealousy. If God sent the famine to effect Joseph's reunion with his father and brothers, why did the entire region have to suffer? Why include the lands that weren't part of the patriarchal scenario? Why Canaan? If Jacob's family was not stricken during the famine, what is the point of bringing famine to the rest of the land? Was it not possible to bring Joseph and his family together without involving the entire Middle East?

Shammai Engelmayer

Let's get right down to it: God does not go around making innocent people suffer in order to move a plot along. If there was a famine in the region, that is nature taking its course. Famines happen. If God takes advantage of the famine to bring father and son together again, that shows His resourcefulness, but is not a comment on His morality.

Of course, it could be argued that, since we know how corrupt the local cultures of the region were, God was only settling up accounts. That is not the case here. If it were, we would have been told so. The Torah is not shy about such things. This is not an example of payback time.

Everything God does, with extremely rare exceptions, is based in nature, not outside of it. Consider His punishments: Lightning bolts do not come from heaven to mete out justice. Rather, there are floods, violent storms, droughts, famine, pestilence, and fast-spreading communicable diseases; not every occurrence is God's punishment, but God makes use of them when they do occur.

Nine of the ten plagues have natural explanations. Creation, the greatest miracle of them all, can be explained through nature. The Baal Shem Tov (the founder of modern chasidism) was correct in stating that miracles happen every day, but that we do not see them. What he meant was that we do *see* them; we just do not recognize them as the work of God because God works within nature.

In other words, God uses nature to advance His cause. The famine would have happened even if Yoseph was still safely ensconced in his father's tent.

More important in this case, the region did not suffer all that much. Pharaoh's dream gave sufficient advance warning of the famine to mitigate its effects. Egypt became the food distribution center for the region when the dry spell came. Now that *was* God's doing and it had everything to do with moving the plot along. If anything, in order to reunite father and son,

God spared the region from naturally induced suffering that it would have otherwise had to endure.

The question asks why so vast a region needed to be struck by the famine. It is only natural. Droughts are not very selective. Sure, it can rain on one side of the street and still be sunny on the other, but more often than not it is pouring all around. This was not the first time drought struck the entire region, nor was it the last.

It is hard to know, however, how extensive this drought was. The Torah apparently resorts here to hyperbolic flourish as a literary device. It describes the severity of the famine by saying it covered *kol-p'nei ha'aretz*, literally "all the face of the land," rather than the more traditional phrase, *p'nei kol ha'aretz*, "the face of all the land." The transposition of the word *kol*, meaning "all," suggests that "the whole world" is meant.

What we know for certain is that the immediate region of our concern was engulfed. That is not a lot of real estate, compared to "the whole world." If the Hyksos were the rulers of Egypt at this time, as I believe they were, it is still early days for them, meaning that the "Egypt" they ruled was in and around the Nile delta. We do not even know whether all of Egypt suffered from the famine. From the delta, it is but a short hop (or a forty-year walk, depending on the route you take) to Canaan.

Finally, let us deal with the midrash that states that Ya'akov and his family were spared the ravages of the famine and that he only sent his sons to Egypt so as not to make his neighbors jealous. This is not a nice midrash, despite its seemingly benign nature.

The Torah makes it clear that Ya'akov and his family had as little as did their neighbors. It quotes Ya'akov as saying: "Go down and procure rations for us there, that we may live and not die"(Genesis 42:2). And the Torah itself states: "And when they had eaten up the rations which they had brought from Egypt, their father said to them, 'Go again and procure some food for us'" (Genesis 43:2).

Now, you may argue that "live and not die" refers not to famine, but to fear of attack by the starving masses all around Ya'akov. In that case, he sent his sons to Egypt to hide the fact that he had plenty of food already. But, how can you argue such a point in light of the second quotation?

Frankly, I would like to believe that if Ya'akov had the food, he would have shared it with his neighbors. This Ya'akov, after all, is Yisrael—a changed man from his earlier self. But even if he would not have done so, there is no way he could have kept it a secret from anyone. Were the people all around Ya'akov blind and deaf? They would have had to be blind and deaf in order not to see and hear the fat, happy cows, sheep, and other livestock; they would have had to have been blind not to see the lush green fields and deaf not to hear the field hands reaping the abundant harvest. So whom would Ya'akov have been fooling? No one.

So why the midrash? Because some rabbis of old (like many today) have a problem with *Tanakh* (the acronym for *Torah*, *Nevi'im* or "Prophets," and *Ketuvim* or "Writings," which together comprise the Bible): They insist on taking everything that is said in it literally, without allowing for the possibility of religious hyperbole. Psalm 37:25 (which ends the *Birkat Ha'mazon*, the Grace after Meals) and the verses that follow it explain what I mean: "I have been young and am now old, but I have never seen a righteous man abandoned, or his children seeking bread. . . . [The Lord] does not abandon His faithful ones."

If this is literally true, Ya'akov and his family must have escaped the effects of the famine. So is born the notion that Ya'akov had the food, but he sent his sons to Egypt to hide that fact.

This insistence on literalism gets them in special trouble when they deal with Iyuv (Job) and his problems. The literalists bend over backwards trying to find sins in his past to explain away Iyuv's suffering, since God does not cause the righteous to suffer, according to the verses just cited and many more like them.

The most often cited sin has Iyuv, Yitro (Jethro, Moshe's father-in-law), and Bilaam (he of talking she-donkey fame) acting as advisers to the Pharaoh of the Exodus. His sin in that version is that he failed to speak up when Pharaoh ordered the death of the Hebrew male children.

Now, throughout the Book of Job, Iyuv's "friends" did the same thing—they insisted that he had to have done terrible things and should have confessed his sins. God Himself set them straight when He first praised Iyuv for his honesty in proclaiming his innocence and demanding an explanation from God. Then God berated the friends for speaking lies to Iyuv. In effect, He says, "Bad things happen to good people and that's the way of the world. You have no right to read anything more into that than that."

Any attempt by Iyuv's friends or by well-meaning sages to prove God wrong is wrong-headed. It also goes against other rabbinic teachings and sacred writings that do assert that bad things happen to good people.

So why am I making a big deal about this? Because this midrash only exacerbates the problem with the question itself. Now, not only did God send a famine throughout the region just to unite Ya'akov and Yoseph, but He then spared Ya'akov from the famine so that he had no need to go to Egypt. It's no longer that everyone else is forced to suffer along with Ya'akov, but that they alone suffer, and it is because of Ya'akov.

For the pretend gods of Mt. Olympus, this kind of behavior is normal. For the God whose "voice" shook Mt. Sinai, who framed His 10-clause preamble to the Law so that it is mostly about how we deal with other people rather than how we deal with Him, who gave Israel a Torah that is low on ritual and high on civil legislation rooted in justice and equality, for *that* God, this is dangerously close to blasphemy.

That is not your intention, nor is it the intention of those who first proposed the midrash. But all too often, in our zealousness to protect and enhance God's public relations image, we only make things much worse by creating a *chilul Ha'shem* (profanation of the Name of God) where none existed previously.

This brings me to my final point: Not every word spoken by *tannaim* and *amoraim* (the rabbis of the Mishnah and the Gemara respectively; together, they comprise the rabbis of the Talmud, the Oral Law) comes from God. It is not all *torah mi'sinai* (laws handed down to Moshe on Mt. Sinai).

Without a doubt, the Oral Law began at Sinai. The Torah does not give "laws" as we understand them. They are chapter headings only. "You shall not seethe a kid in the milk of its mother" demands definitions and parameters. "You shall do no manner of work on the Shabbat" demands definitions and parameters.

In that very real sense, the Oral Law is Sinaitic in origin. The process of putting meat on the bare bones of the Torah law had to have begun the moment a Torah law was first promulgated. But this Sinaitic stamp pertains only to the laws of the Oral Law, not to the debates and discussions over recordings in the Talmud or its contemporaneous literature. Merely because some *tanna*, once upon a time, came up with the idea that Ya'akov and his family were well provided for during this famine does not make it so.

It is also unfair to cite his opinion as "Jewish tradition." It is not. There are far more rabbis of that period and throughout history who accepted the Torah's version of events.

The same holds true for all *midrashim*. Nothing proves that better than the number of *midrashim* that openly contradict each other. A perfect example here is the midrash cited above about Iyuv, Yitro, and Bilaam. In that one, Bilaam counsels Pharaoh to kill the Hebrew children; Yitro counsels him to deal kindly with them; and Iyuv is silent (which was his sin, according to this midrash). Another midrash has Yitro and Amalek as the Pharaoh's advisers—and both advise him to deal harshly with Israel. Bilaam in this one observes events from afar, while Iyuv is nowhere to be found. So which midrash is "Jewish tradition"? Which do we cite as holy writ to make a point?

There is much value to be learned from the midrash, but let us not confuse the word of a *tanna* (or some other rabbi of another age) with the word of God.

Joseph Ozarowski

This week's question is one with no definitive answer. After all, why do events ever happen as they do? Occasionally, we get a glimmer of an explanation. But only the Almighty knows the ultimate reasons for and patterns of things, and He (or is it She?) isn't telling.

It may be possible to explain the events surrounding the famine and Ya'akov's family, as connected to the subsequent experiences involving the slavery and redemption of our people from Egypt. *Midrash Tanchuma Shemot* 4 states, "Because of Ya'akov, they [the Jewish people] were redeemed from Egypt." The famine, Joseph's elevation to chief minister of Egypt, the family reunion, and their life in Egypt all had a direct bearing on the Egyptians' subsequent enslavement and mistreatment of our people. After all, the events that led to Joseph's high position must have in turn led to Egyptian anti-Semitism and resentment at the privileged positions of Jews. Later on, Pharaoh, in the first chapter of Exodus, tries to blame the Jews for all their problems. If this sounds chillingly familiar, it should, for it follows the classical pattern of historical anti-Semitism.

The midrash (*Vayikra Rabba* 23) states, "Because of the merit of the Torah and the people Israel will the world be saved." This is certainly as true today as it was then. Whatever destiny our people of Israel might have will somehow affect the rest of the world. Whatever fate God has in store for us somehow still affects the entire Middle East and the World.

Just read today's newspapers!

David Sofian

When you ask, why inaugurate a region-wide famine in order to effect a family reunion, you are really asking why God chose the history reported in the *parshah*? Why not some other history, some other chain of events without the problems you raise? We would have to presume to know God's mind in order to directly answer your question. Certainly it is possible for God to have brought Joseph and his family together in some other way, but the story is told as it is. Why not deal with the narrative as it is, unpack the story as it is?

This point of view is excellently illustrated in a well known midrash on the very first letter of the Torah. *Midrash B'reishit Rabbah* tells us in Chapter 1:10 that the letter *Bet* begins the Torah in order to teach us what is more productive to investigate and what is not. The lesson is derived from the shape of the letter itself. Just as the *Bet* is closed at the top, back, and bottom and is only open in the front, so one is not to ask what is above and below, what was before or behind.

In other words, our limitless curiosity causes us to wonder about questions that are beyond our capacity to answer because we are finite humans and not God. Some questions inevitably lead us nowhere. We are told in Bar Kappara's name that speculation is fruitless about what was before the act of creation or why creation is as it is instead of some other way.

The same would apply to the Torah's descriptions of God's specific choices. This midrash counsels us to look forward out of the front of the *Bet* and confront questions that are better dealt with.

In a way, this attitude may underlay some of the *B'reishit Rabbah* material on *parshat Miketz* (Chapter 91). In section three, instead of trying to get into God's mind, so to speak, the rabbis used *B'reishit* 42:3 and its emphasis on the ten brothers to ask the more manageable and practical question of how we know that a minyan is ten. They then launch into a very involved discourse. Not only do they ask questions about a minyan in general, but they wind their way into such things as who can recite the blessings over the Torah and who counts in a minyan for *Birkat Ha'mazon*.

As I initially looked over this material to see if it offered an insight into your question, its very silence on your issue, and its actual choice of subject, remade the point of this midrash about the letter *Bet*. Your question can be asked, but not really answered.

This does not mean the rabbis of this section of midrash were content only to open practical questions that might be raised tangentially from the text. Reading the text carefully, the midrash looks for hidden significance within its words. The very first paragraph of Chapter 91 focuses on *B'reishit* 42:2. The midrash notes that Jacob specifically used the Hebrew word *shever* (corn) in referring to the stores in Egypt.

Since he could have used a variety of words, the midrash concludes this word must be hinting at a special importance. The midrash proposes that *shever* might be read as *sever* or hope. If so, then Jacob actually would be instructing his sons to go down to Egypt because hope is there.

This hint certainly has many possible significances. Perhaps Jacob knew somehow that Joseph was alive in Egypt and that his presence there represented hope. It could also be understood more generally. This reference to hope may refer to the more comprehensive and profound hope, the complete realization of God's original promise to Abraham. We can see this because, from our vantage point, we know that this small clan will become a great people in Egypt. From Egypt, God will redeem them and ultimately bring them to the Land of Israel as the great nation originally promised.

I find this way of interpreting the hint to be particularly attractive, for it points us back to the Torah's primary story, the story of God's covenantal relationship with Israel.

Can we really explain why the covenant unfolds precisely in the way it does and not in some other way? Can we really explain why God included Canaan in the famine, or for that matter why God destroyed the world with a flood and not by some other means, or why there were ten plagues instead of just one? Can we presume to know God's mind? On the other hand, the midrash wants us to see the layers of possible meaning within the story as it is told.

Va'Yigash:
Genesis 44:18–47:27

Prophetical Reading
Ezekiel 37:15–28

Overview of Torah Portion

Moved by Judah's offer to substitute himself for Benajmin as Joseph's slave, Joseph reveals himself to his brothers. The brothers go back to Canaan and return to Egypt with Jacob and his extended family. They settle in Goshen. Joseph continues to steer the Egyptian economy during the remaining five years of the famine.

Key Verses

"And Jacob tore his garments and put sackcloth on his loins and mourned for his son many days. And all his sons and daughters rose up to comfort him and he refused to be comforted" (Genesis 37:34–35).

"And Israel said to Joseph, 'Now let me die, since I have seen your face, that you are still alive'" (Genesis 46:30).

Discussion Question

A FAVORITE SON: Jacob's sorrow, his inconsolableness when Joseph disappears, is understandable. His own child, his most-beloved son, is gone, supposedly torn to shreds by a wild beast. But the other patriarchs faced similar, if not quite as dramatic, challenges involving a son. Abraham obediently followed God's command to offer Isaac as a sacrifice. Isaac coped for 22 years without Jacob, who was in Haran escaping the wrath of

Esau and finding a wife. Isaac and Jacob were their fathers' sole link to the promised continuity of the Chosen People, yet their fathers accepted the loss with apparent equanimity. Jacob still had 11 living sons who would become the progenitors of the Hebrew tribes, yet that fact didn't appear to console him. Why? Was he mourning for the loss of flesh and blood or for the incomplete fulfillment of God's promise? Was his reaction to Joseph's disappearance comparable to Abraham's and Isaac's behavior in similar situations?

Shammai Engelmayer

First, let us deal with a fallacy in the question. Avraham, at least as far as the Torah's text is concerned, never had to put up with a "loss" of Yitzchak, nor did he have to accept it with equanimity. Yitzchak did not go anywhere and nothing much happened to him. Avraham's knife was stayed in mid-air by Divine interjection. At best, he had three bad days in which to contemplate a possible loss, but that is all.

What we do not know for certain is whether Avraham would really have killed Yitzchak had the heavenly voice not intervened. Remember, this is the man who argued with God for the life of the Sodomites. His total silence during the *Akedah* story is too pat; his robot-like acquiescence is too contrived. If Avraham was going to make a stand, it most likely would be at the scene itself.

"Look, Lord, here I am, poised with my knife, prepared to do as You ask. But first, tell me this: Did You give me a son after so many years just to take him from me? Having glorified Your Name by giving Sarah a son in her old age, so that all sing Your praises for the miracle of that birth, are You prepared now to tell the world that his birth was nothing but a cruel joke? If it is through Yitzchak that Your promise to me will be fulfilled, as You have said, tell me how that will be possible, if I now slit his throat in Your service?

"I am not arguing with You about killing Yitzchak, nor am I asking You for Your reasons in wanting me to do this thing. You are God and that's that. But I think I have a right to know the answers to my questions before I do this deed for You. I have spent my life glorifying Your Name and spreading Your cause. If now I kill Yitzchak at Your behest, I will become a laughingstock and Your Name will be diminished in the eyes of the world. People will see You as nothing more than the idols they call gods—arbitrary, capricious, even a liar. Have I thus misspent my life? Is this how

You want the world to know You? See, my knife is poised over Yitzchak's throat. Tell me, is this really what You want me to do?"

The fact is, these questions and many others must have gone through Avraham's mind. It is inconceivable that he did not already believe that he knew the answer. It is also inconceivable that he would not demand an answer from God before completing the deed. And, until he had that answer, there was no "loss" for him to endure.

Now, I do believe he suffered a loss. As I read the text, I see strong suggestions that Sarah left him after the *Akedah* and that Yitzchak, too, moved away from him. Indeed, Yitzchak would seem to have parted with his father on the spot. But that is a loss Avraham had to accept with equanimity. His apparent acquiescence to what was surely an unreasonable demand was responsible for that loss.

Yitzchak, too, had little to mourn. For one thing, he had no need to "cope" without Ya'akov since he preferred Esau in any case. Besides, Ya'akov had deceived him in a big way. For another, it was his preference for Esau that led to Ya'akov's having to leave home. So here, too, the loss could be borne with equanimity. It might have been different if it was Esau who left.

Ya'akov's loss *was* different. His "Esau" *was* gone. His favorite son was no longer at his side. Yoseph meant the world to him, if for no other reason than he was the living link to his one true (and too soon departed) love, Rachel.

That alone would make him inconsolable, but there was more. He had to have realized that he was responsible for that loss. He had denied his father the first-born of Yitzchak's heart, so now he was denied the first-born of his heart.

But I also believe that he knew, deep down, that Yoseph did not die at the hands of some wild beast. He who had deceived his father with clothing must have seen through the deception now before him. He was already suspicious of the brothers and their reaction to Yoseph's dream, and he was only too aware of their propensities for violence. He must have realized that it was his other sons who killed Yoseph (why else was he so dismissive of their efforts to console him in his grief, and why would he be so fearful of letting Binyamin go with them to Egypt?), just as he must have realized that it was his overtly preferential treatment of Yoseph and his disdain for Leah (mother of six of his sons and adoptive mother of two others) that were at the heart of that murder.

So, not only did he have to grieve over Yoseph, he had to also grieve over his role in Yoseph's death (including the fact that, despite his suspicions, he sent Yoseph to find other brothers) and grieve, too, for the fact that at least some of his sons were cold-blooded murderers, something he had suspected ever since Shechem.

Now, grieving over his responsibility for Yoseph's death is not the same thing as Avraham or Yitzchak having to cope with the realization that their actions brought about their loss. This loss was much worse because, in effect, Ya'akov had lost all of his sons at the same time. If he believed they had murdered Yoseph, he could no longer accept them as his sons. For 22 years, he kept silent because he had no proof (nor was he anxious to attain any); but that only made his grief even stronger.

That is why he was so anxious to see Yoseph before he died. It was not so much that he would be reunited with Yoseph (that was not possible, as I will explain), but that he would see with his own eyes that his sons were not guilty of the crime he thought they had committed. That is why, too, we do not see Ya'akov castigating his sons for having thrown Yoseph into the pit and then selling him into slavery (whereas, yet again, he castigates Shimon and Levi for leading the attack on Shechem). None of that mattered to Ya'akov when compared to the revelation that they had not killed their brother, after all.

That did not remove his sense of loss, however. This is dramatically brought home to us by the way he blessed Yoseph's sons and what he adds as an aside to future generations, which only heightens our understanding of how great a loss Ya'akov actually suffered. In the next week's Torah portion, we are told:

"And [Ya'akov] blessed Yoseph, saying, 'The God in whose ways my fathers Avraham and Yitzchak walked, the God who has been my Shepherd from my birth to this day . . . , may He bless the lads. In *them* may my name be called and the names of my fathers, Avraham and Yitzchak.'"

Now, something seems to be wrong here. The Torah tells us that Ya'akov "blessed Yoseph," but he did not. He blesses Yoseph's sons.

The Torah does not make that kind of mistake. Clearly, it is trying to tell us that there is no greater blessing for a parent to receive than that his or her children should grow up to be good people. By blessing his grandsons, Ya'akov was giving his son the greatest blessing possible.

Then Ya'akov did something else—he passed on a request to all of us. He says to his two grandchildren, "By you shall Israel invoke blessings, saying, 'God make you like Ephraim and Menashe.'"

Ya'akov is telling us how we should bless our sons. And, from that day to this, for over 3,000 years, this is how we bless our sons: "God make you like Ephraim and Menashe."

This may not sound significant, but it is.

Forget for a moment how Ya'akov phrased the blessing he wants us to use, and consider how he did not phrase it. He did not say, "May God make you like *my* sons, like the 12 sons of Ya'akov."

Why not? The 12 sons of Ya'akov are, after all, our direct ancestors. They are the fathers of the tribes of Israel. By *their* names are *we* known.

The Torah portion we will read in two weeks, the first parshah in Exodus, makes that clear from the very outset: "These are the names of the Children of Israel."

Why did Ya'akov not want us to bless our children by invoking the names of his sons? Because he knew his sons. And, what he knew, he did not like.

The next portion, *Va'yechi*, reflects this. In the central scene of the Torah portion, Ya'akov, from his deathbed, curses his three eldest sons—Reuven, Shimon and Levi. And, while he does not say anything bad about most of the others, he does not have much good to say about them, either.

In fact, based on his last words, the only two sons he has any respect for are Yehudah and Yoseph. The only one of those two he truly loves is Yoseph. Unlike his brothers, Yoseph was always a good son.

As an adult, he was what Ya'akov should have been, but was not: a fair and honest man; a humble, God-fearing man who remained humble and God-fearing even after becoming the second most powerful man in the world; a man concerned about the well-being of all people, no matter who they were, or in what they believed.

Yoseph was better than his father was, and Yoseph's sons followed in his ways. This, then, is what Ya'akov meant by his instruction to us: If we are good people, then may our children be good people, too, just as Ephraim and Menashe are. If we are not so good, if we display the kinds of character flaws Ya'akov had, then may our sons rise above our ways, just as Yoseph rises above his father's ways. In no ways, however, should our sons be like the sons of Ya'akov.

That is the blessing Ya'akov wants us to bestow on our sons. The only conclusion we can draw from this is that Ya'akov's loss was not of Yoseph alone, but of all his children. The reunion with Yoseph and the realization that his other sons had not killed their younger brother was not sufficient to heal the breach.

As for that reunion, the Yoseph who Ya'akov loved was no more. This Yoseph was grown up and very preoccupied with affairs of state. They could meet on occasion and they could enjoy each other's company, but the little boy who was such a comfort to Ya'akov was gone forever. Ya'akov knew that before he even left for Egypt, so much so that it appears he did not plan to stay there for very long.

Joseph Ozarowski

I am not sure that each of the situations you describe are analogous to each other. Abraham never really lost his son. Of course both he and Isaac must have been deeply affected by their experience at the *Akedah*. However, the actual sense of loss was only a few minutes, or at most, if we include the preparation time, a few days. Without minimizing the *Akedah*, it is still not the same as completely losing a child. While Jacob may have been away for decades, it was assumed he went to live with family and was alive. Jacob's leaving was his mother's idea and also blessed by his father. Jacob's flight did not affect God's promise to the patriarchs and matriarchs regarding the future of the incipient Jewish people.

I do not sense that Jacob's lament of Joseph was due to his doubts about God's future for his descendants. As you pointed out, there were other children who would form the core of our people. His emotions probably stemmed from the assumption that his beloved Joseph was presumed dead, and that this loss was violent and sudden. Also, Joseph was Jacob's favored son, and this must have affected his feelings. Yet, there is also a rabbinic tradition that Jacob never fully gave up hope for finding Joseph. This is hinted at in Genesis 43:14, where Jacob sent the brothers to Egypt a second time for food.

This time, they needed to bring Benjamin and desired to free Shimon. Before they leave, Jacob said, "And may God Almighty give you mercy before the man, that he may release unto you, your other brother and Benjamin." In Hebrew, the words "brother" and "other" are reversed. If one inserts a comma between them, the verse reads, "And may God Almighty give you mercy before the man, that he may release unto you your brother, the other and Benjamin." "The other" in Jacob's words hinted at his secret hope that the lost brother Joseph, whose loss is so deeply felt and whose name is not openly spoken, might yet be still alive.

I believe that the Torah offers us Jacob's emotions to teach us about grief, hope, and the parent-child relationship.

David Sofian

Raising the issue you do is very understandable. Many of our traditions group together the *Avot*, the patriarchs. This classification is so common that it is difficult to think of one of them without the other two. For example, the opening words of the *Tefilah* prayer; *Elohey Avraham, Elohey Yitzak, v'Elohey Ya'akov* (the God of Abraham, the God of Isaac, and the

God of Jacob) are among the most familiar words in the Siddur. Already by *Shmot* 2:24, the Torah itself bundles the patriarchs together as a unit.

The Babylonian Talmud, Berakhot 16b makes it clear that the *Avot* are to include only Abraham, Isaac, and Jacob. And the rabbinic teaching of *Zekhut Avot*, the merit of the patriarchs as a group, or the recognition of the patriarchs special worth, is well known. This said, I tend to see differences where you see similarities. It seems to me that the situations you bring together are very different, and perhaps more significantly, the personalities involved are also very different.

Let's begin with the situations. To start with, in the *Akedah*, Abraham is responding to God's command to offer up Isaac. God certainly did not command Joseph's brothers to treat him as they did. Definitely, if Abraham had completed the task of turning Isaac into an *olah* offering, it would have meant the loss of a beloved son, even as Jacob believed he had suffered the loss of his beloved Joseph.

However, as we know Abraham is stopped, the loss doesn't occur. Whatever happened to their relationship after the *Akedah*, both Abraham and Isaac are very much alive and aware that the other lives. The *Akedah* is about Abraham's and Isaac's willingness to respond to God's command, not about the inconsolable grief that resulted from the apparent untimely and unfortunate death of a child.

As you point out, Isaac and Jacob were separated for many years. In that sense, Isaac lost Jacob for a long period of time. However, if we put aside any speculation that suggests Jacob knew Joseph was alive all along, the text itself has us see that Jacob is grieving over the death of a child, a permanent loss. Isaac has to cope with a long, but temporary, separation. It seems to me that these cases are more different than similar.

I think we also have to emphasize the very different personalities of the patriarchs. In my comment to *parashat Va'yetze*, I indicated that the Torah tells us very little about Isaac. We find Isaac only as a supporting character either in Abraham narratives or Jacob narratives. This makes it difficult to explain how he coped with Jacob's absence.

Yet his tendency towards passivity is shown in the *Akedah* and in the story of Rebecca's plot to get Jacob the blessing. Isaac lets life swirl around him. Life seems to happen to him rather than he taking hold and shaping the events of his own life. Regarding Jacob's long absence, he must have reacted in a similarly passive way.

We certainly do not think of Abraham as passive. He responded to God's command to leave home without hesitation. We wonder why he didn't hesitate in the *Akedah*. He challenged God over Sodom and Gomorrah. Certainly, if God had allowed him to complete the offering up of Isaac, he would have grieved.

But he also would have understood that grief within the context of his relationship with God and the trials God repeatedly put him through. This is the way Abraham understood every episode in his life from the very moment we met him.

The Torah's narratives teach us a great deal about Jacob's life in terms of his relationships with other people. The Torah shows us his faults in terms of those relationships and his growth. Jacob's profound grief over the loss of Joseph should be seen in this context. Through it, we are able to see the depth of his love for Rachel. We can also see how his unfortunate favoritism of one child over the others returned to him in the form of pain and sorrow.

This theme of Jacob's behavior yielding trouble for him later was also seen when he became the victim of Laban's deceit, even as he had been deceitful in his youth. Whatever interpretation we might finally place on his grief, it would have to fit with what we know of Jacob's personality.

Then, in answer to your question, in my view, neither Abraham nor Isaac faced the situation with which Jacob had to deal. However, even if they did, we should not expect Jacob to react the way either of them might have.

The Torah does not present us with idealized characters. Rather, each personality is unique. So much of the richness of the Torah lay precisely in these differences and in the different situations they encounter.

Va'Yechi: Genesis 47:28–50:26

Prophetical Reading
1 Kings 2:1–12

Overview of Torah Portion

Jacob, about to die, has Joseph pledge to bury him back in Canaan. Jacob blesses his grandsons and sons. After Jacob dies at age 147, his sons and a large entourage carry his body back to the cave of the Machpelah in Hebron. Joseph dies at the age of 110 and is embalmed in Egypt.

Key Verses

"And Jacob came to Luz . . . and Deborah, Rebecca's nurse, died. . . . And God appeared to Jacob again . . . and blessed him" (Genesis 35:6–8).

"And Israel said to Joseph, 'Behold, I am dying, but God will be with you and bring you back to the land of your fathers' . . . And Jacob called to his sons and said, 'Gather yourselves and I will tell you what will happen to you in the end of days'" (Genesis 48:21, 49:1).

Discussion Question

DEATH AND BLESSINGS: Jacob's life continues a pattern that is evident in the lives of his father and grandfather. God blesses each of them after another person's death; after the death and burial of Sarah, "The Lord blessed Abraham in everything"; "And it came to pass after the death of Abraham that God blessed Isaac his son." And, in Jacob's case, he was blessed after Deborah's death.

The other parallel: Isaac and Jacob, the patriarchs whose blessings of their sons are described in the Torah, took action when their own death seemed imminent. "Isaac . . . called Esau, his older son . . . and he said, 'Behold, I have grown old, I do not know the day of my death . . . , make me savoury food . . . that my soul may bless you before I die.'" (Jacob, of course, received the blessing intended for Esau.) Again, in Jacob's case, he gives his blessings, his prophecies of his sons' eventual fates, with his last breaths.

What do these patterns mean? Why does God bless each of the patriarchs after someone died? Why do Isaac and Jacob bestow their blessings when they sense their own deaths? What is the relationship between God's blessings and the fathers' blessings?

Shammai Engelmayer

It is true that blessings come at the time of death scenes in the Torah, but they also come at other times, as well. In God's case, for example, He blesses Potiphar's house for Yoseph's sake (Genesis 39:5), not because Yoseph had died, but because he was promoted to overseer of Potiphar's estate.

People also give blessings while they are very much alive. In Genesis 28:3, Yitzchak blessed Ya'akov a second time, not for the reason he stated earlier, that he is old and does not know how much longer he will live, but because Ya'akov was leaving home.

What these "blessings" are is another matter. In effect, when a person delivers them, they are a way of transmitting something of value—such as a share in an estate, the passing on of clan leadership, and so forth. Beyond that, these blessings are little more than the person's hopes for the one being blessed.

Ya'akov's blessings in Genesis 49, for example, did not all come true. It is from Levi, not Yoseph, that national leadership emerges in the four centuries that follow Ya'akov's death (Moshe and Aharon); indeed, the Yoseph tribes are insignificant until Yehoshua (Joshua), an Ephraimite, assumes command, then passes back into insignificance upon his death, re-emerging again only when Yaravam (Jeroboam) of Ephraim rebels and divides the country in two, which we can hardly call a blessing fulfilled. Zevulun, says Ya'akov, "shall dwell on the seashore," yet the allotted territory the tribe receives is inland.

With the possible exception of Shimshon (Samson), Dan offers no leaders to Israel, yet "Dan shall judge his people." Indeed, the judge Devorah (Deborah) chides the tribe for its lack of military participation against the Canaanites; such a lack certainly offers no hint of leadership.

As for the scepter never departing from Yehudah, it departed. When the Chashmoneans sat on the throne of Judea, the scepter passed (albeit temporarily) back to Levi, who was never supposed to have it in the first place.

It is because of Ya'akov's blessing and the covenant God makes with David that we believe the Mashiach (Messiah) will be of Yehudah, thus restoring the validity of this promise. Until the *Mashiach* comes, we can only judge by what is, not what may be. Besides, there is a big difference between "never depart" and "come and go and come again."

God's blessings are another matter. When He blesses, it is not as a hope for the future, but as a validation of reality. Potiphar's house flourishes with Yoseph in charge, not because of Yoseph's actions, but because of God's blessings. Potiphar's new-found success is the visible symbol of that blessing. This is not ordinary success that we are dealing with; we must assume that it is success beyond expectations, beyond the norm, because otherwise it would be credited to a person's talents, not God's benevolence.

While blessings can come at any time, from God and from people, it is true that they often seem to come at the time of death. A person's blessings at such times are, as stated earlier, more in the nature of last wills and testaments. What difference did it make to Esau whether he "inherited" Seir or Canaan? What difference did it make to Ya'akov? Neither inherited either in any real sense. The "blessing" was just a promise of something that would happen long after both brothers were gone.

The real blessing was who was to inherit Yitzchak's leadership of the clan. Because it was in the form of a blessing, it could not be revoked, but it nevertheless was little more than the passing on of leadership.

God's blessings have a similar purpose in this regard, but there is an essential difference: They are substantive, immediate, and visibly perceived because they are meant to establish the continuity of the covenant. God was with Avraham, but was He with Yitzchak? Yes, for look at how prosperous Yitzchak was. Was He with Ya'akov when Yitzchak was gone? Yes, because look at how well he has done, at least financially.

From a personal standpoint, none of the patriarchs did well. Avraham chased Yishmael away and, it would seem, created an unbreachable gulf with Yitzchak when he tied him to the altar; Yitzchak saw his family disintegrate because of sibling rivalry; and Ya'akov lost his favorite wife, then his son Yoseph.

With that loss, he effectively lost his other sons, as well. This very likely includes Binyamin, Rachel's second son and Yoseph's younger brother. He may have held Binyamin close to him only because he was Rachel's son and, thus, his only living link to her. His "blessing" of Binyamin here, however, suggest that there was little true warmth in that relationship.

If there is a relationship between God's blessings and the blessings the fathers give to their sons in the Torah, it is coincidental. Yitzchak's blessing of Ya'akov and Esau proves that. It was his intention to bless Esau, not Ya'akov. What if he had? Would it have made a difference? Would it have changed God's mind about who would be the father of Israel? Hardly.

That Ya'akov stole Esau's blessing does not change the coincidental nature of any relationship between the two. It is offensive to think that God maneuvered events in that way in order to prevent Yitzchak from interfering with His plan. God has no need to turn sons into thieves and deceivers of parents; indeed, honoring parents is one of His basic commandments to humankind.

To this day, we have no idea what would have happened at the moment of blessing had Ya'akov not deceived Yitzchak. Would Yitzchak have gone through with blessing the real Esau the way he blessed the fake one? Would God have intervened and told Yitzchak he was making a big mistake? We will never know. All we can know is that, whatever would have happened, the only blessings that count are the ones that come from God. Nothing that would have happened in that tent that day would have changed God's intentions.

Joseph Ozarowski

Blessings have many purposes. Some patriarchal deathbed blessings (such as Isaac's) are meant to convey a positive message to the survivors, much as ethical wills through our history have conveyed moral ideas and heartfelt wishes. (For some wonderful examples, see Riemer and Stampher's *Ethical Wills in Judaism*, New York: Schocken, 1983). Some of the blessings are (as you pointed out) prophetic in nature and others (such as Jacob's) can be mildly termed "constructive criticisms."

Divine blessings require a little more study to understand their intent. What exactly does the Torah mean when it says, for example, that Hashem blessed Isaac after Abraham's death? A most beautiful talmudic passage (Sotah 14a) sees God's blessing of Isaac after his father's death as the classic model for *nihum avelim*, comforting the bereaved. "Just as He comforts the bereaved, so too you comfort the bereaved . . . ," say the rabbis. Thus, the heavenly blessing is really a Divine form of *gemilut hasadim*, pastoral care of mourners that we are bidden to imitate in human form. In essence, God's presence at times of crisis and sadness can be seen as a comforting blessing.

For a fuller treatment of this theme, see my book, *To Walk in God's Ways—Jewish Pastoral Perspectives on Illness and Bereavement*, Northvale: Jason Aronson, 1995, where I develop this idea into a basis for a Jewish pastoral theology.

David Sofian

The moments when we human beings encounter death are moments when we are filled with questions. Those moments, when we realize that our most precious commodity is the very limited time we have, are the moments when we also realize that life is more dear than words can describe. The reality of death forces us to ponder life. We wonder about the meaning of life. We wonder if there is any ultimate significance and purpose to our own lives.

So it is not surprising that within the biblical text, we find God comforting the patriarchs with blessing after encountering death, or that we find individuals expressing themselves in profound ways at those points where they themselves encounter death. Some examples of such expression, in addition to Jacob's remarks to his sons, are: Joseph making a dying request of his people (*B'reishit* 50:24); Moses offering farewell words of warning, instruction, and hope (*D'varim* 32:1), and David's advice to Solomon (*M'lakhim aleph* 2:2ff).

As we look at Jacob's words carefully, we see that even though Chapter 49 is often referred to as Jacob's blessing, it is in fact mixed in texture, richer than a simple blessing. Jacob has much he wants to say before he dies. He blesses. Of Joseph he says, "The blessings of your father surpass the blessings of my ancestors, to the utmost bounds of the eternal hills. Let them be on the head of Joseph, on the brow of the prince of his brothers" (*B'reishit* 49:26). He curses. Of Shimon and Levi he says, "Cursed be their anger so fierce, and their wrath so harsh" (*B'reishit* 49:7). He exalts. Of Judah he says, "You, O Judah, your brothers will praise" (*B'reishit* 49:8). He chides. Of Issachar he says, "When he saw how good was a resting place, and how pleasant was the land, he bent his shoulder to the burden, and became a toiling serf" (*B'reishit* 49:15).

Jacob's farewell words to his children expressed a moment of clarity, a precious moment of meaning. He expressed himself to his sons by telling them what he really thought. He wanted to bestow the truth he saw. Nothing is held back.

Thinking about this subject led me to a book that has long rested on my shelf. Part of the JPS Library of Jewish Classics, it is called "*Hebrew Ethical Wills*" (Jewish Publication Society of America, 1976). A long tradition has developed of the departing generation, bestowing the truth it sees to the following generation. Parents want to leave more to their children than material objects. They also want to leave them their wisdom, insight, and values.

This can be done with the writing of an Ethical Will. Judah Golden wonderfully describes the motivation for such instruments at the end of his introduction to the book.

> For although there may be varieties of terror crowding in as one tries to imagine extinction, it is intolerable (so long as there is life) to acquiesce to being silenced—not to being silent, but to being silenced. There is still something left unsaid, still something to tell to one's flesh of his own flesh, or mind of his mind.
>
> And within those to whom right attitude and action and loyalty to the faith of the fathers are the supreme government of life, there is a compulsive wish to speak from beyond the grave. They know how close lies chaos to the disorders of the living, and they want the volume of their warning not to be reduced. They want to be heard across the deadening silence. . . . The Hebrew ethical will is not mere valediction, but an audacious attempt at continuing speech from fathers in the grave to children in a reckless world. The teacher's absence is not the end of instruction. It was said a long time ago, when the dead are quoted, their lips move [p. 19].

In answer to your question, it seems to me that God blessed the patriarchs as a form of comfort when the reality of death was encountered. However, Isaac, and particularly Jacob offered their words as an "audacious attempt at continuing speech from fathers in the grave to children in a reckless world."

Shmot/Exodus

Shmot: Exodus 1:1–6:1

Prophetical Reading
Isaiah 27:6–28:13; 29:22–23

Overview of Torah Portion

A new Pharaoh enslaves the Children of Israel, who have multiplied and grown strong. Pharaoh's command to kill newborn Hebrew sons is foiled by God-fearing midwives. Pharaoh issues a new order—to drown Hebrew boys; the infant Moses is saved by his mother, who puts the 3-month-old child in a small ark that is set afloat and found by Pharaoh's daughter. As an adult, Moses kills an Egyptian taskmaster and flees to Midian, where he marries into the family of Yitro the priest and encounters God on Mt. Sinai. Moses returns to Egypt to free the Hebrews from bondage.

Key Verses

"**A**nd there went a man of the house of Levi and took a daughter of Levi. And the woman conceived and bore a son; and when she saw that he was good she hid him three months" (Exodus 2:1–2).

"And the child grew and [Moses' mother] brought him to Pharaoh's daughter . . . and she called his name Moses, and said, 'Because I drew him out of the water'" (Exodus 2:10).

Discussion Question

AN EGYPTIAN NAME: God had a role in naming the patriarchs—Abraham, Isaac, and Jacob/Israel. Jacob and his wives named their sons. But an outsider, a non-Jew, Pharaoh's daughter, gives the greatest Jewish prophet his name—Moses. (Moshe, his name in Hebrew, is derived from the word *"to draw out"—m'shetehu*, "I drew him out.")

Granted, the Torah uses the Hebraicized form of the name, not the Egyptian version that Pharaoh's daughter undoubtedly assigned. But why do we continue to use the name she gave? Joseph also received a name from Egypt's ruling family, from Pharaoh himself, but Joseph is known exclusively by his Hebrew name. Moses remained with his own family for three months, long enough for him to be circumcised on the eighth day and be given a Hebrew name. Why is it not recorded in the Torah? Why is Moses' ultimate name not assigned until he grows up?

Shammai Engelmayer

What an appropriate question for a parshah entitled "names"! The name Moshe is not a Hebrew name, but an Egyptian one. This accords with the Torah, which says that Moshe is the name given to him by his adoptive mother, a daughter of the pharaoh.

Actually, it is less a complete name than it is a syllable used in constructing names during the Egypt of this period, especially among the royal house and the priestly class. Several of the kings of the Eighteenth Dynasty (the one before the Ramesides) bore it as part of their names. Records from the Ramesside era, in which the Exodus must be placed, show that the name was still common then.

A priest named Mose is known in this period. Also, from the waning days of Mernephtah, the most likely pharaoh of the Exodus, we have records indicating that someone named Mose deposed a high official, probably the vizier, from office.

According to the Egyptologist Sir Alan Gardiner, "this 'Mose' must have been a personage of the most exalted station, and it seems inevitable to identify him with an ephemeral king Amenmesse, whose brief reign may have fallen either before or within that of" Mernephtah's son and successor, Seti II. (Sir Alan Gardiner, *Egypt of the Pharaohs*, Oxford University Press, 1961. page 277). Amenmesse is reportedly the son of one of Rameses II's daughters. If true, then Mose was still a common name even in the royal household when one of Rameses's daughters named her adopted son Moshe.

Clearly, the rabbis of blessed memory shared the curiosity inherent in the question, because in BT Sota 12a, there is a discussion of what Moshe's real name was. (Note: There are two Talmuds—the Babylonian Talmud, identified by the acronym BT, and the Jerusalem Talmud, identified by the acronym JT.) Rabbi Meir claims that it was Tov, while Rabbi Yehudah insists it was Tovia. Both base their conjectures on Exodus 2:2, which states that Moshe's mother looked at her child and saw *ki tov hu*, that he was a goodly child.

We do not know Moshe's real name because it is not the name by which he was known. More importantly, since he is the original author, it is not the name by which he wanted to be known. The man was 80 years old when he returned to Egypt on his mission. For most of those years, Moshe was what he was called and what he called himself.

We are not even certain that his birth parents even gave him a name at his *brit*. Names in the Torah are often given with the future in mind. What name would you give to a child whose almost certain and immediate future is death by drowning? (If his parents had any inkling of what his real future would be, my guess is that they would have called him Nissim, meaning "miracles," but I doubt that they did.)

We content ourselves, therefore, with relying on the meaning of the Hebrew homonym (Moshe—"he draws out") because it so closely reflects the child's future.

As for why he did not receive even his Egyptian name until he "grew up" (meaning when he was weaned, not when he became an adult), that is one of those little things that speak so loudly to the authenticity of the biblical narrative. As Nahum Sarna notes in his commentary to Exodus 2:10, "The high infant mortality rate in the ancient world dictated that formal adoption and naming by the adoptive parent be postponed until after the weaning, which took place at a far later age than it would in modern societies." (*The JPS Torah Commentary, Shemot*, 1991, p. 10.)

Joseph Ozarowski

Many classical commentaries discuss the origin of Moshe's name. Rashi, for example, suggests several possible Hebraic origins for the name. Tosafot (eleventh-century Western Europe) proposes that Pharoah's daughter actually learned Hebrew from the local Jewish slaves. Ibn Ezra (twelfth-century Spain) writes that Moshe is actually the Hebrew translation for the original Egyptian *Monios*. Or Hahayyim (Rabbi Hayim ben Attar—eighteenth-century Italy/Jerusalem) considers why in the case of other biblical names, the discussion of the name in the Torah was prior to the actual naming, while here the name is first given and the reason given after.

None of this directly addresses your question. But when I discussed the issue at our Shabbat table, a giant grin materialized on my daughter's face. She shouted out, "Daddy, look at this!" The *d'var torah*, which she had brought home from school, quoted a midrash stating that ten people who knew Moshe, including family members, gave him other names tied to various events surrounding his life and circumstances (see *Yalkut Shimoni Shemot* 166).

> His father called him Haver ("connection") because through him (Moses), he connected with his wife whom he had divorced. . . . His mother called him Yekutiel ("God will nourish") because she nourished him at her breasts, and God returned him to her. . . . His sister called him Yered ("going down") because through him they went down after him to the Nile to know his end. . . . His brother called him Avi-Zanoah ("father of abandonment") saying, "My father abandoned my mother but now returned to her. . . . His grandfather called him Avi-Sukko because he was hidden in a *sukka*-like boat. . . . And the people of Israel called him Shemaiah ("God has heard"), son of Netanel because in his days God heard their cries.

(This last name is most odd because Moses' father was Amram, not Netanel.)

None of these names are recorded in the Torah. So I asked my kids why, of all the names in the midrash, was the Egyptian princess's choice the name by which we know Moshe Rabbenu. My oldest son's friend Alan, who was our Shabbat guest, suggested a remarkable answer. The name Moshe, given by Pharoah's daughter, means, "I drew him out of the water." As the Torah points out, the name Moshe/Moses is connected to the act of saving the life of this little Jewish baby. In a time of suffering, slavery, torture, and genocide, the Torah highlights for us the enduring message that saving a life is the most precious gift anyone can bestow.

As the rabbis say elsewhere, "He who saves a Jewish life, it is as if he has saved an entire world." While there were many names that could have been used for Moses, the Torah reminds us via Moses' name that saving human life is the highest value. Thus, the greatest of Jewish prophets and teachers, the one who led his people out of slavery, taught them God's Torah, and spoke face-to-face with the Almighty, was ultimately named by a kindly Egyptian princess who may have risked her life to save his.

David Sofian

God changed Abram's name to "Abraham" right when the covenantal promise is reiterated in *B'reishit* 17:4. This clearly marks the importance of the event. Several verses later (17:15), the same happens when Sarai's name is changed to "Sarah." The fulfillment of the covenantal promise begins with God informing them that she will be blessed with a son.

These name changes clearly reflect pivotal points in the covenantal narrative. The same can be said of the announcement of Jacob's name change to Israel (*B'reishit* 32:29). Jacob is returning to the promised land and is about to carry the covenantal narrative to the next stage.

Recognizing the connection between a name change and a key moment in the covenantal narrative might lead us to think that the withholding of Moses' Hebrew name is in order to dramatize a subsequent name change. If so, the moment for such a change would have been at the burning bush. Moses there receives his mission. The events that will lead to the Exodus and eventually Mt. Sinai are about to begin.

Yet, such an anticipated name change never occurs. The area of wonder, then, for me, is not only why Moses' Hebrew name isn't recorded in the Torah, assuming he had one, but also, given his lack of a Hebrew name, why doesn't God point out the next pivotal stage of the covenantal account with a name change?

Perhaps the rabbis quoted in *Shmot Rabbah* and *Vayikra Rabbah* were responding to your concern in their discussions of Moses' name. In *Shmot Rabbah* 1:20, Rabbi Meir teaches us that Moses' actual Hebrew name was *Tov*. He bases this on *Shmot* 2:2 where, in description of the child, it says, *kee tov hu*, "that he was good." Rabbi Meir sees the word *tov* as an appellation rather than a description. So, perhaps, Moses did receive a Hebrew name. As is often the case, the midrash supplies what the Torah leaves out.

Vayikra Rabbah carries the discussion much further in a very long section, 1:3. First, this section tells us that the Book of Chronicles was included only for the purpose of drawing midrash from it. Having established their intention not to read the text in a straight-forward way, they use Chronicles 4:18 to teach that there were actually ten Hebrew names associated to Moses. The midrash adroitly expounds the names given in the Chronicles verse, so that they refer to Moses.

It is the end remark, however, that I find most intriguing. There, the Holy One told Moses that of all the names applied to him, God would call him by that name which Bitiah, the daughter of Pharaoh, called him, "Moses." This midrash is emphasizing the point that God never had a name change in mind for Moses. Indeed, no other name but Moses will do.

Now why would this be God's choice? Ibn Ezra (as mentioned in the Soncino *Chumash* edited by A. Cohen, 1997 p. 325; comment to verse 10 — "her son") suggests an answer. Let us ask ourselves: What if Moses had not been raised in the royal setting? What if he had not had the benefits denied his people? What if he, too, suffered from the same slave mentality they suffered from? Would the slave experience have prepared him to lead his people? Would his people have been willing to be led by him if he were a mere slave and did not possess the demeanor of their masters? Would he have possessed the courage to stand up to the Egyptian abusing one of his brothers or been able to help Jethro's daughters?

Perhaps the Torah wants us to see that it was his early separation from his people that made it possible for him to later lead them away from Egyptian slavery. It was because he grew up as Bitiah's son that he could lead his people from Egyptian subjugation. Hence, his Egyptian name is the only one given and maintained. Just as the name changes referred to above point us to pivotal moments in the covenantal narrative, here the lack of a true Hebrew name at any point in his life points us to a pivotal moment in the covenantal narrative.

That point, easily overlooked, is where and how he grew up. Moses is exactly the right person to move the story forward, precisely because he is the Israelite who grew up as Pharaoh's daughter's son, an Israelite who carried an Egyptian name.

Va'Era: Exodus 6:2–9:35

Prophetical Reading
Ezekiel 28:25–29:21

Overview of Torah Portion

God repeats his command to Moses: Tell Pharaoh to release the Hebrews from slavery. Pharaoh refuses to listen to the message of Moses and Aaron. The plagues begin: water turned into blood; frogs; gnats; beetles; murrain; boils; fiery hail.

Key Verses

"And Moses and Aaron went to Pharaoh and did so, as God commanded, and Aaron cast down his rod before Pharaoh and his servants and it became a serpent. And Pharaoh also called for the wise men and the sorcerers, and also they, the magicians of Egypt, did likewise with their secret arts" (Exodus 7:10–11).

"And the Lord said to Moses, 'Tell Aaron to take your rod and stretch your hand over the waters of Egypt . . . that they become blood.' And Moses and Aaron did so. And the magicians of Egypt did likewise with their secret arts" (Exodus 7:19–22).

"And the Lord said to Moses, 'Tell Aaron to stretch your hand with your rod over the rivers, over the canals and over the pools, and cause frogs to come up upon the land of Egypt.' . . . And the frogs came up and covered the land of Egypt. And the magicians did likewise with their secret arts" (Exodus 8:1–3).

Discussion Question

MIRACLES AND MAGIC: God knows the limits of the Egyptian magicians' powers. He knows what transnatural acts they can duplicate and what they can't. Yet, the first three demonstrations of His power that he has Moses and Aaron perform before the court of Pharaoh—the rod *cum* serpent, and the first two plagues—are clearly within the magicians' capability.

Why does God open with such light ammunition? Does He expect Pharaoh to be impressed by parlor tricks that his own servants can do? Assuming that God doesn't want to open fire with his heavy artillery, such as slaying of the first born, why doesn't He begin with gnats, the third plague, which Pharaoh's magicians can't duplicate?

Shammai Engelmayer

To begin by answering the specific question, out of context of the entire narrative: The only way to refute the charge, which is certain to be leveled, that Moshe used black magic, rather than the power of God (as, indeed, Pharaoh himself charges), is to first defeat the magicians. This, God does. The magicians are forced to admit, early on, that the plagues are beyond their vaunted abilities to match; in other words, magic is not being used to bring on the plagues.

This is consistent with the various views that see the plagues as overt demonstrations of God's power. According to one view, for example, the plagues are rightly seen as an attack on the gods of Egypt, thus demonstrating that they are not gods at all; that only God is God.

There is also the fact that the first nine plagues are actually three sets of three plagues each. Each set is said to have a different purpose: The first is to establish the existence of God (thus, the magicians have to concede defeat before this set is over); the second is to establish God's presence in this world, not just on some unearthly plane; and the third is meant to show the power of God.

That is the simple answer, but there is a deeper question lurking here and it is the one question that never seems to go away. No matter how many times it is asked and answered, it gets asked again. For good reason: From as far back as the rabbis of the Talmud (and probably a lot farther than that), people have been uncomfortable with God toying mercilessly with the Egyptians. He is God, after all; He didn't have to go through this elaborate scenario to free Israel from bondage. Innocent people did not have to suffer. All He had to do was take Israel out.

It is a fair question (albeit one based on a warped notion of God, as will be seen later on). In many ways, the Egyptians were innocent people. It was not they who enslaved Israel, but their leaders—the pharaohs and the royal ministers. And a good case can be made to exonerate even these Egyptians, since the enslavement of Israel really was God's idea, one He readily shared with Avraham (see Genesis 15:13–14).

Yet God not only punishes Egypt (something else He told Avraham about at the time), but He does it slowly, stretching it out over ten plagues (and possibly ten months), each plague progressively worse than the one preceding it. Is this the same God who demands of us, "Justice, justice shall you pursue" (Deuteronomy 16:20)?

He is—and that is the heart of the problem. Whatever God wants to accomplish, He can accomplish it just by willing it to be (as He did Creation, for example). So all of this was unnecessary. All God needed to do was to put it into Pharaoh's head that Israel should be let go. Thus, no answer to the basic question satisfies us.

The least satisfying answer is that God does what God does. Whatever His reasons, we do not know them and are unlikely ever to find out for certain. All we can do is take it on faith that God knows what He is doing and that what He is doing is just.

Not being a species that can take anything purely on faith, we nevertheless seek to discern God's motives. In this instance, it is quite possible that we have even succeeded somewhat, although there is no way to prove it: God did what He did precisely because He is a just and righteous God.

Sure, as the current version of the question puts it, He could have started off by sending the tenth plague, the death of the firstborn, and it would have done the trick. That was an extreme punishment, however, and God prefers to accept plea bargains—confess your sins and repent, and get a lighter sentence. The sooner you do so, the lighter the sentence.

If Pharaoh had heeded Moshe's request when it was first made, Egypt would have been spared all of the plagues (although, not the natural events that God adapted to His purpose). The only punishment would have been the economic loss Egypt would have suffered by losing such a large work force overnight. Each time the pharaoh denied Moshe's request, the punishment became a little more severe, until finally the punishment was so great that the only punishment left beyond it would have been to destroy Egypt itself. So, the pharaoh said, "Enough. Go, already. We can't take any more of this."

The problem with this answer is that the Torah itself seems to refute it. Ten times, we are told, in one way or another, God hardens Pharaoh's heart. So, even if Pharaoh had wanted to seek a plea bargain, he was prevented from doing so by God Himself.

There are other possible answers, as well, such as this one: If God merely took Israel out of Egypt, who would have been impressed? The whole point of the enslavement, after all, was that it led to the Exodus, which led to the renewal of the Covenant and the giving of the Law. But if the Exodus happened matter-of-factly and undramatically, would Israel have been so quick to go along with the rest of the plan? Even with the high drama, God had trouble keeping Israel convinced that it was getting a great deal instead of a raw deal. How much more so if Israel woke up one day and found that Pharaoh, for no apparent reason, had told them to leave?

Would Israel have believed that it was God's doing, not Pharaoh's? Would Egypt have believed it? Would anyone?

The problem with this answer is that God did not have to make people suffer in order to make an impression. Being God, He could have come up with something else without much trouble at all.

So, which answer is the right answer?

Actually, all of the above are correct. There is no one answer to the question. Whatever the mind can discern as a just reason is correct as far as it goes. The reason we are not satisfied with these answers is because of our conception of God. We insist on seeing Him as the puppeteer and human-kind as the puppets. The Torah, especially in the Exodus saga, would seem to bear that out.

It is wrong. We have free will (the Torah makes that abundantly clear, as well). That means that God is not pulling strings. What happens in this world is our doing, not God's. He may make use of it for His own ends, but we initiate it.

The same is true of nature. There is a natural order to things. Floods happen naturally. In one specific case, the Nile turned "bloody" naturally and, when it did, it chased out that which could breathe on land and killed that which could not. Sea creatures rotting on hot desert sands brought swarms of insects, and so on. God did not make such things happen, other than creating nature in the first place.

On the other hand, He used nature to further His ends. (That is why the tenth plague was needed. If all of the plagues had been *inside* nature, it would have been possible to say that God had nothing to do with them. God needed the one exception—the plague *outside* nature—to prove that nature itself was His greatest miracle. Recently, however, a theory was put forth that even this plague was a natural event. If so, that only confirms the fact that God works through nature.)

When God created everything, he literally "programmed" in every possible permutation of all that would happen. There is an end goal, but how we get there is our business. Although God does not interfere, He did account for each individual's choices in his original programming. I hate to use it as an example, especially considering the film's setting, but *It's a Wonderful Life* is perfect for explaining this. The slightest change can make a world of difference. In the film's case, Jimmy Stewart's character learns how different his hometown would have been if he had not been born.

God, in his programming, accounts for each possible choice each of us can make, but He also accounts for the choices our parents can make, including not having children (in which case, any programming involving us directly or indirectly goes unused).

The first nine "plagues," as we call them, would have happened regardless of whether Israel was enslaved. God did not arbitrarily cause them to happen. Thus, He is not guilty of the charge of making people suffer needlessly. Instead, He used the natural sequence of events to His advantage. This He did by controlling when the events began and ended, and very likely the severity of each, as well, and this was sufficient to prove the points He wished to make. Again, He did this in the original programming: If the pharaoh did X, He would have Moshe do Y, but if the pharaoh so much as looked cross-eyed at him, then He would do Z, and so forth).

As for hardening the heart of Pharaoh, too much has been made of this over the millennia. Pharaoh is as stubborn as they come. The more he was pushed to the wall, the more stubborn he grew. Thus, rather than making things easier, each plague only made things worse.

That is all that is meant by the hardening of his heart. How many times have we been in situations in which we felt we wanted to do something but we held back (or were advised to hold back) because anything we would do would only make things worse? When the text says that God hardened Pharaoh's heart, it is merely saying that a plague that caused him grief, pain, humiliation, or a combination of these, made things worse. Instead of softening Pharaoh's heart, it hardened it because he himself chose to dig in his heels.

The pharaoh of the Exodus made his own choices. He could have relented at any point and a different program would have kicked in. He decided which program would run. He and he alone is guilty of making Egypt suffer.

We need to stop thinking of God as a puppeteer. We are responsible for our own actions. Our actions are responsible for the actions and reactions of others. If this was not true, then God would truly be cruel and *teshuvah* (repentance) would be impossible for us because God, as puppeteer, causes Israel's misdeeds and then punishes it for having committed them; and no matter how much someone may wish to repent, that is not possible until the puppeteer pulls the strings. The whole concept is alien to Judaism—or should be.

Once we accept this, we can accept the answer to the basic question: What God "did" to Egypt was just and proper, and demonstrated His capacity for mercy and forgiveness, as well as His ability to punish evil.

Do not hold up the Torah as the proof that God is a puppeteer. The Torah, as the rabbis of blessed memory keep telling us, speaks in the language of man. There is no way we can understand how God really does what He does, and the Torah does not even try. Instead, it reduces what God does to intelligible metaphors. God has no hand that He can stretch out over Egypt, for example, but that is a concept we can understand and, so, that is how the Torah describes what God did.

God "speaks" to Moshe, not the way people speak, but in some other way. What difference is it to us, however, or to the truth of the story, since the point is that somehow God communicated with Moshe? If "speaks" is something we understand, then "speaks" is the word used. On its level, it is no less true than what actually happened; it is just not how it actually happened.

So it is with every other description of God in the Torah. They are true, but only on a certain level, a level our minds are capable of understanding.

Joseph Ozarowski

Ammunition is the right word, at least according to the midrash. The rabbis (*Tanhuma Shemot*, 182; *Pesikta Rabbati* 17) suggest that all the plagues, including the first two, followed a classic military pattern. While the rabbis probably used a Roman battle model, it does not take much reinterpretation to see modern tactics within. First, God stopped the water supply (blood). Then, a "shouting army" (frogs) was brought in. Third, arrows were shot at the Egyptians (lice). Fourth, God directed "legions" (wild animals) at the Egyptians. Following this, God caused an epidemic (pestilence—we would call this today biological warfare). Then, God poured *naphtha* (boils— today we would call this chemical warfare) on them. Seventh, God catapulted stones (hail—today, we would say bombs) on Egypt. Eighth, God ordered in the troops (locusts). Ninth, God threw the Egyptians into prison (darkness). Finally, God got rid of the leaders (the firstborn).

Somehow, though, it does not seem likely that the purpose of God's action was to imitate Roman or other military tactics. It was not the Divine purpose to compete with Egyptian sorcerers. Some of my members pointed out that, even though the Egyptian magicians were able to duplicate the initial plagues, they were unable to rid Egypt of these problems. Instead, they simply brought on more of the same! Imagine the poor Egyptian peasants coming to their leaders to complain about the bloody water and frogs, and all the royal advisors do is make more! Does this situation sound familiar, like dealing with any of our governmental leaders today?

It is also possible to see the plagues as a gradually ascending crescendo of God's judgment against the Egyptians. Abarbenel points out that Rav

Yehuda's famous plague acronym in the Haggadah, *d'tzakh, adash, b'ahav*, is actually a way to show the patterns of the plagues in three segments.

D'tzakh, the first set of three, shows God as Creator. These plagues show God's sovereignty through plagues that are somewhat annoying and affect property.

Adash, the second set of three, shows God as Lord of History, who cares about the people of Israel. The plagues began to affect the property of the Egyptians in a major way.

B'ahav, the last four, show God as Lord of Nature, omnipotent, universal to all life. Thus, these plagues were inescapable and affected every Egyptian's life.

Another fine explanation involves seeing the plagues as directed against the Egyptian deities. God spelled it out at the conclusion of the plagues (Exodus 12:12), "And against all the gods of Egypt, I will do judgment, I am the Lord," and repeated it again in the summaries of the Exodus (Numbers 33:4). The first plague was directed against the Nile, deified by all Egypt, showing that it, too, was subservient to the Creator of the Universe. The second plague was directed against the frog fertility God, Heqt. All the other plagues can be seen in this way as well. As the rabbis in the midrash (*Shemot Rabba* 9:8) put it (It rhymes in Aramaic but not in English!), *Mahei elohaya viva'atun komraya*, or "Strike the gods and the priests will tremble!" Thus, the first two plagues were certainly not meant as cute entertainments, but important Divine signs with multiple purposes.

(For further reading on the plagues as directed against Egyptian gods as well as the other purposes of the plagues, see Sarna, (1986), *Exploring Exodus*, p 79, New York: Schocken, 1986, Nechama Leibowitz's "The Purpose of the Plagues" (1976) in *Studies in the Weekly Torah Portion* (Exodus), Jerusalem: WZO, 1976, and "The Ten Plagues—Their Purpose and Effect" in *Meditations on the Torah* by B. S. Jacobson, Tel-Aviv:Sinai, 1977).

David Sofian

In order to respond to your question, first let's look back to the preceding parshah, where Moses encountered God at the burning bush (Chapter 3). In that critical episode, God commissioned Moses to go to Pharaoh and set the Israelites free. Moses objected that the people may not have believed him. God assured him by indicating that he, Moses, will perform signs to convince them. We learn in *Shmot* 4:3 how Moses is to cast his rod on the ground. When he does so, it becomes a snake (*nakhash*). This is to be one of the signs by which he will convince his people.

Shortly thereafter, Moses and Aaron go to Pharaoh and inform him of God's command to let the Israelites go. Pharaoh challenges them by asking, Who is the Eternal that he should let Israel go? Moreover, as a result of this clash, Pharaoh instructed the taskmasters and foremen to make matters worse for the Israelites by no longer providing them with straw yet still requiring the same quota of bricks. The Israelites blamed Moses and Aaron for their predicament. Frustrated, Moses enquires of God why things are turning out as they are, and God assures him that this is just the beginning and God's might will prevail.

In our current parshah, in the key verses you relate, Moses and Aaron are going to Pharaoh a second time. This time they are not going with words only. God instructs them, as they were instructed when they came to the Israelites, to offer signs when Pharaoh challenges them to do so. The sign is similar to before. God tells Moses to have Aaron take his rod and cast it down before Pharaoh; only this time it will turn into a dragon or crocodile (*taneen*). It is this change which is helpful in answering your question. Why is it a *taneen* this time?

Your question presupposes that the contest is between Moses and Aaron on the one side and Egypt's magicians on the other. It seems to me that is why you want to know why God begins with demonstrations that are also within the magicians' power. I think the actual contest is between God and Pharaoh. That is why God begins with a demonstration that has meaning within the cultural context of Egypt. That is why this time the rod turns into a *taneen*. Its home is in the Nile, and the importance of the Nile to Egyptian culture goes without question. Then, if the *taneen* represents Egypt, taking control of it symbolically would have held real significance. Shmot 7:12 tells us how the showdown between Aaron and the magicians ended with Aaron's rod swallowing the magicians' rods. Aaron's *taneen* consuming the magicians' *taneeneem* would have communicated Aaron's ability to take control of Egypt. Aaron is God's agent. God is communicating how God can take control of Egypt in this act.

The same now can be said of the first two plagues. In each of these, God strikes through the Nile. This would have been seen as a strike at the very heart of Egypt. And God makes it perfectly clear that doing so is for the purpose of showing Pharaoh who really has power and control. Shmot 7:17 tells us how God declares to Pharaoh straight out that the water turning to blood is so "you will know that I am the Eternal."

Following this same theme in the second plague, the waters of the Nile swarm, are defiled, with frogs. And when Pharaoh seems to have finally submitted to God's power and appeals to Moses and Aaron to plead with

God to remove the frogs, Moses tells him that such will happen on the next day, "that you will know there is none like the Eternal our God" (*Shmot* 8:6).

In answer to your question, God is not beginning with light ammunition. It is not important whether or not the magicians can duplicate the feats. Rather, God is using manifestations of the primary symbol of Egypt, the Nile, as a means of demonstrating supremacy.

Bo: Exodus 10:1–13:16

Prophetical Reading
Jeremiah 46:13–28

Overview of Torah Portion

God brings the final three plagues on Egypt: Locusts, darkness, and killing of the firstborn. Pharaoh finally relents and lets the Hebrew people leave Egypt. God instructs Moses about marking the new moon, observing *Pesach*, and consecrating the firstborn. With unleavened bread and their Egyptian neighbors' riches, the Hebrews depart.

Key Verses

"And the Lord said to Moses . . . 'I will harden Pharaoh's heart and multiply My signs and wonders in the land of Egypt'" (Exodus 7:1, 3).

"And the Lord hardened the heart of Pharaoh" (Exodus 9:12).

"And the Lord said to Moses, 'Go to Pharaoh, because I have hardened his heart, and the heart of his servants, that I might show these signs in his midst'" (Exodus 10:1).

"And the Lord hardened Pharaoh's heart and He did not let the children of Israel go" (Exodus 10:20).

"And the Lord hardened Pharaoh's heart and he would not let them go" (Exodus 10:27).

"And the Lord hardened Pharaoh's heart and he did not let the children of Israel go from his land" (Exodus 11:10).

"And the Lord spoke to Moses, saying . . . 'I will harden Pharaoh's heart'" (Exodus 14:1, 4).

"And the Lord hardened the heart of Pharaoh, king of Egypt, and he pursued after the children of Israel" (Exodus 14:8).

"And the Lord said to Moses . . . 'And I, behold, will harden the heart of the Egyptians'" (Exodus 14:15, 17).

Discussion Question

Pharaoh's hard heart: The obvious question is, why does God harden the heart of Pharaoh, over and over? Most commentators agree on the answer—Pharaoh and his people have to learn about God's sovereignty; Pharaoh has to release the Hebrews for the right reason, out of his free will, not because of the plagues.

Another question remains: Why is Pharaoh's state of mind so vital? Why do the children of Israel remain in slavery while Egypt's ruler comes to appreciate God's power? Is rehabilitating the criminal more important than saving the victim?

Shammai Engelmayer

Although I dealt with these two questions—especially the hardening of the Pharaoh's heart—in the answer to *VaYera's* question, there is more to be said.

To repeat, too much has been made of this hardening of the Pharaoh's heart. He had no choice but to dig in his heels. The Ramesside kings were the first of the pharaohs to identify themselves, not *with* the gods as previous pharaohs had done, but *as* the gods incarnate. Thus, this "god" saw himself locked in a battle with "another" for supremacy. The basis of his very authority was at stake. How could he, the physical manifestation of Egypt's most powerful god, allow himself to be defeated by the God of slaves?

The more he is pushed to the wall, therefore, the more stubborn he grows. He cannot afford to lose the battle because then he risks losing control of Egypt, as well. So, when the text says that God hardened the Pharaoh's heart, it is merely saying that each plague made it that much harder for the Pharaoh to relent.

This may explain the big mystery in Ramesside history. Following the death of Mernephtah, the most likely Pharaoh of the Exodus and Rameses's thirteenth son (all the others before him had died), Egypt fell apart economically and militarily. Some Egyptologists actually believe Mernephtah died chasing the Hebrew slaves.

Egypt had been at its most powerful under Rameses II (dubbed "the Great" for good reason), and Mernephtah supposedly held on to his father's expansions. Yet, immediately upon Mernephtah's death, the country goes to pieces, a condition it will take generations to recover from (and Egypt never recovers to the point where it again reaches the level it achieved under Rameses II).

Not only does the country fall apart, but so does Mernephtah's monarchy. His son, Seti II, is to rule in his place but is prevented from doing so by one Amenmesse (also apparently known as *Mose* in the existing records), who was the son of one of Rameses II's daughters. Amenmesse apparently had enough support among the people and, possibly, whatever military there still was, to be able to hold the throne for at least five years before Seti II can reclaim it.

Regarding the military collapse, this is a supposition based on the existing evidence. It surely was at its height during the reign of Rameses II; the historical record makes that clear. It apparently remained so under Mernephtah, as well, unless his court records are total fiction. Yet, on his death, not only does an obscure nephew usurp his throne without much resistance, but invaders from Lebanon seize and hold portions of the Delta. More important from our point of view, Israel is never troubled by Egypt in the 40 years of its desert sojourn, even though we know from the records that both Rameses II and Mernephtah had the entire region, up to Canaan itself, well fortified and manned. On a number of occasions, the records tell of escaped slaves being captured by Egyptian patrols. That this never happens to Israel, coupled with the other events that we know of from the historical (as opposed to the biblical) record, including a series of urban riots throughout Egypt that the military fails to put down, forces us to consider the possibility that Egypt's military suffered a great calamity in the waning days of Mernephtah to make it so powerless in his wake.

Although the Ramesside era will continue, Seti II is the last king descended from Rameses I, founder of the nineteenth dynasty. When Seti II dies, the throne is again usurped, apparently with the help of a Syrian butler, who later usurps the throne for himself. (This, too, points to a chaotic situation and a moribund military.) An obscure Egyptian retakes the throne from the Syrian and establishes the twentieth dynasty, although he names his son Rameses III, after the great kings of the nineteenth.

Obviously, the name "Rameses" still carried much weight. Thus, it would seem that it was Mernephtah specifically who was rejected, not Rameses. Something happened in Egypt that caused the people to doubt Mernephtah's claim to the throne. Doubting him to be the embodiment of Ra would be such a cause. Such doubt would be cast if Mernephtah emerged the big loser in a head-to-head confrontation with an alien deity.

An aside: Rameses ruled for 67 years, Mernephtah for 13. That totals 80 years. Moshe is said to be 80 when he takes Israel out of Egypt and has lived during the reign of two pharaohs. Coincidence? Sure, just like the coincidence that, 400 years earlier, meaning at exactly the right time in history, a Hyksos named Yakob-Her rules Egypt for 17 years, precisely the number of years the Torah tells us that Ya'akov was in Egypt before dying and being given what, when comparing the Genesis text to ancient records, clearly is a royal, not just a state, funeral. Although there is some question as to what the full name of this Hyksos was—some sources say Yakob-Her; others read it as Yakob-Baal; still others as Yakob-El or Yakob-Al—no one disputes the reading of Yakob. And the identification of Yakob-Her with our Ya'akov is accepted today by some scholars.

In any case, the pharaoh of the Exodus, whoever he was, made his own choices, as I said in the last parshah. He and he alone is guilty of the consequences.

Now, this whole scenario was less about punishing anyone and more about establishing that God alone is; that there are no others. He does so by co-opting and, perhaps, intensifying, natural events that would have occurred in any case. He can do this because He created nature and exists outside it. The plagues can be seen as an attack on the gods of Egypt, demonstrating that they are not gods at all; that only God is God. They also can be seen as first establishing God's existence; then His presence in this world; and finally the extent of His power.

Israel, by the way, is not a victim here. The enslavement and ensuing Exodus are at the core of our being. Everything we are and all we are supposed to be and do derive from those two linked events. The Decalogue and Book of the Covenant that follows it are both immediately dependent on them. Even the Shabbat, originally a memorial to creation, is given an Enslavement/Exodus theme in its restatement in Deuteronomy. So basic is the Exodus that it is the first of the six *zechirot* we are required to recall each day, followed by the Theophany, Amalek, the sin of the golden calf, Miriam's crime and punishment, and the Shabbat.

Indeed, our time in Egypt was part of the covenant promise from the very beginning, as God Himself told Avraham.

It could not be any other way. Look at Ya'akov's sons (or re-read his supposed "blessings" in Genesis 49; he is brutally frank). Do they individually or collectively exhibit any signs of being worthy of being a "treasured nation" and "kingdom of priests?" With the possible exception of Yoseph, do any of them even recognize who they really are, or what their destiny is? One wonders whether they even fear God, considering their readiness to kill their brother and their brutal assault on Shekhem.

(As to the latter, there is no justification for it. Once the men of Shekhem circumcised themselves and agreed to enter into the covenant, their slates were clean. In effect, they had done *teshuvah*. For Ya'akov's sons to use a holy act as a pretense for murder is a blatant *chilul ha'shem*, a profanation of God's name. Shekhem himself deserved to be punished for defiling Dinah, but no one else had to pay for his crime.)

These twelve scions of the patriarchal family clearly could never develop into Israel on their own. That explains why God promises a covenant to Avraham, Yitzchak and Ya'akov, but He offers only generalizations (the land, a large nation, etc.); He does not provide them with any details. Thus, for example, they are told that through Israel the world will be blessed, but there is no explanation provided as to how. The details must wait until after Egypt, because it is in Egypt that this family is to be stripped of all its pretenses and haughtiness and forged into a nation capable of being God's chosen messengers to the world.

That is what the Torah means when it says a family went down into Egypt, but a nation went up from there. We were no longer the children of Ya'akov, but *Ahm Yisrael*, the people Israel. Just as Ya'akov, at the Yabbok, confronted his own shortcomings and was worthy of being called Yisrael, so now were we worthy of the name.

Why did God set things up so that Israel would have to be enslaved? He did not, but He understands human nature. If you have been told over and again that you are unique, that you are the receiver of God's special blessings, it will go to your head sooner or later. That kind of "I am better than you" attitude is incompatible with Israel's mission. On the other hand, a former slave cannot say, "I am better than you." He or she also cannot argue against feeding the hungry, clothing the naked, sheltering the poor, welcoming the stranger, paying a decent wage in a timely fashion, allowing employees and even work animals one day's rest out of every seven, and so on.

Ya'akov's family is the raw material; Egypt is the factory; we are the product.

Joseph Ozarowski

There are really several questions here, and I will try to answer them one at a time.

While many commentators agree, as you pointed out, that the plagues and the subsequent hardening of Pharaoh's heart were part of his re-education process, there are other approaches to this question. Albo (fifteenth century Spain) and S'forno (sixteenth century Italy) suggest that "hardening of the heart" is not a removal of free will, but rather a toughening of the endurance to bear difficulty. Thus, any decision Pharaoh made to let the Jews go was still his own, rather than from the pressure of the plagues.

Rambam (Maimonides), offering a totally different approach, believes that after a certain point, the "hardening of the heart" was part of Pharaoh's punishment and consequences. In this type of drama, there comes a moment when one has lost the capacity to make intelligent, rational, and moral choices. Psychologically, this could be seen as one who countenances and encourages injustice for a long period. The person becomes immune, not losing any sleep over the atrocities. One could easily compare this to many of the Nazis and their allies, whose hearts were hardened as they became completely insensitive to the horrors they were perpetrating. After a point, whatever they themselves suffered in war became part of the consequences. After all, if Hitler had said in 1944, "I do *teshuvah*!" would the war have stopped at that point? Thus, we are not dealing with Pharaoh's state of mind as much as his state of heart and morality.

The issue of why the Jewish people had to stand by while Pharaoh endured the plagues can be settled, I believe, by accepting the rabbinic tradition that slavery stopped at some point during the plagues. This makes rational sense, as well, for while the Egyptian economy and society were being battered by the plagues, it would have been difficult to continue mistreatment of the Jews as had previously been done.

I am not sure whether rehabilitation of the criminal is more important than saving the victim. We all know that the Jewish people, the victims, were indeed delivered from Egypt. But there is a delightful midrash that states that after the splitting of the Red Sea, Pharaoh escaped and settled in Nineveh, Assyria. He was chosen (elected?) king and, in fact, was the King of Nineveh in the Book of Jonah. When Jonah came with the message of God's threatened imminent destruction of Nineveh, Pharaoh no longer hardened his heart. He had seen the consequences of this and immediately repented, bringing his entire community with him! In the end, this midrash teaches us that *teshuvah* is indeed possible, and criminals truly can be rehabilitated. That is, I suppose, one of the many reasons why we read Jonah on Yom Kippur afternoons.

David Sofian

I agree that the obvious question is why God hardens Pharaoh's heart over and over again. However, I do not agree with what you describe as the accepted answer that Pharaoh has to release the Hebrews for the right reason, out of free will, not because of the plagues. Indeed, the tradition is clear that the purpose of the plagues was to make God's name renown in the world.

But once that is said, it seems to me that God's hardening of Pharaoh's heart prompts the opposite thought. These verses from the Torah are telling us that God controlled Pharaoh, therefore Pharaoh had no choice. The question arises because, on the one hand, the Torah tells us God is holding Pharaoh responsible for not letting the Israelites out, and at the same time is keeping Pharaoh from letting them leave.

How can God hold Pharaoh accountable if all his actions were predetermined by God? What are the implications for human freedom given God's repeated hardening of Pharaoh's heart? I am not alone in seeing this theological problem. Rabbi Johanan asks in *Midrash Vayikra Rabbah* 13.3, does God's hardening of Pharaoh's heart not provide heretics with an argument that Pharaoh was denied the opportunity to repent? In other words, the ability to make a free choice was removed from Pharaoh.

Even Rabbi Shimon ben Lakish's retort to Johanan in the continuation of that passage validates Johanan's important theological question. Shimon ben Lakish tries to counter Johanan by replying that the heretics would be wrong, for God warns human beings up to three times, and if they do not repent by then, God's heart is closed to repentance so that God may exact vengeance. In other words, he is not disagreeing with Johanan that God removed Pharaoh's freedom. He differs only regarding the circumstances of the removal. God only took control after first giving Pharaoh a chance to repent.

His comment certainly runs counter to the predominant rabbinic notion that the gates of repentance are always open. Johanan is correctly pointing out the theological problem in the Torah text. Shimon ben Lakish doesn't disagree with Johanan. He only hopes to soften the problem.

The *Mekilta de-Rabbi Ishmael* acknowledges this issue as well. Yet it too finds no real solution. Instead, that ancient midrash uses this problematic passage to draw a moral lesson. In tractate *Beshallah*, we learn that Pharaoh was the first to sin, and so he was also the first to be punished. Therefore, using the interpretive method of *Kal vahomer* (if something is so in a comparatively light case then certainly it must be so in a comparatively heavy case), it can also be said that, if in the case of punishing evil deeds, which is of less importance, he who sins first is first to be punished, how much the more so when rewarding good deeds, which is of greater importance.

In other words, faced with the theological problem at hand, instead of dwelling on it and possibly drawing unwanted theological conclusions about human freedom, divine retribution, and God's willingness to accept repentance, the commentator turns us to our positive relationship with God and encourages us toward the doing of good deeds by pointing out God's quickness to reward them. It seems clear to me that the tradition has no other way to come to terms with our problematic passage. I see no better position than the *Mekilta*'s, for although the problem is far from solved, at least a difficult matter is turned to show us how to derive a positive moral lesson.

Turning to your second question, I do not think the issue is Pharaoh's state of mind, but rather the Israelites' state of mind. Frequently, the Torah indicates that our ancestors were reluctant to accept Moses and the message he was bringing to them. *Midrash Shmot Rabbah* has a wonderful way of expressing this in a comment to *Shmot* 5:1. At the end of chapter 4, Aaron greets Moses, and they return to the Israelites. Aaron then speaks to them and convinces them, by performing the signs God had told Moses to do, that God has indeed seen their affliction and remembered them.

Immediately thereafter, *Shmot* 5:1 begins by telling us that Moses and Aaron came and spoke with Pharaoh. The midrash wants to know where were all the others, and why are the elders not mentioned in this verse? It asks this because the Holy One had said in chapter 3:18 that they were explicitly supposed to accompany Moses and Aaron. *Shmot Rabbah* tells us that the elders did go with them at first, but gradually stole away one or two at a time, until only Moses and Aaron were left by the time they reached the palace.

Clearly, our ancestors needed additional convincing. It was their state of mind, their lack of confidence which necessitated the ensuing events. They are the ones who need convincing that God has remembered them and that their redemption is at hand.

Beshalach:
Exodus 13:17–17:16

Prophetical Reading
Judges 4:4–5:31

Overview of Torah Portion

Pharaoh regrets his decision to release the Hebrews; he sends his army after them in the wilderness. God splits the Red Sea, rescuing the children of Israel, then sends the water back to its original position, drowning the Egyptians. Facing famine, the Hebrews complain to Moses. God provides water, manna, and quail. The Amalekites mount an unsuccessful attack against the wandering Hebrews.

Key Verses

"And Moses told Aaron all of God's words with which He sent him and all the signs with which He commanded him. And Moses and Aaron went and gathered together all the elders of Israel. And Aaron spoke all the words that God had told Moses and did the signs in the sight of the people. And the people believed" (Exodus 4:28–31).

"And the Lord said to Moses, 'Stretch your hand over the sea that the waters return over the Egyptians. . . . ' And Moses stretched his hand over the sea and the sea returned . . . and the Lord overthrew the Egyptians in the midst of the sea. And the Lord saved that Israel that day from the hand of the Egyptians, and Israel saw the Egyptians dead on the seashore . . . and the people . . . believed in the Lord and in his servant Moses" (Exodus 14:26–31).

Discussion Question

A MATTER OF BELIEF: The first time Moses presents himself to the children
of Israel as God's messenger, to bring them out of Egyptian slavery, he
relates God's command and performs two relatively simple, but miraculous,
acts—he turns a rod into a snake and displays a leprous-then-clean hand.
And the people believe. After the series of plagues, after the Exodus from
Egypt, after the splitting of the Red Sea and the drowning of Pharaoh's
army, the Torah repeats that the now-free Hebrews believe in God and
Moses.

Why does the people's divine faith have to be repeated? Why now? Had
their belief lagged? All the miracles that brought the Hebrews' release
weren't enough for them? It seems that their standards for faith in God
have risen—from a few demonstrations of God's power, to massive,
destructive reversals of nature. Have the Hebrews become spoiled? Has
their spiritual level sunk?

Shammai Engelmayer

Yes, "And the people believed"—but for how long? No sooner did Moshe
return from the pharaoh with the news that they now had to make bricks
without straw than the people turned on Moshe: "May the Lord look upon
you and punish you for making us loathsome to [the] pharaoh and his
courtiers—putting a sword in their hands to slay us" (Exodus 5:21).

It only gets worse. Moshe complains to God, blaming Him for the new
troubles. Says God to Moshe: Do not worry; it is all going according to
plan. "But when Moshe told this to the Israelites, they would not listen to
Moshe, their spirits crushed by cruel bondage" (Exodus 6:9).

It was a perfectly reasonable development. The last time Moshe tried to
help, 40 years ago, he ended up killing an Egyptian overseer and having to
run for his life. Now he comes back to Egypt, does some parlor tricks that
impress them and give them temporary hope, and they start packing their
bags. But rather than win deliverance, they gain more work: Now they have
to gather their own straw before they can make their daily tally of bricks.
This guy Moshe is bad news.

We know he is not, but they do not. Sure, those plagues were impressive,
and the magicians could not duplicate most of them, but so what? These
were all natural events, so what was there to believe? As for plague number
ten, the people only had Moshe's word that it happened. They could see the

bloody waters, the hail, and the locusts, even the darkness—but they only had Moshe's word that all of Egypt's firstborn, and only the firstborn, died that night. After all, Israel left Egypt as soon as it was light.

Okay, so maybe they were freed by their God. Maybe. They really do not know this God (with apologies to the midrashists who maintain otherwise). They have some vague recollections of His promise to their ancestors, and they believe in Him in some vague way, but for 400 years, they have languished among the likes of Ra, Horus, Aton, Isis, and their ilk. More important, especially after the heresy of Akhenaten, which occurred in the Eighteenth Dynasty (meaning the one immediately preceding the Ramesside era), the Egyptians very likely cracked down on any monotheistic type of worship within their borders. That would have put an even greater distance between Israel and its God (and may even explain why Israel was enslaved).

As it was, the forefathers of the Israelites themselves had only a vague idea of God. He never had anything to do with any of the twelve sons of Ya'akov, except for Yoseph (and that contact was peripheral, at best). He was the "God of Avraham, of Yitzchak, and of Ya'akov," but was He also the God of Reuven, Shimon, and Levi, etc.? They had no idea; He had not been around for 400 years, and they had no traditions suggesting interaction between their patrynomic ancestors and God. Maybe He brought these calamities on Egypt—or maybe these calamities are natural events and Moshe was able to con the pharaoh into thinking otherwise; the people did not know.

Which brings us to the morning matzah that we read about in the last parshah. It is here that we see in concrete terms just how doubtful the people were about what was happening.

In Exodus 12:8, Moshe is told matter-of-factly that "they shall eat matzah with bitter herbs." We get the feeling that we should know what matzah is, but we do not. Only later on in the text (verse 34) are we told why matzah is the dietary requirement—because the people had no time to bake bread for the journey—but it makes no sense. They knew the night before that they were leaving; Moshe had told them. They had made these elaborate preparations for their final meal before departing. So there was plenty of time to make the dough rise. It is a long stretch between midnight and dawn; a whole bakery's worth could rise in that interval.

Why did they not prepare bread (and other provisions) for the journey? For one thing, because they did not fully believe Moshe. For another, because no one told them to do so. These people, being slaves, are used to following orders, not thinking for themselves. They were told to collect gold and silver, and so forth, but no one told them anything about food. That was their idea, at the last minute. And the food they prepared was the food they were most familiar with—the inexpensive, quick-to-make bread of slaves.

Why did no one tell them to prepare food for their exodus? Precisely because of their doubts (the same reason that, this week, they have to enter the waters of the *Yam Suf* [see the end of this answer for an explanation of this term] before it completely parts): They had to show a willingness to believe that Moshe was sent by God and that God, not Moshe and not nature taking its course, was the cause of their freedom. This they were supposed to do by putting their fate in the hands of God by following Moshe's instructions. This included believing that God would provide them with sustenance on the long journey ahead.

The matzah in the morning thus becomes a symbol of their lack of faith as much as it symbolizes their freedom. At the last minute, they expressed reservations about the ability of their Creator to create food for them on the way. They needed something to eat, and the bread of slaves was a proven staple.

When they saw the Egyptians pursuing them and their backs were to the sea, their lack of faith seemed vindicated. Once again, Moshe had done them in.

It took the splitting of the sea to get the people once and for all to "believe in the Lord *and in Moshe His servant*." It is the first real proof they had that Moshe was the special servant of God, that there was more going on here than that they were part of the road company production of "The Mad Magician from Midian."

It was vital that they believed that Moshe was, indeed, God's servant, because he was their only sign that God existed. When God spoke, He spoke through Moshe. God is unseen, unrepresented iconically and anthropomorphically. He is invisible. Even if they had begun to believe—in their hearts, if not in their brains—that God was more than a vague memory, they nevertheless still had to accept that Moshe was His servant, because Moshe claimed to be the vehicle through which God talked to them.

As subsequent events show, however, their belief was of the moment and as fleeting as a desert mirage. Even the amazing salvation at the sea comes to be seen by them in a natural light. This people again and again will doubt that God is God, constantly challenging Him to prove them wrong. And in the concurrent rebellions of *Korach*, *Datan*, and *Aviram*, they will demonstrate their disbelief that Moshe was God's servant.

A good question to ask here is why God did things in such a way as to continue the ambiguity. Why did He not once and for all prove who He was? The answer, of course, is faith. It is no trick to believe in God if you know for certain that He exists and that He is everything He is cracked up to be. It is more important that you believe in Him despite the lack of concrete proof—in other words, that you take Him on faith.

In the end, these people prove that they have no faith, so their story will end in the desert. God will give Israel Canaan, but it will be an Israel that is prepared to step into the sea, to "believe in the Lord and in Moshe His servant." For that, a new generation must arise, one that knows only Moshe, not Egypt; one whose beliefs are built on hope and not broken by the taskmaster's whip, "their spirits crushed by cruel bondage."

Finally, a few words are necessary here regarding my reluctance to translate *Yam Suf*, the Hebrew name for the body of water that God divided so that Israel could escape the pursuing Egyptians. Is *Yam Suf* the "Red Sea" or "Sea of Reeds?" The Septuagint, the Greek translation of the Bible prepared 2,200 years ago, rendered *Yam Suf* as "Red Sea." *Suf* does not mean "red," however; it means "reed." So many modern translators prefer "Sea of Reeds." That is a different body of water from the Red Sea, so this is not semantics.

More traditional translations prefer "Red Sea," but only because that is the inescapable and incontestable translation of *Yam Suf* as it appears in 1 Kings 9:26. That, however, presents logistical problems vis-à-vis possible routes for the Exodus. More likely, the *Yam Suf* in the Torah is not the actual Red Sea, but one of its tributaries.

Because neither "Sea of Reeds" nor "Red Sea" is fully satisfying as a translation, I prefer using *Yam Suf*.

Joseph Ozarowski

Comparing your two quotes about the people's faith is instructive. At the beginning of the story, following Moshe's two miracles in chapter 4, the Torah tells us, *"Va-ya-amein ha-am,"* and the people believed. Note that the Hebrew grammar is in the singular, though this is not reflected in the translation. At the end of the entire drama, following the splitting of the Red Sea, we are told, *"Va-ya-aminu baHashem . . . ,"* or "and the people believed in Hashem and in Moshe His servant." The Hebrew grammar here is in the plural, again not reflected in the translation. The singular at the beginning might reflect the "group effect," the result that occurs when, say, a mass of people sees impressive magic tricks. Some of the people may be cynical about the magic, but everyone ends up uttering "oohs and ahhs," being so impressed with what they see. While Moshe's miracles were far more than mere magic, the popular response may have been similar to a magician's response.

However, the effect does not last long. In chapter 5, the people become ornery when they are told that Pharaoh will not free them, and that their lot will become even more difficult. By the middle of chapter 6, the people are not even listening to Moshe because of their "shortness of spirit and hard labor."

After the finale at the splitting of the Red Sea, the singular grammar teaches us that, by now, each individual Jew could accept what he or she had seen. This was no longer a group effect but a true spiritual elevation. Rabbinic tradition teaches that each Jew at the Red Sea experienced prophecy and rose to the highest spiritual levels. They did not need to be convinced.

Your last line about our ancestors being spoiled and having a sinking spiritual level, of course begs the larger question of their general relationship with God over the Torah's time period. Immediately after their major expression of faith in Hashem after the split Red Sea, they start *kvetching*—first about the water and then about the food. And later, after the greatest event imaginable, the giving of the Torah, they continue to *kvetch* in constantly increasing ways.

Imagine—the greatest weekend retreat ever at Mount Sinai, with the finest scholar-in-residence, the Lord God, Sovereign of the Universe, and they still go out and worship the golden calf. The constant complaining, in spite of all the miracles one could imagine, is one of the major leitmotifs of the rest of the Torah.

In defense of that generation's behavior, however, it could be said that they still retained the slave mentality all the way through their experiences. This explains their seemingly contradictory behavior of deep spirituality and belief on one hand, but also deep ingratitude and outright rebellion on the other. Perhaps they were simply never ready to live as a free people serving the Creator of the Universe and living a life guided by Divine Law. Maybe it was inevitable that 40 years and the death of the entire generation were necessary for the Jewish people to finally emerge, able to settle in the Promised Land.

David Sofian

Throughout the entire encounter with Pharaoh, miracle after miracle occurs. One might think these experiences would be enough to convince the Israelites. One might think that the new problem to contend with would be Israelite overconfidence and arrogance. Why weren't they at least self-assured in the knowledge that God was working miracle after miracle on their behalf? Perhaps they were.

A cursory reading can give one the impression that they were so convinced. Once God had dealt with Moses' own objections to being God's message bearer to the Israelites and to Pharaoh, the drama moves to a new stage as Moses and Aaron assemble all the elders of the children of Israel to convince them that God had taken note of their situation and was prepared to do something about it. The people saw the signs, the text says, "and the people believed."

This phase of the Exodus story later concludes with the dramatic scene at the sea. The miracle of the splitting of the sea occurs as Pharaoh's army draws near, and when the people see the Egyptians lying dead on the seashore, it says, "they believed in the Eternal and in Moses, God's servant." So perhaps the answer to your question of why this statement needs repeating is that it forms a frame for this crucial part of the story, emphasizing for us that God's miracles provided the solid foundation needed for Israelite faith.

The problem with this way of looking at it is that these miracles do not provide the solid foundation needed. Shmot goes on to tell us that immediately after the splitting of the sea, a mere three days after crossing into the wilderness, the people come to Marah and are already grumbling against Moses about the lack of sweet water. Hadn't they just declared their belief in the Eternal and in Moses, God's servant? Where is their faith and their confidence now?

God works another miracle, instructing Moses to throw a piece of wood into the water to make it sweet. We might think that now their belief in the Eternal and in Moses would be secure. Yet, immediately after the miracle of the sweet water, they begin grumbling again. This time, they complain that, when they were in Egypt, they ate their fill of bread. Again God takes care of them with a miracle.

In the evening quail appeared and in the morning dew appeared. After the dew lay the fine flaky substance that came to be known as Manna. Were these miracles sufficient to bolster their belief? Again the answer is "no," for we see that the Israelites ignored all the accompanying instructions. They are told to gather an Omer per person, but some gathered too much and some too little. They were told not to leave any over until morning. But they paid no attention to Moses. They were told to gather enough on the sixth day to last through the seventh day. Yet some of them went out on the seventh day to gather anyway.

It seems to me that all this material and for that matter the material that follows in subsequent *parashot*, is teaching us a very different lesson than the one implied in your question. No, the miracles that brought the

Hebrews' release were not enough for them. But it was not because their standards for faith in God had risen.

Rather, I think the point is that real faith cannot be established through the experience of miracles alone, if through miracles at all. Without the context of an entire religious way of life, no number of miracles would have been sufficient to establish true faith. The Israelites who left Egypt had not been raised in the context of the Covenant, of relationship with God through the discipline of ongoing Jewish life. They remained the dependent, downtrodden people they had been in Egypt. In this regard, they were not prepared for the experiences that would follow. They could not respond except with the whining dependency that resulted from their day to day lives as slaves in Egypt.

The text is teaching us that religious character is built on our experience of living routine life. The way we experience the regular or even ordinary aspects of human living is what profoundly determines our behavior and attitude toward life. Solid faith is constructed on a whole pattern of living, not on momentary experiences, no matter how dramatic.

This is perhaps the most powerful argument for a disciplined Jewish context for the entirety of our lives. Certainly, contemporary Jews and the modern movements to which they belong differ on the requirements of a disciplined Jewish life appropriate for today. Yet there should be no disagreement on the absolute necessity for maintaining the discipline of day-to-day Jewish practice. The instant society in which we live may tempt us to try to find religious fulfillment in fleeting experiences, such as attendance during Yom Kippur, an occasional Bar or Bat Mitzvah service, or a *Pesach Seder*. These experiences can produce a short-lived warm feeling, which we can mistake for the essence of the Jewish religious enterprise.

When we make this mistake, we shortchange our religious selves. Judaism is built on our covenantal relationship with God and is intended to encompass the entirety of human living. The story of our ancestors' short-lived religious faith helps us understand that, when these experiences are disconnected from the bulk of the rest of our lives, nothing of lasting, rich substance can be built upon them.

Yitro: Exodus 18:1–20:23

Prophetical Reading
Isaiah 6:1–7:6, 9:5,6

Overview of Torah Portion

Moses is reunited in the wilderness with his father-in-law (Yitro), wife (Zipporah), and two sons (Gershom and Eliezer), who he had left behind in Midian. At Yitro's suggestion, Moses delegates men to help rule on the people's legal disputes. Amid thunder and lightning, God at Mount Sinai proclaims the Ten Commandments. God commands Moses to have the children of Israel make an altar on which to offer burnt sacrifices.

Key Verses

"And Jacob vowed a vow, saying, 'If God will be with me, and will keep me in this way that I go, and will give me bread to eat and clothes to wear, and cause me to return in peace to my father's home, then the Lord shall be my God'" (Genesis 28:20–21).

"And Moses ascended to God, and the Lord called to him out of the mountain, saying . . . 'And now if you will indeed listen to my voice and keep My covenant, then you shall be My treasure from all the people, for all the earth is Mine. And you shall be to Me a kingdom of priests and a holy nation'" (Exodus 19:3–6).

Discussion Question

HOLY CONDITIONS: The Torah relates numerous instances of God offering the children of Israel specific rewards and punishments, contingent on their loyalty to His laws—if they obey Him, or if they do not obey Him. But only here, at the foot of Mt. Sinai, three days before His revelation to the

114

entire Jewish nation, does God make the entire relationship conditional, linking the Hebrews' status as the Chosen People to their fealty.

Why now? Is the relationship between God and the Jews really open to renewal, dependent on their obeying the covenant? If Jacob, who was soon to become Israel—the namesake of the Jewish people—apparently established similar conditions for the supposedly eternal relationship, does this indicate that both parties can terminate the covenant? What is the relation between Jacob's statement to God and God's to Moses?

Shammai Engelmayer

The covenant with the patriarchs was always conditional. Indeed, it was less a covenant than the promise of one. There was always more left unsaid than said, and for good reason: The time was not right for God to reveal His terms, because the people themselves were not ready either to understand those terms or to accept them.

We discussed this previously in *parshat Bo*. The Exodus and the Enslavement that preceded it are the core events of our very existence as God's treasured nation. To repeat from that answer:

> Look at Ya'akov's sons. . . . Do they individually or collectively exhibit any signs of being worthy of being a "treasured nation" and "kingdom of priests?" With the possible exception of Yoseph, do any of them even recognize who they really are, or what their destiny is? One wonders whether they even fear God, considering their readiness to kill their brother and their brutal assault on Shekhem. . . .
>
> These twelve scions of the patriarchal family clearly could never develop into Israel on their own. That explains why God promises a covenant to Avraham, Yitzchak, and Ya'akov, but He offers only generalizations (the land, a large nation, and so forth); He does not provide them with any details. Thus, for example, they are told that through Israel the world will be blessed, but there is no explanation provided as to how. The details must wait until after Egypt, because it is in Egypt that this family is to be stripped of all its pretenses and haughtiness and forged into a nation capable of being God's chosen messengers to the world.
>
> That is what the Torah means when it says a family went down into Egypt, but a nation went up from there. We were no longer the children of Ya'akov, but *Ahm Yisrael*, "the people Israel." Just as Ya'akov, at the Yabbok, confronted his own shortcomings and was worthy of being called Yisrael, so now we were worthy of the name.

Even now, after 430 years in Egypt, including time spent in bitter slavery, this people is not ready for the task God has established for it. Israel still has its doubts; it remains too primitive in thought to understand the truth about what is happening. Thus, the people fashion a golden calf—not as a god itself, but as the representation of their God; the text is clear on this. They cannot fathom a deity who is all powerful, all knowing, and absolutely without form of any kind. He cannot even be said to be invisible because that implies the possibility that He ever could be visible, which in itself is anthropomorphic, imposing limitations on God that are unwarranted. The people standing before Mt. Sinai cannot comprehend this.

So God begins to reveal His terms in order to move their development along, but He obviously scales them down. He allows primitive ideas into their system of belief, such as sacrifice instead of prayer, to make it easier for them to understand Him.

Can the Covenant be terminated by either party? Not by Israel, to be sure; and probably not by God, either.

A covenant, at least in this context, is not just a contract between two parties. Its existence is not dependent on performance. If it were, the Covenant would have been scrapped almost immediately because that is how long it took until it was breached. The Covenant is everlasting because God says it is from the outset. And part of that Covenant is a set of penalties for violating its terms.

Israel, on the other hand, has no ability to suspend the terms, but that is what it agreed to, so it has no cause for complaint.

As for the relationship between Ya'akov's deal and this event, it is precisely through the fact that Ya'akov can suggest such a deal that we see how unprepared he and the family he was soon to have were for God's message and His mission.

"[T]he ground on which you are lying I will give to you and to your children," God tells Ya'akov. "Your descendants shall be as the dust of the earth. . . . All the families of the earth shall bless themselves by you and your descendants."

What is Ya'akov's response to this? "If you keep me in food and clothes and keep me safe from harm, you will be my God." God promises Ya'akov the future, but all he cares about is himself and the present.

God's Covenant with Israel is about the future. It is about responsibility to the world God created; to teach that world the moral path and thereby avert a second Flood. It is about caring about others at least as much as you care about yourself.

God made a promise to Ya'akov, as He did to Ya'akov's father and grandfather—but he leaves the terms blank until Sinai. Ya'akov's "deal" with God at Beth El is part of the reason why the terms stayed blank for so long.

Joseph Ozarowski

After reflection and discussion with both my congregants and my family at the *Shabbos* table, I have to question the entire premise of your inquiry. None of us thought there was a relationship between Jacob's personal vow to Hashem and Hashem's covenant with the Jewish people through Moshe. An individual's vow to God in times of trouble has a validity of its own; in fact, many of the talmudic commentaries see Jacob's statement as the basis for the concept of individual vows in general, and more specifically in times of difficulty. (See *Tosafot* on Hull in 2b quoting the midrash; Mordechai [Mordechai ben Hillel Hakohen, thirteenth century Germany] on chapter 4 of *Baba Kamma*; and the *Torah Temimah*'s commentary [R. Barukh Ha-levi Epstein, nineteenth century Russia] on the verse of Jacob's vow.) But it does not really resemble God's choice of our people and our people's positive response at the foot of Mt. Sinai.

Jacob's choice of words indeed has moved commentators to consider the implications. Abarbenel questions how Jacob could put conditions on a vow of faith. Many of the other classic commentators (see Ramban and Rashi) suggest that Jacob's commitment was not neccesarily accepting God's presence per se, for God had already promised that in verse 15, "Behold I will be with you and watch you wherever you will go. . . ." Rather, when God brings Jacob through the coming unknown period, then he will be able to return home, build a house for God, and tithe ten percent of his wealth. Ramban specifically translates the Hebrew *im* not as "if" but as "when." Hirsch suggests that Jacob was not asking for physical protection during his journey, but rather spiritual protection. If so, Jacob's responses of tithing and building are appropriate.

I have to query other aspects of your question. Jacob really was not "soon to become Israel—the namesake of the Jewish people." This did not occur until Genesis 32, some 20 years later, after the sojourn with *Lavan* (and the period of study at *Yeshivat Shem vaEver*, according to the midrash). Jacob does not become Israel until after another experience—his encounter and struggle with the stranger, and his subsequent meeting with Esau. After preparing for both a peaceful encounter as well as the possibility of a violent fight, Jacob prays. And his prayer has no hint of conditions!

"I am not worthy of all the mercies and all the truth which You have shown. . . . Deliver me, please, from the hand of my brother, the hand of Esau, because I fear him, lest he come and attack me, mother and children. . . ." (Genesis 32:11–12.)

No ifs, whens, or buts here. See also Harold Kushner (1981), *When Bad Things Happen to Good People* who develops this idea into a model for prayer.

All in all, I would not term Jacob's promise a covenant or even a model for a covenant. Rather, it was a very personal vow made in time of trouble.

What about God's covenant with our people at Mount Sinai? Can it be terminated? While there are many statements through the Torah stipulating that the *brit* is contingent on our behavior and loyalty to *Hashem*'s Torah (Leviticus 26:14–16, Deuteronomy 8:19–20, 11:13–21, 28:1–69), the Torah also makes clear (in some of the same passages, for example the end of Leviticus 26) that the covenant will not be completely forgotten or broken by *Hashem* in spite of our behavior. Jewish history and teaching, as found in the prophets, embellished and proved this idea. In spite of our people's idolatry and misdeeds, and the suffering and destruction which accompanied the end of the First Temple period, the covenant was still in force.

The famous midrash in which God holds the mountain over our people's heads and threatens them to accept the Torah or die in the desert makes the covenant seem less than a voluntary acceptance, in spite of the people's response of *na'aseh v'nishma*, "We will do and we will hear." First, I would suggest that the midrash can be understood psychologically, reflecting the people's state of mind at that moment. A group of runaway slaves in the middle of a lonely desert, they really had no choice but to accept what God was offering them. And yet, after the destruction of the First Temple, the rabbis suggest (Shabbat 88a) that when the Megillah of Esther says *Kiyemu v'kiblu*, "The Jews fulfilled and accepted," it means that they finally fulfilled the Torah that they had forcibly accepted earlier. In other words, they voluntarily renewed the covenant.

It has been suggested by some modern theologians that, following the Holocaust, God has broken the divine end of the covenant. Being the child of Holocaust survivors, I have very deep and mixed feelings about the open question of God during the *Shoah*. But I might suggest that the rebirth of the modern Jewish State of Israel after the Holocaust, as well as our people's ongoing survival in the diaspora, tenuous as both of these may at times seem, proves (at least to me) that the covenant is still in force and will always remain in force.

David Sofian

You raise an interesting question: Is our covenant with God conditional or not? The agreement that connects God and Israel has certainly not always been smooth. Generally when we think of this particular *parashah*, we focus on the experience at Mt. Sinai and the establishing of the covenant with the entirety of the Jewish people.

Yet, nearly every episode during the time our ancestors spent in the wilderness is one that tests the durability of the covenant. All we need do is look several *parashot* ahead to *Ki Tisa* and the golden calf to see this. However, can the covenant be cancelled? Is the Jewish people's relationship with God eternal or not? This question provides us with an opportunity to see the difference between reading and understanding the Bible in its own context, and reading and understanding it through the lens of rabbinic teaching.

If we look at your question in terms of the Bible itself, scholars tell us that the covenant God made with our ancestors is similar in form to ancient Hittite vassal treaties. To be sure there is a key difference: Israel entered into it willingly as opposed to having been conquered. Recognizing this fact, it is no longer surprising that the expression of covenant you draw us to in the key verses (*Shmot* 19:3–6) takes the form of God's conditional expectations of Israel under the covenant, just as a conquering king expressed expectations and dictated conditions in the treaty.

Yet, it is more important to me to understand how Jews read and understand the Bible, than it is to contemplate how the Bible came to be. Different ideas have developed and have been emphasized in response to new conditions. In terms of the question you currently pose, the emphasis on the eternity of the covenant comes in response to changing reality.

There can be no doubt that Judaism lives today, because the classical rabbis found a way of adapting the institutions of biblical Judaism after the destruction of the Second Temple. Just as Deutero-Isaiah emphasized a trust in God who would restore Israel after the destruction of the First Temple, Judaism's survival required emphasizing a theological interpretation of the devastating loss of the Second Temple that maintained the eternity of the covenant.

This was necessary not only to bolster a devastated community, but also to refute any who would claim the destruction confirmed God's total rejection of the Jewish people. Therefore, when we look at rabbinic material, we find a clear conclusion. The rabbis stressed that God punishes Israel, but never terminates the covenant.

The relationship between God and Israel may be strained, but it cannot be broken. The rabbis then go the additional step of claiming that not only is the destruction of the Temple not an indicator of God's rejection, but it is an indicator of God's love. It is out of love that God punishes Israel's sinfulness.

There are innumerable rabbinic passages concerning God punishing

Israel for her sins. One from *Yomah* 9b makes the point specifically in terms of the destruction of the Temples. There we learn the First Temple was destroyed because of idolatry, immorality, and bloodshed. And then we are told the Second Temple was destroyed because of baseless hatred. The passage concludes that hatred without fair cause is as weighty as the other three combined.

However, we must see that God's justice is tempered with God's mercy, for there are also many passages that indicate God continued to love Israel in spite of her sinning. In the *Yomah* 56b, a heretic tells Rabbi Hanina that the destroyed Temple means the Jews are defiled and God no longer dwells among them. Hanina steadfastly replies that God continues to dwell among Israel, even in the midst of their uncleanness.

In *Shmot Rabbah* (*Terumah*, 33:2), God responds to the nations that claim an irreparable rupture in the relationship by attesting that God will not abandon them, but dwells with them. And in *Aicha Rabbah* (*Proem.* 24) we find an anguished God who, having punished Israel with the destruction of the Temple, nevertheless grieves with them in their suffering.

It is the Bible viewed through the rabbinic lens that makes your key verses problematic. Yet, the Judaism we have inherited was shaped by the rabbis through their interpretation of the Torah's text. Therefore, along with the rabbis, we must answer your question by affirming the eternity of the Jewish people's covenant with God.

Mishpatim:
Exodus 21:1–24:18

Prophetical Reading
Jeremiah 34:8–22, 33:25–26

Overview of Torah Portion

God gives Moses a series of moral and economic laws, ranging from treatment of slaves and punishment for murder to restitution for damaged property and treatment of the less fortunate. Moses relates the commandments to the Hebrews; they accept "with one voice." God calls Moses up to Mt. Sinai to receive tablets on which the commandments are written.

Key Verses

"He that kills a man who dies shall surely be put to death. And if a man does not lie in wait, but God causes it to come to his hand, then I will appoint a place to which he may flee" (Exodus 21:12–13).

Discussion Question

A Divine sentence: God establishes cities of refuge on both sides of the Jordan for someone who accidentally takes another's life. But the Torah clearly states that such a killing occurs only if God wills it. Commentators agree that a person becomes an instrument for bloodshed—even, apparently, by accident—when he or she is guilty of some major offense for which punishment is deserved.

Why this indirect form of punishment? Either a person is guilty of murder, or he is innocent—if he is innocent, why not exempt him from all punishment? Is the inevitable feeling of guilt for the "accidental" murder not sufficient punishment?

Shammai Engelmayer

I am at a loss. I cannot answer this question. Let me explain why. A man is on his way home from the office after a particularly good day. The roads are slippery and visibility is poor, but his mind is less on the driving than on the day he had, especially how he closed a really big deal. A 7-year-old returning from basketball practice stops at the corner, looks both ways, then proceeds to cross the street. The man, his mind elsewhere, misses the stop sign and upon realizing his error hits the brakes. The car goes into a skid, sending it across the intersection and back-ending it into the 7-year-old, who is instantly killed.

Now here is the real question, based on the one posed here and upon Rashi's explanation: How many intentional murders did the 7-year-old commit before God punished him by sending someone who had already committed one unintentional murder (in secret) to commit a second one, this time in front of qualified witnesses? As the Talmud tells us (BT *Shab.* 32a): "punishment is wrought through the hands of a guilty person."

For what crime did He punish the 5,400 people who died in the 1995 Japanese earthquake, beyond question an "act of God?" (For those who say that non-Jews do not count, then we can eliminate the practice of letting out drops of wine from our cup as we recite the Ten Plagues during the *Seder*, and expunge from the midrash the reference to God being angry at the heavenly host, who cheered as the Egyptians were drowning, oblivious to the fact that the Egyptians, too, were God's children.)

But why stop at accidental deaths? As the Artscroll *Chumash* explains the verse, "It is a fundamental principle of the Torah that events are not haphazard. *Always there is the guiding hand of God*" (emphasis mine). Thus, shall we say that God exacted punishment when a 6-year-old girl is raped and murdered by a psychotic degenerate? Shall we say that the 167 people killed in the bombing of the federal office building in Oklahoma City, nearly a hundred of whom were children in a day care center, deserved to die?

Shall we say (heaven forbid) that the Six Million deserved to die?

In a sense, of course, everything does happen because God causes it to happen. As I noted in discussing the hardening of the pharaoh's heart in Va'era, "When God created everything, he literally 'programmed in' every possible permutation of all that would happen. . . . He accounted for each individual's choices in his original programming."

In effect, "If A does X, then Y will happen to B," and so forth. In that sense, *and only that sense*, can God be blamed for every senseless death and act. How the program plays out depends on our own individual input. We, not God, are truly responsible.

This is true even for natural disasters. We choose to be in a certain place at a certain time. We may not know an earthquake is about to hit, and therefore do not know that we are putting ourselves in jeopardy, but the choice of where we are when that earthquake hits is ours; God did not pull the strings to put us there.

How dare we blame God for killing that 7-year-old? How dare we, at the same time, mitigate that blame by accusing the 7-year-old of having secretly committed an act of willful murder, or some other crime punishable by death (a punishment to which minors are not subject in any case)? How dare we suggest that a child who was brutally abused and then slain ever did anything to deserve that?

Perhaps then, the punishment is for a crime carried out in a *gilgul acher*, an earlier existence? I will accept this only from those who will also state that there is no punishment in the afterlife, for why else would God exact a punishment from someone who was already punished before being reborn in a new *gilgul*?

How far are we to carry this kind of misrepresentation of God? As I write this, I am reminded of an incident several years ago in Israel, when a bus carrying children was in an accident and several of them died. One prominent rabbi declared at the time that the children died because the *mezuzot* in their homes were not kosher. And I wonder about an event that occurred on January 22, 1995: Twenty people were killed by a suicide bomber at a bus stop outside Netanya, Israel. Who will write to their parents and loved ones explaining that these people were not innocent victims of a crazed murderer, but the receivers of God's justice at the hands of His chosen avenger?

As for Rashi, not only can't I accept his answer, I can't accept his logic. I can't because Rashi is not the least bit sloppy in his commentaries. I have to assume, therefore, that he knows the truth, but seeks to deflect us from seeking it by deflecting our vision elsewhere because, being in *galut* and thus without cities of refuge, we might act on our impulses if nothing existed to stay our hands.

He begins by attempting to explain why the Torah seems to be so redundant on the issue. Each word is absolutely necessary, he says. Thus, he notes that here, in Exodus 21:12, it states that "one who strikes *a man* so that he dies, that one shall be put to death." If only this verse appeared,

Rashi wonders, then "from where [are we to learn that he is so punished if] he hit a woman or a minor?" He also wonders how we would know that a minor who commits a murder is not put to death.

It is to clarify matters, Rashi explains, that Leviticus 24:17 states: "And a man who kills *any human soul* shall surely die." On the other hand, if only the verse in Leviticus appeared, Rashi states, then we would assume that anyone who kills an unborn child also is punishable by death, but from the verse in Exodus it is clear that "a person is not subject [to the death penalty] until he strikes a viable child [a "human soul"] who is capable of becoming a man."

If we are to follow this logic, especially the latter part about the "viable child," then we have to assume that a person who kills a little girl is not punishable by death because she is not capable of becoming a man. Similarly, because "a man who kills" (Leviticus) clarifies "one who strikes" (Exodus) not only minors but women, too, and should therefore be exempt from the death penalty.

Rashi's logic is faulty as well, in regards to the death of the fetus. There is no reason why these two texts are needed to make this clear, because Exodus 21:22 states it explicitly. If that is not sufficient, then we can also infer it by pairing up that verse with Numbers 35:31, which prohibits accepting monetary compensation in the case of capital murder. Since we can accept compensation for causing a miscarriage, it follows that a fetal death is not considered the death of a person.

Rashi knew all of this full well, just as "the School of Rabbi Yishmael" in BT Shabbat knew full well that God is not the reason why people die in accidents.

And the Torah knows it, too. Indeed, the Torah is very careful with its language here. "And if a man does not lie in wait, but God causes it to come to his hand, then *I will appoint a place to which he may flee.*" The speaker is God; this is clear throughout the parshah. More to the point, God is not afraid of personalizing His actions. Mistreat the widow and orphan, "and My anger will blaze forth and I will put you to the sword" (Exodus 22:23). Be on guard on account of the Law, for "I am sending an angel before you . . ." (Exodus 23:20). Heed the Law and do right before the Lord, "And I will remove sickness from your midst. . . . I will let you enjoy the full count of your days. I will send forth My terror before you, and I will throw into panic all the people among whom you come, and I will make all your enemies turn tail before you. I will send a plague ahead of you . . ." (Exodus 23:25–28).

If God meant for us to know that He is the ultimate cause of unintentional homicide, He would have said so. "And if a man does not lie in wait, *but*

I cause it to come to his hand, then I will appoint a place to which he may flee." That is not how the text reads, because that would be untrue.

That is the reason the Torah is so redundant on the homicide issue, briefly returning to it in Leviticus 17, expanding the subject in Numbers 35, and having it repeated by Moshe in his personal reiteration of the law in Deuteronomy 19. (In none of these places is it suggested that God is the ultimate killer.) It is Moshe, in fact, who provides the key when, in Deuteronomy 19:6, he explains of the *go'el hadam*, the blood avenger, "for his heart will be hot."

The Israel of Exodus 21 is an Israel that had lived among the paganism of Egypt for 400 years. There, it was believed that the gods controlled every aspect of life and death. Anuket nourishes the fields. Sebek and Apepi are responsible for evil. From Nefertum comes life; Osiris rules the dead. How better to cool the hot heart than to attribute accidental death to God, rather than to circumstance and pure carelessness (without any divine component)? It is a concept these Israelites can readily understand.

Even today, 3,500 years later, our hearts run hot and our emotions get the better of us. Only now we have no cities of refuge to block our paths and allow us time to cool off. It is only when we consider the possibility that God played a role in the death that we back off from our heat.

Thus, when Gavin Cato was killed by a Lubavitch chasid in Crown Heights, the local community rioted. During those riots, Yankel Rosenbaum was killed in revenge for the young boy's death, but the Lubavitch community did not then rise up and kill in turn. Its belief that everything begins with God stayed the hand of those whose hearts ran hot.

Everything does begin with God, but once again the caveat: God is not a puppeteer. He does not spend His days making so-and-so do this while He is doing that to whomever. We are responsible for what we do to ourselves and to others. There is such a thing as an "innocent victim."

And so, I cannot answer a question about an "indirect form of punishment," because there is no such thing here. It is not fair to blame God because we let a hammer fly out of our hand, killing another person. It is just as unfair to claim that the person who died because of our carelessness deserved to die because of some hidden crime.

Joseph Ozarowski

There are two aspects to your question: The issue of Divine involvement in the manslaughter which the Torah implies, and the purpose of the exile to a city of refuge for the guilty party.

It is not easy to explain God's involvement in the manslaughter to a rational twentieth century mind. The classic rabbinic explanation, found in the Talmud tractate *Makhot* 10b in the name of Rabbi Shimon ben Lakish, is as follows: ". . . And God has caused it to come to his hand." Of what is the verse speaking? Of two people involved in murders; one who murdered on purpose and the other inadvertently (our case of manslaughter). This one has no witnesses, and neither does the other (which under Torah law cannot be a basis for any of the biblically-mandated punishments). The Holy One, blessed be He, "invites" them both to an inn. The one who murdered on purpose sits beneath the ladder and the one who killed inadvertently goes down on the ladder, falls on the other and kills him. The one who murdered on purpose is killed, and the one who killed inadvertently is exiled.

This approach, followed by most of the classic commentators, suggests that the incident of manslaughter may be God's way of righting a terrible wrong. We might not be able to comprehend the Divine justice, but our tradition teaches that there is a reason for this tragedy, a Divine *tikkun* rectifying an injustice. (See how the Artscroll *Chumash* expresses this thought.) We may not fully understand what has befallen us, but we may take some comfort knowing that in the divine scheme of things, there are purposes and explanations beyond our knowledge.

This concept is not always spiritually satisfying to some, especially if they have been in such a manslaughter situation. Who is to say that my relative or friend who died in a car accident deserved what he or she endured? Why do people who are good and decent become victims of manslaughter? And is every perpetrator of manslaughter a repeat offender? These questions are not easily answered and are probably beyond the scope of our book. I would never suggest the above-mentioned answers when playing the role of pastoral caregiver to a grieving family suffering the loss of a loved one through a tragic accident of negligence. Even *Tosafot* on *Berakhot* 46b questions the theology of the special *shiva* house grace after meals, which states, "He takes back souls in *din* (judgment)." Even though Tosafot leaves the phrase in the prayer, the commentary writes, "There is death without sin and there is suffering without transgression." In other words, death and suffering are not necessarily meant as punishment.

Yet for a believer, one cannot but concede the theological given that *yesh din v'yesh dayan*, "there is judgment and there is a Judge." Somewhere, perhaps only at the Divine level, there must be a pattern to things even if we find this difficult to accept at a given moment.

Should the feelings of guilt be sufficient punishment for the perpetrator? I would say not. There is no guarantee that there will even be a feeling of guilt. Then as now, many people feel a callousness for life, and it probably is even worse now than it was in biblical times. Besides, how many cases do we know of hit-and-run drivers, cases of people under the influence of alcohol or drugs who have no intention to kill, or people who do not keep their vehicles in good order and end up snuffing out innocent life. The Torah says that guilt is not enough. There must be some tangible response by the man-slaughterer acknowledging his or her responsibility. The Torah's law of exile, in this case, is unique.

There are several reasons for cities of refuge for the guilty parties. There is obviously a social aspect. Rather than throw the murderer in jail, we send the person into exile, forcing him or her to rehabilitate themselves in the cities of refuge. These were Levitical cities. The Levites were the teachers and spiritual leaders of ancient times. Thus, the murderer was forced to uproot his or her life and live in a strange place, but with holy people influencing them.

The concept of the go'el hadam, the right of the victim's family to blood vengeance outside the city of refuge, can also be seen socially as the societal means to get the murderer into the city. The needs of the murderer had to be taken into consideration as well. The city had to have all the basic amenities for a normal life. If the murderer was a teacher (rabbi?), the students went along as well. (See chapter 2 of Talmud Makkot and the commentary of Maharsha [Rabbi Shlomo Eidels, Poland—sixteenth and seventeenth centuries] for more on the social aspect of the cities of refuge.)

The Talmud itself, however, gives a different reason for the consequence of exile. The rabbis refers to this as kappara, atonement. Besides the social aspect of the cities of refuge as therapy for the manslaughterer, there is a religious aspect as well to the exile. The murder may not have been premeditated, and the murderer bore no malice toward the victim. Yet, a life and human being, created in the image of the Almighty, has been snuffed out. Not only does this have societal implications, but it has moral and spiritual ones, as well. Thus, the perpetrator must give up something of him- or herself. The talmudic commentaries suggest that this is similar to the offering of a korban, a sacrifice, in the cases of unintentional shogeg misdeeds when life is not lost. This approach may partially explain why the only amnesty for the murderer is when the High Priest, leader of religious life, dies.

All in all, the Torah requires us to take responsibility for our actions. If there is a wrong we have committed, we are bound to right it. We are bidden to be careful with our actions, for we do not get off scot-free when someone else is hurt. Even if we cannot accept the traditional explanation that God ultimately rights those wrongs, we must realize that our actions have effects that we cannot visualize.

To better understand the concept of cities of refuge, the reader should carefully study the other biblical references to this idea and law in Numbers 35 and Deuteronomy 19:1–10. Also see "Stamping Out the Blood-Feud" (Leibowitz 1980) (Numbers) and "The Manslayer's Asylum—Purpose and Rationale" (Jacobson 1977).

David Sofian

Your question to *parashat Shelach Lecha* is similar to the one you ask here. There, triggered by the episode of the spies, you wonder why God needs to ask questions. Does God not already know the answers? Here you are questioning the text's description of a divine behavior also. Since no killing could take place without God willing it, the perpetrator must be God's instrument. Why then does God not declare decisively on the guilt or innocence of that person instead of creating the cities of refuge?

In my answer to *parashat Shelach Lecha*, I referred to Neil Gillman's book, *Sacred Fragments*. Gillman indicates that the image of God described in classical western philosophy/theology is very different from the image of God described in the *Tanakh*. As I suggested there, the problem you raise results from applying the philosophical/theological image of God to a biblical text.

Let me summarize what I said there. Western philosophy sees God as perfect, which means God is omnipotent and omniscient. Within this metaphor for speaking about God, there would be no room for divine inconclusiveness. Along with you, we would ask, "is God in charge or not?" If innocent, why not declare the person the same without any form of punishment? However, the God of the Torah is not the God of western philosophy. Within the Torah's metaphor for speaking about God, we find a God whose mind can be changed and who is often frustrated. We find a God who is not perfect and whose plans are often conditional.

Recognizing this means the Torah itself will not address the philosophical/theological questions western philosophy raises. The Torah wants us to see God is concerned with and interested in this individual who needs a place of refuge.

Since rabbinic Judaism looks to the Torah as the basis for resolving all issues and problems, the commentaries are left to deal with your point and try to find a way of harmonizing an image of God who is in charge with the key verses you assign. How can God cause it and yet the perpetrator be punished?

In particular, Rashi is troubled by your question. Beginning with the theological position that, since God is in charge no occurrence really is an accident, he suggests that our difficulty with this passage evaporates if we elucidate a proper context for it (which he then does by paraphrasing a talmudic argument). Perhaps the person inadvertently killed was a murderer himself and deserved death. Suppose there are two men, one who killed inadvertently and the other who killed intentionally.

However, because there were no witnesses to either act, neither are punished. God brings them together at an inn. The intentional murderer sits under a ladder, and the inadvertent killer, having ascended the ladder, falls upon the other and kills him. Justice is done all around in that the true murderer is put to death, and the death of the person inadvertently killed is dealt with by his killer's exile. Yet those sitting in the inn are unaware of the real circumstances, and so may misconstrue what happened.

Granted Rashi gives us a somewhat convoluted context, but he makes his point. For him our questions only arise due to our lack of perspective. It is not the case that the person is either guilty and deserving of punishment or innocent and not deserving. Rashi is convinced that only God has the broad perspective necessary to make these decisions and mete out absolute justice.

Trumah: Exodus 25:1–27:19

Prophetical Reading
1 Kings 5:26–6:13

Overview of Torah Portion

God gives Moses the details for constructing the Tabernacle—the portable sanctuary—and the vessels to be used in holy service. The materials are to come from the Hebrews' donations of precious metals, animal skins, and cloths.

Key Verses

"And they shall make Me an ark of accacia wood; its length two and a half cubits; its width a cubit and a half; its height a cubit and a half" (Exodus 25:10).

Discussion Question

GOD IS IN THE DETAILS: This Torah portion is a series of specific construction details: Measurements and materials. For the ark, the staves, the tabernacle's table, the curtains, and so forth. All of this is for objects in which the tablets bearing the commandments will be stored. But no similar details are recorded for many of the actual commandments that we consider the essence of Judaism—for example, the kosher slaughter of animals or the punctilious observance of the Sabbath.

Why does the Torah go to such lengths, literally, to ensure that pieces of furniture and accompanying implements, objects with a limited time of usage, are built precisely? Why are the details, the actual *halakhot*, of such eternal Jewish practices as *kashrut* and Sabbath observance hinted at in the written Torah and reserved, in large part, for the Oral Law? Since most Jews were born after the generation in the desert, how can we feel we can fulfill the commandments surrounding the building of the Tabernacle?

Shammai Engelmayer

There are two questions here. The last, how we can fulfill the *mitzvot* surrounding the *Mishkan*, the portable tabernacle, is easy.

The *Mishkan* represents two separate facets of Judaism as religion: Sacred service and ritual practice. Aside from the three fixed times for prayer, anyone can pray at any time of the day or night, and in almost any location, although an abbreviated prayer on the road is preferable to an extended prayer in a ruin (see BT *Berakhot* 3a). On the other hand, sacred service implies communality; in other words, in our day it implies the congregation. Whatever can be done to benefit the congregation, from helping to make a *minyan* to contributing to the upkeep and even the refurbishing of a synagogue and a study hall, fulfills this aspect of the *Mishkan*.

The other facet is ritual, which the *Mishkan* is all about. Since the days of the Second Temple, ritual is something that has its place in the home; indeed, from the fall of the Temple in 70 c.e., the home has been the primary site for ritual. We make *kiddush*; light Shabbat, *havdalah*, and Chanukah candles; conduct *seudot mitzvah* ("ritually-ordained meals," for example, on Purim, at a *brit*, or bar/bat mitzvah, and so forth) participate in the *sedarim* on *Pesach*, and so on. We even *daven* at home more often than in *shul*, especially in the mornings, when *davening* also involves ritual—the donning of *tefillin* and *tallit*.

So we fulfill this aspect of the *Mishkan* by preparing for these rituals by buying the best and most aesthetically pleasing *menorot* and *chanukiot*, *seder* plates, *kiddush* cups, and so forth. We care for these, making certain that they do not lose their luster and thus detract from their beauty, or the beauty of the day or event they are intended to enhance. In the cases of *mezuzot* and their boxes, *tefillin*, and even *tallitot* (for an explanation of these terms, see my commentary to the next reading, *Tetzaveh*), we see to it that they remain kosher and that their outward appearances remain pleasant. We buy the best foods for our ritualized meals and set aside our best clothes for our holy days.

When we engage in ritual, we linger over them. We do not merely light the *chanukiah*, we stay a while, sing some songs, and play some games. We do not mumble our way through the *Haggadah*. Through reflection and prayer, we build up to the moment that we don our *tefillin* and *tallitot* (or, at least, we should).

In such ways, we fulfill the *mitzvot* surrounding the Tabernacle. This is one of the two main reasons the Torah lingers on the issue out of proportion to everything else—to teach us the importance of not taking ritual casually.

The other main reason pertains to the first question posed this week. The *Mishkan*, the Tabernacle, is fixed in time and place; the *halakhot* of the Torah are, with a few exceptions, meant for all times and all places.

We are given details of how the *Mishkan* was constructed both to allow us to visualize this most sacred structure and to enable us to recreate it if ever the need should arise. It is one thing to look at a table or an altar and say, "This one is wearing away; let me build another to replace it," and to actually build it. You cannot just rebuild a part of the Tabernacle; you must use certain materials, but not others; you must use certain tools, but not others; you must employ a particular system of weights and measures. And, when it is all gone and long gone, you have to know how to start all over again, if that is the will of the Lord. The blueprints are necessary.

The *Mishkan*, although portable, is also meant to remain within the borders of Israel. Once it crosses the Jordan, it never can leave there and still retain its sanctity. It is the *Mishkan* only in the Land of Israel. Not even the land of the two and a half tribes (the first *diaspora*) is suitable.

Halakha, on the other hand, is not so static. Indeed, it is not static at all. It is a living organism, meant to be fed and bred. It is meant for all time and every place. That is why the Torah does not provide *halakha* as much as it provides chapter headings for the *halakha* to come.

Thus, we are told to "observe" and "remember" Shabbat. How does one observe and what is entailed in remembering? We may not work on Shabbat, but what is "work?" We may not light a fire, but how does one define the verb "light" and the noun "fire?" We may not cook on Shabbat, but what does "cook" mean?

The answers to these questions must change over time as circumstances change. From a commandment not to stir from our homes on Shabbat, we expand the law to allow for walking measured distances and for the creation of legal devices to allow for even more than that. From a commandment not to cook, we evolve the laws of *kli rishon* and *kli sheni*, allowing us to reheat food on Shabbat under certain guidelines. (A *kli rishon* is the original pot in which a food is cooked; once cooked, the food may be transferred to a *kli sheni*, a secondary pot, after which reheating of sorts is permitted on Shabbat, but only if very strict and controlled guidelines are followed.)

How do I get from "You shall not boil a calf in the milk of its mother" to not having chicken parmigiana for dinner if not for an evolving process of law? Of what practical relevance to an apartment dweller is "You shall not move the boundary marker of your neighbor" if not as a prohibition against unfair competition?

The *halakha* of the Torah needs defining, refining, updating, expanding. Set it in stone, so to speak, and it remains set in stone. Leave it as chapter headings, and the Oral Law becomes Sacred Law.

What is the Torah, after all? It is not a law book in the traditional sense. It is the legitimate, revealed word of God; it is "life" itself, as Moshe will make clear later on. Choose to observe the law and you choose life.

Human vision is very limited. We can see the here and now, and perhaps can glimpse a few decades or a century or two into the future. The laws we write, therefore, cannot withstand the test of time and place. The word of God is for all times and all places. It must meet the needs of all times and all places.

How do we know the Torah is the legitimate, revealed word of God? Because 3,500 years later, we still live by its rules, even though the people from Moshe's day would not understand almost any of what we do today. We can still live by the Torah precisely because it does not provide the blueprints for the *halakha*, as it does for the *Mishkan*, but offers only the rough sketches. It leaves the actual construction to the "architects" and "engineers" of every generation.

Thus, a current debate surrounds the definition of "fire" and the use of electricity. Fire, according to the talmudic definition (derived from discussions in BT *Shabbat* 134a and BT *Pesachim* 75a), must turn that which is burning into charcoal or ashes (consumption alone is not enough) and must by its nature have a flame.

In BT *Shabbat.* 134a, the debate is over whether it is permissible to heat mustard grain on a *yom tov* in order to sweeten it. The answer is yes, if a "burning coal of metal" (very hot metal) is used, rather than a "burning coal of wood," because the wood becomes charcoal and ash.

In *Pesachim* 75a, the issue is the meaning of "roasting on fire." If meat is cut up and placed on wood coals, "Rabi says, 'I say this is roasting on fire,'" because the wood coals by their nature produce flame, and flame is required for roasting.

Electricity, by its nature, does not have a flame, although it can start a fire and it can roast meat without a flame. Running through metal wires, it neither consumes nor produces any ash or charcoal. Does electricity, then, qualify as "fire" under the *halakha*'s definition? Not even every Orthodox authority agrees that it does (just as not every Conservative authority agrees that it does not).

The issue does not stop there. Assume for a moment that all agree that electricity does not fall under the definition of fire. Does that mean it can be used indiscriminately? Can I turn on the television to watch the New

York Giants trounce the Buffalo Bills? It may make for an enjoyable Shabbat afternoon for those who enjoy seeing Buffalo trounced, but is that the proper kind of Shabbat enjoyment?

Starting with Torah chapter headings, then, we would have to create new *halakha* to meet the new circumstance (electricity). This is not possible if the Torah fixed every law in stone.

The Torah, therefore, does not give *halakha* short shrift; it gives it eternal life.

Joseph Ozarowski

A snowy weekend gave our family added opportunity to discuss some truly good questions. After all, what can we learn from details? Rabbi Joseph Soloveitchik, of blessed memory, developed a whole theology based on the minutiae of *halakha*. What about these details of the *Mishkan*, the Tabernacle that served our ancestors in the desert and for many years after until the Temple was built?

My oldest son, Eli suggested that while the minutiae of *Halakha* as found in the Oral Torah are essential for living an observant life, there are not always ethical, moral, or spiritual teachings one can learn from the details. However, the details of the *Mishkan* construction have things to teach us, especially if these teachings relate the building of this earliest sanctuary to our own synagogues, the *mikdashei me-at* (mini-sanctuaries). I pointed out to him that this explanation might fit the approaches of Abarbenel and *Akedat Yitzhak* (Isaac Arama—fifteenth century Spain), both of whom see all sorts of allegorical meanings in the details of constuction. However, Maimonides, in the *Guide for the Perplexed*, as well as the *Sefer Hahinukh* (Aaron Halevi—thirteenth century Spain), both reject looking for meaning in too many details, preferring to stick to generalities about the meaning of the *Mishkan*.

My son Shalom proposed that it was more neccesary to write down the details of the *Mishkan* because people would not remember such specific instructions if they were relegated to the Oral Torah. Also, the details may not be useful in the future, as this building was a one-shot deal (Okay, three shots if you include Solomon's Temple and the Second Temple, neither of which followed these exact specifications, but were in part based on them).

One of my congregants added to this that the Jews here were a group of runaway slaves with little or no professional training in engineering or building. True, they had worked as slaves on royal projects for Pharoah, but they were inexperienced in drawing up blueprints. Hence, God in the Torah had to spell it out for them. The rest of the Torah, however, was meant *l'dorot*, for all future generations, so the details did not need to be spelled out immediately.

I pointed out that if we follow the Torah's chronological narrative, then all the laws had not even been given yet. Just the basics had been taught, the rest were to come. But the major project facing our people at this point was the building of this sanctuary. Therefore, in terms of the people's needs and the structure of the Torah at that point in time, the *Mishkan* had to be spelled out. The rest could wait, as it was part of the living process of Oral Torah that would grow to guide the people as time went on.

David Sofian

Midrash Shmot Rabbah 34:1 gives us a context for answering your question. There, in a long comment on *Shmot* 25:10, Judah Ha-nasi teaches, in reference to Job 37:23, that God comes to each one according to that person's strength. He explains *D'varim* 5:22, "If we hear the voice of the Eternal our God any more, then we shall die," to mean that, if God had approached Israel with full divine might and strength, they would not have been able to withstand it.

Instead, God's call is as Psalm 29:4 indicates. There it says, "The voice of the Eternal is with power." Judah Ha-nasi notes how it does not say, "with God's power," but rather, "with power." This shows us that God encounters each with appropriate power for that individual. God does not overwhelm us but reveals only what is appropriate for each.

Assuming this same lesson applies to the Israelite people as a whole, our ancestors must have been focused on the subject of the tabernacle, because that is what was appropriate for them to receive at that stage of their development. Now why is this the case?

An interesting discussion is found in the sources regarding the sequencing of the incident of the golden calf and the construction of the Tabernacle which is useful in answering this question. We first hear the commandment to build the Tabernacle in our current parshah. Further into *Shmot*, in *parashat Ki Tisa*, we read of the incident of the golden calf. Then the Tabernacle is once again commanded in *parashat Vayakhel*. The repetition leaves the order of the events unclear. Did God command the building of the Tabernacle first, or did the calf happen first?

Rashi on *Shmot* 31:18, along with other sources, informs us that since there is no earlier or later in the placement of events in the Torah, we should understand the incident of the golden calf to have preceded the commandment to construct the Tabernacle. Furthermore, Tanhuma on *parashat Terumah*, paragraph 8, goes on to tell us that, by recognizing this order, we can understand the genuine purpose for the Tabernacle. God's command, "Let them make Me a sanctuary that I may dwell among them" (*Shmot* 25:8), shows all the nations that the golden calf had been forgiven.

Shmot Rabbah and Tanhuma point this out in a beautiful way by explaining that the gold and jewelry collected for the tabernacle would atone for the gold and jewelry collected to build the calf. In other words, the building of the Tabernacle marked an essential reconciliation with God after the terrible sin of fashioning the golden calf.

We have already learned God does not overwhelm but reveals what is appropriate. The sin of the golden calf demonstrates that our ancestors in the wilderness were not ready for a relationship with God without tangible manifestations of that relationship. This, then, is why the Torah goes to such lengths to describe the Tabernacle and its furnishings.

Tetzaveh: Exodus 27:20–30:10

Prophetical Reading
Ezekiel 33:10–27

Overview of Torah Portion

God commands Moses to obtain oil from the Children of Israel for the Eternal Light that will burn in the Tabernacle. God gives the specifications for the "holy garments" that Aaron the priest and his sons will wear while ministering in the Tabernacle, for the sacrifices they will bring to consecrate their service, and for the altar on which they will offer the sacrifices.

Key Verses

"And you shall make holy garments for Aaron your brother, for honor and for splendor. . . . And they shall be on Aaron and on his sons when they go into the tent of meeting or when they approach the altar to minister in the holy place, that they not bear iniquity and die. It shall be an eternal statute for him and for his seed after him" (Exodus 28:2, 43).

Discussion Question

CLOTHES MAKE THE PRIEST: The details for the priests' holy garb are intricate—robe, girdle, breastplate, and other accoutrements. No such uniform was required for Moses, the prophet and lawgiver, or for Abraham, Isaac, and Jacob, the patriarchs. Why? What is different about the priests' service? What do the clothes signify? Are they for the sake of the priests or of the Hebrews whom the priests serve?

Shammai Engelmayer

It is not true that Moshe and the patriarchs were not required to wear "uniforms." Moshe, being a member of *Ahm Yisrael*, was required to wear what all the people were required to wear and not wear what the people were commanded not to wear.

And Israel, being a "holy nation" and "a kingdom of priests," had its "uniform." Specifically, Israel must wear at least one specific type of garment—a covering cloak (Deuteronomy 22:12) that is cut in such a way that it ends in four corners, to which are attached a specific type of fringe called *tsitsit*, which itself must include a unique thread called *techelet* (after its color) as part of its composition (Numbers 15:37–41). That "cloak" is today confined to the garment we call a *tallit*, or prayer shawl. There is a *tallit gadol*, which is the prayer shawl most Jews are familiar with, and the *tallit katan*, a square-cornered garment usually worn under one's shirt, thus making it possible to completely fulfill the commandment regarding *tsitsit*.

We also know of one other item to be worn by Jews as part of their "uniform." Once in the Torah we are told to "bind them as a sign upon your hand and they shall be for a memorial between your eyes" (Exodus 13:9). Three other times we are told to "bind them as a sign upon your hand and they shall be for symbols between your eyes" (Exodus 13:16, and Deuteronomy 6:8 and 11:18).

What these verses actually mean we do not know. Beyond these verses, both the Torah and the rest of the *Tanakh* are silent on the matter. The two references in Deuteronomy, however, have an added component, to "write them upon the door posts of your home and on your gates," meaning *mezuzot*, thus forcing us to the conclusion that this is not a metaphorical statement, but a commandment that requires the wearing of something on the arm and on the forehead.

What that something is has been interpreted as *tefillin*. This is not a rabbinic invention. Archaeology has proven the existence of *tefillin* as far back as the second century B.C.E., and that they were worn by both the priestly class (Zadokites) and the emerging class of scholars (Pharisees) who would evolve into the rabbis. Since these two classes rarely agreed on anything, with the Zadokites being strict constructionists of Torah law, it is a fair assumption that the use of *tefillin* to fulfill the "bind them" commandment goes much further back and is based on an authority that was considered Torah-based and could not be challenged by either side.

Adding to this belief is the fact that the Mishnah, the codification of Jewish law that was completed in the second century C.E., is almost completely silent on the issue of *tefillin* (unlike the Gemara, which has an extensive discussion in BT *Menachot* 34a–37b). Considering that, again based on archaeology, there were serious differences in the composition of *tefillin*, we can only assume from this silence that the notion of wearing *tefillin* was so long-standing and basic to Jewish life that the rabbis of the Mishnah (who we know wore *tefillin* themselves) felt no need to expound on the subject, and that what went into the *tefillin*, and in what order, was not considered as important as the wearing of them.

Also adding to the belief of the antiquity of the practice is the use of the word *tefillin* to describe these symbols. How they got their name is not known from the early rabbinic literature. Thus, by then, the name was commonly accepted and understood, and it required no explanation.

Based on all this, it is fair to assume that: (a) the fourfold "bind them" commandment was indeed a commandment to wear something and that (b) early on in Israelite history (if not from the very beginning), that "something" was interpreted as excerpts from the Torah, written by a scribe on pieces of parchment, and encased in black boxes that are to be placed on the left arm and "between the eyes."

Just as surely as Israel is commanded to wear *tsitsit* and either *tefillin* as we know them or some other kind of symbol (although it is hard to imagine such an alternative), so Israel is specifically commanded not to wear garments that are mixtures of wool and linen (Leviticus 19:19 and Deuteronomy 22:11).

This mixture is known as *sha'atnez*, a word that defies any attempt to explain its meaning, although the rabbis of the Mishnah (*Kil.* 9:8) did propose a clever solution from which they then derived the specifics of how the law is to be observed. In truth, though, we neither know what the word means (or even from what it derives), nor can we fathom a reason for the prohibition. That leaves us to conclude that there is no reason beyond that this is how God wants Jews to dress—by wearing clothes that do not mix wool with linen.

Thus, based on the Torah itself, we know that Jews must wear garments made wholly of the same kind of fiber and that the covering garment must end in four squared-off corners; and that Jews must wear some kind of symbol of the law both on their arms and foreheads.

Finally, there also are other laws relating to appearance, such as to "not round off the side-growth on your head, or destroy the side-growth of your beard . . . , [and] not make gashes in your flesh . . . or incise any marks on yourselves," meaning not tattooing or making other kinds of permanent marks on our skins (Leviticus 19:27–28). These, too, relate to appearance and thus qualify as part of a "uniform."

That brings us to the question of why. Put in terms of this week's question, what does all this signify? Taken individually, the question is unanswerable. Why this and not that is something only God knows. Taken together, however, they serve to differentiate Israel from everyone else. In other words, together they call attention to the Israelite walking down the street. He does not wear his hair the way others do. His cloak is long and squared-off at its base, with fringes hanging down from the four corners thus created. To his head and arm are bound strange devices.

This person will stand out in a crowd.

And that is the point. Israel is a "holy nation" and "kingdom of priests." Its people are supposed to teach the world the ways of the Lord by living that way themselves and thereby teaching by the example of their own lives. Only, if no one is paying attention, the effort is wasted. God wants people to pay attention, so He orders up the uniform.

At the same time, God wants to make certain that we understand who we are and what we are about. The uniform not only calls attention to us, but it reminds us that we have an obligation to fulfill. Why can I not mix wool and linen? Because I do what God commands and He commands this. Why must I wear these fringes? "And you shall see them and be reminded of all My commandments." What is the purpose of these devices on my arm and forehead? They are a "sign" and a "symbol" of my obligations to God.

Our uniform, however, is completely different from the uniform of the priests, especially the High Priest. This, too, is deliberate. Sacrifices and other cultic practices were not part of God's original game plan for Israel. Indeed, the biblical text shows Moshe, God's spokesman, being completely disinterested in sacrifices until something occurs to change his (and God's) mind, probably the incident of the golden calf. Thus—

—Unlike the patriarchs of old following their encounters with God, Moshe offers no sacrifice and builds no altar after meeting God at the burning bush.

—When his wife saves him from God's wrath in Exodus 4, he again offers no sacrifice and builds no altar.

—No sacrifice is called for by him as the Exodus gets underway. The Passover "sacrifice" in Exodus 12:21 is less a sacrifice in the traditional sense and more a way to guarantee that the lamb the people ate that night was roasted, not boiled in water.

—No sacrifice is called for by him before and after Israel is rescued from Egypt's attack at the sea. Indeed, the Song of the Sea would seem to indicate that Moshe saw prayer, not sacrifice, as the proper way to worship God.

—When his father-in-law Yitro invites Aharon and the elders to join him as he sacrifices to Israel's God (Exodus 18:12), Moshe is conspicuously absent from the guest list, suggesting that he may not have wanted to participate in what he saw as an alien, pagan ritual.

It is because Israel shows its inability or unwillingness to understand the true nature of God, insisting instead on reverting to pagan practices, that sacrifice and cult ritual are introduced as a compromise (just as the Torah's restrictive rules regarding the eating of meat are a compromise with God's intention that we eat only fruits, vegetables, and grains). That is what *Yishayahu* (Isaiah), in God's Name, meant when he said of sacrifices, "Who asked that of you" (Isaiah 1:12)? That is what *Yirmeyahu* (Jeremiah), also in God's Name, meant when he said: "For when I freed your fathers from the land of Egypt, I did not speak to them or command them concerning burnt offerings and sacrifice" (Jeremiah 7:21–22).

In fact, these two inheritors of Moshe's mantle are very graphic in conveying God's disgust for these rituals, especially since they did not do what they were supposed to do: Keep Israel on the straight and narrow path of God rather than on the wider paths of heretical belief and pagan practice.

The special dress of the priests thus serves a twofold purpose: For as long as sacrifice and cult remain a part of Israel, the priestly garb is meant as a part of the ritual, designed to be awe-inspiring. At the same time, it is meant to convey the message that this is not part of the true worship of God. That is only achieved through fulfilling God's mission by fulfilling His commandments. For that, there are different clothes—the uniform of the Israelite.

In fact, the priestly clothes cannot be worn outside the sacred precincts of Tabernacle and Temple. Moshe cannot wear them, nor can any other Israelite. They cannot be worn in Borough Park or in Barclay Square. They cannot be worn anywhere if there is no Tabernacle or Temple.

The uniform of the Israelite, on the other hand, is eternal and universal, just as the mission of the Israelite is eternal and universal.

Joseph Ozarowski

Clothes are important. Not so important as to completely define us in terms of "You are what you wear," but people certainly perceive us by how they see us. True, *Ethics of the Fathers* 4:27 bids us "not to look at the jar, but what is inside it." Nevertheless, clothing has its place in the Torah. Adam and Eve were unclothed before they became self-aware; their being clothed comes with their initiation into real life. God Himself (Herself?)

fashions Adam's and Eve's first clothing following their expulsion from the Garden of Eden (Genesis 3:21).

A number of modern commentaries (among them Benno Jacob [nineteenth and twentieth century Germany and England] and Hirsch) speak of clothing in terms of civilization. Animals do not wear clothing. Among earlier commentators, *Akedat Yitzhak* speaks of clothing symbolizing moral qualities, using the Latin term for clothing, *habitus*, to refer to clothing helping us define ourselves. (An illustration from a completely non-Jewish source is the term for a nun's garment, "habit.")

The Torah says, "And you shall make Holy Garments for Aaron your brother for honor (*kavod*) and splendor." Maimonides suggests that the clothing reflects the grandeur and majesty of the ceremonies led by the priests. This was to have an esthetic and emotional effect on the lay participant. Ramban, connecting the idea of clothing to both Esther and Joseph, whose clothing is highlighted by Scripture, proposes that clothing suggests royalty. The priests were to act in this fashion. Thus, at least one school of thought believes that the priestly garments were for the benefit of the Jewish people, who witnessed them in use at the Tabernacle and later the Temple. Malbim (nineteenth century Romania) on the other hand, comments that Moses was told to fashion clothing for his brother. But the next verse tells us that the wise-hearted artisans were to do this task (Exodus 28:2–3). The double tailoring suggests that the outer clothes made by the artisans were a symbol of the Moses-made "inner garments" for the priests' inner souls.

In other words, the soul must be clothed in splendor, as well as the body. Malbim suggests that in order for the priests to affect others, they must improve themselves spiritually; this was symbolically meant by the clothes that Moses made. Thus, according to Malbim, the clothes were for the direct benefit of the priests, and only indirectly for the participants. So in answer to your question, the clothes were both for the sake of the priests (inner-directed) and the Jews who were served by the priests (outer-directed).

I cannot help but refer to one of your previous year's questions on this Torah portion and my response in this context. You asked, "Where was the honor and splendor if most of the time, the High Priest was busy with sacrifices, getting these wonderful garments bloody, greasy, and dirty?" I would offer that there can be honor in getting dirty. One often gets *schmutzedik* in doing honorable work; this does not detract from the honor, and can often enhance it. The Gemara in *Nedarim* 39a tells how the great Rabbi Akiva visited a sick, lonely, and unnamed student. He swept up and cleaned the student's room, thereby giving the student life and health. The Hebrew term for "sweep and clean" used by our sages in this Gemara is *kibdo*, which also means "to honor." By cleaning up the *schmutz* of this lonely, ill, and anonymous student, Rabbi Akiva was also honoring him.

It is possible to offer honor by engaging in dirty work, if that effort is for a good cause. (For more on this wonderful Gemara, see chapter 3 of Ozarowski (1995).)

David Sofian

Your question indicates that there are two choices for understanding the priestly garments. It seems to me that there are three possibilities. Let us look at the two options you present first.

Ramban tells us that these elaborate clothes should be understood as the Israelite equivalent of aristocratic dress. These intricate garments enhanced the prestige of those who wore them, increasing priestly respect among the people. In other words, they were for the people who the priests served. The priests were distinguished and made recognizable by them. Since life was centered around the *Mishkan* and the *Korbanot*, it would have been important that the priests, and especially the High Priest, be easily discernible by their clothing.

We have a modern version of this thinking in the robes judges wear in court and clergy wear in their pulpits. That garb is meant to enhance the prestige and respect of those who wear them. Even though rabbis are not clergy in the Christian sense of the word, many contemporary rabbis favor the wearing of a robe when functioning on the *bima*. They argue, in similar fashion to Ramban, that within our society this is the accepted means of distinguishing for everyone else the rabbi as the rabbi.

The other alternative you suggest is that the garments were for the priests themselves. This is also possible if we no longer think of the clothing creating the correct impression on others but think of them as expressing the wearer's inner reality, or at least expressing the inner reality the wearer was striving to achieve. The priest's goal was to be of the highest character and spiritual strength. In this view, the richly enhanced clothing as meant to reflect the richly enhanced reality of that kind of inner being.

Again we can find an example of this thinking today in the *kittel*, or white robe, that is worn on Yom Kippur. On Yom Kippur, we seek forgiveness from one another and from God in order to renew and purify our lives. The white garment is meant to reflect that inner state.

Above I mentioned I thought there was a third possibility. In *Midrash Shmot Rabbah* 38:8, there is a discussion of the stones on Aaron's breastplate and of the priestly garments worn on Yom Kippur. The passage tells us that these stones, and the garments themselves, were worn so God could look upon them when the priest entered the Holy of Holies on Yom Kippur.

By way of explanation, the passage continues that this should be compared to a prince whose teacher wanted to go in before the king to plead on his son's behalf, but was afraid that those standing by might attack him. The king clothed the teacher in his own royal purple cloak so that all who saw him would be afraid of him. So, too, with Aaron, who repeatedly entered the Holy of Holies on Yom Kippur. The angels there would have stopped him were it not for the many merits which entered with him. Thus God gave him garments like the holy garments (so to speak, God's own garments), just as the king gave the teacher the purple cloak.

In other words, the priestly garments were not so much to identify the priests for the people or as an expression of the priests' inner selves, but were to help God remember the many merits that entered into the Holy of Holies with Aaron. What made them so special and important was that the garments helped achieve divine forgiveness. Looked at this way, we can see why nearly an entire chapter of Torah is devoted to the details of these most extraordinary garments.

Ki Tisa: Exodus 30:11–34:35

Prophetical Reading
1 Kings 18:1–39

Overview of Torah Portion

Moses receives from God directions for taking a census of the Children of Israel. God instructs Aaron and the priests to wash their feet as part of their service in the Tabernacle and commands Moses to anoint Aaron and his sons. God appoints Bezalel to supervise construction of the Tabernacle's vessels. The Hebrews, alarmed by Moses' failure to return at the end of 40 days on Mt. Sinai, persuade Aaron to make a golden calf to serve in Moses' stead. Moses, angered by their behavior when he descends from the heights, shatters the tablets on which God had written the Law. Sinners die at the hand of the Levites and of God. Moses returns to Mt. Sinai to receive the Law on a second set of tablets, which he carved.

Key Verses

"And the Lord said, 'I have surely seen the affliction of My people who are in Egypt and heard their cry because of their taskmasters. . . . And now, the cry of the Children of Israel has come before Me. . . . Come now, and I will send you to Pharaoh that you may bring my people, the Children of Israel, out of Egypt'" (Exodus 3:7, 9–10).

"And the Lord spoke to Moses, 'Go down, because the people that you brought up out of Egypt have behaved corruptly . . . ; they have made a golden calf and have worshipped it. . . . Now leave Me alone that My anger may wax hot against them, that I shall consume them and make you into a great nation'" (Exodus 32:7–10).

145

Discussion Question

INSTANT PUNISHMENT: God hears the anguished cries of the enslaved Children of Israel for hundreds of years in Egypt before He dispatches Moses to effect their freedom. At Sinai, God observes the mutinous building of the golden calf and threatens to destroy His Chosen People in an instant.

What was God's rush? If He could tolerate the sounds of their suffering for so long, why would He not propose a second chance when they went astray? Moses, who had trekked through the wilderness to return to Egypt, could have been sent down immediately from Mt. Sinai to rebuke the sinners. Some commentators assert that God did not intend to destroy the Hebrews but was testing Moses' reaction. What lesson about God, Who describes Himself as a long-suffering Deity, would Moses learn from this apparent demonstration of heavenly anger?

Shammai Engelmayer

Let us understand something about this people, Israel. In all, 430 years have gone by since they arrived in Egypt. That was their choice, not God's. They had been promised by Him that He would be their protector; that, for believing in Him, they would want for nothing. Yet, Ya'akov and his family decide to accept the pharaoh's invitation to live in the comfort and security of Goshen rather than to trust in the Lord's promise.

That God came to Ya'akov on the way and told him all would be well does not change the fact that the choice was Israel's to make. Ya'akov never asked God if he could again leave Canaan. And his own words make clear that the intention was for a brief visit, not for a prolonged stay (see Genesis 45:27–46:4).

God knew that was going to happen; indeed, he told Avraham that it would and, more important, He knew how it would turn out. He did not remind Ya'akov of that precisely because Ya'akov and his family had a choice to make and they made it. It was the wrong choice, although it was the one God knew they would make.

For much, if not most, of their time in Egypt, Israel was either a welcomed guest or a tolerated foreigner. During that time, the biblical evidence suggests they had little to do with their God, for they had no need of Him or His promise. They were doing quite well, thank you, without the responsibilities necessitated by a covenantal relationship. To them, God was still their God, but a very distant one. The more the years went by, the more distance they put between Him and themselves.

(The rabbis of the Talmud acknowledged this in the midrash that explains why the deliverance could not wait for Rabbi Akiva, although, had he delivered Israel, there would never be another *galut*. It was because by Moshe's day, Israel's degree of impurity had reached the red line. It would have overloaded long before Rabbi Akiva, making it impossible for him to deliver them.)

When things went sour, however, they remembered God and His promise. Suddenly, they needed Him. And He heard their cries—not for 430 years (Exodus 12:40, but see below), but only for a short while. He sent Moshe to them and, immediately, they rejoiced. Things got worse instead of better, however, and the people began their incessant carping. Then came the plagues and the Exodus. Their joy was unbounded—until three days later, when their backs were to the sea and the Egyptians were rushing towards them. Then they again began to carp and complain. The sea parted and they rejoiced in that event, but then the water dried up.

And so on. This Israel was no better than the Ya'akov who, at Beth El, assured God of his loyalty so long as God clothed him, fed him, and protected him from harm.

God had waited a long time for Israel. He had depended on the sojourn in Egypt and the enslavement to recast the people into a different mold. Nothing had changed, however. And now, despite His explicit warning against it, they turned the national treasury into a golden calf and proclaimed that it had taken Israel out of Egypt. It did not matter that the calf was not a god but merely the representation of the One True God; it was a violation of His word, directly given to each and every one of these people, without Moshe or any other intermediary.

God's anger was real. On the other hand, He understood what was really going on. It would take a long time to mold this people, much longer than four centuries. Indeed, four times four centuries might not even be enough.

Because God is infinite, so is His patience. He could wait Israel out. He could modify His program to fit their stages of development into His kingdom of priests, His holy nation and treasure (i.e., providing an "eternal light" as a symbol of His Being; a Tabernacle as a symbol of His Presence; sacrifices as a transition to pure prayer; and acts of *chesed* as the true form of sacred service).

However, He could not guarantee that the leaders of this people would be as patient. Moshe was only human, and his successors would be human. Human patience will run out, just as Moshe's finally runs out towards the end of the desert period (see Numbers 11). God needed assurance that their leaders would stick by this people no matter what they did.

And so he "tested" Moshe, fully expecting Moshe to respond as he does here. And when Moshe finally does lose it, God, too, switches sides, becoming their protector in the sense that He diminishes Moshe's leadership by elevating the elders to a higher status, thus assuring that the people would never be subjected to the whim of one person alone.

That incident makes clear that the lesson is not for Moshe, but for all who come after him. Israel is not to be abandoned merely because it sins against God. If it sins, the leaders have failed somehow and must work harder at keeping Israel on the right track. They do not have the option of saying, "Because we are righteous, God will not desert us. So, let us leave this people to disappear from the earth, and we will become God's people in their place." God made a non-renewable and non-transferable offer, and it was rejected, as He intended it to be.

Each of us is responsible for all of us, physically, emotionally, and spiritually. No matter how righteous we think we are, He will desert us individually if we desert His People.

Sadly, there are people among us today who will have nothing to do with us because they see themselves as the true believers and we as unworthy of their fellowship. And I do not mean only the Orthodox attitude toward Conservative and Reform. I also include the attitude of the extreme Orthodox toward the centrist and modern Orthodox sects; the Reform attitude toward "the Orthodox;" the traditionalist's attitude toward the more liberal Conservative, and vice versa; and so forth.

God put us all in the same boat; He expects us to oar together.

Now for a digression. Was Israel in Egypt for 430 years, as the Torah text tells us? Or was it in Egypt for only 210 years, as some of the rabbis would have it?

The answer is that the Torah knows better how long Israel was in Egypt. The problem that the rabbis of blessed memory had accepting this stems from the genealogy of Moshe, as given in Exodus 6:16–20, which makes Levi Moshe's great-grandfather, meaning that there was no way for 400 years to have gone by from the time Levi went into Egypt with his father Ya'akov until his great-grandson Moshe was born. This, however, ignores the genealogy of Yehoshua (Joshua), as given in 1 Chronicles 7:22–27, which puts a full ten generations between Moshe's aide and Ephraim, Levi's brother, which is consistent with a 400-year span. Clearly, the Torah's genealogy is incomplete, for whatever reason.

There are, on the other hand, very good reasons for insisting on the Torah's number at face value. The period of 430 years fits too perfectly into historical realities.

The Torah tells us that the Hebrews, once enslaved, were employed on massive building projects, including the construction of the cities of Pithom and Rameses. We know that these two cities were built by Rameses II, a pharaoh of the thirteenth century B.C.E. A stele erected by him at Bet Shean even boasts that the city bearing his name was built by foreign slaves, at least some of whom were Semites. The stele also brags about his subjugation of the "Asians," a term the Egyptians often used to refer to Semites from the Canaan area.

The Torah's account also makes it imperative that the seat of government for Egypt at the time had to be in close proximity to the areas in which the Israelite slaves lived, namely the Nile Delta region. This, too, is a staple of the pharaohs of the Nineteenth Dynasty, the beginning of the so-called Ramesside Era. It is during this period, then, that the Exodus, if it occurred, would have taken place.

Other signposts also point the way to this period, including the archaeological evidence of the fall of Jericho and other cities on the west bank of the Jordan River, many of which seem to have occurred (although there continues to be considerable debate about this) during the thirteenth and late twelfth centuries B.C.E., just the time when the former slaves would have arrived in Canaan had the Exodus taken place during the Ramesside era.

There is also Israel's encounter along the way of such kingdoms as Moab and Edom, which most scholars continue to believe only came on the scene during the reign of Rameses II. Thus, Israel could not have left Egypt before Rameses II; coupled with the archaeological evidence in Canaan, we must conclude that Israel could not have left much later, either. We have thus limited ourselves to Rameses II or Mernephtah, his thirteenth son and successor, as the pharaoh of the Exodus.

Now, retracing our steps back 400 years from the time of Rameses, we find conditions on the ground that would allow for a Semite (Yoseph) to rise to the position of vizier. For example, the Torah's version of events makes it mandatory that the Egyptian seat of government again be located in the Nile Delta (not where the Egyptian capitals usually are located); in fact, we find it virtually on the same spot as in the later story of the Exodus.

Going back four centuries puts us in a period in Egyptian history in which at least a portion of the country was ruled by Semites, who apparently came from the same region of Canaan as did Ya'akov and Yoseph. These interloper pharaohs, known as Hyksos (meaning "rulers of foreign lands"), made the Nile Delta their capital seat. In fact, the later Ramesside capital was built on the same spot. (They also introduced into Egypt the horse-drawn chariot, a feature of the Yoseph story.)

It is simply too hard to accept that the Torah's version of events— including the location of the capital at both ends of the story, the presence of friendly Semites on the Egyptian throne at the beginning, and the various narrative clues at the end that have been given dates by archaeology—is wrong, and that rabbis of blessed memory who lived thirteen centuries later knew better how long Israel was in Egypt.

Those rabbis, by the way, knew that they were not always correct in their descriptions of past events. They gave their laws absolute force ("whosoever transgresses the law of the Sages deserves death"; see BT *Berakhot* 4b, based on a discussion in BT *Eruvin* 21b), but not their non-halakhic material.

Joseph Ozarowski

In our weekly discussion in *shul* based on the question, my erstwhile chairman of the board pointed out the obvious problem surrounding the entire issue: Anthropomorphism. How does an omnipotent Deity, Creator of the universe, get angry at all?

Ramban attempts to answer this by suggesting that when *Hashem* says, *haniha li*, "leave Me alone that I shall wax angry at them and consume them . . . ," God means that the divine attribute of mercy will be put aside, and the attribute of judgment will rule. Both of these are certainly Divine prerogatives.

Another explanation may simply be to invoke the rabbinic aphorism, *Dibra Torah bil'shon bnei adam*, or "the Torah speaks in human terminology." The language is simply colorful, written in a way that all generations, including ours, can understand.

In discussion of the actual question, both my children and my congregants suggested that there were different purposes in the Divine anger at the calf and Divine patience during the slavery. The slavery took so long for a reason—the need to allow the incipient Jewish people to grow, and to effect a change, a *tikun*, for all the impurity and assimilation of Egypt. It was simply neccesary to endure all those years of suffering in order for the divine plan to unfold. The golden calf, on the other hand, was a frustration of the Divine plan. Everything that *Hashem* developed up to this point would be put to waste by the actions of the Jewish people. Could anyone blame even a long-suffering Deity for being upset and wanting to start over the Divine plan?

However, there may be yet another approach to understanding God's reaction to the golden calf incident. Steve hints at it when he suggests that God may have been testing Moses' reaction. Steve must be referring to *Midrash Shemot Rabba,* where the rabbis compare the story to a King (God) who becomes angry with his son (the People of Israel) and threatens to kill him. (How many parents sometimes feel like killing their kids? Unfortunately, the increased spate of parental violence directed against their own children makes this tongue-in-cheek comment far less humorous than in the past.) Yet the son's teacher (Moses), standing outside and hearing this argument, correctly assumes that the King wants him to go and settle this dispute. Thus, as the modern commentator Benno Jacob explains, while, *haniha li* literally means "leave Me alone," in effect God is really saying, "Do not leave me alone!" At this point, Moses begins to pray, by indirect invitation of God.

However, I would go much further and suggest that God's entire threat, not just the statement to Moses, is meant to bring about the positive conclusion of reconciliation. The Talmud (*Avoda Zara* 4b) teaches, "Says R. Yehoshua Ben Levi: [The people of] Israel only made the calf to give a *pithon peh* (an opening) to *ba'alei tshuva*—to penitents."

God could have prevented the entire incident if He chose to do so. Yet the golden calf was allowed, precisely to teach our people about the inevitability of sin and the possibility of return. People are going to sin—that is human nature. But we can also recognize our shortcomings and our potential to do better through *teshuvah*—repentance and return.

We are also assured that our *teshuvah* will be accepted if sincere, just as after the golden calf. This is why we always refer to God's post-calf words of forgiveness, the thirteen Divine attributes of mercy and kindess, at *Selichot* services and especially as the core refrain during Yom Kippur prayers.

David Sofian

The first part of your discussion question draws us to the contrast between the seemingly excessive time that elapses before God hears the anguished cries of our enslaved ancestors and God's immediate response to the calf. As I began to think about this contrast, speculating in particular about the lengthy period of slavery, I realized anew how easy it is to assume that God's attention is constantly fixed on Israel, since the Torah essentially is about the relationship between God and the Jewish People.

It is this presumption which causes us to wonder why God took so long to respond. Amos' words in the ninth chapter of his book come to balance this. In verse 7, he reminds us that Israel is much like the Ethiopians, the Philistines, and Aram in God's eyes. Israel's covenant is special, even critical, to God's plan, but Amos wants us to take note that Israel is not God's only focal point.

If nothing else, the length of time before God acts in the narrative reminds us that, even as we exult in our own sacred story of our relationship with God and the attention we receive from God, we should not conclude that it is the only such story or that we are the only objects of God's attention. We should not come to believe that God's relationship with the Jewish people excludes all other relationships.

I think this also helps us come to an understanding of why God's threat is so instantaneous after the calf. By creating the contrast between the gap in God's attention to the developments in Egypt and the immediacy of God's attention to developments at Sinai, the Torah is emphasizing just how paramount the time of connection at Sinai was. The experience of Egyptian slavery and Exodus is only the prelude to Sinai. God is fully present to the Jewish people at Sinai. We know this from the intensity in God's immediate and decisive response when the people stray with the calf.

Regarding your second point, I think it is productive to see God's expression of anger as God testing Moses. This helps us understand why God refers to the Israelites as "your people" while informing Moses of the events below. It also helps us with God telling Moses, "leave Me be that My anger might blaze forth against them and that I might destroy them and make of you a great nation." It is almost as if God is first reminding Moses that the people are his responsibility and that, because they are Moses' responsibility, he should not leave God be.

With this choice of words, God seems to be asking Moses to plead their case. Perhaps God knows that Moses will be tempted after seeing the calf to conclude that enough is enough. Would it have been unreasonable for Moses to have decided that this flock could not be shepherded effectively? If so, God's way of communicating is meant to prompt Moses to assume the role of shepherd once again. The reverse psychology works. Moses intervenes on their behalf with success.

Ibn Ezra emphasizes this by suggesting that verses 11–14 of chapter 32 would be better placed after verse 31 of the same chapter. In Ibn Ezra's sequence, Moses would acknowledge the people's great sin first in verse 31, then his plea would follow in verse 11. With that order, first Moses is informed of the great sin and God's anger over it. Secondly, Moses descends and sees for himself the terrible events. Then, only after the destruction of the calf, does Moses plead for his people.

This reading resolves the conflict of God renouncing the punishment in verse 14 and Moses nevertheless saying in verse 30 that perhaps he would win forgiveness. It also dramatizes the moment prior to his intercession. There is a moment of uncertainty. Would Moses intercede, or was there perhaps a part of him that wanted to accept God's offer? Maybe it was God's hint in the initial conversation, "let Me be," that caused Moses not to let God be at the critical point.

Finally, you ask about the lesson Moses might have learned about whether God is long suffering or easily angered. Clearly, parts of the Torah show us a God becoming angry and other parts show us a God who is forgiving. However, if we assume, as we have been, that in this case God is goading Moses by being angry, and that God actually wants Moses to recommit to his leadership of the people by successfully interceding on his people's behalf, then God who is long suffering and slow to anger is affirmed here.

VaYakhel: Exodus 35:1–38:20

Prophetical Reading
1 Kings 7:40–50

Overview of Torah Portion

Moses assembles the Children of Israel and relates God's instructions for the Tabernacle's materials and construction. The Hebrews willingly provide more than enough materials. Moses announces Bezalel's selection as the Tabernacle's master craftsman. Bezalel and his crew build the designated items, according to the specifications, which are repeated here.

Key Verses

"And Noah did according to all that God commanded him, so he did" (Genesis 6:22).

"And Bezalel made the ark of acacia wood; two cubits and a half was its length, a cubit and a half was its width, a cubit and a half was its height. And he overlaid it with pure gold . . . and he cast for it four rings of gold . . . and he made staves of acacia wood . . . and he made an ark cover of pure gold" (Exodus 37:1–6).

Discussion Question

FOLLOWING ORDERS: Two biblical building projects—Noah is commanded, directly by God, to construct an ark, which will house the remnants of mankind and the animal kingdom; Bezalel is instructed, through Moses, to build the portable sanctuary and its vessels, as the centerpiece for the Hebrews' worship of God in the wilderness.

The Torah relates just the barest specifications about the ark's construction and it indicates, in nine Hebrew words, that Noah complied with a task that occupied 100 years. The Tabernacle is a much simpler project—its construction took four months; yet the Torah provides intricate building details and repeats them when Bezalel does his work. Why the discrepancy in the Torah's treatment of the two cases? Is one intrinsically more important than the other? Why not simply state that Bezalel acted according to his holy command, without repeating every act he actually carried out?

Shammai Engelmayer

The basic assumption of this week's question is correct: There is a difference between the way the Torah treats the ark of Noach and the Tabernacle. The question, however, is framed in assumptions which are not correct; we will deal with these further on in this discussion.

It is true that the Torah lingers over the construction of the *Mishkan*, the Tabernacle. In fact, as noted earlier in our answer to the question for *Parshat Terumah*, it lingers on the issue out of proportion to everything else.

There are several reasons for this, as noted in the earlier answer. One reason is to teach us the importance of not taking ritual casually. The other is simply that direct communication between God and humanity begins and ends with Moshe. No one before Moshe "saw" God up close and personal; no one had live, face-to-face, one-on-one conversations with Him. No one will after Moshe is gone. Thus, this is the one and only opportunity to provide the building plans and specifications for a Tabernacle that, being composed of earthly matter, will eventually rot, break, or tear (depending on which part of the structure or its appurtenances is involved).

Will any wood do to rebuild that table, or just acacia wood? There is this really great material that just arrived from Sidon; can I not use it for the replacement curtains? There are so many more people now; should we not double the size of the Tabernacle?

Because indirect answers from God can be misinterpreted, the Torah provides the exact plans and specifications so as to eliminate any possible question of what is right and what is wrong in maintaining the Tabernacle's structure through the centuries.

Noach's ark, on the other hand, is a one-time-only project. No one will ever need to repair it or to reconstruct it from floorboard to ceiling board.

To these reasons, we add another specific to this question. The *Mishkan* is the place where humans go to commune with God and learn His way. The Lord's way means life, as Moshe himself states in Deuteronomy 30:15–20. The *Mishkan* thus represents life itself (as does the Torah), and life deserves to be dwelt upon. *Noach*'s ark, on the other hand, represents death. True, it preserved life by saving *Noach*, his family, and the animals, but it would never have been necessary if not for the global holocaust raging outside its portals. It is sufficient to dispense with such death swiftly.

In a similar vein, the *Mishkan* represents service to God, while *Noach*'s ark represents disservice to God.

(This raises a question: In *Terumah*, the issue posed by the question was why the Torah dwells so long on the *Mishkan*, as opposed to *halakha*. The answer said that it was because the two were so different. Here, we seem to be equating the two. The *halakha*, after all, represents life and service to God. The differences, however, outweigh the similarities. As already noted in the earlier answer, the *halakha* is for all times and all places, whereas the *Mishkan* is limited in time and space. Also, each *halakha* is sacred in itself. The *Mishkan* is sacred only when all of its pieces are assembled and in place. Thus, merely because there are similarities between the two, there are no contradictions between this answer and the one given in *Terumah*.)

This week's question is flawed, however, in three respects—the length of time it took to build *Noach*'s ark, its complicated nature, and the "skimpiness" of its building plans.

There is nothing either complicated about the ark or skimpy about its plans as given in Genesis 6:14–16. This is quite literally a case of "what you see is what you get." God said to *Noach*: "Take some gopher wood and pitch, and build yourself a giant wooden rectangle. On the inside, divide it up into three levels. Put one window up near the top and do not forget to put in a door."

This is not a boat. It has no bow or stern, no rudder or mast. There is nothing to propel it, either, not even an oar hole. After all, this is not meant for going anywhere; it is only meant as shelter from the terrible rains and flooding outside. This is a floating box, pure and simple. It has no feature that requires a Frank Lloyd Wright, a Leonardo Da Vinci, or a Rembrandt. Using the plans given in Genesis 6:14–16, even a child can build a duplicate; all he or she needs to know to get it exactly right is what a cubit is (estimated between 17.55 inches and 18 inches or so). If gopher wood is unknown or unavailable, any shipbuilding wood that will float may do.

The Tabernacle, on the other hand, is made up of many parts, involving exact measures, specific materials, and intricate designs. Only highly skilled craftsmen can create these many parts; the ordinary individual does not have that kind of ability. Thus, it is the Tabernacle that is the more complicated structure.

As for the time it took to build the ark, a midrash states matter-of-factly 120 years, and this is picked up as *torah mi'sinai* from then on, aided by its mention by Rashi and then other commentators, such as Radak and Ibn Ezra.

The midrash (*Genesis Rabbah* 30:7) bases itself on Gen. 6:3, in which God, clearly beginning to despair about the behavior of His two-legged creatures, shortens the life span of the human to 120 years. No reasoning is given by the midrash for its exegetical co-opting of this verse, but we can make an educated guess: The rabbis of blessed memory were troubled by the notion of God wiping out the whole world without giving any warning. Since mention of the 120 years appears immediately before God gets so disgusted that He decides to bring the Flood, the rabbis solved their dilemma by declaring that Genesis 6:3 implies that it took Noach 120 years to build the ark.

That means that Noach would have had to have built the ark at the rate of about 10.5 cubic cubits a day. At that pace, a snail could probably cover more ground in an hour than Noach could in a month. Rather than serve as a warning to anyone, Noach would appear ridiculous to all who saw him, and his efforts would be seen as the biggest joke ever.

The rabbis understood this, too, so they did not suggest that Noach actually built the ark every day for 120 years. Instead, they had him planting the trees he would use for the wood; cutting them down when they were big enough to use; planting new trees in their place; cutting those down in time; and so forth. It was this activity, the midrash tells us, that caused the people to question Noach about what he was doing.

The midrash has its homiletic purpose, but it should not be taken so seriously that it is used to compare the ark of Noach to the *Mishkan*. It is fair to assume that the ark was built in a very little amount of time, far less than it took to construct the far more complicated *Mishkan*.

On the other hand, what may have taken a very long time was assembling the animals for the floating zoo. I agree that God would not have destroyed the world without first providing ample warning, and it is entirely possible that 120 years went by. Rather than the time being used to build the ark (or to grow the trees needed for the wood), the time could have been spent gathering the animals and bringing them to their temporary home.

Now that would have been a sight that not only would have brought questions, but also tourists. As Noach's collection of animals grew in size, his fame (or infamy) would have spread far and wide; people would have come from all over to marvel at the animals and the ridiculous-looking rectangular box around which the animals had gathered.

In that way, God's message of impending doom would receive the widest possible airing.

Joseph Ozarowski

The last line of your question carries a separate but significant issue which is probably beyond the parameters of this week's question: Why all the repetition of *Mishkan* (Tabernacle) building at the end of Exodus? For a discussion of this, the reader is urged to see "The Recapitulations" (Leibowitz 1976), and "Why Are the Items of the Tabernacle Listed So Often?" (Jacobson 1977).

While modern commentators such as Buber (quoted in Jacobson) suggest a linguistic connection between the *Mishkan*, the human-made home for God's Presence, and the Genesis account of Creation, God's home for the human presence, I have yet to find any of the commentators, classic or modern, who compare the massive *Mishkan* building project to that other massive biblical building project, Noah's Ark. It seems that, while these two projects represent the Torah's contributions to the field of construction, they are also polar opposites in content (as you correctly point out) and in theme. Many of the classic commentaries (Ramban, *Or Hahayim*) point out that the *Mishkan* was a labor of love (and perhaps that is why its details are repeated so many times).

As a model for all subsequent Jewish houses of worship, every detail is lovingly recounted again and again, with possible symbolic significance for the future (see my response to the question for *Parshat Terumah*). The ark, on the other hand, was a labor of survival. The ark was necessary for the family of Noah, as bearers of the human spirit, along with the elements of the animal kingdom, to endure the flood. But it certainly had no religious or theological significance. It was a *hora'at sha'ah*, a temporary measure. Notwithstanding all the explorers and TV shows that go off "in search of Noah's ark," the ark had served its purpose once the flood was over and was of no further interest. Thus, its details are not important for the Torah to record.

There may be another dimension to this contrast. The ark, along with the rest of early Genesis, represents the universal side of the Torah as the story of all humankind. The ark represents the story of human corruption and decency as found in Noah's survival. Judaism includes the universal element. But the *Mishkan* represents God's particular interest in a small, weak, struggling people as the bearer of the title "Chosen."

Even though other religions claim the "Old Testament" as their own, we assert that the Torah is ours, and its messages as well as its responsibilities belong to us. Thus, the details of this *Mishkan* are important to us as the prototypic model for Jewish worship.

David Sofian

The comparison you raise is an intriguing one. Yet, even though these undertakings are similar in that each involves divinely commanded human construction at a pivotal point in the narrative, I find them to be more dissimilar than alike. These projects are different in at least two important ways. Noah and Bezalel are different in the way each sets upon his task. And, more importantly, the purpose for God's command to build is also different.

Let us begin with Noah and Bezalel. In his comment to *B'reishit* 6:14, Rashi tells us that Noah occupied himself with the building of the ark for 120 years. He goes on to suggest that this very lengthy time period was not because the project was so difficult or complicated, but because Noah was hoping the delay would give people the opportunity to repent and thereby avert God's decree of destruction. This reason is certainly laudable.

However, *B'reishit* 6:11–13 makes it clear that God meant the decision to stand. God makes the decree in such a way that repentance was not possible. Noah is hindering God's plan, not furthering it with his delay. On the other hand, *Shmot Rabbah* 50:5 makes it clear that everything Bezalel did was done with self-sacrificing devotion.

The midrash emphasizes this by pointing out how Bezalel was rewarded for each and every facet of his work because of that devotion. Perhaps this is the reason Bezalel's work is detailed so completely in contrast to Noah's.

The contrast of these episodes is even more significant when we look at the context for God's command in each. What is the goal for each endeavor? Again, let us begin with Noah. As I just pointed out, the beginning of *parashat Noah* makes it clear that God had decided to destroy creation as a result of its corruption. God does not issue the decree in hopes of moving anyone towards repentance. We are to conclude it is too late for that. The only purpose for building the ark is to save a remnant of creation with which to start over.

Now what is the point of the building of the Tabernacle? This is a more difficult question, but let me continue the point of view I expressed in my answers to *parashat Terumah* and *parashat Ki Tisa*. If we follow Rashi and understand the golden calf to have preceded the construction of the Tabernacle, then we can see the construction of the Tabernacle as a kind of atonement for the calf. The people get in trouble with the calf because they need a physical object as a focus for their worship. God lets them atone for the calf and accepts their need for the desired physical object in the form of the Tabernacle.

The Tabernacle is essentially different from the calf only in that God commanded its building and not the calf's. The contrast between the two situations is unmistakable. Unlike God's dealings with the generation of the flood, God here is making it possible for the generation of the calf to atone.

This is another reason why the Torah relates more details of the building of the Tabernacle than it does for the building of Noah's ark. The details of building the ark are unimportant. What is important is that it effected a new beginning. The Tabernacle is crucial because, by establishing an acceptable physical focus for their worship, God made it possible for our ancestors to repent.

These details we need to know, for by showing us how God makes repentance available even for the generation of the golden calf, the eternal acceptability of our own repentance is affirmed.

Pekudei: Exodus 38:21–40:38

Prophetical Reading
1 Kings 7:51, 8:1–21

Overview of Torah Portion

The Torah gives an accounting of the materials used by Bezalel and his workers in making the Tabernacle. Moses blesses their completed work. God commands Moses to set up and establish the Tabernacle, and to anoint Aaron and his sons as His ministers. Moses carries out the command. The Hebrews continue on their journey.

Key Verses

"And the Lord spoke to Moses, saying, 'On the first day of the first month you shall establish the Tabernacle of the Tent of Meeting . . . and you shall take the anointing oil and anoint the Tabernacle and everything that is in it, and shall sanctify it, and it shall be holy.'" (Exodus 40:1, 9).

Discussion Question

A HOLY TASK: God's prime imperative to the freed Children of Israel is to be holy—to behave in a way that He deems correct. But how do people, God's creations, make an object holy? What does it mean that we sanctify something?

The Tabernacle, once built, clearly would be fit for use without further action by the Hebrews. Why the command to Moses to sanctify the Tabernacle? True, the root for the Hebrew word for "sanctify," *l'kadesh*, means "to make separate," but the Tabernacle by its very uniqueness, grandeur, and purpose is already distinct. How could Moses' action, in setting up and anointing the Tabernacle, make it any more separate? For whose benefit was the sanctification command given?

Shammai Engelmayer

Very simply, the anointing of the Tabernacle is not what makes it holy. As the question suggests, the assembled *Mishkan* is already holy in and of itself. The anointing, however, does add an aura of mystery and magic to the "sanctification" process, precisely because this is a people who need to see to believe.

Let us reprise our thesis of the generation of the desert and of the institution of sacrifices. This Israel is a primitive Israel, for too long influenced by the paganism in which it grew from a family into a people. Within that pagan system, the "gods" controlled every aspect of life, from conception and birth, to death and afterlife. There were "gods" to explain natural events and others to explain good and evil. And each "god" had an attendant ritual, including sacrifice, gift-bearing, and magical incantations.

Along comes Moshe and says that God is the one and only; that He is everywhere at once and always unseen; that He has no form of any kind, not of human, or beast, or anything else; and the way to serve Him is through prayer and proper ("holy") behavior. In other words, the people are supposed to accept a complete overhaul in their thinking, beliefs and expectations. The Rambam (Maimonides) likens the situation "to the appearance of a prophet in these times who, calling upon the people to worship God, would say: 'God has given you a law forbidding you to pray to Him, to fast, to call upon Him for help in misfortune. Your worship should consist solely in meditation without any works at all'" (*The Guide of the Perplexed*, 3:32).

The Rambam's point, of course, is that Moshe's message was beyond the people's ability to understand or accept.

Of course, this generation knew of its God before Moshe; He had contacted their ancestors and made certain promises to them. However, that was more than 400 years ago. As far as they knew, He was only a tribal God, in any case, and One who apparently functioned within a confined geographical area (Canaan). After all, if He was anything more, why were His promises to their ancestors rooted in real estate, and where had He been for the last 430 years, when they were facing an ever-deteriorating situation in Egypt?

When they saw Moshe do his parlor tricks for them, they believed in God; but when they saw their work increased, they stopped believing. When they saw that the plagues brought about their freedom, they believed; when they saw the Egyptians coming after them, they stopped believing. When they saw the waters part and the attacking army destroyed, they believed; when they saw the heat of the sun and the dearth of water, they stopped believing.

And so it went. For them, seeing was believing, because that is the way it was in all other religions, so they fashioned a golden calf to represent their deity. And they sacrificed to that calf, because that was the only way they knew how to serve a god.

Clearly, this was not a people that was ready for anything more sophisticated and sublime. They and their descendants had a long way to go before they could understand the truth about God. Until then, something else was needed to help deflect them from repeating the golden calf incident by pursuing idolatry and paganism in the name of God.

That something was an elaborate system of sacrifices and "magical" rituals adapted from the pagan world around them. Adapted, but not adopted; the sacrifices and rituals were cleansed of their paganism and redefined in a strictly God-oriented vein. They were not meant as the permanent way of serving God, but as a transition from paganism.

(The proof of this is in the place-bound nature of sacrifices versus the boundless venue of prayer. Sacrifices were limited to one place—at first before the door of the *Mishkan* and then the Temple in Jerusalem. In the desert, when the nation was small and all in one place, it would have been possible for a person to fulfill all the sacrifices required of one, but the more populous the nation became, and the farther away from the cult center the people spread out, the more impossible it became for all but a small minority. And sacrifice became impossible for all once the Temple was gone.)

(Prayer, on the other hand, is possible at home, in synagogue, on the road, in Israel and outside it. Prayer continues regardless of whether the Temple stands and regardless of where a person resides. If God had intended sacrifices to be the legitimate and ideal mode of service to Him, He would not have placed such serious limitations on them.)

One example of how such adaptation works should suffice. In BT *Berakhot* 2a–2b, there is a discussion of when a *kohen* who was impure may enter the Temple gates to eat his *terumah* portion. The answer, based on a verse in the Torah (Leviticus 22:7), is when the sun goes and a new day begins. And yet, the *kohen* (the priest) has not yet brought the appropriate sacrifice. How is this possible?

Because the sacrifice is an obligation imposed by the sacrificial system, but not a magical cleansing device. The period of impurity is fixed. When it ends, it ends. The sacrifices are powerless by themselves. Bring them too early and the impurity remains. Do not bring them at all and the impurity is washed away in any case, because its time has elapsed.

This would seem to be contradicted numerous times in the Torah, especially in the Book of Leviticus. It is clear in those instances that a sacrifice is required, but the reasons for them have less to do with magical cleaning powers than more practical considerations.

A people that cannot fathom a God without form or substance cannot accept that the mere passage of time removes impurity. Thus, the prescription for sacrifices is given. It is because that is what pagans would do to cleanse themselves. Because Israel needs to see to believe, because it only understands the modes of worship current in the pagan world, it, too, gets a sacrifice, but the sacrifice is denuded of any supernatural connotation.

We see the same rationale in the *halakha*, as well, when the need arises. Thus, for example, it is forbidden to utter incantations over wounds, "but if the victim's life is in danger, permission was granted" provided that an incantation would "settle [the victim's] mind and strengthen his feelings," even though incantations obviously "are of no use." (Rambam, *Mishneh Torah, Hilchot Avodat Cochavim*, 11:11; the *Mishneh Torah*, subsequently abbreviated as MT, is Maimonides's codification of the Oral Law.)

So it is here with the *Mishkan*. Moshe anoints the Tabernacle to "make it holy," not because the act makes it holy, but because, to borrow from the Rambam's phrasing, it "settles the people's minds and strengthens their feelings."

Eventually, Israel will realize that pouring oil over acacia wood helps preserve the wood but does nothing to add to its "holiness." Eventually, Israel will come to understand that it has no need for pagan trappings to serve God. However, that will take a long time.

Indeed, "eventually" may not yet be here even today, 3,500 years later. The sacrifices may be gone (albeit not by our choice), but each community of Jews has its own superstitions adapted from the surrounding culture, such as the Eastern European custom of putting a red cord around an infant's wrist to ward off evil spirits.

And we still have this belief that "impurity," which is invisible and intangible, somehow mystically transfers itself to the "pure." True, this is a belief that begins with the Torah itself, but for the reasons already stated: the people, conditioned in paganism, could not completely shake off these beliefs. Today, however, rather than isolating these beliefs (but not abrogating them; they are *mi-d'oraita*, "from the Torah," after all, and thus cannot be casually dealt away, no matter how we explain them), we have added to them even as the rabbis of the Talmud did not do so.

Thus, for example, following a ruling of the Ramban (Nachmanides), some men refuse to allow a woman to even touch a Torah scroll because, if they are menstruating, they will pass on their impure state to the *Sefer Torah.*

And yet, in BT *Berakhot* 22a, the *tanna* Rabbi Yehudah ben Bathyra II tells us specifically that "the words of the Torah are not susceptible to uncleanness." (Two centuries later, this view is the accepted standard, according to the *amora* Rav Nachman bar Yitzchak.) Indeed, in BT *Megilla* 23a, the Talmud declares that a woman *ab initio* (from the start) may ascend the *bima* to read one of the seven *aliyot* on Shabbat, but that this is not done "out of respect for the congregation," a euphemism for "the men would get angry." Nowhere in that brief discussion is there even a hint that a woman is prohibited because she may be impure.

Even more to the point, because it does not involve "the words of the Torah," is the case of *tsitsit*. The ritual fringes are themselves "holy," yet in BT *Menachot* 43a we are told: "Rav Yehudah attached *tsitsit* to the aprons of [the women of] his household. . . ." In the ensuing discussion, the only issue is whether *tsitsit* is a time-bound commandment (from which women are usually exempt); there is no discussion of whether a woman's impurity could be passed on to the *tsitsit*.

Clearly, the rabbis of blessed memory did not see this as an issue worthy even of dismissal. They understood the difference between hocus-pocus and *halakha*. Today, however, the most common answer given to why a woman cannot even touch a Torah scroll (much less receive an *aliyah*) is that she may be in a state of impurity. Thus, we continue to be ruled by superstition.

While on the subject of women and *aliyot*, a digression in itself from the original question, another interesting digression is in order—whether women can sing before the congregation. The prevailing wisdom among the Orthodox and some Conservatives is no, because a woman's voice can be seductive. In fact, "singing" is how an *aliyah* was fulfilled in the days of the Talmud and for centuries thereafter. There was no "Torah reader"; the person who was called to the Torah for an *aliyah* was called to *read* a portion; if only one person in the congregation was capable of doing so, then that one person would ascend the *bima* for the first *aliyah*, descend at its completion, go back up for the second, go down again, and so on. "Reading" the Torah is inaccurate, however; we do not *read* the Torah, but *chant* it according to specific musical notations. In other words, *we sing it*. Thus, the discussion in BT *Megilla* 23a also means that a woman's voice *ab initio* may be heard by the congregation. Here again, then, superstition gets in the way of *halakha*.

Now an objection can be raised on this point. We read in BT *Berakhot* 24a, "Shmuel said: 'The voice of a woman is *erva* [lewdness], for it is said [in Song of Soloman 2:14], "For your voice is sweet and your face is comely.'" From this, the *Shulchan Aruch Orach Chaim* rules that a woman's voice may not be heard singing during prayer.

While the ruling in a sense fits the context in which Shmuel, the first century *amora*, made the statement, there are several problems with this interpretation.

The first, of course, pertains to the rabbinical view of *Shir HaShirim*, The Song of Songs. As attested to by Rashi, the phrase in question is God speaking to Israel. It is also preceded by "Let me hear your voice." It is hard to imagine taking such a positive statement and turning it into a negative one. Shmuel's interpretation would be more palatable if the verse read: "Let me *not* hear your voice, for your voice is sweet and your face is comely."

It is also hard to imagine that this view of Shmuel's was the accepted one in the *amoraic* period because of the off-handed discussion of *aliyot* in BT *Megilla* 23a. If the rabbis of the period had agreed to the view, then someone would have mentioned it there, either as an addendum to "out of respect for the congregation," or as an alternative to it. Not even the Rambam raises the issue in reprising the reason women do not get *aliyot* in his *MT Hilchot Tefilla* 12:17.

Shmuel, by the way, is considered authoritative only in matters of civil law, especially those dealing with financial issues. On matters of ritual and practice, however, it is the opinion of Rav Abba bar Arikha (Rav) that usually prevails. Unfortunately, we have no statement on the issue from Rav. We must assume, however, that this statement of Shmuel's is an opinion of his, but not necessarily a generally-held belief at the time.

There is also the matter of the context of this statement. The immediately preceding discussion relates to reciting the *Shema* in bed when others are in the same bed (especially one's nude wife). Shmuel's statement and the others included here relate to the recital of the *Shema*. One can assume, therefore, that they relate specifically to the recital of the *Shema in bed*. Thus, it can be argued that what Shmuel is saying is that a woman's voice is seductive to a man when she is nude and lying next to him in bed, and thus he should not recite the *Shema* while she is singing. Shmuel may have an entirely different view when the woman is fully clothed and nowhere near the man.

In passing, it must be added that much of what Shmuel says in the entire discussion of the nighttime *Shema* directly contradicts the rulings of the *tannaim*. That his fellow *amoraim* at times uphold him over the *tannaim* (something that is almost never done in the Talmud) suggests that the rabbis of Babylonia may have been motivated by factors other than purely *halakhic* ones. (The statement about a woman's voice carries no discussion, so we do not know whether the *amoraim* agree with Shmuel on this point, or whether his view is in concert with or in contradiction to *tannaitic* doctrine. We assume they accept it, however, because it is included in the Gemara without further comment.)

We have come a long way from the generation of the desert, but we still have a long way to go.

Joseph Ozarowski

When I presented this question to my daughter, her Shabbat guests, and later to my congregants, they all came up with the idea that Moses' action was for others to see. Not everyone was privy to the divine instructions regarding the sanctity of the *Mishkan*. Thus if people—Jews or travelers— saw Moshe sanctifying the *Mishkan*, they would realize its significance and feel the Divine Presence.

I would go a large step further. Besides whatever publicity or teaching value Moses' action may have had, I think the Torah teaches us a major point on the very definition of *kedusha*—sanctity. God, by definition, is *kadosh*—separate, unique, and completely identified with sanctity. But God expects us to do our share in making the world and our lives *kadosh* as well. Moses' action—itself a mitzvah, a holy commandment ordered by God—was to act and sanctify the Tabernacle.

By doing this, Moses showed that we all have the ability and are expected to sanctify the world around us. The *Mishkan* was the prototype for our future houses of worship and a reflection of *Hashem*'s very creation of the world (see the previous response). Both *shuls* and the world may have intrinsic *kedusha* (holiness and sanctity), but the *kedusha* does not count for a lot without human involvement. Unlike non-Jewish approaches to holiness (Rudolf Otto's idea of the "numinous" comes to mind, as well as some Eastern religious ideas), the Jewish idea of holiness and sanctity is not otherworldly, heavenly, or separate from human endeavor. On the contrary, it is very much centered in this world through our actions. Thus Moses had to add his human efforts to fully make the *Mishkan* holy. And this was truly God's instruction and wish.

David Sofian

It is a beginning to acknowledge that the root of *l'kadesh* means "to make separate;" however, we need a broader understanding of this word, "holiness." The word expresses much more. *Sifra*, the early midrash to *Vayikra*, is helpful in providing us at least two further layers of meaning.

The first such layer is along the lines of your comment at the opening of your discussion question that to be holy is to behave in a way God determines is correct. *Vayikra* 20:7 tells us, "You will sanctify yourselves and be holy, for I am the Eternal your God." Beginning with the idea that holiness necessitates separateness, *Sifra* 91d comments on this verse that holiness is not so much a matter of being separate by avoiding idolatry, but rather separateness is a matter of our actually observing God's commandments.

Then, in the context of the Tabernacle, holiness is not so much a matter of forestalling pagan worship, but it is a matter of worshipping God in the way commanded. Possibly this nuance cues us to what it meant for Moses to sanctify the Tabernacle. His act of sanctification is an act of recognition. It represents the people's recognition of the Tabernacle's importance not only in forestalling another incident like the golden calf, but more importantly in providing our ancestors with the means of worshiping in the way God determined was correct.

Sifra 93d helps us with another nuance in its comment to *Vayikra* 20:26, "You shall be holy to Me, for I the Eternal am holy, and I have set you apart from other peoples to be Mine." *Sifra* begins again by telling us this means that, since God is separate, Israel is to be separate. But then it focuses on the end of the verse, "to be Mine," and adds that, if you wish to belong to God, you must separate yourselves. It says to us in God's voice, "If you sever yourselves from the other peoples, then you belong to Me; if not, you belong to Nebuchadnezzar."

Not only does God make Israel holy by making it separate, but Israel must make itself holy by recognizing itself to be separate. This is the meaning of belonging to God. We come close to God by recognizing our own distinctness, by our own willingness to be apart. God made the Tabernacle special, separate, and holy in its own right. However, Israel also has a role in this by recognizing that through it, they made themselves distinct. Moses' act of sanctification is also about acknowledging this.

Then, in answer to your question, Moses' act of sanctification is in fact an act of recognition, a declaration, with several nuances. *Sifra* shows us that these nuances at least include Israel's recognition that, through the Tabernacle, they can forestall the idolatry of another calf; through it, they are given a means of observing God's commandments regarding proper worship; and through it, they can act to separate themselves and thereby belong to God. Viewed this way, God's command to Moses to sanctify the Tabernacle is very much for Israel's benefit.

VaYikra/Leviticus

VaYikra: Leviticus 1:1–5:26

Prophetical Reading
Isaiah 33:21–34:23

Overview of Torah Portion

God gives Moses the laws for bringing various sacrificial offerings—burnt offering, meal offering, peace offering, sin offering, guilt offering, and offerings for people who have committed other particular offenses.

Key Verses

"And if anyone sins, that he hears the voice of adjuration—he being a witness, if he saw or knew, and does not tell it—then he shall bear his iniquity; or if anyone touches any unclean thing . . . the carcass of an unclean beast or the carcass of unclean cattle or the carcass of unclean swarming things, and it is hidden from him . . . or if he touches the uncleanness of man . . . and it is hidden from him, and when he knows, he is guilty; or if anyone swears with his lips to do evil or to do good, whatever a man utters with an oath and it is hidden from him, and when he knows, he is guilty. . . . it shall be . . . that he shall confess . . . and shall bring his forfeit to the Lord for his sin . . . and the priest shall make atonement for him" (Leviticus 5:1–6).

Discussion Question

BIBLICAL CONFESSIONS: For the first offerings to be brought as expiation for various sins, or as an expression of thanks to God, the Torah prescribes the appropriate sacrifice—an animal, or the meal sacrifice of cooked flour. Only in certain cases—a witness who fails to give testimony, or someone who contracts ritual impurity, or an individual who does not fulfill a vow—does the Torah mandate oral confession, *vidui.*

If the purpose of the sacrifices is to inspire repentance, or *teshuvah*, in a sinner, why does the performance of confession not fulfill that requirement? Why is a physical sacrifice still needed? Why is a confession specified only in these certain cases? What do they have in common with each other, and how do they differ from the other categories for which a sacrifice is brought?

Shammai Engelmayer

It is not true that "[o]nly in certain cases . . . does the Torah mandate oral confession." In Numbers 5:5–7, we are told: "And the Lord spoke to Moshe, saying, 'Speak to the Children of Israel: When a man or a woman commits any sin . . . , thereby committing sacrilege against the Lord . . . , they shall confess the sin that they committed. . . .'"

From these verses, the Rambam states the law explicitly (*MT Hilchot Teshuvah* 1:1): "If a person transgressed against any commandment of the Torah, be it a positive or a negative [commandment], whether [the transgression was] willful or in error, when he atones and returns from his sin, he must confess before God, blessed be He. . . . This is a verbal confession. This confession is a positive commandment [number 73]."

Thus, not just in the three instances cited here in Leviticus 5:1–6, but in all transgressions, whether accidentally committed or with malice aforethought, confession is a prerequisite for atonement.

Nevertheless, the question is correct in noting that only in these three instances are we specifically enjoined to confess. Clearly, there is something about these three wrongful acts that caused the need for confession to be highlighted.

The obvious answer is that, in all the other cases in chapters 4 and 5, the wrong committed is already known. If the *Kohen Gadol* (High Priest) or the nation as a whole commits a wrongful act, clearly it is known. In the case of a communal leader or an ordinary Israelite, we are told that the wrong is pointed out to him or her. Further on in Leviticus 5, the penitent actually is accused of doing wrong and swears falsely that he is innocent; again, the matter is known.

Not in these three cases, however; here, the wrongdoer does wrong, but no one else knows it. A person has information that is relevant to a case being tried; only the person with the information knows that (although others may suspect it). A person makes a vow to do something; only the one making the vow knows it. In both cases. the problem is that no one can see into someone's head, and the wrongdoer is unaware that his or her action is a violation of God's law.

As for the carcass case, it is evident from the text that no one was around when the person touched the offensive creature; otherwise, he or she would have known instantly about the wrong because it would have been pointed out.

Thus it is that the person is specifically bidden to openly confess, lest he or she think that, because the wrong was hidden in the first place, no one need know why he or she is atoning.

That is the obvious answer, but it does not satisfy me. There simply is no way that a person who deliberately withholds testimony does not know he or she is doing wrong. The same goes for going back on a vow. These are conscious acts. And, frankly, the same holds true for the middle entry, the carcass. How can someone touch a dead pig, say, and not know he or she touched a dead pig?

To my mind, what is really at issue here is not that the person does not know the act was wrong, but that he or she disagrees that it is wrong. Perhaps, in order to remain in good standing with the community after the matter has become known, the person may bring an offering of expiation, but deep down inside this person is not convinced that there is anything for which he or she must atone; God is better served some other way.

Looked at in this way, the public confession is not about the wrongful act itself; that confession is already required. Rather, the confession spoken of here is an acknowledgment of the additional wrong—disagreeing with the law itself.

(We are not dealing here with a person who rejects a particular law because he or she also rejects God's law in general. Such a person is not expected to stand up before the community and say, "I have sinned;" for him or her, the punishment of *karet*—"cutting off"—is the only solution. For an explanation of *karet*, see my answer to the question for *parshat Tzav*.

(We are also not dealing here with a person who believes a law is no longer valid, but continues to follow it because it has not been changed. A perfect example of this is my belief that the sacrificial system was pagan in origin and was adapted by Moshe and God for use only until Israel could make the transition to a higher form of service and worship. Until I know for certain, however, that this is true, I continue to recite the appropriate prayers for a resumption of the sacrificial cult, because I also believe that laws can only be changed through the *halakhic* process. In the cases here, the assumption is that the individual can decide on his or her own to ignore a law.)

Let me give you an example. The Torah states in Deuteronomy 18:10–11, "Let there not be found among you . . . one who inquires of the dead." From this, Rambam declares (*MT Avodat Kochavim* 11:13), "Anyone who performs an act in order that a dead person should come to him and give him information is [given] lashes. . . ."

It does not matter even that the deceased was a great sage or prophet. After all, Shul sinned when he went to the witch of Endor in order to summon the dead Shmuel to advise him (see 1 Samuel 28).

Consider the following hypothetical case: A certain congregation became so attached to its rabbi that members were accustomed to inquire of him whenever they needed advice or felt the need for a blessing for something or other. Unfortunately, this rabbi, being a mere mortal, eventually died. By then, however, the congregation had become so convinced of his saintliness that its members continued to visit the rabbi to ask for his help. They were convinced that their rabbi would continue to plead with God on their behalf.

While the case is hypothetical, it is based on numerous real cases. It goes without saying that no one involved in such behavior thinks this is a violation of God's law. In other words, what they are doing disagrees with the law as stated in the Torah (in this case, inquiring of the dead in order to obtain assistance from beyond the grave), but they do not see that a violation is involved. When they finally realize that it is a violation (if they ever do), they will be obligated to confess both the sin of inquiring of the dead and the sin of disagreeing with the law as stated in Deuteronomy 18:10–11.

Having thus established that confession is required each time an offering of expiation is brought, we can deal with the second part of the question— why a sacrifice is required in addition to confession of the sin.

The answer, once again, is that a sacrifice would not have been required at all if the early Israelites had been able to shake off their pagan beliefs. They could not; to them, the only way to make "the gods" forgive people was through bribery. So it must be with their God, as well. And so, God gives them the offering of expiation.

Let us face it: If sacrifice was truly intended to be a part of atonement, no Jew would have been forgiven for his or her sins in the last 1,925 years. Make that 2,581 years for the majority of Jews, since a majority of us have lived outside the land since the First Temple was destroyed. In other words, confessing does indeed fulfill the requirement. The midrashic compilation *Pesikta Rabbati* (45) makes this clear when it says, "Repentance is valued above sacrifices." The sacrifice is intended only to pacify the people, who need to see to believe.

There is, however, a more practical aspect to these sacrifices than merely playing up to the people's pagan side. Talk, as the saying goes, is cheap—and people do not respect "cheap." Throw in a financial penalty, and now you have something people do respect. They are more likely to take the act of confessing more seriously if it puts a dent in their pocketbooks.

Joseph Ozarowski

Hatat, the sin offerings, were brought by individuals in many cases of negligent misdeeds, called *shogeg* in Hebrew. The circumstances for these *shogeg* misdeeds were not accidental but were also less than intentional. Ramban points out that textually, the three cases of a failed witness, negligent ritual impurity, and inadvertant non-fulfilment of a vow are the only cases of *hatat* mentioned by the Torah as requiring *vidui*, or confession. Yet Ramban quotes rabbinic and midrashic sources (*Sifre Zuta* Numbers 5:5 and *Sifre* Numbers 2) that say that *vidui* was required in all cases of *hatat*, not just these.

In other words, these three were just examples of sin offerings that needed confession. But really, all sin offerings were accompanied by a confession reminiscent of the Yom Kippur confession (see the *Torah Temimah's* comments on this). The only reason these three *shogeg* cases are pointed out in the Torah is that normally, *hatat* offerings were required for sins whose intentional versions would have been punished by *karait*—a spiritual cutting off of the soul (see the next question and answer). These three sins, when done intentionally, would not have been punished by *karait* and were therefore singled out by the Torah as the examples for *hatat* accompanied by *vidui*.

David Sofian

You ask several difficult questions. As you will see from my comments below, the need for both a confession and an offering should have been evident for all the times a sin or guilt offering was required, so why it was specified only in these particular cases is difficult to explain. However, perhaps these three cases are grouped together because of their private nature.

The first case, withholding testimony, is about the lack of appropriate speech. Such an offense might easily remain unknown and private. Regarding the second case, as is pointed out in the commentary to this verse found in the U.A.H.C.'s Torah Commentary (1981), it was not sinful in and of itself to become ritually unclean. The sin occurred when an individual in such a state did something like eating consecrated food. This, too, is the kind of offense that would likely remain private.

Regarding the third case, swearing falsely, the *tannaitic Midrash Sifra* tells us that, since violation of oaths regarding civil matters are treated later in verse 20, the oaths violated here are of a religious character. Conceivably, personal religious oaths referred to here were also likely to remain private. No one else knowing made these offenses easily disregarded.

Perhaps this is the reason the offering itself was not sufficient. In order to underline the sinful nature of these offenses and help guard against their dismissal, an oral statement of confession was required.

You also ask: Why was confession not enough, why is the actual offering still required? It is because these offerings were for the purpose of repentance that a simple confessional statement would not be enough. We are taught over and over again that the gates of *teshuvah* are open. However, we should not assume that statements of *teshuvah* mechanically produce God's forgiveness.

How strongly this is expressed in the well known passage from *Mishnan Yomah* 8:9 that a person who says, "I will sin and then repent, sin again and repent again," is denied the chance to repent. From the rabbinic point of view, repentance is more than simply saying the right thing. It must be meant, and the test of proper intention is whether or not the sinner ceases committing that particular sin.

To simply utter a confession would be meaningless. The making of the actual offering concretizes the intention of the words. The penitent's sincerity is confirmed in the offering.

Even if we assume that the sin in question is unintentional, the point still holds that a simple confessional statement is insufficient. The offender should not conclude, at the point of realizing a sin had been committed, that since the sin was unintentional, it is insignificant. True forgiveness requires a demonstration of sincerity in this case as well. How easy it would be to brush off such a sin with the mere words, "I'm sorry." I am reminded of how a child will repeatedly say, "I'm sorry," when explaining to a parent that whatever was done was not done on purpose.

The oral confession is usually not enough. Such a child needs to take some concrete action in order to learn to show greater care. As before, the making of the actual offering concretizes the penitent's intention.

The same point pertains if you had asked your question in reverse. We might have asked why the offering itself does not suffice? This time we find the lesson taught in *Midrash Vayikrak Rabbah* 2:12. There we discover that a person should not think that merely bringing a bull with much flesh will automatically yield God's acceptance, no matter how abhorrent or grievous the deed. The midrash is pointing out to us that the offering may be counterproductive unless accompanied by the confessional statement.

Again, God's forgiveness is not automatic without the proper intent and sincerity. We concluded above that words of intention were confirmed with a tangible offering. Here, we conclude that the meaning of the tangible offering is confirmed with sincere words, that is, the offender's ability to offer words of confession.

Although I am not sure precisely why only the three cases are singled out as they are with the requirement of confession, it is clear that in matters of repentance both confession and concrete acts are necessary.

Tzav: Leviticus 6:1–8:36

Prophetical Reading
Jeremiah 7:21–34, 8:1–3, 9:22, 23

Overview of Torah Portion

God gives Moses the details for the priests' bringing of sacrificial offerings—tending the fire, wearing the priestly garb, the preparation, burning, and eating. God orders Moses to anoint Aaron and his sons in view of "all the congregation."

Key Verses

"And the flesh that touches any unclean thing shall not be eaten; it shall be burnt with fire. . . . But the soul that eats of the flesh of the sacrifice of peace-offerings, which are the Lord's, and his uncleanliness is upon him, that soul shall be cut off from his people. And a soul that touches any unclean thing . . . and eats of the flesh of the sacrifice of peace-offering, which are the Lord's, that soul shall be cut off from his people" (Leviticus 7:19–21).

"You shall eat no fat, of ox, or sheep or goat. And the fat of that which dies of itself, and the fat of that which is torn of beasts, may be used for any other purpose, but you shall certainly not eat it. For whoever eats of the fat of the beast . . . the soul that eats it shall be cut off from his people" (Leviticus 7:23–24).

"You shall eat no blood. . . . Any soul that eats any blood, that soul shall be cut off from his people" (Leviticus 7:26–27).

Discussion Question

MAKING THE CUT: *Karet* (or *karait*), cutting off a soul from the Jewish nation, is a heavenly punishment reserved for a particular class of offenses that strike at the basis relationship between God and His Chosen People—the covenant of circumcision, disobeying the *kashrut* regulations of Passover, desecrating the Sabbath. Just as one's actions cut an individual off from "his people" in this world, God will cut him off, by an early death or deprivation of a place in the next world.

Why does this group of dietary prohibitions—eating certain sacrifices in a state of ritual uncleanliness, eating banned fats, eating blood—rank in the category of the Torah's fundamental commands? Why does someone who eats an animal's fat, admittedly a sin, deserve this form of spiritual exile? What separates these violations from the larger group of *kashrut* violations, for which a more traditional rabbinical court-based punishment is called?

Shammai Engelmayer

The first question we need to ask is, "what is *karet*?" Other than that it means "cutting off," that is not an easy question to answer.

Virtually all rabbinic authorities agree that *karet* involves premature death. In the minor Babylonian tractate *Mo. Kat.* 28a, there is a debate over whether *karet* means death at age 50, or somewhere between 50 and 60. The problem with the latter opinion, which was expressed by Rava, is that the prophet Shmuel (Samuel) died at age 52. As for a person who has already passed this age when he incurs the punishment of *karet*, the rabbis of blessed memory seem to agree that the punishment is exacted through the manner of death.

Clearly, there is a difference between *karet* and "death by the hands of Heaven," but the rabbis were not certain what that difference was in practical terms. So they argued that the latter was a death that occurred at age 60.

Karet may also be fulfilled through the death of children (or perhaps in the guilty person's childlessness, *ariri*, based on Leviticus 20:21). A person with no heirs is effectively "cut off" from Israel.

On the other hand, there is an indication in the Torah that *karet* does not always involve death but banishment. For example, in Leviticus 20:17, a brother and sister who marry each other are subject to immediate *karet*, "in the sight of their people." This suggests banishment, not heaven-sent death.

It would appear, then, that *karet* actually is a little bit of both. Where the sin is known, banishment is the solution (or lashes; the Talmud says lashes usually obviate the need for *karet*). When the sin is not known, *karet* is God's domain exclusively and is accomplished through death of some kind.

The specific crimes referred to by the question are punishable by the divine form of *karet* because they are crimes only the perpetrator and God know about. How is anyone else to know if someone has suffered a discharge that makes him or her unclean (and thus unfit to handle a sacrificial offering), or that the meat that person is eating was "torn of beasts," or that behind closed doors he or she enjoys a bloody rare steak? No one can; thus, no one but God can carry out punishment.

The issue here is purity, by the way, not *kashrut*; *karet* is not a punishment for violations of *kashrut*. The fact that the perpetrator is violating *kashrut* is incidental here. It is the purity issue that brings about the divine punishment. The perpetrator deliberately violated a rule he or she understood to involve the invisible stigma of ritual impurity yet kept it a secret and even was willing to participate in sacred tasks while in that state.

This is unacceptable to God because Israel is His kingdom of priests, His holy nation.

What the perpetrator did was say, "I do not want to be a priest of God. I do not want to be holy. I do not want a divine mission. I want no part of any covenant. I just want to be left alone to live my life as I see it."

Thus, *karet* provides God's response. You do not want to be God's priest? Fine; you are cut off from Israel. You want to live your own life your way? Okay, but remember that it was God who gave life and it is God who decides when life ends.

Now, it is true that deliberately violating *kashrut* (or any other laws of God) has the same effect. The person is saying the same thing; sending the same message. So why not the same punishment? Because he or she is challenging God, but not directly attacking Him. There is no element of destroying the sacred.

In the instances enumerated here, however, the issue is not that the person thought himself or herself to be impure because of a deliberately sinful act meant to bring on such impurity. Rather, it is that the person deliberately meant to pass on that impurity within sacred precincts. In a sense, it was an attempt to make God impure. This is what turns an ordinary sin into an extraordinary one deserving of an added punishment of an equally extraordinary nature.

Joseph Ozarowski

Karet, the cutting off of a soul from the collective body of the people of Israel, is a difficult concept to explain. As you pointed out, the traditional rabbinic approach is to assume that this is a Divine, rather than human-inflicted punishment. Either the person will die early, the traditional rabbinic explanation, or God will somehow take away the person's *olam haba*, the portion in the next world. We have no way of knowing whether people who are uncircumcised, ingest bread on Pesach, eat on Yom Kippur, break the laws of family morality, deny the Shabbat, or commit the other offenses for which this punishment is prescribed, live less than people who observe these *mitzvot*. We do know that the punishment is a spiritual one.

The offenses for which *karet* is threatened all seem to be part of the fundamental structures of basic Judaism. Yom Kippur, *Pesach*, Shabbat, morality, *brit mila*, and the rest form the backbone of Jewish life and practice. In denying these, the individual Jew can be said to cut him- or herself off from the Jewish people and Judaism. In this way, *karet* can also be seen as a self-inflicted punishment.

This brings us to your question. The rules regarding ritual uncleanliness, blood, and *chaylev* (fat) must all represent some fundamental value within the Jewish scheme. The denial of these values would cut the perpetrator off from God and the Jewish people. It is possible to easily explain two out of three. *Tum'ah*, ritual uncleanliness, comes from a contact with death. The primary conveyor of *tum'ah* is direct contact with a human corpse. The Temple was a human life-affirming place, and the sacrificial service could not be tainted with *tum'ah*, any connection with death. Thus, someone who knowingly did so denies a major part of Judaism and is cut off (or cuts him- or herself off) from God and the Jewish people. Similarly, blood symbolizes life, and drinking blood symbolizes violence and idolatrous practice. To drink blood goes against one of the ultimate goals of the Torah, which is to teach us to be less bloodthirsty. But what does *chaylev*, the fatty materials of the animals, symbolize? Cholesterol? Calories?

The *chaylev* in the Torah is the fatty substance sometimes referred to as suet and found in the front of the animal. Unlike the fats that are found inside and adjacent to the meat and are kosher, forbidden *chaylev* is easily removed in a process known as *treberrn* in Yiddish or *nikur* in Hebrew. And as the *Or Hahayim* points out, our verse, while in the context of sacrificial offerings, also includes eating *chaylev* in non-sacrificial animals and would, therefore, apply today. In fact, the process of *treberrn* is still done today by kosher butchers or in the kosher slaughterhouses.

Rabbi Samson Raphael Hirsch in *Horeb*, 454, speculates on the reasons for certain foods being kosher and other *trafe*. He divides all food into three categories: 1. foods that symbolize passivity and are kosher (plant life and all kosher animals); 2. foods that symbolize activity and are non-kosher, including most non-kosher animals, *ever min ha'chai* (tissue from a living animal), and blood; and 3. foods that symbolize dullness and are non-kosher, including non-kosher fish, worms, animals not in the right physical condition to be considered kosher (*trefa*), non-kosher slaughtered animals (*nevela*), and *chaylev*.

These fats are "bare of movement, having become alien to the animal itself, nourished by inactivity." *Chaylev*, in effect, is the opposite of blood which, ". . . is of the utmost activity, bearing on the animal's whole physical being ('for the blood is the life,' Deuteronomy 12:23), representing . . . the body in flow." Thus blood and *chaylev* are opposites, and both are forbidden by the Torah on penalty of *karet*. But even Hirsch, the great rationalist and seeker of reasons behind the Torah's commandments, admits that his ideas are speculation.

In the end, these rules, while fitting into the framework of nature, are from God, and that is their ultimate reason. This is why blood and *chaylev* are considered to be *hukim*, laws which may not have an easy or rational explanation and whose aspects and consequences may not be fully explainable.

David Sofian

Your question could open up the whole subject of the meaning of *kashrut*, but I will limit my remarks to the verses you determined. However, one general observation is in order. Significantly, by focusing our attention on these three aspects of forbidden eating, we can immediately see that *kashrut* is more than the Torah's attempt to promote good dietary hygiene.

In your question to *parashat P'kudei*, you raised the issue of the meaning of God's imperative to Israel to be holy. Here, too, the focus needs to be on the nature of Israel's holiness. There I referred to the ancient *tannaitic Midrash Sifra* and its comment to *Vayik.* 20:26, "You shall be holy to Me, for I the Eternal am holy, and I have set you apart from other peoples to be Mine." The midrash there directs our attention to the end of the verse and the words, "to be Mine."

According to it, these words mean that if you sever yourselves from the other peoples, then you belong to God; if not, you belong to Nebuchadnezzar. Israel is not only separate due to God's command but also must actively and meaningfully make itself distinct, sever itself. The dietary cases raised here are examples on the biblical level of means for Israel to do precisely that.

Israel is set apart and sets itself apart through the maintenance of ritual purity, currently expressed in the dietary prohibition emphasized in your first set of key verses, Leviticus 7:19–21. Since the *Shelamim* offering could be handled by common Israelites away from the sanctuary, it was particularly relevant to make this point here. Its importance is further emphasized with the warning of the penalty of *karet*. Ritual purity is not only a matter for the priests. The penalty of *karet* makes this point absolutely clear.

The fat referred to in verse 23 is the same fat described in chapter 3:3–4. This fat covers the internal organs and entrails of the animal and was particularly designated as God's. Taking the extra step of not eating this fat was an important way of acknowledging the truth of Psalm 24, the earth is God's and all its fullness.

This tangible act of recognition sets Israel apart by making Israel continually self-aware of its relationship with God in the ongoing preparation of food. Again, attaching the penalty of *karet* emphasizes the importance of this point.

The prohibition connected with consuming blood is found several times, indicating its importance. This weight is yet furthered by affixing the penalty of *karet*. We are to see that the very life of the animal is manifest in its blood. Being that the same is true of humans, the blood expresses a bond of commonality between us and animals as living beings created by God. The necessity of taking the animal for food is recognized, but our most basic bond with it cannot be violated by consuming the essence of its life.

Here, too, Israel sets itself apart with a tangible act that recognizes continually the commonalty of life that pervades all of God's creation. Israel expresses its reverence for life in this act and thereby eloquently expresses its reverence for God.

It is unclear to me why these violations in particular are distinguished from other matters of *kashrut* with the punishment of *karet*. What is clear to me is that each of these cases expresses a crucial value, and that value is emphasized by the attached penalty.

Shmini: Leviticus 9:1–11:47

Prophetical Reading
2 Samuel 6:1–7:17

Overview of Torah Portion

Moses orders Aaron and Aaron's sons to offer sacrifices eight days after their anointment as priests. Nadav and Avihu, Aaron's sons, offer incense on a fire that God had "not commanded" and are consumed by heavenly fire. God gives Moses the laws of *kashrut*.

Key Verses

"And it came to pass on the eighth day, Moses called Aaron and his sons . . . and he said to Aaron, 'Take for yourself a bull-calf for a sin offering, and a ram for a burnt-offering, without blemish, and offer them before the Lord'" (Leviticus 9:1–2).

"And the Lord spoke to Moses, saying . . . 'When a woman delivers seed and bears a male, she shall be unclean seven days. . . . and if she bears a female, she shall be unclean two weeks. . . . and when the days of her purification are fulfilled . . . she shall bring a year-old lamb for a burnt-offering, and a young pigeon or a turtle dove for a sin offering'" (Leviticus 12:1–7).

"And the Lord spoke to Moses, saying, 'When a man or a woman clearly utters the vow of a Nazarite, to dedicate oneself to the Lord, he shall abstain from wine. . . . no razor shall come upon his head. . . . he shall not approach a dead body. . . . He shall consecrate to the Lord the days of his Naziriteship. . . . When the days of his consecration are fulfilled . . . he shall present his offering to the Lord, a year-old lamb without blemish for a burnt-offering and a year-old ewe without blemish for a sin offering'" (Numbers 6:1–14).

Discussion Question

SINFUL SACRIFICES: A sin offering is brought when someone has clearly, negligently, committed a forbidden act. But Aaron and his sons were commanded to be anointed as priests; women, as the child-bearing part of the family unit, are vital to the commandment, strictly addressed to the male, to be fruitful and multiply; one is permitted, though not commanded, to accept a Nazarite's life of self-denial. Then why a sin offering in each case? Other types of sacrifices—which indeed, are called for—would seem more logical. What sort of sin is implied? What do the anointed priest, the post-partum mother, and the former Nazarite have in common?

Shammai Engelmayer

You have to understand the mind of the ancient Israelite. Stuck in the mire of paganism, he or she is unable to see too far beyond its beliefs and practices. Thus, to the Israelite, "impurity" is on a par with sin. A person who is impure brings a sin offering.

Sometimes, this is carried to extremes. The ancient Israelite believed (as did the pagans) that certain diseases were "unnatural" and, thus, were divinely ordained as punishment. People suffering from such a disease bring sin offerings after the disease has run its course. To accommodate those beliefs (or, more likely, to imbue them with a sense of holiness in order to remove them from the profane and allow the people to develop spiritually), God provides for the sacrifices and how they are to be performed.

That people held such beliefs in the ancient world is clear from the records we have. It is also clear from our own texts, especially the Book of Job. Here was Iyuv (Job), a man as pure as can be and as steadfast in his love of God as is humanly possible. Yet, when calamity strikes him and disease afflicts him, his so-called friends demand that he admit his sins and repent, for if he was blameless, none of these disasters would have befallen him. It simply was not possible for people in the ancient world to separate happenstance from divine intervention.

It is God Himself Who sets them straight, incidentally. One must wonder whether the real purpose of the Book of Job is to argue against such superstitious beliefs.

As for childbirth, there is no sin in it, nor in the process by which a child is conceived. Childbirth, however, involves blood and, thus, impurity. The sin offering is not brought because the woman had a child, but because she became impure in the process. (There is also the possibility that the woman who gave birth might have sinned without realizing it, perhaps by uttering an oath of some kind while in extreme pain. She likely would have no memory of it, so the sin offering is pre-emptive; just in case she made a vow she does not remember and, therefore, cannot fulfill.)

The Nazarite, on the other hand, does commit a sin. The whole concept of the Nazarite is alien to the normative practice of Israelite religion, then or now. We are commanded to be fruitful and multiply, not to live in celibacy. We are commanded to *live* by the law, not retreat from life because of the law. There may be legitimate reasons why a person chooses to become a Nazarite for a time, and rules are set forth to allow for those, but it nevertheless goes against everything for which the Torah stands.

The sin offerings of Aharon's sons referred to here are of a different nature. They are not meant as atonement for their sins but of the people as a whole. The priests bring their own sin offerings, as well—for eight days, no less. These, too, are pre-emptive. On Israel's part, it is meant to wipe the slate clean as God enters into the midst of the community through the assembling of the *Mishkan*; for the priests, it is meant to allow them to begin their sacred service with their own slates clean.

In other words, there really is no connection from one to the other.

Except, perhaps, for one thing: That, even before God's decree in each case, the people already believed that an offering was required; that somehow God had to be bought off the way pagan gods had to be bought off. That is the real sin—forcing God to adapt pagan practice for Israel's use because Israel is too stiff-necked to understand how God truly is to be served; and forcing Him, as well, to allow the people to hang on to their pagan superstitions for the time being.

This may also explain why Aharon and his sons had to go through the eight days of purification and atonement before beginning their service. It was Aharon, after all, who actually made the golden calf, that tangible symbol of Israel's inability to comprehend or accept the true nature of God or how to serve Him. Aharon (and probably his sons) thus helped Israel perpetuate its pagan notions, thereby requiring a higher degree of atonement.

This may also explain why Nadav and Avihu were killed when they brought "strange fire" into the Tabernacle.

Rabbi Akiva, among others, argues that this "strange fire" came from their own ovens, when it should have come from the altar itself.

Some commentators insist that Nadav and Avihu were punished for sins they had committed earlier. For example, it is suggested that they looked brazenly upon God when they joined their father Aharon, their uncle Moshe and the elders on Mt. Sinai.

Other commentators argue that it was for a sin of the moment that they died. A verse in this week's parshah, for example, suggests they may have been drunk. Another verse, in *parshat Acherei Mot*, suggests they had penetrated the Holy of Holies, something not even Aharon was permitted to do, as yet. A third explanation is that they ignored their teachers, Moshe and Aharon, by not asking them what was proper.

We do not need to look that far to solve this mystery. The answer is right there for all to see. It is contained in the very next verse, when Moshe tells a startled Aharon: "This is what the Lord meant when He said, 'Through those near to Me I show Myself holy, and gain glory before all the people.'"

The import of this statement is clear; Nadav and Avihu were not near to God. Their action was not meant to glorify God before the people, but to glorify the people before God. As religious leaders, they were too willing to follow the whims of the people over the word of God.

Their act demonstrated that Nadav and Avihu were as enthusiastic about the sacrificial cult as was Israel itself. So enthusiastic were they that they could not even wait for the fire of God; they had to rush forward with fire of their own. In effect, they were saying: "What does it matter that this is not what God really wants, not what He originally intended? It is what the people want. Let them see that, unlike the reluctant Moshe, we will give them what they want."

That was their sin and that is why they died. They failed to live up to their responsibilities as religious leaders. Because they believed that it was in their best interest to do so, they put the whims of the people before the words of God.

And God said: "No. This is not the way a religious leader should behave. By all means, serve the people with compassion, mercy, and justice. See to their needs and accommodate their desires, but do not put their whims before My words."

To repeat, then, the common denominator (if one exists at all) is the people's belief that a sacrifice is required at all. This belief preceded God's decision to inaugurate the sacrificial cult and was the reason for the decision. It is for the sin of forcing God to adapt pagan modes of worship that these sin offerings are brought.

Joseph Ozarowski

Before we try to find the common thread binding the three cases of *hatat* (sin offerings), let us deal with the two cases from outside the *sidra* to determine why they require such an offering. Ramban, basing himself on the comments of Rabbi Shimon Ben Yohai (*Nida* 31a; *Bereshit Rabba* 20:17), suggests that the *hatat* was to atone for any unseemly comments the mother may have made during the pain of childbirth, such as words insulting or rejecting her husband. In fact, the *Meshekh Hokhmah* of Rabbi Meir Simcha of Dvinsk (nineteenth century Lithuania) says that her *hatat* as a turtledove symbolizes the (hopefully) continuing relationship between the new mother and her husband, the new father. Having been through four childbirths myself in the labor and delivery rooms with my wife, I can attest to the truth of this idea.

The mother's pain of delivery is not easy, and the hormones are flowing. Many things are said by the child-bearing mother in the heat of the moment which are not really meant or intended. The Torah does not forbid these comments, yet the Torah still requires a *hatat* for these before re-entry into the Temple.

There is a most interesting dispute in the Talmud *Taanit* 11a–b regarding the one who, ". . . sits in a (constant) fast," for example, an extreme ascetic. Rabbi Elazar considers this individual holy, based on the description of the Nazirite as holy. On the other hand, Shmuel considers that person to be a sinner, because the Torah requires the Nazirite to bring a *hatat*, a sin offering. The reason for the sin offering is because as a Nazirite, the person did not imbibe wine. While the Nazirite was permitted by the Torah to deprive himself of wine, yet that deprivation requires a sin offering.

Now we come to Aaron in our *sidra*, who is required to bring a *hatat* before beginning his officiating duties in the *Mishkan*. A number of the classic commentators (Ramban, *Or Hahayim*, *Kli Yakar* [Rabbi Ephraim Lunshitz—sixteenth and seventeenth century Poland and Bohemia]) see this sin-offering as an atonement for Aaron's role in the golden calf story. In fact, they suggest that this is why Aaron's *hatat* was a calf! *Kli Yakar* further points out that the other calf offering, on behalf of the entire Jewish people, was not considered a *hatat*. Rather it was an *olah*, or burnt offering. This was because their role in the golden calf story was clearly an intentional sin, at least in terms of the role of those who were directly involved with the incident. Aaron's role was somewhat murky—not totally the cause for it and yet still bearing some measure of responsibility.

Here, now, is the connection between the cases. All three of our examples involve issues where the person did something permitted (or even encouraged) by the Torah. Yet within these acts came actions not fully in consonance with the spirit of the Torah, and for which the person must bear some responsibility: The childbearing mother who made nasty comments to her husband while delivering, the Nazirite trying to elevate himself but by doing so isolating himself from society and depriving himself of normal life, and Aaron, who with all good intention tried to placate the people in Moshe's absence and ended up being a part of the golden calf incident. So before coming back into the normal sphere of spiritual life (the mother wishing to enter the Temple, the Nazirite re-entering society, and Aaron beginning his duties), all three must bring a *hatat*.

My son Shalom and one of my congregants pointed out that each of these cases—the childbearing mother, the Nazirite, and Aaron—are cases of elevated holiness. Each of these was or is involved in doing a *mitzvah*. Perhaps what may seem like trivial offenses under normal conditions (nasty comments to a spouse, abstention from wine, and placating the people seeking a leader) are considered, under these circumstances, much more severe offenses. Thus, a sin offering is required. It seems, like the old Standard Oil commercial, we expect more from people who are holier, but we do not always get it. So they bring a *hatat* to make up for it.

David Sofian

Basing himself on talmudic sources, Solomon Schechter (in *Aspects of Rabbinic Theology: Major Concepts of the Talmud*, in his chapter on "Forgiveness and Reconciliation," 1909), teaches that the majority of the rabbis understood that, for the sin offering to be meaningful, it had to be accompanied by repentance and the confession of sins. What mattered was not so much the offering itself, but the quality of the intention and purpose which motivated it in the first place.

The offering is not an automatic escape procedure to expiate sin; rather, it expiates sin because it is an expression of a genuinely contrite spirit. It is this genuine disposition that really matters. In other words, God accepts the offering and the offerer's repentance because of the purity of intent out of which the sin offering was brought. Therefore, the expression of true repentance reconciles us with God, and this reconciliation makes it possible for us to begin afresh.

This is the key to answering your question. Your question assumes that some specific sin, some forbidden act was committed—in the process of the priestly appointment, in the delivery of a child, or in a Nazarite's vow— which required a sin offering. It seems to me that it is mistaken to look for that specific sin. We should not be looking at this offering as a curative to some particular forbidden act, the nature of which is unclear and unexplained. Rather the *hatat* ought to be understood as part of the general preparation for the new existence that comes after these events. In each case, the person involved stands before God at a new level of holiness.

To use the example in this actual Torah portion, Aaron and his sons are about to embark on a new stage of their lives, ministering to God as priests, a new level of holiness. The woman giving birth who shares with God in an act of creation, motherhood, is entering a new level of holiness. Admittedly my approach is not so evident in the case of the Nazarite, in that the sin offering is made after the completion of the vow.

Here, we could follow Ramban, who indicates an actual sin is being committed when the Nazarite forsakes his vow and is again ready to defile himself with worldly passions. I prefer to follow Rambam, who saw the very act of taking the vow negatively. Maimonides opposes the vow and its resulting abstinence as excessive and beyond the requirements the Torah intends. Following this perspective, the Nazarite effectively lowered his level of holiness by becoming a Nazarite.

If so, then he, too, is moving to a higher plane of holiness upon the completion of his vow. In order to be ready for this, each is required to offer a *hatat* in true repentance and desire to be reconciled with God. It is their genuinely contrite spirit which makes it possible for them to enter their new levels of holiness, their new roles in life, be it the priesthood, parenthood, or the return to usual life after the completion of a vow.

Tazria: Leviticus 12:1–13:59

Prophetical Reading
2 Kings 4:42–44, 5:1–19

Overview of Torah Portion

God gives Moses the laws for purifying oneself after childbirth, or if biblical forms of leprosy are found on the body or one's clothing.

Key Verses

"And the priest shall look at him on the seventh day, and behold, if the plague remains in its appearance and the plague has not spread in the skin, then the priest shall shut him up seven more days" (Leviticus 8:5).

"[Second *aliyah*] And the priest shall look at him again on the seventh day, and behold, if the plague is dim and the plague has not spread in the skin, then the priest shall pronounce him clean—it is a scab, and he shall wash his clothes and be clean" (Leviticus 8:6).

Discussion Question

MAKING THE BREAK: The ancient rabbis who divided the week's Torah readings, based on an oral tradition, end each section for which a person is called up to the Torah on an upbeat note. Each *aliyah* is supposed to provide spiritual optimism.

What is optimistic about seven more days of separation for someone suspected of having contracted leprosy? The very next sentence describes a clean verdict after the additional seven-day period. Why doesn't the *aliyah* end there? What is the rabbis' implicit message?

Shammai Engelmayer

The question starts with the premise that the glass is half empty. Actually, it is half full.

The first *aliyah*, in fact, does end on a positive note. The priest discovers that the afflicted person is not suffering from leprosy after all. The skin anomaly has not spread. In seven more days, the afflicted one will be "pure." (The sixth *aliyah*, in which afflicted clothing is discussed, ends similarly, by the way.)

If there is a special lesson meant here, it is that an *aliyah*, whenever possible, should also begin on a positive note. If the first *aliyah* had ended after the next sentence, as the question suggests, then the second *aliyah* would begin on a down note.

Even if the first *aliyah* did end on a sour note, this does not necessarily conflict with the rule since, according to a variety of sources, it has nothing to do with individuals. What the Torah reader is urged not to do is end on a note detrimental to Israel. (Maimonides, among others, does not limit the rule to Israel only. The *Shulchan Aruch*, on the other hand, seems to so limit it. I say, "seems" because the qualifier is added by the commentators; see, for example, the *Mishnah Berurah* on the subject. (The *Mishnah Berurah* is a commentary on the *Shulchan Aruch* written by Rabbi Yisrael Meir Ha-Cohen, z'l, known also as the *Chafetz Chaim*. The plain text, however, offers no limitation.)

Common sense provides the reason. Reading the Torah is supposed to be a positive experience. Ending a section on a sour note, therefore, is to be avoided in order to keep the experience positive.

It must be pointed out that this is not a rabbinic decree with a capital "R" (meaning the sages of the talmudic age, whose decisions carry the imprimatur of *tora mi'sinai*). Even during the days of Maimonides, where each *aliyah* began and ended was still at the discretion of the reader(s). When the rule was finally promulgated to keep the ending upbeat is uncertain; but it is certain that the talmudic sages had no such hard and fast rule.

This can be seen in an interesting discussion in BT Megillah 31b regarding the blessings and curses of Leviticus 26. The reading of Leviticus 26 should begin before the section and end after the section, and no break may be made in between. On the other hand, we are told, the blessings and curses section in Deuteronomy 28 may be broken up at the discretion of the reader. The difference between the two is that, "In the former, Israel is referred to in the plural and Moshe pronounced them (the curses) on behalf of the Almighty, while in the latter Israel is referred to in the singular and Moshe pronounced them on his own behalf."

This would suggest two things: That there was no hard and fast rule against ending an *aliyah* on a sour note; and that, if such a rule did exist in talmudic times, it was restricted to sour notes about Israel as a whole, not individuals. Even this has its exception, as the *aliyot* for *Ha'azinu* (Deuteronomy 32) demonstrate. In any case, the rule is not violated here. The verse refers to an individual, and the note is a positive one.

That leaves us with the question of why the *aliyah* did not end with the next sentence, which is decidedly more upbeat. The answer would seem to be because the verse that follows it is a negative one and should be avoided whenever possible.

Why it should be avoided requires returning to the discussion in *Megillah*. There, the premise was that the curses section in Leviticus had to be read as one section. The rabbis of blessed memory ruled that verses from before and after should be added, however, in order that blessings not be made on curses. (The blessings in question are the blessings made before and after each *aliyah*.)

It is possible that, in sectioning each parshah into seven parts, the decision was made to avoid starting *aliyot* on a negative note in order not to make a blessing on such topics.

Joseph Ozarowski

The Torah *aliyot* are indeed supposed to end, if not on a positive note, then at least on a neutral or non-negative note. So how can we explain that this *aliyah* ends advising the *metzora*—the sufferer of this skin disease, called in Hebrew *tzara'at* (which is most definitely not the same as the medical malady known today as leprosy)—to stay in isolation another seven days, when the plague has stopped spreading but has not gone away?

In fact, the Torah does this again later in the *sidra* regarding *tzara'at* of the clothing (13:54): If the plague has not spread but remains on the garment, "Then the *Kohen* shall command that they wash that in which is the plague and isolate it for another seven days." And this marks the end of the seventh *aliyah*!

I decided to attempt to find something positive in this second isolation. There are several approaches to the whole question of *tzara'at*. A minority approach, hinted at by a few medieval commentators, as well as some pre-moderns, assumes that there are medical and hygienic elements to the treatment of the *metzora*. (See Ibn Ezra on 13:2, though later on 13:45 he suggests a different approach—that *tzara'at* may be punishment for evil actions; see also Ralbag on *tzara'at* of clothing; see also Hertz's introductory comments to the *sidra*.) According to this approach, there is no real explanation for the break at the verse regarding the second isolation. Besides, as the dermatologist in my *shul* who is so fond of this section of the Torah always explains to me, there is no modern medical support for any of the measures suggested by the Torah for any known skin disease today.

Another minority view (Abarbenel, for example; see also Hertz) views *tzara'at* totally in a context of *tum'ah* and *tahara*—ritual purity and impurity, but not necessarily as a result of Divine punishment for evil deeds. According to this thinking, I also could not find or develop a reason for the break.

The vast majority of commentators, from the rabbis (Hazal) through most of the classic commentaries, as well as almost all Traditionalist moderns, assume that *tzara'at* is God's punishment or result in Biblical times for the sin of *lashon hara* (speaking slanderous gossip against one's neighbors). One proof for this approach is the incident where Miriam spoke ill against her brother Moshe, and was struck with *tzara'at* for it (see Numbers 12 and Deuteronomy 24:8–9). It is possible to see the various practices and rituals surrounding the treatment to the *metzora* as having social significance, and many of the commentaries interpret the two *sidrot* this way. We might say that the isolation has therapeutic value, teaching the *metzora* that there are consequences from living with other people.

Thus, when the plague has stopped spreading but has not fully gone away, the sufferer stays in isolation for another seven days. The same procedure is followed with clothing mentioned before the seventh *aliyah*. If the isolation is seen as therapy, then the second isolation can be viewed not as a bad thing, but as a necessary and good thing. Anytime one is trying to cure him-or herself of various emotional or psychological maladies, the process itself can be seen as beneficial.

In modern-day thinking, people recovering from drug or alcohol addiction (perhaps an example of a modern-day *metzora*?) can see their recovery as a good thing. Thus, the Torah specifies a second isolation, noting that the plague has stopped, but some more therapy is necessary. This is not a negative note but a positive one and an appropriate place for an *aliyah* to stop.

David Sofian

Let's begin by noting that a similar question could have been asked about the break between the sixth and seventh *aliyot* in this parshah. There, the subject is a garment suspected of *tzara'at*. The sixth *aliyah* ends with

Leviticus 13:54, "then the priest will command and they will wash that which the plague is in, and he will shut it up a second set of seven days."

Although now we are only considering a garment, we could nevertheless ask "what is optimistic about seven days more of separation for a garment suspected of having *tzara'at*?" And again, the matter is resolved in the very next verse. Given that the parshah discusses *tzara'at* in terms of people first and then garments, and, that we find the *aliyot* dealing with each broken in a similar fashion, it is clear that this is not an accident, that the rabbis intended to teach something with this division.

Rashi points us towards a possible understanding in his comment to chapter 13:46. The Torah tells us in this verse that the one afflicted with *tzara'at* shall be unclean and will dwell alone outside of the camp. Rashi, referring to the classical rabbis, explains why this person is not placed with others who are unclean. Why must this one dwell alone? He says it is because the *tzaru'a* caused a separation through evil talk between a husband and a wife, or between a person and a friend. Therefore, in like manner, the *tzaru'a* is separated from the community. Thus Rashi is teaching us that the *tzara'at* is a punishment for the moral defect of using slanderous or divisive speech.

S'forno helps us also in his comment to Leviticus 14:36. There, the Torah is speaking about *tzara'at* in a house and how the house in question was to be empty before the priest would go and see it. S'forno comments that the house had to be empty to give the owners time for repentance and prayer. The plague, again, is a punishment for moral defect, hence time is allowed for proper repentance.

Now, let's return to the actual question. Where is the spiritual optimism in the additional seven days? If we understand the plague of *tzara'at* as punishment for a moral defect, then we can also understand the Torah's mandating a period of waiting as a gift of time so the one afflicted can properly repent and pray.

The rabbis repeatedly teach that the gates of repentance are always open and that God forgives the truly penitent. It is this notion, hinted at in the breaking of the *aliyot*, that is spiritually uplifting.

Metzora: Leviticus 14:1–15:33

Prophetical Reading
2 Kings 7:3–20

Overview of Torah Portion

God gives Moses further laws for purifying oneself after contracting a biblical form of leprosy and for purifying a house or other belongings that have become ritually impure.

Key Verses

"And the Lord spoke to Moses, saying, 'This shall be the law of the leper in the day of his cleansing. He shall be brought to the priest . . . the priest shall look, and behold, if the plague of leprosy is healed in the leper . . . [the priest] shall pronounce him clean . . . and he that is to be cleansed shall wash his clothes and shave off all his hair and bathe himself in water, and he shall be clean; and after that he shall enter the camp, but shall live outside his tent seven days. And it will be on the seventh day that he shall shave all his hair off his head and his beard and his eyebrows . . . and he shall wash his clothes and shall wash his flesh in water and he shall be clean'" (Leviticus 14:1–9).

Discussion Question

BIBLICAL SHAVE: A scarlet letter in the Torah? An individual who returns to his community *sans* all hair is unmistakably marked as a former leper—someone in whom the symptoms were found, but is now ruled clean. Where is the concern for the person's public embarrassment? His right to privacy? If leprosy is considered a punishment for certain types of sins, are the plague itself and the quarantine punishment not in themselves? Why add the additional public shame?

Shammai Engelmayer

There is no scarlet letter here, only a visible assurance that this person is just fine, thank you, and there is no need for him or her to be shunned.

Consider what is going on here. Because the people are unable to loosen the hold paganism and its attendant superstitions have on them, they tend to see things through warped lenses. Thus, visible skin ailments of the kind discussed in Leviticus were seen as punishments from God for sins of some kind. (The traditional view is that this particular skin disorder was a punishment for evil speech.)

However, they were also seen for what they were—potential threats to public health. Many of these ailments were contagious and, in the close quarters of an Israelite encampment (and later, village), contagious diseases could have had a devastating effect on the population.

Because of the paganistic proclivities of the people, it made sense to put the responsibility for the public's health in the hands of the priesthood. After all, who better to deal with heaven-sent matters than the man of God? The people were more likely to obey the priests in such matters than secular authorities.

For the priests, that meant having to act quickly to separate a potentially infected person from the rest of the community, and to determine as soon as possible whether that person was truly contagious. Those who were truly infected and contagious were isolated for as long as it took, even if that meant for the rest of their lives. Those who were not contagious, or whose diseases ran their course, were just as quickly reintegrated into society as they were excised from it.

Removal of the hair from face and scalp was a prerequisite to such determination. The priest needed to view all of the skin, not just a part of it. He needed to know for certain that no other lesions were lurking on the body of the afflicted person. Facial and scalp hair have a tendency to obscure such lesions (and any other anomalies). Thus, all of this hair had to go before the person could be released from isolation.

When that person returned to camp, however, the lack of hair did not cry out, "Sinner!" Rather, it testified to the fact that this man or woman was not infectious, and it was safe to go up to him or her and say, "welcome home."

Even if you did not trust the abilities of the purifying priest, you could be assured of this person's "purity" because you could see for yourself that there are no lesions, even in places normally hidden from view.

At the same time you, who cling to your paganistic beliefs, can see with your own eyes that this person is free of sin; that "punishment" has been lifted; that the hairless person is worthy once again of being part of *Klal Yisrael*. The lack of hair is thus a badge of honor, in that respect, and not a scarlet letter.

Joseph Ozarowski

Your question is compounded when one realizes that the Torah prohibits shaving certain body parts and facial hair because this seems to imitate various idolatrous rites. (See the *Meshekh Hokhma* of Rabbi Meir Simcha of Dvinsk, who frames the question, but unfortunately does not provide an answer!)

Before we explore possible answers, it is important to note that there is some halakhic question as to how much body hair is to be shaved. The halakhic midrash *Torat Kohanim* mentions two opinions. Rabbi Akiba requires all body hair to be shaven, except nasal hair that cannot easily be seen. Rabbi Yishmael requires only hair normally visible to the eye to be shaven and does not require underarm and pubic hair to be shaven. Maimonides rules like the first view.

It is not necessary to view the skin disease *tzara'at* or its treatment as punishment. Following my answer in the previous section, we can see several possibilities. If *tzara'at* is a health issue, then the shaving of hair can simply be seen as a health measure or consequence. After all, people undergoing various cancer therapies often lose their hair. While this may look strange to some, it certainly is no punishment or shame. If this is the case, then the community must provide an extra measure of understanding for the individual.

However, if the treatment of the *metzora* is seen as therapy for the sin of *lashon hara*, then the isolation procedure, while not considered punishment, is indeed not enough. My kids and congregants agreed that shaving is part of the *metzora's* reintegration into society. And, because the sin of *lashon hara* is so great, perhaps the sufferer must undergo a last bit of public exposure because of the damage he or she has done to others with words.

The Torah highlights three segments of hair to be shaved: The head, the beard, and the eyebrows. *Kli Yakar* suggests that these are symbolic of the three types of misdeeds for which one is struck with *tzara'at*. *Gasot ruach* (haughtiness of the spirit) is symbolized by the head. In English, the phrase, "when something goes to one's head," denotes an inflated ego. *Lashon hara* is symbolized by the beard that surrounds the mouth. *Tzarot ayin* (narrowness of the eye) denotes miserliness and looking at the world or other people angrily.

According to *Kli Yakar*, the shaving of the hair is not meant to publicly embarrass the *metzora*. Rather, it reminds him or her that before he or she re-enters the human community after isolation, there is a social reason for the isolation that the *tzara'at* required.

David Sofian

Judging from some of the rabbinic reaction to the *m'tzora*, the concern with this disease was certainly great. In *Midrash Vayikra Rabbah* 16:3, Rabbi Johanan prohibited going near a person so afflicted. Rabbi Meir would not eat eggs that came from the vicinity of lepers. Resh Lakish would throw stones at a leper seen in the city and, Rabbi Eleazar ben Rabbi Simeon would hide if he saw one.

If we read this rabbinic attitude back into biblical times, it would not be surprising that Vayikra would be more concerned with making sure that everyone knew the disease was no longer present than with the possibility of the former leper's public embarrassment. It could have been argued that it was to the person's advantage to be singled out in the way the parshah describes.

The public nature of the elaborate purification rite would have reassured everyone that the skin disease was gone and the person had been pronounced clean.

At this point it is appropriate to ask about this rabbinic reaction. Why did they react so harshly? Could it simply have been the fear of contagion? If so, that would explain avoiding those who were sick but it wouldn't explain Resh Lakish's willingness to throw stones at them. That level of hostility is much harder to grasp. I think this response comes from a sense that the *metzora* deserves the disease.

In my comment to *parshat Tazria*, I pointed out that Rashi associated the disease of *tzara'at* with evil talk. Rashi wants us to look at this disease as Divine punishment for using improper speech. *Midrash Vayikra Rabbah* makes this same point with its famous comment on the word *metzora* itself. *Vayikra Rabbah* teaches in chapter 16:1 that the word *metzora* alludes to a person who utters evil reports.

This conclusion is reached by playing on the sound of the word *metzora*, breaking it apart into *motzee shem ra*—someone who brings forth an evil report. In other words, according to this, whenever the Torah uses the word *metzora*, it is not so much talking about a person with a skin disease as it is talking about a person with a moral defect.

The disease is God's punishment for the hurtful speech. The sufferer deserves his suffering. Resh Lakish's willingness to throw stones is an expression of his disdain for the sinfulness of the *metzora*.

I bring this up because it not only explains Resh Lakish's hostility but also may help explain the need for a public rite of cleansing. Given the view that the illness is divine punishment, then being cured must be a sign that God has ended the punishment and forgiveness has been granted.

The Divine initiation and termination of the disease is also emphasized when we consider that, throughout these sections of *Vayikra*, the priest never does anything to cure the disease but only determines the status of it and then acts accordingly. Whether the one afflicted continues to have it or is cured is in God's hands alone.

S'forno's thought also mentioned in my comment to *parshat Tazria* is relevant here, as well. S'forno tells us that the reason a house thought to have *tzara'at* must be empty before the priest goes in to see it is to give the owners time for repentance and prayer.

In other words, the way to cure the disease is to correct the moral defect with prayer and repentance. The same would apply in terms of the person healed. Seen this way, the elaborate cleansing process is not about singling the person out as a former leper but is expressive of the successful internal cleansing, the real *teshuvah* that the person has completed.

Having said all this, I must add that I personally find any notion that disease is a form of deserved divine retribution to be completely unacceptable. This way of thinking about God is horrific, for it easily leads to the conclusion that God intends for everyone who is suffering to endure that suffering. This would mean that even children stricken by disease somehow deserve that disease. Those rabbis mentioned who avoided people with *tzara'at* were bad enough in that they contributed to an atmosphere that fostered blaming the victim for his distress. But to scornfully throw stones at them, as is reported about Resh Lakish, is disgraceful.

Rather than seeing those who are afflicted as deserving of their pain and therefore contemptible, we should follow the example found in tractate Sanhedrin of the Babylonian Talmud, which relates a story about Rabbi Joshua ben Levi and Elijah. It is an involved story, but when Joshua ben Levi asks Elijah where he can find the *Mashiach*, Elijah tells him to look near the gate to the city sitting among the poor and the ill. Joshua ben Levi finds that the *Mashiach* is there taking care of these people.

As I read this passage, it is clear that such people are not being blamed but require our compassion and concern. This is the example we should follow and the attitude we should have toward the sick and suffering.

Acherei Mot:
Leviticus 16:1–18:30

Prophetical Reading
Ezekiel 22:1–19

Overview of Torah Portion

God tells Moses the proper conduct for Aaron and the priestly class, as well as the proper decorum for all the Hebrews' bringing of sacrifices. Commanding the Children of Israel not to emulate the Egyptians or Canaanites, God lists banned sexual relationships.

Key Verses

"And Moses said to Aaron and to Eleazar and to Itamar, his sons, 'Do not let the hair of your heads go loose, and do not rend your clothes, that you die not'" (Leviticus 10:6).

"And you shall not go from the door of the tent of meeting, lest you die" (Leviticus 10:7).

"And the Lord spoke to Aaron, saying, 'Wine and strong drink you shall not drink, you and your sons with you, when you enter the tent of meeting, that you die not'" (Leviticus 10:8–9).

"And the Lord said to Moses, 'Speak to Aaron your brother, that he not come at all times into the holy place . . . that he die not'" (Leviticus 16:1–2).

"And [Aaron] shall put the incense upon the fire before the Lord, that the cloud of the cover may cover the ark-cover, that he die not" (Leviticus 16:13).

Discussion Question

AVOIDING DEATH: Aaron and his sons are originally assigned the priestly duties as a means to educate the Children of Israel, to aid the process of repentance. Now, following the death of two of Aaron's sons for offering a "strange fire," the emphasis shifts from the carrot to the stick—do this or that so you won't die. Is this change more apparent than real? Was the erring sons' malfeasance sufficient to radically change all the priests' prime incentive? Does this indicate that we should perform *mitzvot* mainly to prevent death, rather than to serve some more noble purpose?

Shammai Engelmayer

This is the *karet*-and-stick approach to *halakha*: Stick to the rules, or suffer *karet* (death at God's hand when He decides to impose the penalty).

Nothing has changed since Aharon's sons brought their strange fire. These death threats are part of a system of belief rooted in paganism and superstition. The people—and their teachers, the priests—wanted the system and believed in it. So God uses the system's own mechanisms to moderate behavior.

In the ancient world, the presumptive gods were feared for their pettiness. Ba'al will get even someday for a slight. Horus will make you pay for your lack of support. As for the Olympians, to them people are nothing but toys to play with. In any case, read Homer.

The Israelites, as already noted, believed such things. They did not believe Moshe when he said this is not the way of God. And from the moment they began to collect the precious metals for their golden calf, it was clear that Moshe was not going to change their minds. The sacrificial system that served as the main mode of pagan worship was adapted, therefore, to the worship of the one true God.

It was stripped of its pagan veneer and turned into a sacred service, but its effectiveness was only as lasting as the people's beliefs in the pagan. As soon as they wised up to the truth--that God had other ideas about how He was to be served—the system would collapse and make way for the three T's: *teshuvah*, *tefilla*, and *tsitdkut* (penitence, prayer, and performance of righteous acts, or three Ps in English).

Until that time, of course, the easiest way to gain compliance was to use superstition. "You believe that if you cross a god he or she will kill you?

Fine, then cross Me and I will kill you—in My own time and in My own way."

In fact, that is the beauty of *karet*. Since you never know when the sinner will meet up with his or her punishment, whenever that person dies and in whatever manner can be attributed to God. It is a no-lose proposition for Him. People will die in any case; if others believe the death was a penalty executed, so much the better.

I think the real question here is not whether anything has changed, because *karet* came before Nadav and Avihu's tragedy and extends to all Israel. The question is why the special emphasis in the selected verses on the priests.

That is related to Nadav and Avihu. Their deaths quite literally put the fear of God into Aharon and his sons. God understood that the sacrificial system He adapted could easily be turned back into the pagan system from which it arose. He knew that, having invested a priesthood, He was at their mercy, for they could lead the people astray. So He let them know that the Lord fights strange fire with friendly fire—His own. The graphic message in the deaths of Nadav and Avihu was reinforced by repeated references to sudden death if the priests violated God's rules.

Having seen what happened to their kinsman, the priests had no choice but to believe.

Joseph Ozarowski

It was incredibly strange to encounter your question this weekend. You see, my grandfather died this past Friday, and the circumstances of his death were rather odd; they have been on our minds this entire Shabbat. He was not sick at all; in fact, he was so healthy that in spite of his ninety-plus years, he had a disdain for doctors and hospitals. Yet, he had checked in for cataract surgery, which was quite successful.

At some point in the middle of the night, it seems he attempted to get out of bed when he should not have. Knowing him, he would have never asked for help, for he was feisty and independent. He was found at the foot of his bed in a pool of blood. He lapsed into a deep coma from which he never came out. So, all Shabbat, we were second-guessing ourselves about what we should or should not have done to prevent this tragedy.

In the same way, it is possible to approach this entire chapter and your question as reaction to the sad death of Aaron's two sons. Everything is being second-guessed—"Don't do this or that, lest you shall die." Once one has been touched by death, everything becomes an issue, and people are just naturally extra sensitive to each action. Rashi's comments on Leviticus 10:6 and 16:2 follow this idea: If you do this, you will also die thusly.

As the funeral took place and the week of *shiva* went on, we all realized that there was very little anyone could have done to prevent my *zeidie's* death. The hospital staff were super, and it did not seem as if there was negligence or malfeasance. In the same sense, the warnings of death do not have to be seen exclusively as a reaction to the tragedy. Both my congregants and my kids in discussion suggested that the danger of being too close to the source of Divine energy was there all along.

The tragedy just made it more apparent. We all know that there are areas that one is simply not supposed to enter because of danger. The image of the skull and crossbones and the note, "Warning—authorized personnel only," on electrified fences comes to my mind. It only seems more recognizable after the tragedy. As *Sifte Hakahmim* (a super-commentary on Rashi) on Leviticus 16:2, 16:13, and Ramban on 10:7, put it, "*Mi-mashma lav, ata shome'a hen*," implied from the negative, one can hear the positive. The Gemara in *Yoma* 53a suggests that, while the threat of the consequence of death was emphasized after the tragedy, the warning in 16:2, "for I appear in the cloud . . . ," was uttered before the tragedy. Sometimes, people need negative reinforcement to teach a positive lesson.

There are, of course, other connections between the tragedy and the penalty warning. Many of the commentators (see Hirsch, for example, as well as Nehama Leibowitz's essay on the subject) suggest that Nadav and Avihu acted out of a religiosity without guidelines; this is what the term *aish zara* (a strange fire) means. The Torah wants our devotion and religious fervor, but within halakhic parameters. Otherwise, it could lead to the type of unbridled passion that incurs tragedy. We have all seen how nations inspired by religious fervor and devotion to a deity commit the most horrifying atrocities one can imagine.

We as Jews are not immune to this danger. The horrific and tragic assassination of Israeli Prime Minister Yitzhak Rabin in November 1995 by a *kipa*-wearing, God-fearing religious Jew is an ample illustration of this. The purpose of halakhah is to give a structure for our religious passion. And we must know that there are both good as well as tragic consequences for our religious acts. Thus, death was referred to in the subsequent warnings to Aaron and his descendants regarding their religious leadership.

David Sofian

Midrash *Vayikra Rabbah's* twentieth chapter is also very interested in the tragedy of Nadab and Abihu's deaths. Although the material there is specifically about their deaths, several options for answering your question are suggested.

To begin with, *Vayikra Rabbah* wonders if we are capable of understanding in a meaningful way why God allows certain consequences to flow from our acts. Our inability to comprehend God's motives is expressed in the first paragraph of chapter twenty by giving biblical examples of how the same consequence resulted from both righteousness and wickedness. In one of the illustrations given, it is pointed out that both King David and the sinner Nebuchadnezzar ruled for forty years, even though David built the Temple and Nebuchadnezzar destroyed it. (This midrash credits David with building the Temple because it was his idea, and he would have followed through if God had not stayed his hand.)

It is beyond our understanding why God treats the righteous and the wicked the same in this case. The second paragraph of the chapter goes even further with this point by having God acknowledge that personal righteousness does not even necessarily result in personal happiness. Again, several biblical examples are given of righteous people whose righteousness vexes them. For instance, the midrash reminds us that Abraham was blessed with a son when he was 100 years of age, but he was also told by God to offer Isaac up as a burnt offering. His righteousness did not bring him happiness.

We are additionally told how Elisheba, the daughter of Amminadab, Aaron's wife, did not receive happiness in this world. Even though she had the joy of being Moses' sister-in-law and Nahshon's sister, she nevertheless suffered the loss of Nadab and Abihu. Her righteousness did not bring her happiness. God's motive for this is not within our grasp. It is simply not fruitful to try to determine God's motives here.

This resigned response to the reality of unexplained or undeserved death is dramatically brought home in the next paragraph of the midrash. There, we find a story of a dignitary who, at the marriage feast for his son, sends that son upstairs to bring down a barrel. As the son is doing so, a snake bites him and he dies. The house is turned from a place of joy to one of mourning. The story ends with the father saying to the guests, "you came to bring my son under the bridal canopy, now you must carry him to his grave."

We do not know why this has occurred, particularly at the time of the fulfillment of a *mitzvah*. Just as Aaron responded with silence to the deaths of Nadab and Abihu, the father here is resigned to reality. He only knows what must be done next.

These sections of *Vayikra Rabbah* then offers a kind of response to your question. Just as the young man's death goes unexplained but accepted, so, too, we must accept the assurances of death in your key verses as the warning they are, without genuinely explaining why they are made.

The appeal of this approach is that it recognizes that, for us, death is part of the profound mystery at the core of life.

The last paragraph (12) of chapter 20 gives us another approach. Here, instead of counseling a form of resigned acceptance, an attempt is made to draw a positive lesson from the deaths of Nadab and Abihu. This approach does not necessarily explain God's motives, yet it does find a comforting reason for the reality as presented. The conclusion is not so much that we know God acted in order to teach the given lesson, only that the lesson can be learned from what God did.

This is accomplished, in our case, by noting which events are in close proximity in the Torah text and then giving reasons for that proximity. Rabbi Judah concludes that the proximity of Aaron's death to the discussion of the breaking of the tablets teaches that his death was as grievous to God as the breaking of those tablets. Rabbi Abba ben Abina concludes that the proximity of Miriam's death to the discussion of the Red Heifer's ashes teaches that the death of the righteous effects atonement.

In like manner, Rabbi Hiyya ben Abba concludes the same lesson, only he derives it from the proximity of the death of Aaron's sons to the Day of Atonement. The noble purpose in the key verses might be found by applying this lesson to these verses. Comfort is derived in the knowledge that, should the priest's death result, that death atones for the sin committed.

A third approach is the one I find most appealing. We should see the key verses not as threats or warnings, but as declarations of God's love and concern for Aaron and the priesthood. Assuming a negative motivation to performing God's commands was perceived by the priests, that negative motivation would have resulted from the very deaths of Nadab and Abihu. Since they died without clear explanation, the key verses are providing that explanation.

Effectively, with these verses, God explains what Aaron and the priesthood must avoid so as not to make Nadab's and Abihu's mistake. These verses are not expressing judgment, they are expressing mercy.

The rabbis in chapter 20 of *Vayikra Rabbah* reflect this approach also. Material there also tries to clarify what Nadab and Abihu did wrong. For example, paragraph six tells us that their deaths were caused by their own impudence. We learn that they gave a legal decision in their master Moses' presence. Following God's example in the key verses, the rabbis want us to understand Nadab's and Abihu's mistake so that we can avoid it.

Then, to me, these key verses do not represent a change in incentive to performing the mitzvot in order to avoid death. They are warnings emanating from God's love. God does not want us to die, but to live. I would read these verses in the light of Ezekiel 33:11, "Say to them: As I live—declares the Eternal God—it is not My desire that the wicked shall die, but that the wicked turn from his ways and live. Turn back, turn back from your evil ways, that you may not die, O House of Israel."

Kedoshim:
Leviticus 19:1–20:27

Prophetical Reading
Amos 9:7–15

Overview of Torah Portion

God tells Moses a series of ethical, agricultural, sexual, and ritual laws. Among the precepts are: honor for one's parents, consideration for the less fortunate, and favorable judgment of one's neighbor.

Key Verses

"Do not stand by your neighbor's blood" (Leviticus 19:16).
   "Any person from the Children of Israel, or of the strangers who reside in Israel, who gives of his seed to Molech shall surely be put to death. . . . And if the people of the land hide their eyes from the man when he gives from his seed to Molech, not putting him to death, I will set My face upon that man, and upon his family, and will cut him off" (Leviticus 20:2–5).

Discussion Question

Taking a stand: The Torah, in commanding the Jewish nation not to stand by a neighbor's blood, is issuing a societal imperative in idiomatic language—when someone is threatened, you must get involved. But the statement, couched in the negative, hardly rings like a call to arms. Why does the Torah not declare, "Help your neighbor!" or call for some other specific action?

In condemning the followers of Molech, an ancient Semitic group that practiced child sacrifice, God unambiguously rejects the ability to say "I didn't see"—if you turn your gaze away from a sin, He will step in. Why not a similar declaration when blood is about be to spilled, when a life is in danger? What is the difference between the specific threat to children of Molechism and the general danger to one's neighbor?

Shammai Engelmayer

Before we can answer these two questions, a third must be asked and answered, for in it rests the answers to these: What in the name of heaven does any of this have to do with the priesthood? Here we are, smack in the middle of Leviticus, *Torat Kohanim*, the Laws of the Priests, and we are being given laws for all Israel regarding such matters as forbidden sexual unions, acceptable foods, the ways of dealing with neighbors and strangers, and so on. What are these laws, most of which have homes elsewhere in the Torah, doing in a how-to book for cult priests?

The answer is simply because Israel *is* a kingdom of priests. Strip away the pagan trappings of the sacrificial cult and you are left with Israel and its mission: to teach, by the example of their own lives, how lives should be lived. When the people wise up to the fact that they do not need to kill animals in order to serve God, a how-to book for cult priests will become passé.

By inserting into its very center the so-called Holiness Code, we are being told that the *Torat Kohanim* is for all time, but especially for when the sacrificial cult is no more, and the people realize that all Israelites are God's *kohanim*. Chip away at Leviticus all you want—this is its heart and here it is not bound by time, place, or family lineage.

And how are "we priests" supposed to act? One way is by extending our hand to all. We are to love our neighbor as we would ourselves be loved (Leviticus 19:18) and, in the same way, also to love the stranger (Leviticus 19:34). And, lest you think that "stranger," or *ger* in Hebrew, refers to the proselyte, the Torah makes clear its intent, when it adds, "for you were *gerim* in the land of Egypt."

Extending our hand also means not standing by idly when a person's life is in danger, be that person a neighbor or a stranger (for "the stranger among you shall be considered by you just as the homeborn," says Leviticus 19:33). However, it is not enough to "help" in such situations; you "shall not stand idly by your neighbor's blood." Your help must truly be of help.

Assume, for example, that a person is drowning in a lake, but you cannot swim. Is it sufficient to call 911? That is helping, but it is idle, meaningless help. By the time a rescue team arrives, that person will be dead. By all means, dial 911; but first get something out to that person that he or she can hold on to until rescuers arrive.

Or, let us use the example cited by the extra-mishnaic commentary to Leviticus, the *Sifra*. There, the situation is a person on trial for his or her life. You have evidence that may save him or her. The *Sifra* says you must reveal that evidence because of this law.

Now, if the Torah had merely said, as the question here proposes, "help your neighbor," it could be argued that contributing to a fund to hire the best criminal defense lawyer in the country fulfills the *mitzvah*. That is not what the Torah says, however. It is more emphatic—"Do not stand idly by your neighbor's blood."

The key is in the word "idly." Your help cannot be half-hearted, "idle." What you do to help must be the most effective in the situation, even if it is not successful. Maybe your evidence will not sway the jury, but it is exculpatory and, therefore, far more effective than hiring Johnnie Cochran, Robert Shapiro, and colleagues. Maybe the log you throw to the drowning person will not save him or her in the long run, but that person has a better chance of surviving with it than without it.

As for *Molech* worship, this has less to do with turning one's gaze away from sin and more to do with how morally depraved you and your society have become.

Molech worship, as the question notes, involved the sacrificing of children. This was acceptable in many parts of the pagan world. However, it is not acceptable to the One True God. This is the point of the *Akedah*. Avraham clearly believes that child sacrifice is a proper mode of worship because he utters no protest. God put Avraham and Yitzchak through the ordeal precisely to stay Avraham's hand and to exchange Yitzchak for a ram. It was His way of demonstrating, as graphically as possible, that He does not condone the sacrifice of human beings, period.

Israel does not need to be given a law against child sacrifice to know that this is not God's way. After all, the people know what happened in the *Akedah* story. Thus, if someone violates God's will by sacrificing a child, be that person an Israelite or a resident alien, that person must die. If he does not die, it is because the community has sunk so low that it sees nothing wrong with this corrupted mode of worship.

The matter goes further, however. Human sacrifice is only a small step from animal sacrifice. In bad times, when normal sacrifices seem to avail naught, someone could get it into his or her head that a higher level of life is required by God. Indeed, at least three kings of Judah—Achaz, Menashe, and his son, Amon—condoned and even participated in child sacrifice, and the neighbors of Yiftach (Jephthah) allowed him to sacrifice his daughter in fulfillment of a poorly constructed and invalid pledge. The prophet Michah would also seem to confirm this when he says (Micah 6:7), "Shall I give my firstborn for my transgressions?" Obviously, his answer is "no," just as God's answer is "no." This is not the way the priest-kingdom of God is to behave.

The situations, thus, are clearly different. In the case of the person whose life is in danger, it is possible for the one who sees the threat to seize the opportunity to save a life. In the case of *Molech* worship gone unchecked, the people are beyond the power to see right from wrong. God must step in before the people sink so low that even He cannot save them.

Joseph Ozarowski

Actually, the Torah does declare and call for positive specific action to help the next person. It is found just two verses later, "Love your neighbor as you would yourself." Rabbi Akiba in the *Sifra* (a rabbinic midrash) considers this verse a *klal gadol*, a fundamental principle of the Torah. As many of the commentaries (Ramban and Hirsch are typical) indicate, we are bidden to act in a loving manner, aiding and assisting others with acts of *chesed* (lovingkindness). Thus, this verse acts as counterpoint to the other one about not standing by your neighbor's blood. The fact is, humans need both positive as well as negative instruction to build a humane society. The Torah has the full measure of both.

The beauty of *parashat Kedoshim* is the richness of law and ethics found within. These include general fundamental principles, as we have just seen, as well as specific rules such as the decrees regarding *Molech* worship. *Molech* worship is considered by the Torah to be particularly heinous because of the atrocity of human child sacrifice involved. It seems to me that *Molech* worship constitutes a particular danger to the moral nature of society.

Thus, the Torah addresses it as a crime from which one cannot easily stand away. If we do, we risk destroying ourselves in the process. In terms of your specific question, we can say that turning away from stopping *Molech* worship is the most extreme example of not idly standing by the blood of one's neighbor.

During most years, *parashat Kedoshim* falls out near *Yom Ha'shoah*, the period in which Jews and indeed many other decent individuals commemorate the horrors that befell our people during the Holocaust. If there is any message that we can discern more than one-half century after the end of World War II, it is that saying "I didn't see" is not a morally acceptable position in the face of horror and atrocity. The Nazis were the epitome of twentieth century *Molech* worship.

Among the six million *kedoshim* (holy martyrs and victims), the Nazis murdered a million and a half Jewish children on their altar of death and destruction. Their's was certainly an idolatry of death. The Torah reminds us that in face of such evil, no one can turn away their gaze; this is what most of the so-called "civilized" world did in allowing the Holocaust to take place.

The Torah tells us not to stand idly by the blood of our neighbor, but even more specifically commands us not to turn away when children are being slaughtered to idolatry. If we turn away, we risk being cut off from the fabric of human existence and the Divine Presence that rests within.

David Sofian

Let's begin with why *Vayikra* 19:16, "do not stand upon the blood of your neighbor," is couched in the negative. Being that the phrase is idiomatic, its exact meaning is unclear. The generally accepted interpretation is that we are not allowed to stand by indifferently while our neighbor is in mortal danger. Rashi explains, if someone is drowning or being robbed, you are not allowed to be detached. You must save him or her. If so, disobeying the commandment would mean doing nothing. Then, putting the commandment in the negative actually communicates a positive action.

Commanding us not to stand upon another's blood is actually commanding positive involvement in the safety of another. Even though this is obvious, I mention it because it indicates that the phrasing of the verse is not weaker due to its negative formulation. "Do not be detached from the problems of another," is just as potent as, "be involved in those problems."

To be sure, phrasing it this way may be even more potent, for it addresses a proclivity to withdraw when faced with the need for active involvement, and this can be frightening. How much easier it often is to remain on the sidelines, to do nothing rather than something?

The Torah is teaching us that this tendency must be confronted. All the more reason to state the commandment as we find it. Passivity is a fault to overcome, therefore, it is passivity which the command forbids.

Furthermore, this idea is also stated positively in the most famous phrase from this section of Torah. Verse 18 of this same chapter commands, "You will love your neighbor as yourself." Extensive commentary has been produced on this wonderful adage. However, for our purposes here, let us note its comprehensive outlook and how it states positively the same orientation to life that verse 16 formulated negatively. How well they complement each other.

Turning to your second question, let us note that the first several verses of *Vayikra* 20 have a different focus. This is why the language is different. The issue now is not only the threatening of human life through inactivity. This threat to children comes from the idolatrous worship of *Molech*. The attraction of idolatry was powerful enough that it had to be condemned in the strongest possible terms.

In response to your questions to *parashot R'eih* and *Shoftim,* I deal with matters of idolatry and how the Torah condemns these practices in no uncertain terms. There, in *D'varim*, the point is made by focusing on the extreme case of someone who entices his own family in secret to idolatry. Here, the concern is the influentially negative example of a person willing to offer up a child. The offender is to be put to death, and if the people refuse to get involved, combatting idolatry is so critical that God personally will act.

This, then, is the difference you ask about. *Vayikra* 19:16 is teaching us about the need to be involved with our neighbor. Chapter 20:2–6 emphasizes idolatry's undermining influence on the meaning of Israelite existence.

Emor: Leviticus 21:1–24:23

Prophetical Reading
Ezekiel 44:15–31

Overview of Torah Portion

God gives Moses the directives for Aaron and the priests: How to maintain their spiritual cleanliness; how to eat the sacrificial meals; and how to bring sacrifices. God gives a comprehensive description of the holy days' observances—the Sabbath, Passover, *Shavuot*, Rosh Hashanah, Yom Kippur, *Succot*, and *Shmini Atzeret*. The priests' obligations in the sanctuary are spelled out. An Israelite man, son of an Egyptian father, is sentenced to death by stoning for blaspheming God's name.

Key Verses

"The person blaspheming God's name shall surely be put to death, all the congregation shall surely stone him. . . . The person who mortally strikes an animal shall pay for it, life for life. And if a man maims his neighbor, as he did, so shall it be done to him, blow for blow, eye for eye, tooth for tooth" (Leviticus 24:16–20).

Discussion Question

DEFENDING GOD'S NAME: Commentators have always interpreted the apparent harshness of the Torah's legal code—an eye for an eye, a tooth for a tooth—as the introduction of economic recompense. The offender does not suffer the loss of a bodily part; rather, he or she must pay for the victim's loss. Yet, the Torah speaks in uncompromising terms of the penalty for someone who dishonors God's name—death by stoning. The imperative is repeated.

Why no equivalent punishment in this case? Why such a strict verdict? God, impervious to the curses of mankind, can afford to be lenient when His honor is at stake. Who is harmed by the crime committed by a tongue?

Shammai Engelmayer

The animal world, humans included, is made up of the hunted and the hunters. There is a physical way to tell them apart: The hunted have eyes on the sides of their faces to improve their peripheral vision. The hunters have eyes in front of their faces in order to better keep an eye on their prey.

Human beings have eyes in front of their faces. We are natural predators.

What is it that keeps us from being nothing but the predators we can be? What is it that keeps us from harming animals, defoliating the fruit-bearing trees of our enemies, keeping the poor person's pledge even in the evening, and standing idly by our neighbor's blood?

The Law is all that stands between us and our darker, more natural, side. And yet, it is not the Law that stays our natures. It is from whom the Law comes that gives it its power.

Tear down God, make of Him a mockery, diminish Him in the eyes of His people, and you tear down the entire structure of the society He created. There will be nothing to stand between us and our basic nature.

That is what makes this crime of blasphemy so much greater and so deserving of the severest punishment. When an animal is set upon, one life dies. When a person is injured, one life is impaired. When God is diminished, all life is endangered.

For Israel, the problem is compounded by the Covenant. Israel exists solely because of the pact it made with God. Without God, Israel (His kingdom of priests, His treasure) has no purpose for being. Thus, not only is society in jeopardy, but the very existence of Israel is threatened.

That leads to another question: Since God is the one being blasphemed, why is He not the one to do the punishing?

For one thing, He is not the real victim. He is still God. Attack Him all you dare, nothing can ever change who He is. He will continue to be, no matter what.

The real victim is the Israelite society. It is this society, in its persona as "all the congregation," that must carry out the punishment.

Another reason is that society must show that it does not believe the blasphemer. For most people, killing another human being does not come easily, at first, because it goes against our moral (i.e., Godly) code. It is only after we have killed that the predator inside us is awakened and murder becomes easier.

If killing someone is difficult, killing someone slowly is even more so. Stoning is a slow and painful death. To kill that way requires a belief that God Himself has mandated it. As bizarre and horrible as it sounds, the people demonstrate their belief in God and their disbelief in the blasphemer by the act of stoning.

Finally, in a very public way, society must make plain what will happen to anyone who seeks to separate the people from their God. It is hard to imagine anyone watching someone being stoned who would want to face a similar death.

Joseph Ozarowski

This week's question was significant for me in that I found it difficult to come up with a good answer! I looked, researched, discussed, and dissected your query. I learned some interesting and important things, which I will share in this response. But honestly, after all is said and done, I still find it tough to compare why the Torah's tort laws of damages to humans or animals involve financial recompense, while blaspheming God is a capital offense punished by stoning.

One of the first places I look when I seek a rational answer for a question on a Torah issue that seems too ancient or unacceptable to the modern mind is in the work of Rabbi Dr. Samson Raphael Hirsch, the great German modern Orthodox scholar. Rabbi Hirsch associates the crime of cursing God with taking false oaths. In other words, when one uses God's name, one is in effect acknowledging Divine rule over everything. To do the opposite is to deny God to ourselves and to others. But when examining the issue of dishonoring God's name, he writes in *Horeb* (1962):

> "Here would be the place to deal with the most abhorrent of crimes, blasphemy, but the author recoils with horror from doing so. Whosoever [sic] hears somebody else uttering blasphemy must tear *kri'ah*, the same as for the dead."

Thanks a lot, Rav Hirsch. We know that cursing God is a major crime, but couldn't you help us by dealing with the reason?

My son, Shalom, pointed out during the Shabbat table discussion that the Torah (Exodus 21:17) also considers cursing parents a capital crime. And since the Talmud (*Kiddushin* 30b and elsewhere) points out that there are three partners in the formation of the human being—the mother, the father, and God—there may be a connection between the crimes of cursing parents and Creator. But again, why?

It is interesting to note that the death penalty in such a case is carried out by the witnesses and judges, who have to place their hands on the perpetrator's head and then complete the execution (see the *halakhic* midrash *Torat Kohanim* on this). How many capital cases could be tried in our country if this were required? Would Judge Lance Ito and the witnesses in the O. J. Simpson case have been prepared to put their hands on his head and then throw the switch on him if O. J. had been convicted? Would the judge and jury in the McVeigh Oklahoma City bombing case be prepared to do so?

Another halakhic fact which ameliorates the question (though it does not answer it completely) is that there is a distinction between cursing (*kilel*) and blasphemy (*nokev*). The Torah says, "Whosoever curses his God shall bear his sin." The commentaries (Rashi, Rashbam [Rabbi Shmuel ben Meir—Rashi's grandson—twelfth century France], S'forno) explain this as cursing God using any number of Divine names, but less than overt blasphemy. The penalty for this is either *azhara*, a warning (a ticket?) from the *Beth Din* or *karet*, Divine punishment by God in some unknown way (see previously where we discussed this concept). Actual blasphemy punished by stoning only involves employing the 72-letter ineffable Name of God, used exclusively in the Temple, and doing it publicly after being warned not to do so. This, of course, makes the actual question a moot one, for we do not even know exactly what this name is.

The Hebrew term for blasphemy (*nokev*), also means "to pierce." One who publicly blasphemes the Holiest Name of God also pierces the sense of Godliness in society. For this, the Torah prescribes a harsh penalty, for the crime goes against the framework of the ideal Jewish society, which is a Godly one. The *Sidra* has other references to this, most notably 22:32, where God says, "And you shall not profane My Holy Name, but [rather] let Me be sanctified among the children of Israel, I am the Lord Who sanctifies you." This idea of *Kiddush Hashem*, making God's Name and His ideals present in the world, contrasted with *Hilul Hashem*, profaning God's name, is a major one in Leviticus and in this *Sidra*. The story of the argument leading to the blasphemy, as well as the punishment emerging from the story, is a most extreme example of this.

There may be a message for us in all this. One of the major issues facing us today is the increasing secularity in our world at the expense of spirituality and holiness. Perhaps the Torah is warning us of the dangers inherent in a civilization and culture where there is no sense of Divine purpose or, worse, hostility to the Divine Presence. This does not necessarily mean that there is a role for religion in government affairs, as some fundamentalist Christian groups have suggested. But it is appropriate to ask whether a society with no religious or moral underpinning can survive.

But, after all is said and done, I still find it difficult to explain for the modern mind why the most extreme case of public pre-warned blasphemy involving the ineffable Name of God is punished by stoning, while torts are punished by monetary compensation to the victim.

David Sofian

The rabbis used several hermeneutical principles to draw out meaning from a given text. You seem to be using one of their principles, *Homer v'Kal*, in the question you ask about Leviticus 24:16-20. *Homer v'Kal* reasons that if something holds in a heavy or serious case (*homer*), you should expect that the same thing would hold in a less serious, or light, case (*kal*).

As I read your question, in your view the *homer* is the case of human bodily loss because someone is actually hurt. The *kal* is the case of blaspheming, or dishonoring, God who, of course, cannot really be harmed by such language. The problem, then, is: Why doesn't the remedy for the *homer* not hold for the *kal*? And more than that, why is the remedy for the *kal* so much more severe (death) than the remedy for the *homer* (economic recompense)?

You ask, in the case of blaspheming, "who is harmed by the tongue?" It is clear to me that the rabbis were certainly concerned with your final question and they did see genuine harm, but they would not have framed the situation as you do. They certainly would not have seen the case of blasphemy or dishonoring God as light or less serious than physically harming a human being.

Midrash B'reishit Rabbah helps me make this point in a comment on the creation story. In *B'reishit Rabbah* 1:5, Rabbi Yose ben Hanina indicates that whoever elevates himself at the cost of his fellow person's degradation has no share in the world to come. How much the more, then, when it is done at the expense of the glory of God! In other words, here the essence of your *Homer v'Kal* is reversed. As bad as degrading or hurting a fellow human being is, and as we see doing such means losing one's share in the world to come, nevertheless, it is even worse to degrade or dishonor God.

We also can see this rabbinic concern for proper acknowledgment of divine authority in BT Sanhedrin 91b. There, instead of condemning the dishonoring of God, the point is made by telling what happens when we honor God. Rabbi Joshua ben Levi teaches that to sing songs of praise of

God in this world leads to the inheritance of the next. And BT Berakot 57a emphasizes this point again by telling us that even saying in a dream, "may God's great Name be blessed," leads to a share in the future world.

These and many other rabbinic passages lead me to conclude that the rabbis were absolutely opposed to any statement or act that denied God's authority and instead emphasized the need to overtly acknowledge God's rule. This was so because the entire rabbinic approach to life stood on recognizing God's authority.

Without such recognition as a foundation, their teachings on reward, punishment, and Divine justice would be meaningless. Without such recognition as a foundation, believing that repentance was part of the way human beings can overcome their fallible state and be judged favorably by God, the ultimate ground of the universe, would be incomprehensible. Without such recognition as a foundation, knowing that Torah is the source of wisdom and God's light for human beings would be impossible.

Therefore, it is not at all surprising that there is no compromise in the penalty for someone who dishonors God's name. God, of course, cannot be harmed, but the great harm done in dishonoring God, in denying God's authority in the world, is the destruction of the entire rabbinic approach to life.

B'Har: Leviticus 25:1–26:2

Prophetical Reading
Jeremiah 32:6–27

Overview of Torah Portion

God commands the Hebrews to observe *shmittah*, the Sabbatical year, and *yovel*, the Jubilee year. God repeats the prohibition against idolatry.

Key Verses

"And [God] said to Avram, 'Know for sure that your seed shall be a stranger in a land that is not theirs'" (Genesis 15:13).

"And it came to pass in those many days that the King of Egypt died, and the Children of Israel cried because of their servitude, and they cried, and their cry rose up to God because of the servitude" (Exodus 2:23).

"And the land shall not be sold in perpetuity, because the land is Mine, because you are strangers and inhabitants with Me" (Leviticus 25:23).

"And if [a servant] is not redeemed . . . he shall go out in the year of Jubilee, he and his children with him. Because the Children of Israel are servants to Me; they are My servants that I brought out of the land of Egypt" (Leviticus 25:54–55).

Discussion Question

STRANGERS IN THE PROMISED LAND: Egypt was a horror for the Children of Israel: they were strangers in a strange land; they were servants, the Egyptians' slaves. Moses promised redemption: no longer strangers, no longer servants. Has God changed His mind? Again, He refers to the Hebrews as strangers. (Though the word *ger* also can be translated as "inhabitant" or "convert," few translators accept that meaning in this

221

context.) Again, they are called servants. What is different about their new, post-Exodus status as strangers and servants? What new meaning do those terms take on for the Children of Israel as they prepare to enter the Land of Canaan?

Shammai Engelmayer

God did not change His mind; there is no new meaning here. From day one, when God called to Avram and told him to go to Canaan, Israel has been God's servant.

Avram understood this and accepted it without question. Why else would he leave kith and kin and travel to a strange land? Why else would he not even attempt to challenge God's request that he sacrifice Yitzchak to Him?

Yitzchak, for all his faults, could never bring himself to directly challenge God's will. Sure, he tried to pass on the mantle to Esau, knowing in his heart that it should have gone to Ya'akov. When the blessing goes to Ya'akov, however, Yitzchak accepts God's will. From that point on, he is a team player, for he is God's servant.

What happened to Egypt supports this view. Egypt had many slaves. Other nations also had their slave class. Yet God intervened only for Israel's sake—and He intervened with tremendous force. Why did God have a need for such a display? We discussed some of the reasons earlier. Here, another reason is relevant: He was punishing Egypt precisely because Egypt had enslaved God's servants. It had taken from God that which belonged to God, namely Israel.

Israel's servitude to God, however, is not like the slavery of Egypt. Avram freely accepted the yoke of heaven, as did his son and grandson, as well as his great-grandchildren, the patrynomic ancestors of the twelve tribes or Israel. Israel itself renewed that acceptance at Mt. Sinai. And, indeed, each generation renews that bond for itself.

Egypt, on the other hand, made Israel its slave by force; it kept Israel enslaved by the taskmaster's whip.

For their service, Egypt gave the Israelite slaves subsistence wages and hovels in which to live. To keep the slave population from becoming too strong, Egypt took many of the male children and killed them while marrying off the more desirable among the female children to other peoples.

For their service to God, Israel gets His land as its *achuzah* (its holding).

So long as Israel remembers that it is solely to Him that it owes its allegiance, all will be well. If not, God will deal forthrightly with it.

As for their being strangers, they are, in the sense that the land is not theirs. "Stranger," in this sense, is equivalent to "tenant." The stranger is in the abode (in this case, the land) at the sufferance of the landlord. Because he is not the landlord himself, he must abide by the rules set forth by the landlord. He has no rights of his own to the property, save those the landlord allows.

This is the relevance to the Israelites who are preparing to enter Canaan.

Joseph Ozarowski

The whole point of these sections in the Torah is to define freedom for both our people and indeed for all people. Referring to our status as servants in the context of the ban on land sales in perpetuity and servile employment in perpetuity teaches us that ultimately, we are here to serve *Hashem*. As the Talmud (BT *Kiddushin* 22b) comments on verse 55, "For unto Me are the people of Israel servants, they are My servants whom I brought forth . . . —they are My servants and not servants to other servants." The whole point of institutions such as *shmittah* (the Sabbatical of the Land), *yovel* (the Jubilee year), and the limitations on Jewish servitude was to teach that message. It is not difficult to interpret this idea for the modern mind. How often do contemporary people find their lives enslaved to "land," symbolic of wealth, or to their employment obligations toward others?

People who work 80 hours a week to satisfy either their employer or their own need to make money, who never see their families, never engage in a spiritual life, or never have a life of their own, are indeed enslaved. By following God's Law, we are truly freed, but for a higher purpose. The Torah chooses to frame this message as a contrast for our ancestors between their servile status in Egypt and their imminent status as freed people in Canaan.

There are other contexts in which the limits in servitude in order to serve *Hashem* can be seen. It is possible to see this idea in the religio-political sense, in terms of the Land of Israel under non-Jewish domination (as it was until 1948). Rabbi Meir Simcha of Dvinsk, in *Meshekh Hokhma*, suggests in his comments on verse 23 that the term, "residents with Me" implies that *Eretz Yisrael* is ultimately God's and therefore ours. God's *shekhina* is on the Land only when we dwell there and the Torah practices relating to the Land can be followed. When we are in exile, this cannot happen.

It is also possible to see these ideas in the cultural sense. *Tosafot* understands Israel in verse 55 as "my servants" to mean "and not servants of Esau." "Esau" was the rabbinic code name for Rome, and, with only a little homiletic license, can be seen as Rome's historic and cultural successors in Christianity and Western Civilization. This could mean that God never wants us to see ourselves as beholden only to these forces around us. Being so close to "Esau" can lead our people to become so completely assimilated that we lose our sense of Jewish distinctiveness. This may very well be the danger today.

One could also see our verses existentially, in terms of our inner relationship with God. Ohel Ya'akov, using language from *Ethics of the Fathers*, says that this world is like a corridor to the next. If we see ourselves as *toshavim*—too deeply rooted in this world—then God is only *ger*, a temporary resident with us. But if we see our presence in this world as *ger* then God's presence is more permanent. We are reminded that we do not live forever. But when we recognize our temporality, it is easier to welcome *Hashem* into our lives and be guided by the Divine Presence.

One last thought. Before we get carried away with the cultural and political definitions of servitude and freedom, as well as our transitoriness and existential condition, the Talmud (BT *Baba Bathra* 10a) does give us another model for our relationship with *Hashem*:

> [The Roman despot] Turnus Rufus asked R. Akiba: If your God loves the poor, why does He not sustain them? [R. Akiba] said, in order to save us through them from *gehenna* [by giving *tzedaka*]. He said, on the contrary, this *tzedaka* condemns you to *gehenna*. A *mashal*: What this is like? Like a human king who got angry at his servant, banished him to jail, and commanded not to bring food and drink [to the prisoner]. One fellow went and fed him and brought him drink. When the king would hear of this, would he not get angry at him? And are you not called servants as it is said, "Because the children of Israel are servants to me. . . ." Said Rabbi Akiba to him: Let me also give you a *mashal*. What is this like? Like a King who got angry over his son, banished him to jail, and commanded not to bring food and drink [to the son]. One fellow went and fed him and brought him drink. When the king would hear of this, would he not give this man a reward? And we are called children, as it says (Deuteronomy 14:1), "You are children to the Lord your God."

So, perhaps, we are servants and strangers to God, but we are also God's children. A great deal of life—politically, culturally, and spiritually, can be spent trying to find the proper balance between these two aspects of our relationship with *Hashem*.

David Sofian

The *Kedushat HaYom* section of the *Yom Tov Tefilah* characterizes Pesach as the season of our freedom. This is obviously a good description, since the story of Pesach is the story of our redemption from Egyptian slavery. The same prayer also characterizes Shavuot as the season of the gift of our Torah. This reflects the rabbinic idea that Shavuot was not simply an agricultural festival but was connected to the revelation at Sinai. In order to understand why the key verses refer to our ancestors as servants, we need to reflect on this connection. We need to ask about the meaning of freedom here.

As our tradition sees it, the point of Pesach is not freedom in the sense of license. Rather, the Exodus from Egypt celebrates the freedom to accept the responsibilities and duties entailed by our relationship with God. We are meant to see that God brought us forth from Egypt to arrive at Sinai and there become God's servants. This perspective may already be evident in God's charge to Moses in *Shmot* 3:12, "And He said, 'I will be with you; that shall be your sign that it was I who sent you. And when you have freed the people from Egypt, you shall worship God at this mountain.'"

This essential Jewish idea that the experience of the Exodus leads to the experience of Sinai is asserted also in the counting of the Omer. *Vayikra* 23:15–16 says, "and you will count for yourselves from the morrow of the sabbath, from the day that you brought the sheaf of the wave offering; seven complete sabbaths; even unto the morrow of the seventh Sabbath shall you number fifty days; and you shall present a new meal offering unto the Eternal."

This fundamental attachment shows that Shavuot is the completion of Pesach on several levels. Biblically, there is the agricultural completion of the grain harvest begun at Pesach with the bringing of the Omer. Tradition sees the historical connection of the journeying begun in the Exodus reaching its apex in the arrival at Mount Sinai at Shavuot. However, most significantly for your question, Shavuot theologically fulfills Pesach.

We learn that the Israelites were brought out from Egypt for the purpose of receiving the Torah so that they would be shaped and defined by the life of Torah. Freedom from Egyptian slavery is meaningful because it leads to the free acceptance of the covenant at Mt. Sinai.

Here, then, is the reason why God refers to the children of Israel as "servants to Me." This is the Israelites' essential identity. They were redeemed in order to serve God within the covenant established at Mt. Sinai.

In like fashion, the Israelites' settlement upon the land is also part of their covenantal relationship with God. Given that verse 23 states unequivocally that the land is God's, their tenancy upon the land will result only from God's covenantal promise which was first articulated to Abraham.

The language here makes sure it is understood that they were not to be owners but rather God's selected tenants. Since the land would not be theirs in an absolute sense, they were to be perpetual "strangers" upon it, continuing to live upon it as long as they continue to enjoy God's favor. Hence, God refers to them as "strangers resident with Me."

In both cases, these terms refer to the essential quality of the covenantal relationship. These terms do not reflect a change in divine attitude but an expression of it. They were brought out of Egypt in order to be God's servants. They will be "strangers," that is "tenants," in the land of Israel in order to be God's servants. Their post-Exodus status, whether in terms of the acceptance of Torah or of life on the land, is that of fulfilling the covenant as God's servants.

B'Chukotai:
Leviticus 26:3–27:34

Prophetical Reading
Jeremiah 16:19–21, 17:1–14

Overview of Torah Portion

God states the blessings He will bestow on the Children of Israel if they keep His commandments, and the curses, if they disobey. He gives more regulations about the Sanctuary concerning vows and tithes.

Key Verses

"But if you do not listen to Me and do not do all these commandments . . . I will scatter you among the nations . . . and your land shall be a desolation, and your cities shall be a waste . . . and the land shall lie forsaken without [the Children of Israel]" (Leviticus 26:14, 33–34).

Discussion Question

A FORSAKEN LAND: Ignore My commandments and you risk severe punishment, God warns —hunger, fear, defeat, and exile. This, the Children of Israel can understand; these punishments will affect them or their descendants. But why should they care what happens to a land, albeit a Promised Land, that they have never seen? (Most of them, in fact, will *never* see the Land of Canaan because of the sin of the spies. God knows this; their attachment to the land should, logically, be even weaker.) Why is the fate of the land included in the list of punishments that will strike the people? Is this comparable to the promised reward and punishment in the World to Come, which also seems illusory in this world?

227

Shammai Engelmayer

To begin with, these people still think they are going from Mt. Sinai directly to Canaan. They do not learn otherwise until after they have sinned by believing the spies and rebelling against Moshe (and God). Anything told them about the land they are to possess, therefore, is directly relevant to them.

On the other hand, what makes the words of the Torah eternal is that these words are not addressed to a single generation or even have the same meaning from generation to generation. The audience changes as the generations change, and the meaning often changes with it. So, anything addressed herein is meant to live beyond the immediate audience.

Consider the law that forbids the moving of a neighbor's boundary marker. It has relevance to those people who own land and use boundary markers. Yet it also has relevance in the dawn of the twenty-first century, because from it is derived the law against unfair competitve practices.

Also relevant today is the question's premise that the people's attachment to the land is somehow voluntary. It is hardly so. The people exist so long as they remain attached to the land in some way. There is no Israel without the land and no land without Israel. You neither need to accept it nor reject it; that simply is the way it is.

Too few Jews today really believe that Israel is their "home," and that the land in which they live is only a temporary dwelling place. Merely because they believe that, however, does not make it so. They cannot exist if Israel does not exist.

Curiously, in the North American diaspora especially, we see this principle at work. For nearly 2,000 years, we were separated from the land, but only physically. We longed for our reunion with the land. Thus, in our hearts the connection remained strong. While, over the centuries, individuals among us prospered, we did not prosper as a nation or as a people.

There were times, of course, when the people-land connection became tenuous. The Jews of *Sefarad* (Spain) believed they were the "new Jerusalem" in many ways. Came 1492, and they were wanderers once again. The Jews of France began to feel diconnected, as well. Liberty, equality, and fraternity had imbued them with a new sense of freedom. Then came the Dreyfus affair.

Here, in North America, our sense of belonging is so strong that our Jewishness itself is collapsing around us. The demographics tell part of the story—a high rate of intermarriage, a high rate of communal non-affiliation, a high rate of voluntary conversions out of Judaism.

Other surveys add to the picture, such as the one that shows that six out of every ten youths in North America who are eligible for a Jewish education do not receive any. Among those who do, how many can really read and understand the basic texts of their heritage? How many really know what it is they are saying when they pray? How many really understand the whys and whats of Jewish practice and ritual?

Most telling, perhaps, are studies that make it clear to fundraisers that the "baby boomers" among us are not turned on by appeals on behalf of revitalizing Jewish life. Only "feel good" themes interest them in giving.

Of course, God does not send a lightning bolt out of the sky anytime someone refuses to stay connected. Rather, the punishment is separation. The Ten Tribes of Israel/Samaria were not put under the sword; they were absorbed into the world into which they were thrust. They disappeared into that world. They became like everyone else.

Jews are not like everyone else. We are God's priests, His holy nation, and the land comes with the job. It is the recompense: "Do the job well and faithfully, and the land is yours. Fail at the job, and you cannot dwell within the land. The land is yours only as an *achuzah* (a holding); it is not a permanent possession. You are tied to the land, and it is tied to you. While you are outside the land, it will not flourish for anyone else. It will remain desolate and barren until your return."

And so it was, as history shows. The land did not thrive during the nearly two millennia of our separation. Now it thrives again. Where once there were swamps, there are orange groves. Where once there was desert, agriculture and industry flourish.

As for the world to come, ours is a system of living, not of dying. It is a system for living in this world, and no other. Perhaps there is a world to come; perhaps not. The Torah speaks nothing of it, because it is irrelevant. What we must do, we do out of faithfulness to our Master, not because we expect to be granted a diamond-encrusted palace in the hereafter.

To put it in terms of 1990's vernacular, the world to come is to die for. Our job is to live.

Joseph Ozarowski

The *pshat*, the plain sense of the parshah, is that these people were expecting to enter the Promised Land; if not for the incident of the spies, they would have done so. God's final words in Leviticus in the *tokheha* have a number of different contexts. Consequences in the Promised Land were certainly ways of letting our ancestors know that there will be unhappy results if they do not keep their end of the *brit* with *Hashem*.

There is a textual proof for this approach. Just before the *tokheha*, the Torah deals in *Parshat Behar* with the laws of *Eretz Yisrael*, the Promised Holy Land. These laws include *shmittah*, *yovel*, and the issues of land rights. In fact, it has been pointed out by commentaries that the 70 years of Babylonian Exile, seemingly predicted by the *tokheha*, corresponded to the number of years that *shmittah* was not observed during the First Temple period. So there is a relationship between the Land and the *tokheha's* dire warnings.

Alternately, as one of my congregants suggested, if our ancestors' feelings toward an unseen Promised Land were not enough to insure their fealty to the Covenant, we could still see the logic of God's use of land in the warnings, since our people had come from Egypt. Egypt was also an agricultural society, though not exclusively. Even as slaves, the Jewish people recognized the importance of land in a nation's life. So, if their loyalty to the Land was not secure, they could still be taught about the results of their actions in terms of land in general. If the Torah speaks in terms all generations can understand, they could certainly see the Covenant framed in terms of land, if not the Land.

Many are concerned about the nature of reward and punishment emanating from this chapter. Ramban's approach is that the *tokheha* only deals with the time when the entire Jewish People are ensconced on their Land. Only communal behavior on our own Land will determine God's relationship with us. Obviously, this means that if I, as an individual, go out and eat a ham sandwich or go to the movies on Saturday, God is not going to strike me down with lightning. But the Ramban explains that there is a special relationship with *Hashem* when we are all on our own Land.

However, there may be ways of seeing the *tokheha* outside of an *Eretz Yisrael*-based context. It does not take a major jump of homiletic license to see the *tokheha's* warnings to a community in a modern context. Can we not imagine God saying, "If you do not hearken to My laws of morality and integrity, protecting the good earth I have given to you . . . then I will deplete the ozone layer and cause pollution in your land, air, and water. . . . I will spread dread diseases among you and cause despair. . . ." This idea does not see the warnings so much as punishment, but as results and consequences of our actions.

The Torah is cautioning us that we cannot escape these consequences. Just as there is an ecosystem in nature, where every action causes results in other parts of the system, so too can we speak of a moral ecosystem in which we cannot detach our actions from their consequences. This is not a fashionable idea in late twentieth century America where people "do their own thing."

Perhaps the Torah is trying to teach us that there is really no such thing as "do your own thing," and we need to be concerned about what we do as a community, an aggregate of individuals.

I do not think the Torah is dealing in illusory issues comparable to the world to come; I think the *tokheha* speaks very much to issues in this world.

David Sofian

It never occurred to me to question the Israelites' attachment to the Land. Your question assumes that only people who actually had the opportunity to live on the Land would have cared deeply about it. It occurs to me now, since you asked the question, that this line of thinking is bolstered by what we know of their responses already seen in the Book of *Shmot*, and what will happen in the Book of *Bamidbar*.

For example, in *Parashat Beshalach* we examined whether or not the miracles the Hebrews experienced during their release positively impacted their level of faith. Already there, we could see their limitations, since lacking a context for an entire religious way of life, their experience of miracles proved insufficient for them to establish a lasting core faith.

Hence, their whining dependency continued and circumscribed their ability to fulfill the covenant. Remembering this and keeping the entirety of their track record in mind, it surely is possible at this juncture also for them only to have responded to the threats of punishments that would have directly affected them, like hunger and fear.

Therefore, it seems to me that it is not so unreasonable to assume that they would have lacked the perspective to relate to the profundity of this threat. However, if so, why indeed is it included in the list of punishments? And more puzzling still, why do the punishments reach their crescendo with this threat?

Even though our ancestors' intractability is clear, time and again foiling God's plans, I nevertheless think this threat, in particular, would have been substantial to them. No matter how obtuse they were, the fate of the Land would have been concrete to them and not illusory. It is included where it is precisely because it would have impacted them powerfully.

Certainly, since the covenant was affirmed with them at Mt. Sinai, and since their lives had been configured by the building of the Tabernacle and the establishment of the offerings, their experience of reality was structured by that Covenant, which from the moment God originated it with Abraham, included the promise of the Land flowing with milk and honey. They absolutely would have understood a threat to this special and highly symbolic piece of land, a threat to utterly destroy it no less, as a threat to their core identity as the peoplehood of Israel.

Because the promise of this good Land was a central facet of Israel's group identity, they most definitely would have perceived the significance of God's warning that, without their fidelity to the commandments, it would be destroyed. The essence of who they were as a people meant that they could not help but care.

Bamidbar/Numbers

Bamidbar: Numbers 1:1–4:20

Prophetical Reading
Hosea 2:1–22

Overview of Torah Portion

God orders Moses to take a census of the Children of Israel, by tribes, counting all males at least 20 years old; the tribe of Levi, consecrated for holy service, is to be counted separately. God declares where each tribe is to be based during their travels through the wilderness, arranged around the Tabernacle. God assigns specific functions to individual Levite families.

Key Verses

"And the Lord spoke to Moses in the wilderness of Sinai . . . , saying, 'Take the sum of all the congregation of the Children of Israel, by their families, by their fathers' houses, according to the number of names, every male, by their polls, from 20 years old and upward, all that can go forth to war in Israel'" (Numbers 1:1–3).

"And the Lord spoke to Moses in the wilderness of Sinai, saying, 'Number the children of Levi by their fathers' houses, by their familes, every male from one month old and upward'" (Numbers 3:14–15).

"And the Lord spoke to Moses and to Aaron, saying, 'Take the sum of the sons of Kohat from among the sons of Levi, by their families, by their fathers' houses, from 30 years old and upward until 50 years old . . . to do work in the Tent of Meeting'" (Numbers 4:1–3).

Discussion Question

MAKING SENSE OF A CENSUS: The general census, ostensibly to determine the number of men who can be mustered into a Jewish army, is also considered an indication of the size of the entire Hebrew nation—commentators extrapolate the total population at more than three million. The count of Levites is clearly for the purpose of certifying how many men in that tribe are eligible for their special service in the Sanctuary; their service starts at 30.

Thus, the census directions seem backwards. The general census should count a greater number of people, starting with infanthood, while the Levite census should be limited to the of-age individuals. Why does the Torah order the general census to survey only men at least 20 years old— excluding the greater part of the nation—while including in the Levite census many underage men who will not be eligible for their designated service for several years? What difference is indicated between the Levites and the other tribes? Are these censuses more than a simple body count?

Shammai Engelmayer

Simple "body counts" are, of course, strictly forbidden by the Torah. These are not simple counts, but counts made for specific purposes.

The general count called for in Numbers 1:1–3 is, as stated in the text, for the purpose of military service. There was an obvious need to know how many able-bodied men were available to fight the coming battle for Canaan. Because the under-20s were not eligible to fight (and because everyone who could fight over age 20, including the senior citizens, was eligible), this count begins at age 20.

The third count (Numbers 4:1–3) is for the purpose of the sacred service. Before anyone could dole out the jobs needed to be done in and around the Tent of Meeting, there had to be a count of how many people were there to do the work.

As for the second count, of Levite males from a month old and upward, the Levites had nothing of their own—no land, no independent source of income, no means of supporting a family. It was the community's respon- sibility to provide for the Levites, who the Torah often ranks with the widow, the orphan, and the poor. It was to determine what was needed to support these Levites that this count was made. If the count began at age 30, the community would have no way of gauging the needs.

One could then ask, "but what about the little Levite girls? Do they not have to be included in such a count?" The answer is that yes, they do, but they are nevertheless excluded. There is no satisfactory explanation given for this exclusion, other than the common (but not necessarily accurate) one that Israel was a male-dominated society in which females did not count. I believe, however, that the opposite is intended here.

Because women were treated as chattel in ancient Near Eastern societies—
and the men of Israel were as chauvinistic as any other—the law deliberately excluded them from the count in order to protect their rights. If
females were counted in what is essentially a "welfare" census, it would
have created an incentive for the ever-poor Levites to keep their daughters
at home long after others their age had been married off. After all, the more
people in the household, the more would be provided to that household.
The women, in effect, would become hostages to the Levite welfare system.

Instead, the law creates the opposite situation: As long as the daughters
remain at home, they add no income to the family, while they siphon off
some of its resources.

Such an interpretation is consistent with the Torah's egalitarian view (all
humans derive from a single source, the hermaphroditic *adam* of Creation,
and thus no one can claim superiority), but without a direct statement of
intent, the text leaves itself open to interpretations that defeat this purpose.
Only the seeming inequality is visible.

Joseph Ozarowski

Why a census altogether? Many commentaries focus on the repeated use of
the Hebrew word *tzava*, which refers to a large organized group. Most
often, including in modern Hebrew, this is used in a military context. That
is why male Israelites were counted from age 20 and up—this was the age
for military service. Levites, on the other hand, were used for religious
leadership (like a chaplaincy in the military) and were not included in the
count.

Hirsch has a slightly different twist to all this, suggesting the general
count from age 20 and up was for a kind of peaceful public service to
Hashem and community. The Levites were pressed as a group for this
service. None of this, though, explains why the Levites were counted from
one month and up.

One of my congregants had a simple, but brilliant, answer. Originally, the
firstborn of each family were to serve as religious leaders in the *Mishkan*.
However, they excluded themselves by their involvement in the golden calf
incident and were replaced by the Levites. The firstborn were supposed to
serve from the age of one month and above, and the exchange with the
Levites had to be equivalent. (This, by the way, is why we redeem the
firstborn in the *pidyon haben* ceremony after 30 days, and the source is in
this *sidrah*—see 3:11–13 and 40–51.) Hence, the Levites were also counted
from one month and up.

Rashi (3:15, quoting *Hazal*), however, suggests that the sanctity of the Levites was not created in the desert. If one counts the number of Jews, the family of Jacob that went down to Egypt toward the end of Genesis, the count is 66. Yosef and his two sons make 69 (assuming his wife did not convert and was not part of the count). This is one less than the traditional number 70. Hazal says that Yokheved, mother of Moses and from the tribe of Levi, was born along the way and thus is included in the count. Hence, Levites were numbered at this early age from the very beginnings of our people.

One of my congregants quoted a midrash that I could not trace but would still share in light of your question regarding the purpose of censuses. Moses, acting as census taker by Divine instruction, had no access to forms, pens, or computers. The Midrash says he went from tent to tent talking to each family and asking about their spiritual needs. In this sense, the purpose of the census is not simply to find statistics or numbers, but rather to deal with the human aspect of knowing who was a part of the Jewish people. In this way, Moses acted as a very good pastoral counsellor when he numbered his flock.

Rashi (3:16) has a different variation on this theme. Regarding the Levitical count, he writes:

> Moses said to the Holy One, Blessed Be He, "How am I to go into their tents to know the number of their babies?" Said the Holy One, Blessed Be He, "You do your part and I will do mine."
>
> Moses went and stood at the door of each tent. The *Shekhina* [Heavenly presence] went ahead of him, and a *bat kol* [heavenly voice] came out of each tent and said, "There are so many babies in this tent." That is why the verse reads, "And Moses numbered them according to the word [or mouth] of God.

From this we see that when numbering must be done, it is done with the utmost respect for the individual, his or her privacy, and personal life. Jewish tradition discourages us from turning people into numbers. That is why when we count people, even for a mitzvah such as a *minyan*, we never count, "One, two, three." Rather, we use a verse with ten words, such as the blessing *Hamotzie*, or at the very least we count, "Not one, not two, not three."

David Sofian

I see no reason not to accept Rashbam's well-known common sense explanation for the census counting those 20 years old and older. The intent was as you voice in your discussion question. It would yield the number of men who could make up an army needed to battle for the Land of Israel. If that is the goal, I don't see anything backwards in the procedure.

Given that the purpose was to prepare an army, the count would arise as it did. Only incidentally would it then be possible to extrapolate an overall total. Accepting this, it remains to explain why the Levites were left out of the process.

It turns out that Moses was concerned about it, too. In Midrash *Bamidbar Rabbah* 1:12, we find Moses filled with misgivings, thinking that perhaps something is wrong with his tribe since God did not want the Levites counted. God's response to Moses here is very helpful in responding to your question. God explains to Moses that since the tribe of Levi drew God close to itself, God would also draw the tribe of Levi close.

Referring to the time of the golden calf, God rewards the Levites for their faithfulness and draws them close by trusting them to be the sanctuary's custodians. In other words, the Levites had proven themselves to be special by proving themselves loyal. Therefore, God had special plans for them. This explains why they were excluded from the census. Loyalty to God is of paramount importance. However, it doesn't yet answer your question of why they were counted differently from the rest when they were finally counted.

The midrash directs us here also. In *Bamidbar Rabbah* 1:11, Moses is standing, wondering why God does not want the Levites numbered. As I already noted, loyalty to God is supremely valued. Now we learn exactly how significant this is.

Here, in answer to Moses' question, it is explained to him that God knew what would soon happen in the episode of the spies. God knew that all of the generations in the wilderness would die, so God does not have them counted because God does not want the Levites included in that fate. The Levites were not going to die in the wilderness, but were going to enter the Land—*Bamidbar Rabbah* 3:7 goes to great pains to demonstrate this.

Learning this from the midrash led me to an understanding of why the Levites were counted from their infancy. This method was an expression of God's special love for them. Since they are singled out from the other tribes and are going to survive and not die in the wilderness, it would be useful to know exactly how many there were. The purpose of this counting is not to find out how many are of fighting age. The purpose here is to find out just how many there are altogether, since they are to be exempt from the judgment the rest are to suffer.

Naso: Numbers 4:21–7:89

Prophetical Reading
Judges 13:2–25

Overview of Torah Portion

God's instructions about specific functions for individual Levite families continue. God gives Moses the laws for a sinner's restitution to a victim, an accused adultress' trial by the miraculous water of bitterness, and a Nazarite's vow of self-denial. The princes of the Twelve Tribes bring gifts of gold and silver, meal offerings, incense, and animals to mark the Tabernacle's anointing.

Key Verses

"And the Lord spoke to Moses, saying . . . 'If any man's wife goes astray and acts unfaithfully against him, and a man lies carnally with her and it is hidden from the eyes of her husband, and there is no witness against her . . . and the spirit of jealousy comes upon him . . . the man shall bring his wife to the priest . . . and the priest shall take holy water in an earthen vessel . . . and let the woman's hair go loose . . . , and the priest shall cause the woman to swear with the oath of cursing . . . [that] this water that causes the curse shall go into your bowels and make your belly swell and your thigh fall away'" (Numbers 5:12–22).

Discussion Question

A BITTER LESSON: The prescribed procedure for dealing with a woman suspected of infidelity ranks among the Torah's most baffling scenarios, depending as it does on a miracle—the accused wife is made to drink a concoction (the so-called water of bitterness) of dust from the floor of the

Tabernacle and a scroll on which God's now-blotted-out Name was written; if guilty, she will suffer a painful death, her sexual organs swelling; if innocent, she will return to her husband and become pregnant.

Equally baffling is the description of the accused woman's role in this trial by water. The Torah refers to her as a man's wife, not simply as a woman; it cites a man lying *with* her, not her lying with a man; the husband's spirit of jealousy, not her certifiable guilt, determines if she is tried. The wife is apparently a passive agent throughout.

Why does the Torah repeatedly refer to the woman in terms of another man, not as an independent agent? Why does the Torah mention the woman's unfaithfulness to her husband before the actual sexual sin of which she is accused? In a society where the uncovering of a woman's hair violated her sense of modesty, why did the priest let loose her hair before she was found guilty?

Shammai Engelmayer

Once again, we need to recall why the sacrificial system and the cultic priesthood were instituted: The people are too rooted in pagan beliefs to accept a wholesale change to a higher form of service to God (and, indeed, the only proper form of service, through good deeds, study, and prayer). They continue to buy into the magical, mystical, hocus-pocus practiced by pagan priests. And, when it becomes evident to Moshe and to God that they are not about to change, all of that is cleansed of its paganism and superimposed on the religion of Israel.

This penchant for superstition provides an opportunity in cases of alleged adultery. The fact is, there are more men who suspect their wives of having affairs than there are wives who are sleeping with other men. Men are more prone to suspicion because they fantasize about the women they meet. Since too many men also have no idea how much work is involved in running a household, they figure their wives have all this free time on their hands. Because men *think* they know what they would do if they had that free time, they assume their wives are doing it.

This assumption becomes particularly strong when the couple is childless. In this superstitious climate, the inability to conceive is seen as punishment for the sin of adultery. And, unless the man has slept with someone else's wife, he knows he is not an adulterer as that term is understood by the Torah. That leaves his wife.

You can talk yourself blue in the face, but you will not be able to knock it out of the heads of such men. Their suspicions eat at them and destroy their marriages. And so their superstitions are used to overcome their suspicions. They may not believe their wives, but how can they not believe God Himself?

That, in essence, is what is behind this "miracle." It is a psychological game that is being played out.

Adultery is not committed in public or before two qualified witnesses. A man and woman may be seen together in public, but that is a far cry both from engaging in illicit sexual relations and from being caught in the act. There is no way to prove adultery, which also means there is no way to prove that adultery had not taken place. And yet, unless the matter is dealt with convincingly, the husband's suspicions could grow so strong that tragedy becomes inevitable. Hence, the trial by bitter waters.

The innocent woman, knowing she is innocent, will trust in God and drink the water. The guilty woman would probably rather confess her sin than risk so horrible a death (although her confession alone, while confirming her husband's fears, is insufficient to convict her). And, if she tries to tough it out, she either will suffer psychosomatic symptoms, or she will get away with it; either way, the issue becomes moot and a potential tragedy is averted.

Letting her hair down in public is part of the psychological game. It is a humiliation and, in effect, she has been stripped naked of all defenses. It is part of the build-up to the trial itself.

Why is this done in public? This answers the question of why the Torah first mentions her going "astray" before mentioning the actual crime of adultery. Husbands tend to be suspicious, but those suspicions usually (not always) need something on which to feed and grow. Perhaps it is the way other men look at his wife, perhaps it is because his wife talked to another man. Whatever the cause, rumors often get started. These only feed the husband's jealousy.

Once he has made his accusation, of course, everyone knows it. If the woman is to be absolved of guilt, therefore, the only fair way is for it to happen in public.

The hocus-pocus aspect of the ritual also serves as a deterrent. If a woman really believes in it, she will be loathe to risk facing so awful a death.

The fact is, the Torah's general view of women and the *halakha's* general view are much the same: Women tend to be practical; men tend to act out of emotion.

Thus, Yitzchak was willing to thwart God's will by giving his beloved Esau the blessing; Rivka, ever the practical one, had to stop him.

Thus, the Talmud tells us (Kiddushin 41a) that a man may not become betrothed to a woman sight unseen because, when he does see her, he may not like her and cast her aside. Presumably, this is because a man often makes such decisions with his hormones, not his brain. A woman, on the other hand, may become so betrothed because she is more practical while at the same time willing to accept a less-than-perfect specimen.

As for the vindicated woman becoming pregnant, we know today that many women can not conceive for psychological reasons (just as many women show physical signs of being pregnant when, in fact, they are suffering what is known as "hysterical pregnancy"). The mind is that powerful, it seems. By passing the test—and having been told that it will lead to conception—it is a safe bet that many women will conceive after the ordeal. (It also helps that their husbands are more likely to make love to them after having been found innocent.)

Until she drinks the water, of course, the woman is a passive player in all of this. That is only natural. She is, after all, the passive player in intercourse (here defined in its absolute sense, not with the broader brush of foreplay and afterplay). She is also not likely to level an adultery charge against herself. And, considering that the adultery very likely is a figment of the husband's imagination, there is nothing she can say or do to eliminate the suspicion.

Joseph Ozarowski

Explaining the section of the *sotah*, the suspected adulteress, is one of the most difficult tasks one could have. Now, if one simply accepts the Torah as the word of *Hashem*, the task is easier. But if one needs to be convinced of the relevance of the Torah, or even if one is already so committed but has a late twentieth century mindset with its emphasis on the rights of the individual, the idea of "innocent until proven guilty," and egalitarianism, then this chapter is a toughie. As one of my congregants pointed out, women truly seem like second-class citizens.

And your question, coming during the week when two hasidic Jews were arraigned in California for suspected sexual harassment of a teenage woman on a plane, caused a rather heated discussion in my weekly class.

First of all, it must be stated that traditional *halakha* is not egalitarian. Men were permitted polygamy until the *takana* (ruling) of Rabbenu Gershom some 1,000 years ago. The Torah never permitted the same for women. This may explain some of the language in our chapter regarding the woman in relationship to the man. Nevertheless, women have extensive rights under *halakha*, but this essay is not the place to explore this important topic.

The *sotah* ritual is only used in certain narrowly-defined cases of adultery. In fact, where the woman admitted her affair, it is not used at all. In such a case there is a divorce, but the woman does not receive her *ketuba* (settlement). The classic case of adultery, a capital offense, only occurs when there are witnesses (public adultery) and formal warnings (a repeat offense). Also, the Talmud clearly states (Sotah 47b) that the *sotah* test can only be used and would only work when the husband himself is "free from sin," that is, has not himself committed adultery or connived to falsely implicate his wife.

In fact, the Talmud (BT *Sotah* 47b and BT *Tosefta Sotah* 14:2) tells us that when open adultery (both male and female) increased toward the end of the Second Temple period, the ceremony usage was cancelled by Rabbi Yochanan ben Zakkai and it has not been used for 1,900 years. Even in the earlier period of our history, the *sotah* test was only used when the husband had evidence that his wife had an affair and he confronted her in front of witnesses, but none of the other above-mentioned circumstances existed. The husband was in a "fit of jealousy" (that is how the late Pinhas Peli translated the Hebrew term *ruah kin'ah* several years ago).

In ancient non-Jewish societies, the husband could simply kill the suspected wife or throw her out of the house. However, according to the Torah, he cannot unilaterally decide her fate but must bring her to the Temple and the Priest. In the Code of Hammurabi, a suspected woman was expected to place her life at risk by an ordeal of throwing herself into the river (also involving water!) for the sake of her husband.

Compared to all these, making the suspected woman drink some dirty water may not have been too pleasant, but it certainly was rather benign in comparison. And if she was guilty, the illness she would suffer had no physiological roots; it could not have come from the dirty water. Rather, as Ramban points out, it must have been God's intervention via a Divine miracle (the only such case in the Torah) that would cause her discomfort. And if she was innocent, the husband's jealousy would subside, and domestic quiet would hopefully return. The point of the whole procedure was to restore some psychological trust to an already rocky marriage. This is why the Talmud says that BT *Sotah* 17a even the name of *Hashem* may be erased (in the scroll which is ground and mixed with the water) to make peace between a husband and wife.

One of my congregants suggested that the whole thing was meant to dramatically convince the parties involved to get the problem out in to the open before the ritual was to take place. A similar idea was proposed by Emanuel Rackman in an article he published several years ago in the *National Jewish Law Journal*, where he termed the *sotah* ritual a psychodrama rather than an ordeal. (Ironically, he was severely criticized by many within the Orthodox right-wing for such an interpretation!) Possibly, it was never meant to be carried out; in fact my son and I, who studied tractate *Sotah* together awhile back, were hard-pressed to find evidence in the Talmud that this ritual ever happened.

My approach does not answer all the questions about the *sotah* chapter, but it does make the section a little more understandable.

David Sofian

The subject you raise is indeed a fascinating one. The ordeal of bitter waters is the only trial by ordeal in the Torah. I believe it is also the only time the usual rules of evidence are avoided. In *Parshah Shoftim, D'varim* 19:15, it is explicitly stated, "a single witness shall not stand up against a person, for any transgression, for any sin, for any sin that may be committed; on the word of two witnesses or three witnesses should the matter stand."

So we need to ask the general question first, "why is the question of adultery so important that the Torah's own due process is supplanted?"

Judith Romney-Wegner's book, *Chattel or Person? The Status of Women in the Mishnah*, is very helpful. This highly insightful book in general, in particular, her discussion of the Mishnah's tractate *Sotah* (page 52), sheds light on the scriptural passage in question. The key to understanding the *Bamidbar* passage is recognizing that in the scripture's view, and in the Mishnah's view, as well, even though a woman herself is not owned by her husband, her sexuality is.

By marrying her, he owns exclusively the right to have sexual intercourse with her and the right to her capacity for reproduction. The text is saying that adultery only can be committed by a wife against her husband. Clearly, all this is designed to protect paternity.

A critical problem arises when it is uncertain if the husband's rights have been violated, and that is exactly the case *Bamidbar* raises. Here, a woman's husband only suspects his wife of adultery. If you will, the husband is jealous of his property rights; that is, he suspects his rights have been violated but lacks the witnesses necessary for due process. A situation of doubtful paternity was unacceptable, so due process is superseded. The husband's need to protect his rights overrides the usual right of due process.

Recognizing this allows us to understand why the Torah text refers to the woman repeatedly in terms of another man. The issue in question is not her independence. It is her relationship to her husband or, more precisely, whether his rights in his relationship with her have been violated. That is why everything is stated in terms of her husband and his jealousy.

This explains the passage as it is. Yet, before leaving the matter, a word about what brought this practice to an end is in order. *Mishnah Sotah* 9:9 tells us that Yohanan ben Zakkai brought the rite of the *sotah* to an end. He reasoned that since adulterers had become numerous, the rite of bitter waters ceased. This would fit with the supposition that since the rite required a *minhah* offering, it would have become obsolete with the destruction of the Temple. However, it may also tell us something about how the rabbis eventually came to view this rite.

Alexander Guttman, in his article, "The Role in Equity of the History of the Halakhah," (found in his collection of articles, *Studies in Rabbinic Judaism*, 1976), suggests that the reason the ordeal of bitter waters was made inoperative was the rabbis' concern for equity. They eventually became uncomfortable with the ordeal's attempt to force God to reveal the truth and with the unfairness of it to women. He bases this on the Talmud's discussion in BT *Sotah* 47b. While commenting on the Mishnah's phrase, "when adulterers became numerous," the Gemara informs us that at the time when the man is free from iniquity, the waters resolve the matter; but when the man is not free from iniquity, the waters do not resolve the matter.

Since it is not now the case that men are free from iniquity, the bitter waters would not affect the *sotah*, so the rite would no longer be useful. The Talmud leaves us with the implied question, "when were men ever without iniquity so that the waters would be useful?"

I find great significance in this passage from BT *Sotah* because it demonstrates to me how the tradition valued fairness and equity. Nothing in the original *sotah* passage ties the effectiveness of the ordeal to the man's rectitude. Yet, that does not stop the Gemara from using this rather weak reason as a way of explaining how the practice was terminated. Yohanan ben Zakkai, motivated by a strong sense of fairness, did what needed to be done.

I believe a willingness to adopt fairness and equity as an overarching value ought to be the basis for applying Jewish law today, just as it was in the case of the *sotah* then.

Beha'alotecha:
Numbers 8:1–12:16

Prophetical Reading
Zechariah 2:14–17, 3:1–10, 4:1–7

Overview of Torah Portion

God instructs Moses how to separate and consecrate the Levites for service in the Sanctuary. Moses and Aaron carry out the instructions, after which the Levites begin their service. God introduces a second Passover for people unable to bring the proper sacrifice on the original date. God tells Moses to make a pair of silver trumpets for calling the congregation together to proceed in their travels in the wilderness or when going to war. The people, longing for Egypt, complain about the manna that sustains them; God brings a monthful of quail. Miriam and Aaron challenge the uniqueness of Moses' prophetical status; God defends Moses, giving Miriam leprosy.

Key Verses

"And Moses' father-in-law said to him . . . 'You shall provide from all the people men of valor, God-fearing men, men of truth, haters of unjust gain . . . and let them judge the people . . . that they shall make it easier for you and bear the burden with you'" (Exodus 18:17–22).

"And Moses said to the Lord . . . 'I am not able to bear all this people alone, because it is too heavy for me.' And the Lord said to Moses, 'Gather to me seventy men of the elders of Israel whom you know to be elders of the people and officers over them, and take them to the tent of meeting that they shall stand there with you. And I will come down and speak with you there, and I will take of the spirit that is upon you and place it upon them. And they shall bear the burden of the people with you that you will not bear it alone. . . .' and it came to pass that when the spirit rested upon them, they prophesied" (Numbers 11:11–17, 25).

Discussion Question

MORTAL MEN, HOLY SPIRIT: When overworked, Moses originally accepted his father-in-law's advice about appointing men to assist in settling the people's legal questions. It made sense to choose individuals with proven leadership skills—valor, truthfulness, and financial rectitude. They had to use their abilities in their new judicial positions. But now, with the people complaining about hunger and Moses declaring that he couldn't single-handedly bear their ingratitude, God declared that He will apportion part of His spirit to the seventy selected men.

Why is Moses commanded to pick men who are already the people's known leaders? Wouldn't the divine gift of prophecy provide the needed wisdom or insight, compensating for any individual shortcomings? Indeed, if Moses chose totally non-distinguished individuals, who would succeed in their adjunct roles only because of their heaven-sent powers, it would serve as a more impressive demonstration of God's power. The Torah provides spare details about how the seventy chosen men actually used their brief burst of Holy Spirit—if we know so much of their selection, why are we told so little of their subsequent actions?

Shammai Engelmayer

The problem with this question is that the text itself is subject to different interpretations, each of which could change the nature of any answer.

For example, the question presupposes that the seventy chosen ones were immediately seized by the Spirit of God, that they began to prophesy, and that this gift of prophecy was momentary; once ended, it never returned.

That it never returned is based on the definition of the phrase in Numbers 11:25, *v'lo ya'safu*, which means "they did not continue to do so." That indeed suggests that this is a one-time event.

On the other hand, two *targums* (translations)—*Onkelos* and *Yonatan*—do not see the phrase *v'lo ya'safu* in their texts. Rather, they read it as *v'lo ya'su'fu*, which means "did not cease." Thus, these two *targums*, one of which became the "official" Aramaic translation of the Torah, insist that the prophetic gift stayed with the 70 throughout the remainder of their lives. (The rabbis of blessed memory urged all Jews to study each week's Torah portion three times—twice in the original Hebrew and once in its *Targum Onkelos* version.)

The fact that we hear so little of these men after their appointment suggests that the traditional reading—that it did not extend beyond the moment—is the correct one. For the moment, we will follow the traditional reading.

That brings us to the "divine gift of prophecy" itself. From a strictly grammatical point of view, no such gift was bestowed on the seventy. Rather, God causes them to behave in a manner believed to be common with prophets, meaning they display some kind of ecstatic behavior. (See Jacob Milgrom's excursus on the subject in *The JPS Torah Commentary*.) The purpose was not to allow these men to prophesy, but to demonstrate to the people looking on that they had been touched by the Spirit of God. This makes considerable sense, especially if the ability was as fleeting as the traditional reading maintains.

Then there is the question of who these people are. The fact that the text refers to them as *ziknei ha'ahm v'sho'terov*—elders of the people and their officers—leads Rashi to suggest that these were the same people who as *shotrei b'nai yisrael*—Egyptian-appointed Israelite overseers—allowed themselves to be beaten when the people under them failed to make their daily quota of bricks, despite the lack of supplied straw (Exodus 5:14).

On the other hand, we already encountered "seventy elders" earlier in the Torah and some commentators believe these are the same seventy. (The question, in fact, seems to follow this view.)

What makes defining terms so important can be seen in how part of our question—why the divine gift of prophecy was not sufficient, thus requiring Moshe to choose from among already established leaders—would be answered, depending on who the seventy are.

If the seventy were the same ones who joined Moshe, Aharon, Nadav, and Avihu on Mt. Sinai, the fact that they were suddenly touched by God would seem redundant.

These people presumably already wore that badge of honor; after all, it is not every Israelite who gets to party in the immediate presence of God. (Many, but not all, of the major commentators believe the original seventy died because they partied too heartily, by the way.) In this case, the question itself would have been posed incorrectly. Rather than ask why the divine gift was not enough, the question would have been, "why the divine gift at all?"

That, then, leads us to a conclusion: This seventy and the first seventy are two distinctly different groups.

Now we can answer this part of the question. This seventy were chosen because of who they were—leaders of some sort. However, who chose them? Moshe. And that is the problem. Moshe is already showing signs of losing faith. The people have worn him down. More importantly, the people are losing faith in him. Indeed, they are on the eve of rebellion against him. So what if he names seventy people to serve with him as the national leadership? What he says carries increasingly little weight with the people.

That is why God must demonstrate that, while Moshe makes the choices, he does so with God's full support. These men whom Moshe has selected are made to act like prophets; the "Spirit of God" touches them, however briefly. God is telling Israel that these men are His choice, too; that Moshe remains God's messenger.

To my mind, this is also one reason why the incident with Eldad and Medad is recounted here. The story—two men, whose names were apparently on the list of the seventy, stayed behind in the camp for unspecified reasons but were nevertheless seized with the same prophetic-like ecstasy—seems out of place. Eldad and Medad play no further role. There is no long-term significance to it. There is not even any apparent momentary significance to it.

Inclusion in the story, however, does make sense when you realize that Eldad and Medad were not the only people left in the camp. For one thing, the youth who brought Yehoshua and Moshe the news was there, too. Presumably, many people were. If Moshe was out of favor with the people, it is likely that many of them would have refused to go to the Tent of Meeting to see "him" crown "his" lieutenants, thereby missing the demonstration of God's sanction of the seventy.

Eldad and Medad, therefore, are left inside the camp; they are clearly seized by the Spirit of God, with Moshe far removed from the scene. Those who refused to go to the Tent of Meeting thus had the message brought home to them, as it were. Those at the Tent, who hear about Eldad and Medad, have additional confirmation that this is from God and is not a conjuring trick on Moshe's part.

Who these men are also dictates the need for a sign of Divine favor. Rashi is likely correct in equating this seventy with the overseers who took the lashes for the people. Moshe had complained that God had "dealt ill" with him by placing "the burden of all these people" on him, as though he were their parent. The overseers, on the other hand, had assumed a heavier burden than Moshe, for they literally had put their bodies on the line for their people. They were beaten by the Egyptians, but they did not take it out on the people, whose inability to produce sufficient bricks was responsible for the beatings. They acted very much like parents who would willingly give up their lives to save their children.

Obviously, these people were popular with their fellow Israelites. There had to have been many more than seventy, however; perhaps seventy times seventy, since it is neither likely nor possible that the Egyptians would have appointed one overseer for every 10,000 or 20,000 people.

Are the seventy whom Moshe chose the best of the lot? Were they chosen, perhaps, because they were more loyal to Moshe than to the people? Do people whose life's work had been to make bricks and oversee the work of others who make bricks have the wisdom and ability to lead a nation? These are among the questions that are answered by God Himself when He demonstrates to Israel that these seventy have His sanction.

The popularity of these people is one reason God bids Moshe to choose from among this group. The other is that they serve as a counterpoint to Moshe in the sense that they have already proven a willingness to bear a burden that includes accepting physical punishment on behalf of the people—a burden far greater than that which Moshe rejects.

As for why Moshe was not bidden to choose nonentities, thus allowing for an even greater display of God's power, His power is not at issue here. These people are meant to relieve Moshe of the burden of administration, just as his earlier appointees relieved him of his judicial burdens. In a very real sense, Moshe had already established a judicial branch; now he was establishing an executive branch. (At this point, the priesthood served as the legislative branch, filling in the blanks left by God in giving His Torah.) These people would be responsible for the mundane tasks of supply procurement, sanitation, traffic control, and so forth. What they needed most was not Godly power, but the people's trust. This group had the people's trust.

This would also explain why we are told so little of their subsequent actions. These were unimportant to the Torah. The seventy were not prophets, after all. They were not lawgivers. They were not even judges. They were simply in place to administer the needs of such a large multitude.

Now, it is true that this seventy becomes *the model* for the future Sanhedrin, which served as the national legislature and supreme court of the Second Temple period and beyond—but this group is *not* the Sanhedrin itself. There is no textual suggestion that they served any special function whatever; the Torah's silence on their activities, in fact, suggests otherwise.

On the other hand, what if *Targum Onkelos* and *Targum Yonatan* are correct—that these people, seized momentarily by a fit of ecstasy in the manner of prophets, *continued* to prophesize for the rest of their lives? In that case, the Torah's silence about their activities cries out for explanation.

I believe the *targums* to be correct. These people had mundane administrative tasks to perform, but they were more than mere officials.

There is one class of people that we know existed in Israel, at least from the time of Moshe's death (and, thus, presumably while Moshe was still alive), for which the Torah apparently supplies no explanation. This class of people was exceptional. From its ranks came those who led and who appointed leaders. In times of national crisis, it was to members of this class that the people turned for guidance. It was from this class that the word of God continued to be given.

This class was concerned with the issues Moshe was concerned with. It functioned in much the same manner as he functioned. In fact, this class was the extension of Moshe into future generations. It was *the class of the prophets of Israel.*

Where did Eli come from? What gave Shmuel the power to lead a nation, appoint kings, and remove them? From where did Natan gain the right to condemn a king? Obviously, their power came from God, but how did the people know that? How did the people know that these people who called themselves prophets were who they said they were and were touched by God?

I think what we see here is the birth of that class. While Moshe lives, there is little need for the prophets, other than to establish them among the people. The Torah, therefore, does not dwell on their activities (which, as noted, were mostly mundane, in any case). We will learn about them later, when they are needed, and when their activities are pivotal to the continuing saga of Israel. For now, it is sufficient for the Torah to provide us only with the basis of their authority.

In this sense, then, this group of seventy is indeed the model of the future Sanhedrin. There is a direct line from the prophets to the scribes to the rabbis of the Sanhedrin.

Joseph Ozarowski

The relationship of the seventy select (according to some it was seventy-two, Eldad and Medad having turned down the job yet still receiving prophecy) to the leaders Moshe picked with Jethro's advice is not completely clear. My first inclination was to consider the choice of the seventy a *hora'at sha'ah*, a temporary measure needed because of the crisis in the people's confidence and their constant *kvetching* (complaining). The advisors picked with Jethro, on the other hand, seemed to me a more permanent judicial presence. However, upon research, I discovered that whole schools of commentators from the Talmud (BT Sanhedrin, first Mishnah and 16b) through Hirsch saw the choice of the seventy as the source of the Great Sanhedrin and obviously meant as a permanent presence.

The language of both chapters have some similarities, notably the need for leadership to help Moshe "carry the burden with you" (Exodus 18:22; Numbers 11:17). There is however, one crucial difference. In Exodus, the leaders simply share the burden of governing, judging issues, and adjudicating people's problems. Here, there is a religious element present when God offers to share the Holy Spirit and prophecy with the seventy.

Maybe this means that for an enduring system of leadership to survive, the leader cannot merely be satisfied with the legal minutiae of law, but he or she must also inspire followers with his or her spiritual leadership, gaining strength and the ability to lead from the Spirit of the Living God. This is a powerful message which all community religious leaders, rabbinic as well as lay, ought to take to heart.

There is another element. Rashi addresses the question of who the seventy really were. He suggests that they were the *mukim*, the Jewish leaders who were responsible to the Egyptian taskmasters in Egypt. Whenever there were problems, the Egyptians set on these individuals first and beat them (hence the name *mukim*). Their claim to leadership was based on the fact that they led people in suffering during terrible times. Thus, they probably had the respect of the people in the pastoral sense of truly sharing their burden of slavery. Now the time had come to translate this empathy into sharing the burden of freedom and living a Godly life. Through their understanding and having gone through the worst with their people, they were worthy of the Divine Presence in order to inspire the people.

This is a fine model for community leadership today. Rabbinic and lay leaders must empathically feel the pain of the common folk if they are to lead. Only if they do so can God's spirit be shared with all. (For more on the need for empathic leadership, see chapter 14 of Abraham Besdin's *Reflections of the Rav* [Jerusalem: World Zionist Organization, 1979], where Rabbi Joseph Soloveitchik develops this idea of empathy based on Moshe's changed role after this whole incident; also see chapter 6 of my book *To Walk in God's Ways—Jewish Pastoral Perspectives on Illness and Bereavement* (Northvale: Jason Aronson, 1995), where I extensively develop this idea of pastoral and empathic leadership.

All in all, we do not have much in the way of specifics about the experience of the seventy. But we do know that their religious and pastoral leadership provided the firm basis for Jewish jurisprudence ever since.

David Sofian

A similar matter will arise later in the Torah's narrative when the focus is Joshua's succession of Moses. The question you ask here about why these men were picked could also be asked about Joshua and his assumption of leadership. In that case, and I more fully go into it in my response to *Parashah Pinchas*, Joshua assumes leadership because he earned it.

In brief, I pointed out there that the midrash makes clear that Joshua had served Moses, the community, and God well, and so he therefore deserved to become leader. In other words, worthiness was the key to Joshua's advancement. The same point pertains here. Of course, God could have taken totally undistinguished individuals. This could have been so anywhere along the line. However, that is not the way God chooses. God especially chooses Abraham, Rachel, and Moses, or any of the other amazing personalities of the narrative, because of their qualities.

Rashi helps clarify this in his commentary to chapter 11:16. Commenting on the phrase, "gather unto Me," he informs us that the complainers punished in chapter 11:1 are the first elders mentioned in *Shmot* 3:16. The reason God destroyed them is to be found in *Shmot* 24:11, where we learn how they acted irreverently when they beheld God. What impudence to eat and drink even as they gazed at God! Rashi teaches us that their punishment was delayed to now because God didn't want to bring about mourning at the same time as the giving of the Torah. In terms of this discussion, they clearly weren't worthy of leadership, and they would have been an inappropriate choice to be endowed with God's spirit.

So then why are these elders chosen? Rashi continues in his comment to "whom you know that they are," utilizing *midrash Bamidbar Rabbah* 15:20, to tell us that these were the same Jewish individuals who had been appointed officers in Egypt. There, in spite of Pharaoh's orders, they had pity on their fellow Israelites when they couldn't meet the quota of bricks demanded, and their pity led to their own additional physical affliction. They chose to accept pain and distress themselves so that their fellow Israelites might not be totally exhausted.

In other words, these individuals were chosen, like Joshua later on, because they had done something to earn leadership and the experience of God's Spirit. Who better than these individuals who had already proven their willingness to help Israel with its burdens and to share the burden of dealing with them now, along with Moses?

God chooses them because they were willing to sacrifice themselves for the benefit of the community. Perhaps this answers your final question also. If they were chosen as the midrash and Rashi suggest, and received glory, greatness, and the Holy Spirit in order to teach the importance of self-sacrifice, particularly for the sake of Israel, the details of what happened to them afterward are not important.

It is the connection of their earlier commitment to their elevation as sharers in the divine spirit with Moses that we are meant to see. Hence it is their selection that is emphasized in the Torah, not their subsequent actions.

Shelach Lecha:
Numbers 13:1–15:41

Prophetical Reading
Joshua 2:1–24

Overview of Torah Portion

God tells Moses to send men to spy out the land of Canaan. They return, after forty days, with a largely negative report, which causes the people to cry for a return to Egypt. Angered at their faithlessness, God vows that the older generation, those twenty years old and above, will not enter the Promised Land but will wander in the desert for forty years; instead, their children will inherit the Holy Land. God gives directions for bringing sacrifices upon entering Canaan.

Key Verses

"And the Lord said to Moses, 'How long will this people despise Me and how long will they not believe in Me, for all the signs that I have performed in their midst . . . ? How long shall I bear this evil congregation that keep murmuring against me'" (Numbers 14:11, 27)?

Discussion Question

A QUESTION OF DEITY: God is angry that the people He brought out of Egypt want to return there and that they accept the spies' negative report about Canaan. First He questions the people's attitude, then His own patience. Why does God ask questions? Does He not know all the answers? If He simply wants to convery His anger, a declarative statement would suffice. Are the questions purely rhetorical? Moses does not offer a direct response to the heavenly queries; he apparently has no answers. Is the dialogue between God and Moses a paradigm for our use of questions and answers?

Shammai Engelmayer

Perhaps this can be viewed as a model for our reliance on questions and answers as the way to understand God and His desires for us.

The Jewish philosopher Philo of Alexandria, writing in the first century, saw three modes of revelation in the Torah—direct revelation, divine inspiration, and God's answers to Moshe's questions. In the sense that, through His questions, we are given a brief look into the nature of God, then this colloquy can serve as a model. For, after all, why do we ask questions if not to pierce the veils of mystery enshrouding Him and His plan for humankind? If God can reveal a bit of Himself through His questions and answers, then we can learn about Him in the same way.

The problem, however, is that God is not asking questions for the sake of getting answers. Answers are not what He is after here. God, being God, knows the answers, in any case; rather, He is trying to get Moshe to understand himself. Thus, in trying to use these questions in order to fathom something about God, we are relying on material God prepared, not to reveal portions of Himself but portions of His respondent's self.

Moshe is on shaky ground at this point. He already doubts whether God can deliver on His promises. And he has had his full of this people.

Or so he says (and probably believes). God needs to get Moshe to see the truth—that it is his frustration that is at its fullest, not his faith in God or his commitment to and love for his people. God, through His questions, forces Moshe to think through his own sense of helplessness.

It is not the first time this conversation is held, and it will not be the last. The previous time, in fact, made this conversation and the ones that follow in parshah *Korach* necessary, because that version saw Moshe on the offensive against Israel, with God in the position of having to calm him down. God, of course, knows Moshe's heart, but He is not certain Moshe knows his own heart at this point; the strain on him has been that great.

There is another issue raised by the question, however, that must be addressed here. If God knows all the answers, He also knows what the future will bring. Thus, He knows in advance what will happen with the spies. By ordering Moshe to choose twelve people to spy out the land of Canaan, then, God is setting up Israel and Moshe. Are we to believe that God could be so perverse? Is God that cruel? Clearly, God is not, so something else must be going on here.

In Deuteronomy 1, when Moshe recounts the story, he says *the people* sent the twelve to spy out the land, not God. That would seem to settle things, but we are faced with a less than clear text this week, thus muddying the waters. This week, God says, "Choose *for yourself* men and send them to spy out the land of Canaan."

Does the text in this *sidrah* suggest God's initiative? So most critics believe, but there are strong objections to such a reading—the most obvious being that He had no need for any intelligence the spies could supply. *Only the people, not yet trusting in the power of God, despite all that had happened (and apparently on the eve of rebellion), needed spies to reassure themselves that Canaan was conquerable.*

Another objection: If God initiated the mission, it would have been sufficient for Him to say, "*Shelach anashim* (send men)." Instead, He says, "*Shelach lecha anashim*," which, literally translated, means, "send *for yourself* men."

Does this prove that God was not the initiator in Numbers? No, because it is possible to read the text this way: "Moshe, I do not need spies, but you and the people want some reassurance, so send for yourself men. . . ." Nevertheless, the inclusion of the "for yourself" strongly suggests that God was not the initiator.

There are additional texts here that make the suggestion a near certainty. In 14:34, for example, God is talking: "Corresponding to the number of days that you spied on the land . . . , a year for each day, you shall bear the consequences of your sin . . . ; and you will know what it is to frustrate Me."

The sentence contains phrasing that is inconsistent with God as initiator of the spying. Indeed, the whole sentence suggests that God is punishing Israel as much for having wanted to send spies in the first place as for having believed their negative analysis of the situation in Canaan. Had God been the initiator, the situation would be untenable: God is angry at Israel because, after He orders Israel to send spies to spy out the land, the spies do their job and report to the people, who believe their report because, after all, is that not why they were sent? In effect, God is punishing Israel for listening to Him in the first place, and that is nonsensical.

If more proof is needed, in both 14:16 and 14:36 we find the phrase, "as for the men whom Moshe sent"; not God, but Moshe. True, these men were chosen by Moshe according to God's guidelines (13:2), but it was Moshe who sent them, not God. (The petulant tone of the phrase suggests that God was displeased that Moshe even bothered to bring the people's request to Him; that Moshe, shaky in his faith in God's powers, was unable to muster persuasive arguments to reassure the people and calm their fears.)

This theme is repeated throughout chapters 13–14 and is consistent with what Moshe himself says in Deuteronomy 1:22–23: "And you all came near to me and said, 'Let us send men before us and they will search out the land'. . . . And [the idea] pleased me. . . ." Pleased me—not God.

That still begs the question: If God knew what would happen, why did He play along? Why did He not warn Moshe and Israel what was in store for them if they pursued this dangerous course?

That brings us back to a point I made in answer to the question in *Parshat Vayera*: When God created everything, he literally "programmed" in every possible permutation of all that would happen. He accounted for each individual's choices in His original programming. There is an end goal, but how we get there is our business. God does not interfere. So, in truth, He did not know what would happen, only what could happen. At every step along the way, the spies and the people had the ability to change the outcome. God cannot be faulted because Israel, exercising its free will, chose the wrong path.

Joseph Ozarowski

The idea of God asking questions in spite of the fact that the answers are known is frequently found in the Torah. The first and classic case is back in Genesis 3:9 where God asks Adam and Eve after they ate the forbidden fruit, "Where are you?" *Hashem* certainly knew where they were. But as Rashi, based on the Midrash, explains, *Hashem* was trying to engage Adam and Eve with words. *Hashem* was offering them the chance to do *teshuvah*, to say they were sorry for transgressing the Divine command (see *Sifte Hakahmim*, the super-commentary on Rashi, who clearly spells this out; see also Ibn Ezra). Rashi suggests several other biblical examples of God engaging the human party with words, including Cain on murdering his brother ("Where is Abel, your brother?"), Bilaam, and Hezekiah. In each case, God is giving the human parties the opening for a dialogue that will hopefully bring them to contriteness and repentance.

Another, more subtle case, is after the golden calf incident (Exodus 32:10), where God does not ask a question but makes an angry radical statement to Moshe, "And now leave Me be . . . that I may destroy them, and I will make of you a great nation." Again Rashi, based on the midrash, explains that up to this point, Moshe was stunned by the people's actions and had no response to God. But God's comment was understood by Moshe as leaving him (Moshe) the opening for prayer, knowing that the ultimate forgiveness of our people would be based on his plea. So again, God is providing a chance to right the wrongs through engaging the human party with words.

Our case of the spies is even more severe. The *Or Hahayim* suggests that God's question to Moshe here was to prevent Moshe from praying to God for forgiveness in the way he did after the golden calf. The sin of the spies and their followers, in open rebellion against God and the divine plan, was so serious that God in essence now says, "Moshe, don't even to try to *daven* this time!" Yet in spite of this, Moshe still prays, choosing his words carefully to supplicate on behalf of his flock. And in the end, God forgives the sins and does not destroy the people, though they are condemned to be in the desert for forty years.

What is the moral of all this? God wants to hear from us. *Hashem* will give us the opportunity to engage in dialogue because our *teshuvah* is preferred. And even when it seems that things are so bad that there is no hope, prayer is still worthwhile and effective.

David Sofian

The case you raise is not the only time God asks questions. Some examples would be the third chapter of *b'reishit* when God asks Adam, "where are you?" In that same parshah God asks Cain, "Where is your brother Abel?" Likewise, when Sarah hears that she is to become pregnant and laughs, God asks Abraham, "Why did Sarah laugh, saying, 'shall I in truth bear a child, old as I am?'"

By asking, "why does God ask these questions?" you are pointing to the incongruity that exists between the God theologians describe and the God we read about in the Torah. Neil Gillman points out in his highly readable and helpful book, *Sacred Fragments* (1990), that the image of God found in classical western philosophy and theology is quite different from the one we find in the Bible. The problem you raise results from applying the philosophical and theological image of God to a biblical text.

Philosophy and theology want to know about our concepts of God. It discusses what, if anything, we can know about God's nature and/or God's attributes. Theologians and philosophers expose our thought about God to the most careful critical analysis. Western philosophy, starting with the Greeks, sees God as perfect, for an imperfect God would not be God. In order to be perfect, God would have to be omnipotent and all-knowing. Anything else would contradict God's perfection.

But then, if God is omniscient, where does that leave human freedom? How can human beings be truly free to make choices, if God already knows the outcome? Does God's foreknowledge not contradict human freedom? This problem occupied a great deal of medieval Jewish thought. And if God is all-powerful, why does God allow evil to exist? How can a benevolent God with the power to do something about it allow evil in the world?

This dilemma, with all its variations in expression, is the most intractable problem theologians face. These are the kinds of questions theologians deal with.

Clearly, within this image of God, this metaphor for speaking about God, God would not be asking questions. As you say, certainly this God must know all the answers. So assuming a philosophical concept of God as a starting point, a serious study of the text leaves us to deal with the questions God asks by using midrashic or interpretive techniques. This can be a very creative process, as the reader of midrash knows.

It was precisely this kind of problem which led me to comment in answer to your question to Parshah *B'ereishit* that, when God asks Adam, "where are you?" the question can only be for Adam's benefit. The other approach to the problem is to recognize that the philosophical and theological image is not the image of God the text is expressing, and we should not try to force it upon the text. Rather, we should try to understand that image for what it is.

Turning to the God of the Torah, we find in this image, God is emotional. As you pointed out in your question, in this parshah God is angered by the people's acceptance of the spies report. The biblical God cares deeply about how we conduct our lives and our social relationships. This God cares and that concern often leads to frustration, which God also often exhibits.

In the Torah, we can read about God's anger and pleasure; about a God whose mind can be changed and Who destroys and saves. This God has desires and plans for humankind that are conditional. As we can see, this God is hardly perfect. God having emotions, desires, and passions means God changes and has needs. A God who is perfect would never need to change. A God who is perfect would never have any needs to fulfill.

So, then, when we recognize that is the biblical image of God, it is not surprising that God asks questions in the Bible. The Torah is not distressed or disturbed in the least by the philosophical and theological questions raised above. The Bible is interested in and committed to showing us that

God is intimately involved with Creation, with human beings, with our ancestors, and with us.

Looked at from the Torah's perspective, the questions God asks should not cause us to wonder about God's philosophical perfection. Rather, these questions help us see an image of God that is interested in us and is involved with the world.

Korach: Numbers 16:1–18:32

Prophetical Reading
1 Samuel 11:14–12:22

Overview of Torah Portion

Korach, a member of the tribe of Levi, leads a rebellion of 250 men who challenge Moses' and Aaron's divine authority. All the usurpers die at the hand of God, drawing the criticism of many Hebrews that Moses caused the death of "the people of the Lord—" God brings a plague in which 14,700 people die. God miraculously vindicates Moses and Aaron by making Aaron's rod bloom almond blossoms in the Tabernacle. God tells Aaron the Levites' duties and rewards.

Key Verses

"And Eleazar the Priest took the brazen firepans that [the followers of Korach] who were burnt had offered, and beat them, for a covering for the altar—as a memorial to the Children of Israel so that no common man, not of the seed of Aaron, approach to burn incense before the Lord, that he shall not be as Korach and his congregation" (Numbers 17:4–5).

Discussion Question

SENSE ABOUT INCENSE: Beaten firepans are to serve as a memorial, a visual reminder, to the actions of Korach's followers. But the action being memorialized is their offering of incense, which seems to overlook their larger sin—they rebelled against Moses' authority as God's chosen leader. Indeed, Moses instructed them to bring the incense, as a test of his divine vindication.

Why does the Torah memorialize the ultimately rejected incense instead of the actual rebellion? What is so important about the incense? Why not save the firepans intact as a more vivid symbol of the uprising?

Shammai Engelmayer

Precisely because the firepans are not saved intact, it is clear that "the ultimately rejected incense" is not what is being memorialized. Rather, because the firepans have become sacred in some way, the metal from which they were fashioned is put to a sacred use—as additional plating for the altar. That this serves as a memorial is purely incidental. To all who see it, that plating is obviously superfluous. It is in this way that it serves as a reminder of Korach's rebellion and its fate.

One could ask why the firepans, having become sacred, were not used as firepans by the priests. The answer would seem to be that, while they are now sacred, they were fashioned for reasons decidedly unsacred—namely, as a challenge to the authority of Moshe and Aharon, and thus indirectly as a challenge to God's authority. (That is why the firepans are beaten out of shape—so they could never be used, even accidentally, as firepans.)

Keep in mind that we are not dealing here with belief in Moshe's word. No matter how much Korach and company insist that they doubt the word of Moshe that he and Aharon are the chosen leaders, they saw with their own eyes that God, in fact, had chosen Moshe and Aharon. And they saw it in a very graphic and very gruesome moment when God demonstrated how He deals with those who presume to act without His authority. Nadav and Avihu were instantly consumed for bringing their strange fire. None who saw that could argue that God had not chosen His leaders.

It is because of what happened to Nadav and Avihu that the firepans and incense are again used to demonstrate God's choices. Moshe sets up an identical situation to the recent horrible event, then gives the conspirators twenty-four hours to prepare. That means he also gives them twenty-four hours to realize the similarity and to repent. That they do not repent only proves that they meant to challenge God, not just Moshe and Aharon.

There is an added reason, however. The text makes it clear that the firepans, when lit and filled with incense, can mean life or death, depending on who holds the pans. When those who are not entitled to carry the firepans do so, they die. Shortly after Korach's firepan-wielding rebels are crushed by God, thousands of lives are saved when Aharon carries his firepan into the heart of an Israelite camp being attacked by an angry God. Again, the message of whom God chose is clear.

Does this mean that there is something special, or even magical, about the incense? Absolutely not. To repeat, the use of incense and firepans here is deliberate—meant to evoke the memory of the fate of Nadav and Avihu, in the hopes that it would inspire repentance rather than rebellion. That the incense is then used to thwart God's deadly anger against Israel is God's way of making certain that no one could ever claim that it was the incense itself that killed the rebels. The incense is nothing but a smelly substance; only God has power over life and death.

In truth, when Aharon ran into the midst of the plague-ridden camp with his burning firepan, he had absolutely no effect on the course of the plague. God killed as many people as He intended to kill and spared all whom He intended to spare.

On the other hand, if Aharon's act had such a chilling effect on a superstitious people that they would not again challenge God's authority, well and good. In fact, for this generation, the challenges and rebellions are at an end. Unfortunately, their acceptance of God and His chosen leaders comes too late to save them from 40 years of wandering and death in the desert.

Having said this, I must add an explanation. In the next portion, *Chukat*, the people "arrive" at Kadesh, where Miriam dies. Because there is no water, the people again challenge Moshe and Aharon. When they refer to the death of their "brothers," there is the implication that this event took place not too long after the rebellions of Korach, and Datan and Aviram. The people also make reference to having personally been taken out of Egypt.

On the other hand, God's statement to Moshe and Aharon that they would not lead this congregation into Canaan suggests that the event took place toward the end of the forty years. Since nearly all of the events depicted from *Parshat Chukat* onward are clearly in the final year of the desert sojourn, it is more than likely that this event also took place in that year. The reference to dead brothers thus would not refer to Korach and company, but to the generation of the Exodus who died in the wilderness.

The reference to be taken out of Egypt poses no problem here. Only the adults who left Egypt were doomed to die in the desert. All those under the age of 20 lived to cross over into Canaan (see Numbers 14:29).

Thus, because we have no record of anything that occurred to Israel between the plague and the return to Kadesh in year 40, we must assume that nothing worth mentioning took place, which is further proof that the rebellions ceased.

Joseph Ozarowski

What symbolism is there in turning the firepans into an altar cover? The *Or Hahayim* suggests that covering the altar was a tangible means of keeping itinerant people away from the altar at non-usage times. While the Torah has warned non-priests numerous times to keep their distance from the altar (including here, see 17:5), *Or Hahayim* writes that a more concrete reminder, based directly on the tragic incident, was needed to insure the altar's sanctity and keep outsiders away, "so that he fare not as Korach and his company . . ." (vs. 5).

There is more to this explanation than meets the eye. My oldest son asked me on Shabbat why Korach's question, "Seeing all the congregation, every one of them is holy, the Lord is among them, and why do you raise yourselves over the congregation of the Lord?" (16:3) is considered so problematic. Didn't God in Leviticus 19:2 actually command the entire congregation to be holy, "Ye shall be holy, for I the Lord your God am holy?" What was the difficulty?

The answer has to do with the nature of Korach's rebellion, which centered around the issues of structure vs. anarchy. In the midrash, Korach taunts Moshe by asking him if a room full of scrolls needs a *mezuzah*, and if a garment entirely made of *techelet*, the blue color required in classical *tsitsit* threads, needs *tsitsit* strings. These are not just clever "*kuntz kashes.*" They describe the nature of Korach's challenge. Korach is saying that we do not need structure, leadership, teachers, or *mitzvot*. Everyone is holy, everything is holy (à la the late Allan Ginsburg), and people should just do whatever they want to achieve holiness because of this.

Moshe's response is essentially that we all indeed do have the potential to be holy, and God wants us to achieve our potential as religious beings. But this must be done through the framework of the Torah. Religion without some structure runs a great risk of going haywire, justifying all sorts of terrible things in its name. The end result is the possibility of being swallowed by the Earth. Religion is not meant to be so dry that spirituality is lost, but it is also not a free-for-all. The Torah's command to be holy attempts to strike that balance between being part of a Divine community religious system that fosters holiness and achieving a personal sense of holiness.

The *Or Hahayim* teaches us that the altar is accessible to all within the Torah's system. Indeed, people from all walks of life—men and women, wealthy and poor, Jew and non-Jew—were represented at the Temple. But it was all done within the framework of the *halakha* and Temple structure. The altar covers, the remains of a chaotic rebellion, were a tangible reminder that, while the Torah allowed all to become close to God through a *korban* at the altar, some structure and distance had to be maintained.

David Sofian

After being introduced to Korach and the rest of the rebels, the very beginning of the parshah tells us that these agitators rose up against Moses. Shortly thereafter, Aaron is also a target. The word *lakhem* in chapter 16:3 ("to you") makes it clear that both Moses and Aaron are being accused of going too far.

Yet, after the allegation that the two of them had raised themselves above God's congregation, Moses stands in the primary role. Moses is clearly hurt by the challenge to him as the leader. Moses responds orally to the rebels and tries to convince them to end their revolt. Moses speaks with God about the situation.

Moses' prominence in the story always left me with the impression that the antagonism was primarily against him and his leadership. This impression was reinforced for me by Moses' own words in 16:11, which can be read as having a condescending tone. It says there, "for who is Aaron that you should complain against him?" I always heard those words faintly hinting at a Mosaic conceit—why complain about him, is deposing me not your real goal?

True, when God appears in verse 19 and speaks in verse 20, it is to both Moses and Aaron, and together they successfully petition God not to destroy the whole community. So the narrative itself made it clear that it is not about Moses alone. But soon after that, the focus returns to Moses, and with it my sense that the challenge was primarily against him. I noticed the wording of your question indicates a similar point of view when you say, "they rebelled against Moses' authority as God's chosen leader."

However, your question about the incense and firepans led me to rethink all this. I found a very different picture beginning to emerge when Moses informs Korach that in the morning God will show who is holy. Both Rashi and Ramban indicate that this phrase, "who is holy," refers to the priesthood. And Ramban elucidates the continuation of this passage, so we see that what is being challenged here is not so much Moses' authority, but the authority of the priests.

As I indicated above, I had never looked at our narrative this way. The idea of choosing firepans and incense to resolve the conflict begins to make more sense when we see that perhaps the primary object of hostility was Aaron and the priesthood.

We find this point of view reinforced in *midrash Bamidbar Rabbah*. Chapter 18:8 reminds us that Israel and the nations are different. Other nations have many religious observances and many priests. Israel has one God, one Torah and one code of laws, and so also has only one altar and one High Priest. The midrash goes on to accuse all 250 rebels of seeking the High Priesthood. This means their offense was their rebellion against the authority of the High Priesthood.

The next section of the midrash continues this emphasis by telling us that, had Aaron taken the priesthood on his own initiative instead of God choosing him, the rebels would have been correct in standing against him. However, since it was the Holy One who gave him the High Priesthood, standing against Aaron is standing against God. And then, just to add the final touch, the midrash makes sure we are reminded of Aaron's worthiness by recalling his piety and modesty. We learn that even as Moses was anointing him High Priest, Aaron expressed a lack of confidence in his own worthiness.

Seeing that this episode may be about Aaron's authority and practice, and not so much about Moses', clarifies why a contest using censers and incense is used to decide the issue. A cultic challenge is resolved with a cultic contest.

This perspective is fortified one more time at the end of the biblical story itself. Aaron is the hero when, in the aftermath of Korach's rebellion, he functions in his priestly role. In 17:6, after the altar had been plated with the firepans, the people turn on Moses and Aaron again, accusing them of bringing death on them. God becomes angry and wants to annihilate the Israelites by sending a plague. It takes Aaron offering incense, standing between the dead and the living, to make expiation for the people.

Then, in answer to your question, the Torah is not memorializing the rebels' rejected incense. It is reminding the Israelites that only someone of Aaron's offspring should presume to offer incense before God. The altar's overlay of copper made from the firepans serves to remind all of what happens when Aaron's authority as God's chosen High Priest, and the functioning of the priesthood in general, is challenged.

Creating the memorial this way, instead of leaving the firepans intact, allowed the reminder to be integrated into the most central spot of priestly functioning. It is hard to imagine a more dramatic, constant symbolic expression of support for Aaron and priestly authority.

Chukat: Numbers 19:1–22:1

Prophetical Reading
Judges 11:1–33

Overview of Torah Portion

God gives Moses the law of the red heifer—an unblemished cow whose sacrificial ashes will purify the ritually defiled. Miriam dies at Kadesh. The people's water supply ceases, bringing a question of why Moses brought them to "this evil place." "Talk to the rock and it will bring forth water," God instructs Moses. Instead, he strikes the rock; the water comes, but for disobeying God's command, Moses is told he will not bring the Children of Israel into the Promised Land.

The King of Edom refuses the Hebrews permission to pass through his territory. Aaron dies on Mount Hor. The King of Arad attacks the Hebrews, taking captives. The victorious Hebrews vanquish him and destroy his cities. Again, the Children of Israel complain of hunger. God sends poisonous, fiery serpents among the people. The King of the Amorites and the King of Bashan attack the Hebrews and are defeated.

Key Verses

"And the Lord said . . .'All the men that have seen My glory and My signs that I performed in Egypt and in the wilderness . . . and have not listened to My voice . . . shall not see the land that I swore to their fathers'" (Numbers 14:20–22).

"And the Lord said to Moses and Aaron, 'Because you did not believe in Me to sanctify Me in the eyes of the Children of Israel, therefore you shall not bring this assembly into the land that I have given them'" (Numbers 20:12).

Discussion Question

THE UN-PROMISED LAND: First, the Children of Israel demonstrate their lack of faith in God's promise, accepting the spies' pessimistic report about the land of Canaan; in response, God denies them entrance to the Promised Land. Now Moses disobeys God's command *vis-à-vis* the rock and God withdraws Moses' mandate to take the people across the Jordan. Does God break His word? The misfeasance of the Hebrews (repeated flouting God's commands) and of Moses (one misinterpretation of a command) are dissimilar both in quality and quantity. Why this—severe—punishment in both cases? Why the same punishment for the leader and the followers? Does the punishment fit each crime?

Shammai Engelmayer

Let us, first off, dismiss the suggestion that God breaks His promises. He does not; and in any case, broken promises are not the issue here.

Dealing with the simple issue first, it was Israel that broke *its* promise. Standing at Mt. Sinai, it said, "we will do and we will listen." The people heartily accepted the Covenant with God. That Covenant granted Israel a leasehold—the land of Canaan—in return for fealty to God and fulfillment of His task for them. Having broken their word over and again within the space of a few short months, it was only fitting that they lose out on the Promised Land.

Any lesser punishment, and God's word would be worthless, for He made clear what would happen if Israel failed to live up to its end of the bargain.

In fact, rather than suggest that God does not keep His promises, this is an example of how protective God is of those promises. Only the generation of the Exodus loses the Land; despite the sins of the fathers, the promise remains valid for the children.

Moshe, on the other hand, poses a problem. At least on the surface, the punishment does not fit the crime. To solve the problem, we need to look elsewhere—especially further on, in *Parshat Va'etchanan.*

"And you shall repeat them to your children in order to teach them;" so Moshe commands us in *Va'etchanan,* as Israel prepares to cross the Jordan to begin the conquest of the Promised Land. So we remind ourselves at least four times a day as we recite the first paragraph of the Shema—twice during *Shacharit,* once during *Ma'ariv,* and once on our beds before we sleep.

The *Shema* is one of the two main features of *Va'etchanan*. And this commandment—to teach our children—is a principal feature of the *Shema*. The commandment is also the key to the mystery of why Moshe was denied the right to cross over the Jordan. At the same time, it is also key to a modern mystery, about which I write more later.

"And you shall repeat them to your children in order to teach them" were not casual words that flowed from Moshe's lips. He could have said, as he does many times—including in the paragraph in *Parshat Ekev* that eventually became the second paragraph of the Shema—"and you shall teach them to your children."

But he does not say "you shall teach them" here. He says, "you shall *repeat them* in order to teach them." It is not enough to sit down one day and tell them the things they need to know about who and what they are. You have to repeat the lessons over and again. And you have to repeat them in such a way as to make a lasting impression upon the children. It is not enough to talk these lessons through. You have to act them out, day after day, year after year.

We, the Jewish people, could never have survived for four generations, much less for four millennia, if we had not observed the commandment to "repeat them to your children in order to teach them;" if we had not, in a meaningful and substantive way, passed on to our children and our children's children the laws and traditions that define our existence.

Failure to fulfill this commandment carries with it a high risk—both for the individual *and the community*, for this command rests not on the parent alone. All of us share in that responsibility. If we fail to carry it out, we all will be punished.

And the punishment for this sin of omission is the severest of all: oblivion.

The risk to the individual can be gleaned from the opening sentences of *Va'etchanan*. Having passed on the mantle of leadership to Yehoshua, Moshe tells us that he beseeched the Lord to let him cross over the Jordan and enter the Promised Land.

This, after all, has been the goal of his life. He has spent the last 40 years pursuing it. He has endured deprivation, rebellion, vilification, and war. What did any of it matter if, at the end of the journey, he could sit, however briefly, under his own vine and fig tree in the land flowing with milk and honey?

Moshe had a right to expect this. Yet God turned him down. "And God was angry with me because of you, and He did not listen to [my plea]."

This does not jibe, however, with what we are told this week, in Numbers 20:12. Here, God specifically says that Moshe was punished because of what happened at the rock.

What, exactly, did happen? The desert was cruel; the people were thirsty. They demanded water—and a return to Egypt. God told Moshe to speak to a rock until it gave forth water to slake the people's thirst, in so doing demonstrating God's glory and His beneficence. But Moshe lost patience with the rock and hit it with his staff. This momentary lapse, we are told, cost him the right to cross the Jordan.

Moshe will repeat this in *Parashat Pinchas*, when he quotes God as saying he could not enter Israel "because you rebelled against Me in the wilderness of Zin." What Moshe did at the rock was so terrible that it outweighed a lifetime of good deeds.

Surely, however, it could not have been for so trivial a matter that so harsh a punishment was decreed. And, indeed, Moshe will tell us in *Va'etchanan* that the reason is "because of you," meaning the people, not because of something he himself had done.

Can the two be reconciled? They can—and in that reconciliation we can understand what Moshe's true sin was when he lost patience with a stubborn stone. For what Moshe is really saying in both instances is that his request was denied *because he was a poor teacher*.

The people who stood before Moshe demanding to be returned to the fleshpots of Egypt never knew those fleshpots; their parents did (see the end of my answer for *Parshat Korach*). Now that the parents are dead, their lack of faith lives on in their children. Clearly, Moshe had not taught the Second Generation well enough about the land they were to inherit to overcome what their parents had told them about the land they had fled.

He had also not taught them well enough about the greatness of the Lord to overcome the lure of false gods. Unlike their parents, this people was raised knowing God alone, yet it soon will rush headlong into the apostasy of Ba'al Pe'or.

Moshe had failed in his mission as teacher. He had taught these people from infancy, yet they grew up as rebellious as their parents—and as ignorant. All that Moshe had done in his life could not overcome this one failure. Who he was did not matter; what counted was what he was not—he was not a good teacher.

So God denied Moshe's request. He would not enter the Promised Land. He would not claim a share in Israel's inheritance. And, in the sense that a parent lives on in his or her children, Moshe's life effectively ends with his death. His children, already barely visible, soon disappear from our view completely.

Indeed, when Moshe dies, there is nothing tangible by which to remember him. There is no physical relic of his to point to in remembrance of his life. There is not even a marker on his grave, the location of which itself is a secret. It is as if he never was, except for one thing—"and you shall repeat them to your children in order to teach them." Ironically, the commandment that cost him so dearly also rescues him from oblivion. He may have failed as a teacher for the second generation, but he succeeded in becoming the teacher *par excellence* for all the generations to follow. He is, after all, *Moshe Rabbenu*, (Moses, our Teacher).

Frankly, however, the punishment still does not seem to fit the crime. To finally solve the Moshe mystery and go on to discuss the modern mystery, we must first solve yet another mystery: Does God punish children, grandchildren, and great-grandchildren for the sins of the fathers?

Judging from the fact that God only keeps the generation of the Exodus from entering the Land, we must assume that He does not carry a grudge. Yet, in the Ten Statements, the reprise of which is the other main feature of *Va'etchanan*, we are told: "For I, the Lord your God, am a jealous God, visiting the sins of the parents on the children, and unto the third and unto the fourth generation of them who hate Me; and showing kindness unto the thousandth generation of those who love Me and keep My commandments."

Can this be? Is God so vengeful that He would punish my great-great-great-grandchildren for my sins? Does this not contradict the Torah itself— both in the fact that the second generation inherits the Land and in a declaration appearing a mere nineteen chapters after Moshe restates the Decalogue—that a person is punished for his or her crime alone? Are we now to believe that God is so cruel and so arbitrary?

No. As a midrash in the *Mekilta d-Rabbi Ishmael* explains regarding the original verse in Exodus, this applies only to children who sin *as their parents sinned*.

This is made even more explicit in the "official" Aramaic translation of the Torah, the *Targum Onkelos*. To the offending verse, "unto the third and unto the fourth generation of those who hate me," it adds a phrase: "when the children continue to sin as their parents had done."

God is not being arbitrary and capricious. What He is saying is that children learn from their parents and from the community in which they live. If the parents sin—if the community tolerates and even condones such behavior—the children will be predisposed to sin themselves. With each successive generation, the sin grows larger until, finally, a generation comes along that is so far removed from Israel's path that it is no longer a part of Israel.

This message is even clearer earlier in *Va'etchanan*: "When you shall have children and grandchildren, and have lived in the land a long time. . . . And you do what is evil in the sight of the Lord your God . . . , you will soon be completely gone from the land . . . , and the

Lord will scatter you among the peoples, and there will be few of you left among the nations."

In a midrash, the rabbis of blessed memory apply a trickle-down theory to this verse. If the head of the Sanhedrin errs in a decision, and neither the presiding judge of the *Beth Din* nor any of the judges challenge him, the people will surely sin, for how can their leaders make a mistake?

It is common sense: Our children, or those who look to us for leadership and guidance, will not take seriously what we ourselves do not take seriously. We cannot tell them Shabbat is sacred and holy—and then head out for a Saturday afternoon of shopping at the malls. Children do not learn by listening; they learn by seeing what we do.

This, then, is how God visits our iniquities on our children—by allowing human nature to take its course. The risk we run by not teaching our children in a meaningful way about their responsibilities and obligations as Jews is a loss of everything that makes us Jews.

This solves mystery number two—and it solves mystery number one, as well. Moshe is not being punished merely because he was a poor teacher. He is being punished because *his failure as a teacher had put the very future of Israel in jeopardy*. If the second generation had succeeded in rebelling against Moshe and against God, either in the wilderness of Zin or at Ba'al Pe'or, Israel's inheritance would have been forfeited.

Thus, Moshe's punishment fits the test of "an eye for an eye." In this case, it is "an inheritance for an inheritance."

This leads us to mystery number three, the modern mystery I referred to earlier: We are Jewish. We will be Jewish until the day we die. Can we say the same thing, however, about our grandchildren and great-grandchildren?

Looking at the statistics, one must have doubts. There is good reason why our communal leadership has placed "Jewish continuity" on top of our agenda, ahead of all the other concerns of Jewish life.

We are losing it. The Jewish future—at least in the diaspora—is no longer certain. Our life as a people is being drained by dozens of wounds, all self-inflicted.

Why is this happening? One statistic stands above all the others and speaks the loudest to us: Six out of every ten Jewish children in North America receive no formal Jewish education of any kind. And of the four out of every eight who do get a formal Jewish education of some kind, too many of them do not want that education and do not understand why they have to learn all these things. (The quality of that education is also wanting.)

Why must they waste their time studying the importance of keeping kosher if their parents, by the example of their lives, demonstrate that keeping kosher is not important?

Why must they miss baseball practice to study about *Shavuot* when no one in their family can even remember what that festival is about, much less when it was last celebrated by them?

Too many Jews learned those kinds of lessons from their parents. They sent their children to Hebrew school and then taught them, by the example of their lives, that Hebrew school was a waste of time. The statistics say that American Jewry, at least, learned that lesson well—so well that most Jewish children do not go to Hebrew school of any kind. And what about their children, and their children's children?

As a people, we survived for four millennia because we heeded the commandment, "and you shall repeat them to your children in order to teach them." Now that we merely pay lip service to that commandment, can we survive even four generations more? It is not likely.

Fortunately, knowing why we will not survive also provides us with the solution to the problem. Education is the key to Jewish survival. Somehow, we must provide for a quality Jewish education for every child in our community, regardless of a parent's ability to pay.

Moshe was punished because he was not a good teacher and, thereby, risked the future of Israel itself. How much more will we be punished if we do not even try to teach while there is still a people left to learn?

Joseph Ozarowski

Ah, one of the classic questions of the *Chumash*: Why could Moshe not go to the Promised Land? Was his punishment appropriate for the crime? The question reappears in *Sidra Va'etchanan*, where in Deuteronomy 3:23–26, Moshe recounts a dialogue between himself and God not mentioned in our *sidra*. There, he recalls how he pleaded with *Hashem* to be allowed to go to the Good Land and see it—perhaps not as a leader, but at least as a "civilian or retiree," or perhaps on a "tourist visa." The Divine response is, in essence, "Don't even bother to talk to me about it any more!" (vs. 26).

There are so many answers to the question of Moshe's sin, and I will focus on three. Firstly, we might directly answer your question, as do so many of the commentaries (Ramban, Ibn Ezra, etc.), suggesting that there really is a different standard for leaders than for common people. What may seem like minor errors in judgment, temper, language, and behavior can be a major misdeed for the major leader. Moshe missed the chance to sanctify God's name publicly by talking to the rock, showing that God's purpose can be achieved through gentle words and not striking the rock. He could have proved that even an inanimate rock, with encouragement, can do the will of God; how much more so can human beings. Thus, Moshe suffered the consequences appropriate not so much to the deed, but to his station in life. A hotel burglary may seem like a petty crime, but when it is authorized by the President of the United States as part of an election campaign, it becomes a major offense. So *Hashem* did not excuse even the leader of his generation from this misdeed.

Another approach is the psychological one. (I first heard the kernel of this idea from my colleague Rabbi Reuven Bulka of Ottawa at a Rabbinical Council of America conference.) Moshe suffered from a classical case of rabbinical burnout. All the symptoms, including the inability to listen to a group of thirsty congregants; the name-calling and loss of temper; the fact that he fell on the ground, and that he not only did not follow God's instructions but repeated the offense (these are mistakes pointed out by *Hazal* and embellished by the *Maharsha*); are all symptoms of the fact that Moshe was truly unable to lead the next generation any longer. He was no longer able to bring them into the Promised Land.

It was time, after forty years, for a change. It is possible that Moshe was upset following the death of his sister, which immediately preceded this. But he did not seem to recognize that even though he called the people rebels (20:10), they were not the rebels their parents had been, only thirsty and tired followers. A leader cannot function like this.

Moshe attempts to explain himself in *D'varim* 3:26 by saying, "And God was angry with me for your sakes (*l'ma'ankhem*) and would not listen to me. . . ." The midrash *Yalkut Shim'oni* understands "for your sakes" to mean, "because of you" (*biglalkhem*).

In other words, after so many years of leading and bearing the *kvetching* (complaining) and difficulties of the desert experience, Moshe became like his people, lowered himself to their level, and was punished as they were in not being allowed to enter the Land. This point, to a large extent, explains the above two reasons but may not be fully satisfying to many. In the end, is it really fair?

There is a third response, which, while not an explanation, may be fitting from a literary point of view and perhaps most true to life. According to *Hazal*, one of God's answers to Moshe's pleas in *D'varim*, is *Avra sha'ata*, "The time has passed." Fairness is not the issue here. A leader cannot lead without a flock, and the new generation was no longer his flock. Moses actually had to die without achieving his beloved goal of leading his people to the Promised Land. This is the saddest reason, of course, but it is also the truest to life.

Many are the times that we work and exert energy toward a cherished goal, only to be stopped before achieving that goal. All of us find ourselves in that situation at times. Our time is up. But we can learn from Moshe that even though we may not see the ultimate fruits of our labors, or as Moshe did, only see them from afar, the goals are still worthy. We should not give up efforts for the future but rather continue them, if not for ourselves, then for our descendants.

David Sofian

I think your question has always troubled readers of the book of *Bamidbar*. How could it be that a single moment's loss of control on Moses' part could result in the loss of his ultimate goal, entry into the Land of Israel? How could God punish Moses that way? The classical rabbis also were disturbed by this turn of events.

Their way of dealing with these events begins with how they understood divine reward and punishment. In *Midrash B'reishit Rabbah* 33:1, Rabbi Akiva explains how God punishes all negative acts sooner or later, and how God deals with the righteous as opposed to the wicked. It says there: God deals strictly with both, even to the great deep. God deals strictly with the righteous, calling them to account for the few wrongs that they commit in this world in order to lavish bliss on and give them a goodly reward in the world to come. God grants ease to the wicked and rewards them for the few good deeds that they have performed in this world in order to punish them in the world to come. In this view, since no one is perfect, everyone deserves some reward for the good deeds done and some punishment for their evil deeds. Rabbi Akiva is expressing the clear rabbinic preference for receiving one's reward in the world to come. God's love for the righteous is revealed by the punishment they receive in this world. God's hatred of the wicked is revealed by their receiving reward in this world.

In *Midrash D'varim Rabbah* 9:9, we find this point of view applied to Moses. Above we saw how Rabbi Akiva taught that out of love, God deals strictly with the righteous in terms of the punishment due for whatever wrongs they may have committed. This passage teaches us that as Moses became resigned to death, God began to appease him by saying, "by your life, in this world you have led my children, also in the time to come I will have you lead them."

This statement is an attempt to deal with the seeming injustice of Moses being denied completion of his goal—that is, leading the children of Israel into the Promised Land. What the statement does is to place Moses into the category of the righteous who are punished in this world—he must turn over leadership temporarily—so that he might be rewarded in the world to come, where he will retake his position of leadership.

This rabbinic approach has the virtue of resolving each of your questions.

God is not being unjust by breaking the divine word; rather, God is expressing divine love for the generally righteous Moses. Of course, Moses is treated differently than the rest of the people. Only someone to whom God wants to guarantee entry into the world to come would be punished as Moses was. And the imbalance of punishment to crime is only apparent. Moses will once again lead the Israelites, but it will be in the certainly preferable local of the future world.

As we can see from all this, the rabbis were immensely concerned with explaining why the wicked often prosper, and the righteous often suffer. Living after the destruction of the Temple in degradation or exile, they needed to affirm somehow that God continued to love them. In order to meet the challenges of developing Judaism in their new circumstance, they needed to maintain their confidence in their relationship with God; they needed to maintain absolute certainty in God's justice.

They accomplished this by showing how their suffering was really a sign of God's love for them. They accomplished this by showing how the determination of who will enter and who is kept out of the world to come can clarify all apparent divine injustice.

We, too, need to affirm somehow that God continues to love us living as we do after the *Shoah*. We, too, feel the need to shore up our confidence in our relationship with God. And we have inherited from the rabbis a model of one way to do that.

Yet, such a clever resolution is not so obvious to us. I, for one, am not able, as the classical rabbis were, to simply assert that God is just and that it is only a matter of proper approach to see that justice. After the *Shoah*, it is not at all clear that God's justice can be taken for granted. We wonder, is there a world to come where all apparent injustice is balanced?

Perhaps we are still too close to the events of the *Shoah* to be left in anything but a state of silent meditation, in a state of struggle and inner turmoil. Therefore, the question you pose is one we must wrestle with year in and year out as we read this parshah. Perhaps that is the great value of this section of the Torah for us now. Perhaps the goal is to force us to ask and grapple with these questions.

Balak: Numbers 22:2–25:9

Prophetical Reading
Micah 5:6–6:7

Overview of Torah Portion

Balak, king of Moab, fearing the approaching Children of Israel, engages the Gentile prophet Bilaam to curse them. Bilaam, insincerely protesting that the royal wish flouts God's will, accedes to the request but is stymied at every turn, blessing the Hebrews instead. At Shittim, near the Jordan River, many Israelite men are enticed into idolatry by the women of Moab. Pinchas, grandson of Aaron, slays a couple who brazenly copulate in public.

Key Verses

"And Balak, the son of Tzipor, saw all that Israel had done to the Amorites. . . . And Balak . . . king of Moab at that time . . . sent messengers to Bilaam . . . saying . . . 'Please come now and curse this people for me'" (Numbers 22:2–6).

Discussion Question

HIDDEN CURSES: The entire story of Balak's attempt to curse the Children of Israel is related in the Torah without their mention. Apparently, the Hebrews were unaware of the evil scenario. If they were not involved and were not actually threatened, why was the unsuccessful attempt recorded in the Torah? With so many details? How did the Children of Israel—or how do we—benefit from the knowledge? Did the actions of Balak and Bilaam somehow affect them—and us—even though the plans remained vicarious?

Shammai Engelmayer

The question raises a serious issue: Is what we today call the Torah truly *torat moshe*, "the Torah of Moses?"

For 200 years now, modern scholars have been debating the question, with all too many of them concluding (I believe erroneously) that, not only is this not "the Torah of Moses," Moshe had nothing to do with writing "the Torah" in any form.

This is not the place for a detailed discussion of that debate. Suffice it to say, however, that the story of *Bilaam* (Balaam) and his stubborn she-donkey is one of the many reasons these modern scholars challenge the traditional view of how the Torah came to be. Like our questioner, they were troubled by the fact that the entire episode sticks out like a sore thumb in the Torah's narrative.

These modern scholars, however, were not the first to wonder about the anomalies strewn throughout the Torah's text, including this one. Questions of authorship and authenticity began long before; indeed, they were a concern of no less a group of scholars than the sainted rabbis of the Talmud themselves.

On the surface, this is inconsistent with the view this same group made a core part of Jewish belief: Not only did Moshe write all of the words in the Torah, but the words he wrote were only those that God Himself dictated. Thus, among those "who have no portion in the world to come," the Mishnah tells us (*Sanhedrin* 10:1), is "he who says . . . the Torah is not from heaven."

Surely, if they believed this, how could they have questioned the authorship of a single word?

The answer is that these rabbis of blessed memory understood *torah* in a way different than we understand it—perhaps because they had different versions of the text from which to choose an "authorized" text, perhaps because they distinguished between laws (*torot*) and narrative, or perhaps a little of both.

This view could be challenged by noting that the *amora* Abbaye, in BT *Megilla* 31b, argues that the restatement in Deuteronomy of the blessings and curses of Leviticus was done by Moshe in his own name, or of his own accord. His opinion, the text makes clear, was also held by others and, consequently, it had an effect on the law relating to how the blessings and curses sections should be read.

The statement by Abbaye and its halakhic consequence suggests that the rabbis did not limit the word *torah* to laws alone, because here they need to clarify that a section of non-laws was spoken, not by God as is normally the case, but by Moshe on his own. At the same time, however, no matter how one translates the phrase *mipi atzmo*—literally, "of his own accord"—the fact remains that the rabbis of blessed memory once again posed a challenge to the Torah as we have it being the *torah* they refer to when they speak of the "*torah* of Moshe" and say it is all "from heaven."

Not everyone is willing to accept this interpretation. The *Tosafot*, a group of commentators on the Talmud who followed Rashi and often disputed him, echoing the majority of traditional post-talmudic commentators, seek to clarify Abbaye's statement by saying that, while Moshe indeed spoke the words on his own, it was only after being moved to do so by the Holy Spirit, thus essentially making even these words "from heaven." Such an amendment, however, undermines Abbaye's logic in ruling that, unlike the blessings and curses section in Leviticus, the companion piece in Deuteronomy can be broken up into separate *aliyot* precisely because it was not "from heaven," but from Moshe *mipi atzmo*.

That the rabbis of blessed memory had a different definition of *torah* surely is the implication in a discussion relevant to this week's question. In BT *Baba Batra* 15a, the question is asked, "who wrote the biblical texts?" With reference to the Torah, the first five books of the Bible, this answer is given: "Moshe wrote his own book [the Torah] *and the portion of Bilaam*," (emphasis added) meaning Numbers 22–24. (In some editions of the Babylonian Talmud, the text of which was "standardized" only after the invention of the printing press, this is referred to as "the *book* of Bilaam.")

Because our version of the Torah includes Numbers 22–24 as an integral part of the whole, and it obviously was back then too, this statement in the Talmud clearly suggests that the rabbis of that era defined *torat moshe* in a way that did not include all of the Pentateuch as we know it today. To some, at least, this week's tale of Bilaam and his she-donkey, while undoubtedly written by Moshe, was not originally included by him in his *torah*. That would explain why the story stands out like a sore thumb: It was not originally meant to be there.

If so, then why did someone come along at a later date and take this secondary work by Moshe and put it into Moshe's primary work, the Torah?

I think the answer is double-edged. On the one hand, its inclusion introduces us to the alien seer, who plays such a pivotal role in the apostasy at Ba'al Pe'or. Only by adding the story of Bilaam and his she-donkey to "the Torah of Moses" can we understand why Bilaam was so willing to reveal Israel's unfaithfulness to its God.

Bilaam was the greatest prophet in the region in his lifetime—until Moshe came along. His reputation was known far and wide. So great was that reputation, in fact, that others recorded his exploits as well, leading him to the distinction of being the only person named in the Torah's narratives for whom we have concrete evidence both of his existence and how well thought-of he was in his vocation.

That he failed to carry out his commission to curse Israel would have been a sore point with such a man who lived by his reputation. Having suffered public embarrassment, he would want to avenge himself. However, since Moshe knew by then that God would prevent him from doing so directly, he devised a plan to allow Israel at Ba'al Pe'or to curse itself, as it were, by lusting after the cult prostitutes of Moab and, before the altar of the god Ba'al and in his name, joining together with those prostitutes in unholy lust.

As we learn in the latter portions of this week's parshah, the plan succeeded only too well. A plague went through the Israelite encampment and 24,000 people died.

Why? Because Israel failed to see what Bilaam saw. Israel wanted in on the good life, not realizing that it had the best life of all. It did not matter that the life Israel had was the life it had chosen of its own free will. All that mattered was that it was a life filled with restrictions and obligations unlike what anyone else had to endure.

What a strange reading is *parshat Balak*. For most of it, this is "The Three Stooges meet Francis, the Talking She-Donkey," and only the she-donkey comes out not looking like an ass. The Three Stooges, in order of appearance, are King Balak, Bilaam, and Israel. The mood is light throughout, until the end. Then the plot turns serious and bloody.

Despite the ending, however, in many ways, this is a comedy. Bilaam, the great seer, cannot even see what his she-donkey sees. The man whose words have such power must depend on the words of an ass to stay alive.

King Balak is a pitiful sight, running from mountain top to mountain top, sacrificing animals left and right, hoping to get Bilaam to curse Israel, rather than bless it.

As for Israel, it is blind to the truth, which brings us to the second reason this story was appended to the Torah: Because there are other truths that lie beneath the comedy and the tragedy. They were truths that Bilaam could see, but Israel could not.

One of these truths is that God will protect Israel as long as Israel protects itself by remaining faithful to Him. Throughout the story, as this week's question itself notes, Israel is not involved. For the first and only time in the Torah since Avraham makes his appearance, Israel is in the background.

Moshe, too, is nowhere to be seen. He wields no staff here; offers no prayer. Indeed, for all we know, he is totally unaware of what is going on atop the mountains surrounding him and Israel. Only God is here—and

He is making it absolutely clear to Bilaam that Israel is His special people and under His Divine protection.

At the end of the parshah, however, Israel is very much in evidence—rebelling against God and paying the price.

The message is clear: As long as Israel is faithful to God, He is faithful to Israel, protecting it even when it does not know it needs protection and is unaware that it is receiving it. When Israel is unfaithful, however, He is there, too; only this time, He is exacting His revenge.

There is another important reason, however, for this chapter being here: To teach us that the God of history will not be thwarted. That is, after all, what God is. He may not get involved in the minute-by-minute machinations of mortals, but He will not allow those machinations to interfere with the Divine plan of history.

It takes awhile, but Bilaam finally figures that out, even if no one else does. Throughout the story, he keeps hoping that God will change His mind and let him curse Israel. When he realizes that nothing will get God to reverse Himself, Bilaam on his own declares how goodly are Jacob's tents; in other words, how fortunate Israel is. No matter who besets it, no matter what it does to itself, Israel will remain God's own treasure. It may be humbled but never vanquished.

This message that the God of history will not be thwarted is even stronger in Bilaam's first blessing: "This is a people that will dwell apart; it will not count itself among the nations."

Four thousand years of Jewish history attest to the accuracy of that prophecy. We have always been a people dwelling apart. Even when we sought to be a part of the people around us, they made certain we kept apart. Paranoia has nothing to do with it. History does not lie. The world is divided between "them" and "us," and "they" never forget it. When we try to, "they" do something to remind us.

Bilaam was right about something else, too. We are an *ahm*, not a *goy*; a people, not a nation. We are tied to each other and to the Divine plan, no matter where we reside—in our own land or spread out across the globe. Try as we may to change that, to assimilate into the culture surrounding us, to be a part of the specific place in which we find ourselves, and to act like "normal people" act, we remain unique and apart.

We read this portion and are surprised that, after three tries, King Balak still does not understand that God alone controls Israel's fate. We are surprised that Bilaam repeatedly tries to get God to change His mind and let him curse Israel. We are surprised that they do not get the message, but let us face it: After 4,000 years, we still don't get it. We still try to assimilate and to be like everyone else. We still run away from our responsibilities as His "kingdom of priests." We still lust after the cult of Moab.

Each time we do, of course, we fail. We made a deal long ago in the desert of Sinai. We made it of our own free will. We entered into a covenant with the God of history. And the God of history will not be thwarted.

That is what makes the story of Bilaam and his she-donkey so necessary to the text. It is, after all, what the Torah is all about. At no time in the Torah is Israel content with its lot as God's kingdom of priests, His holy nation. At no time is Israel faithful to its promise to obey God and follow Him. Yet Israel remains God's chosen. Its story moves inexorably forward. Israel may have to be dragged kicking and screaming, but it will fulfill its destiny. The God of history will not be thwarted.

I also think that is one of the reasons the Torah ends where it does: With Israel still on the west bank of the Jordan River. From the Exodus onward, the goal of the Torah narrative has been to take Israel from the house of bondage to a land flowing with milk and honey. Yet it ends with Israel not only not in possession of Canaan, but not yet even physically in Canaan. That part of the story is accomplished in a book that is not a part of the Torah, the Book of Joshua.

It is as if the Torah is saying Israel's role as the chosen of the God of history is outside the land. The land is its dwelling place, its sanctuary, and its reward, but it is in the world at large that Israel must fulfill its destiny.

Joseph Ozarowski

Your question assumes two points: One, that the people of Israel were not directly affected by the episode of Balak and Bilaam; and two, because the people of Israel were only indirectly affected makes this section inappropriate for inclusion in the Torah. Obviously, the fact that you asked the question means that you—as do I—believe that the chapter does have something important to teach us and does belong here.

The Talmud (BT *Sanhedrin* 105b) tells us that while all of Bilaam's comments started as curses and became blessings, they eventually came true as curses, except *Ma tovu*—"How goodly are your tents O Jacob [referring to synagogues], your dwelling-places O Israel [referring to Jewish schools]." In other words, Bilaam's prophecies came to pass as curses—whether you define "curse" as incantation, evil wish, or nasty comments.

Specifically, this point refers to the observations, "It is a people that dwells alone," yet dies righteously (23:9–10), and, "None have beheld iniquity in Jacob, neither has one seen perverseness in Israel . . . there is no enchantment with Jacob, neither is there magic in Israel . . ." (23:21–23). In fact, one could argue that Bilaam himself made these blessed words

of his come true as curses since Hazal blamed him for organizing the Ba'al
Pe'or incident that follows. During that incident, the Jews did not dwell
alone but "were paired to Ba'al Pe'or" (25:3), and they participated in
perverse, idolatrous, unrighteous, and licentious behavior.

Only our *shuls* and schools, our houses of worship and *yeshivot* have
provided lasting continuity and blessing to our people over the ages.
Perhaps this is why we use the words of *ma tovu*, originally uttered by a
devious non-Jewish prophet, as the first words said when entering a
synagogue. (Note, however, that the commentary of the *Torah Temimah*
argues that the only blessings that turned into curses were the blessings in
chapter 24, excluding *ma tovu*.)

To answer the second point, we might say that even when the Jews are
not the active protagonists, they are still affected by what goes on within.
More importantly, we have much to learn from what goes on. The fact that
God has a relationship with a non-Jewish prophet teaches us that even as
warped as Bilaam might have been, we do not have a monopoly on
spirituality and prophecy. Even the incident of the ass, with brilliant Bilaam
not being able to see the angel of the Lord that his supposedly dumb animal
could perceive, has much to teach us. But that story is, well, a donkey of a
different color.

David Sofian

One possible answer to your question is that this narrative about the
non-Israelite Bilaam provides a contrast to the Israelite prophets. We learn
something crucial about them in comparison to Bilaam. This is Ramban's
view. After Balak tries to entice Bilaam into coming to curse the Israelites
and the wonderful interlude with Bilaam's talking ass, the pivotal moment,
finally arrives, Bilaam is unable to curse the Israelites as Balak wanted. At
this key point in the story, we find the phrase "And God met Bilaam . . ."
(chapter 23:4).

Ramban uses this phrase together with the phrase in chapter 22:9, "And
God came unto Bilaam . . ." to tell us that Bilaam was not a real prophet.
He argues that this is the case because these two phrases are never used with
real prophets. He wants us to see that Bilaam is only God's instrument for
this single occasion, and that he is being used to honor Israel. Chapter 22:5
describes Bilaam's location at the beginning of the story. There, it says Balak
sent messengers "to the land of the children of his people."

In his comment there, Ramban indicates that this phrase is intended to
teach us that Bilaam was a magician just like all the people of his land.

Placing Ramban's comments together produces a clear picture. Ramban wants us to see that Bilaam is really only a magician who held his special status for but a moment. We should not mistakenly think that he enjoyed the same relationship with God that the prophets of Israel enjoyed. He is elevating the Jewish people's relationship with God, in contrast.

For Ramban, this is why the story is told. Future generations of Israel are meant to see that their relationship with God is unique. It is not something of their own invention. It even is expressed and confirmed in God's use of the non-Israelite magician Bilaam.

Midrash Bamidbar Rabbah greatly expands the use of this story in its opening section on our parshah. No longer is it merely a matter of emphasizing Israel's unique relationship with God with a comparatively simply contrast. *Bamidbar Rabbah* 20:1 gives us the reason our relationship is unique. We learn there how God was available to other peoples in exactly the same way God was available to Israel. They spurned the opportunity.

This section tells us that just as God raised up kings, sages, and prophets for Israel, God raised them up for other peoples. Solomon is contrasted to Nebuchadnezzar, David to Haman, and Moses to Bilaam. Whereas Solomon built the Temple and offered songs and supplications, Nebuchadnezzar destroyed and despised it.

Whereas both David and Haman were given wealth, David prepared for the building of the Temple, and Haman used his wealth to try to destroy an entire people. Whereas Moses and the prophets of Israel cautioned Israel against transgressions, Bilaam suggested a plan to corrupt Israel. Moreover, quoting both Jeremiah and Ezekiel, the passage goes on to show us the superiority of the Israelite prophets, in that they nevertheless retained their compassion for both Israel and idolaters.

It is not so with Bilaam. Using an idea found in BT *Sanhedrin* that it was Bilaam who was responsible for the Moabite women luring the Israelite men at Shittim, the passage concludes by explaining that this is the reason the story of Bilaam was written down. The Holy One wanted us to know why the Holy Spirit was removed from the others. Bilaam and the others showed that they would abuse their relationship with God.

This section and others like it want us to see that Israel's special relationship with God results not from being arbitrarily picked or from God displaying unfair favoritism, but from Israel's understanding and acceptance of the responsibilities that accompany the relationship.

You ask how Israel benefits from this story. Given the passages above and many others like them, we can see how this story would have been very comforting to a people whose Temple had been destroyed and who had been dispersed in foreign lands, yet who nevertheless continued to maintain a belief in their special relationship with God.

Bilaam's narrative has the effect of reaffirming the covenantal relationship between God and Israel in the blessing and recognition of a non-Israelite. Given the claims to the contrary by those in whose midst Jews lived, this message would resonate powerfully throughout Jewish history.

At this point we need to ask what meaning the story has for us. We live in a place and time where, by in large, we are not threatened by others and do not need to defend our sense of covenant with God. All the possibilities of that covenant can be pursued openly. To me, Bilaam's words of blessing act as a challenge to what we are intended to be as a covenanted people.

Following the Jewish Publication Society translation, Bilaam says in *Bamidbar* 23:21, "None hath beheld iniquity in Jacob, neither hath one seen perverseness in Israel." Our goal as God's people should be that all who behold us as a people should be able to truthfully say that.

Pinchas: Numbers 25:10–30:1

Prophetical Reading
1 Kings 18:46–19:21

Overview of Torah Portion

God, praising Pinchas' zealotry in slaying the copulating couple, awards him the Covenant of Peace. God commands Moses and Eleazar to take a census—the second—of the Children of Israel. The daughters of *Tselophchad*, whose father had died without sons, petition Moses to inherit their father's property. God tells Moses to install Joshua as his successor as leader of the Jewish nation, and gives details about public sacrifices to be brought daily and on holy days.

Key Verses

"And Moses spoke to the Lord, saying, 'Let the Lord, the God of the spirits of all flesh, set a man over the congregation who may go out before them and may come in before them, and who may lead them out and who may bring them in, that the congregation of the Lord not be as sheep who have no shepherd.' And the Lord said to Moses, 'Take to yourself Joshua the son of Nun, a man in whom is spirit, and lay your hand upon him, and set him before Eleazar the priest and before all the congregation and command him in their sight. . . . at his word shall they go out and at his word shall they go in'" (Numbers 27:15–21).

Discussion Question

LEADER OF THE TRIBES: Joshua was undeniably a man of courage, a man of faith. But was he a man of accomplishment? God tells Moses to appoint Joshua as his successor as leader of the Hebrews, but how has Joshua earned the responsibility? In his previous foray across the Jordan, as part of the twelve spies who spied out the land of Canaan, he and Caleb disagreed with the ten who brought back a pessimistic report. Joshua couldn't change their minds about the inhospitality of the Promised Land. He couldn't persuade them to change their report. How did he merit designation as the man to bring all of the Children of Israel into Canaan? What is the Torah's criterion for leadership?

Shammai Engelmayer

We first meet Yehoshua (Joshua) in Exodus 17:9. There, "Moshe said to Yehoshua, 'Choose men for us and go out and do battle with Amalek.'" There is no further description of Yehoshua—not who his parents are or not where he comes from (although this is material we are supplied with later). It is as if the Torah means to tell us that Yehoshua is someone with whom we should be familiar.

And, indeed, if we were there at the time, we would have known Yehoshua because, almost from the very beginning, he has been at Moshe's side, his strong right arm. Indeed, when we next meet him in Exodus 24:13, he is identified as Moshe's aide who accompanies him farther up Mt. Sinai than anyone else, Aharon included, is permitted to go.

Then, in Exodus 33:11, we learn that although Yehoshua does not share in Moshe's encounters with God, he nevertheless shares Moshe's access to the Tent of Meeting. By the time we encounter him in Numbers 11:28, this access is already presumed and unexceptional.

Thus, virtually from the beginning, Yehoshua clearly is Moshe's aide and designated successor, although not yet formally. This is hinted at most strongly in Numbers 13:16, when Moshe changes his aide's name to Yehoshua, implying a future deliverer.

Because Yehoshua was chosen for the job even before we meet him in the war against Amalek, we cannot say he was chosen because of his proven abilities as a wartime leader (which would be natural, considering that his role was to lead Israel during its conquest of Canaan). He was not chosen for any prophetic abilities he might have because, although he shares Moshe's access to the most sacred precincts, he does not share in the revelations Moshe experiences.

So why was he chosen? Because God chose him, just as He chose Moshe before him, for no reason that we know of or can point to, based on the Torah's text. God chooses whoever He chooses to choose. He needs no reason and, often, gives none.

Why did God choose Avraham? What did that son of idol worshipers ever do to deserve becoming the founder of Israel and the beloved of the God of all things? The sainted rabbis of the midrash offer us many fanciful explanations, but God Himself, in His book (meaning the Torah) chooses not to tell us, just as He chooses not to tell us why He chose Moshe, or Yehoshua.

It is not fair to claim that a person was chosen because of some unspoken piety or righteousness. The Torah makes that clear when it places Aharon at the center of the golden calf fiasco. Despite that tragic event, God chooses Aharon to be *Kohen Gadol* and father of the priestly line.

God chooses whoever He wishes to choose, and for His own reasons. Our conception of that person's worthiness is not an issue and is certainly not relevant.

On the other hand, we have no right to arbitrarily diminish that choice by pointing to an incident that suggests the chosen leader was a bad choice because he shows little capacity for leadership, as does the question this week.

To begin with, just as we do not know why someone is chosen by God, we also do not know for what purpose that person actually has been chosen. When we first learn that God has chosen Moshe, we assume it was because Moshe had the qualities needed to lead Israel from Egypt to Canaan. As the story unfolds, however, we realize that Moshe has trouble leading his way out of a paper bag. He cannot convince the pharaoh to let Israel go (God does that); and, in forty years of trying, he cannot convince Israel that God is God and must be obeyed.

His leadership abilities were not why God chose Moshe. Based on the rest of the story, which includes the fact that even today we claim adherence to "the Torah of Moses," we can assume that God chose Moshe, not to be Israel's leader but its teacher.

Yet even here we are faced with anomalies. Not only is he a bad teacher for his immediate audience, but he who is slow of speech is chosen to speak God's words to Israel and the world, from generation to generation. Only God knows why.

And that is the way God wants it. He wants us to accept His choices because they are His choices, not because we can rationalize why God made those choices.

In Yehoshua's case, of course, a fair case can be made that he was chosen because God knew he would be an excellent military commander, thus leading Israel to the conquest of the Promised Land. After all, is that not precisely what Yehoshua does?

No, it is not. Yehoshua dies before the conquest is complete (and, indeed, it is never completed the way the Torah had outlined it). The northernmost border stops just above Sidon, rather than encompassing all of Lebanon and the territory eastward to the Euphrates; in the south, a strip of land by "the River of Egypt" also remains unconquered; and by Joshua 13, we find that the Philistines have replaced the Anakim in control of a small but significant coastal strip on the west.

True, the text in Joshua 21:41 insists that "the Lord gave to Israel the whole country which He had sworn to their fathers that He would assign to them; they took possession of it and they settled it," but God Himself acknowledges to Yehoshua that this is only figuratively accurate. "Yehoshua was now old and advanced in years," the text tells us as Joshua 13 begins. "The Lord said to him, 'You have grown old, you are advanced in years; and very much of the land still remains to be taken possession of.'"

So Yehoshua was not chosen because he would accomplish the conquest of the Promised Land, for he does not complete the task. We cannot even say that he was chosen because of his leadership abilities since, judging from the biblical text, his hold on Israel seems to have withered well before his death and certainly before the task of conquering the land was completed.

Thus, when the tribes of Reuven and Gad, and the half-tribe of Menashe, return to their territory on the east bank of the Jordan, "the Israelites sent Pinchas . . . accompanied by ten chieftains" to challenge them for an apparent violation of the Law (see Joshua 22:13–14).

Now, it could be argued that Pinchas was sent because the alleged infraction was of a ritual nature. The text, however, pointedly states that "the Israelites" do the sending, not Yehoshua, and he otherwise plays no role in this, even though it involves a potential civil war; yet the text also makes clear Yehoshua is still God's chosen leader.

While we cannot claim to understand why God chose Yehoshua, we must defend him from the suggestion in our question that he failed to convince ten of his colleagues to change their report. That is not evidenced in our text this week.

Let us look more closely at the situation. Calev, not Yehoshua, takes the lead here. Yehoshua deliberately stays in the background. In Numbers 13:30, it is only Calev who stands up to protest the spies' report; only in 14:6 do both men speak up, and even there it is more likely that Calev alone spoke. Thus, not only did Yehoshua fail to convince the ten, he did not even make an effort to do so.

And for good reason. Yehoshua let Calev speak because, as Moshe's aide, anything Yehoshua would say would be automatically discounted.

Yehoshua's position is predictable. Of all the spies, he alone is guaranteed to have a positive report. He alone will not be swayed by contrariness or fear. Calev, on the other hand, is like the other ten—a blank slate. That he, too, demonstrates his faith in God and His promise makes Calev unique.

That Calev may also have been a proselyte, meaning someone with no tradition to support belief in God's promises other than pure faith, makes him still more unique. This uniqueness makes him, not Yehoshua, the ideal spokesman for God's side here.

Put another way, that the spies were sent at all indicates that the people were not buying what Moshe was telling them about God's ability to deliver on His promises. It would be unreasonable, then, to expect them to heed a similar defense coming from Moshe's closest aide and obvious successor. To then blame Yehoshua for not having done what clearly he was in no position to do in the first place is unfair to Yehoshua.

It is also unfair to God. If He wanted us to know what criteria He uses to select leaders, He would have told us. Because He didn't, we have no right to use the apparent failures to question that criteria.

Joseph Ozarowski

What a difference a generation makes! Joshua had extensive early experience as military leader, as well as assistant to Moshe. He had his share of successes—the campaign against Amalek—and also failures (not only the spies' incident, but also his misreading of the Golden Calf episode [Exodus 32:16, "There is a voice of war in the camp. . . ."]). But his standing up to the majority report of the spies, even if he could not convince them and the others to follow him to the Promised Land, showed principle and courage. These attributes, coupled with experience, made Joshua the logical choice.

Or was he? There were probably other candidates for the job. The midrash suggests that Moshe entertained the idea that one of his sons should succeed him. Since the daughters of Tselophchad were able to inherit of their father, why not also the sons of Moshe? Of course, *Hazal* point out that unlike their father, they were not qualified in learning. However, there was probably another obvious candidate who had proved his mettle. Pinchas' patriotic act of zealotry stayed the physical, moral, and spiritual plague that beset our people. To many Jewish loyalists, he was probably the hero of the hour. Even God conferred upon Pinchas, *Briti Shalom*, "my covenant of peace." So, why not Pinchas?

During my weekly Shabbat afternoon *shiur*, a number of congregants suggested that letting Pinchas, Aaron's grandson and future heir to the priesthood, become the people's civil leader would be too much mixing of religion and state. The Torah's vision of government does mix religion and state, but they are not supposed to be identical. The King is not to be the High Priest and vice versa. This issue came back many years later to haunt our people, when the priestly Maccabees also became the civil leaders. So God, at the time of the Torah, chose as leader someone well qualified for the task, but not from the priestly tribe.

I personally believe that there were issues of personality and leadership abilities at play here. Pinchas' act may have been considered meritorious by God, but according to many midrashim, Hazal did not see it as a model to emulate. While his motive may have been pure, he was considered by the Sanhedrin and even by Moshe to have committed a criminal act (see JT *Sanhedrin* 15). The sages did not sanction what he did, and they were ready to try and sentence him. It was the only the "divine pardon" that got Pinchas off the hook. As one of my colleagues once suggested (Rabbi Stanley Wagner of Denver, in the *Rabbinical Council of America Sermon Anthology of 1976*), "Pinchas received the Jewish Medal of Honor, but did not enter the Jewish Hall of Fame."

An act of pious zealotry, even for pure motives and subsequently endorsed by God, is not enough to qualify someone as a leader. And while Pinchas continued to serve our people in positive ways (he was one of the two spies Joshua sent after Moshe died; after the initial war of conquest for Israel, he led the delegation to negotiate with the two and a half tribes who settled in Transjordan [see Joshua 22]; and he served extensively as High Priest), he was not the right man for overall leader.

So what qualities did Joshua have? A cursory look at God's dialogue with Moshe (Numbers 27:15–18), along with Rashi's comments, yields a wonderful definition of leadership.

Verse 15: "And Moses spoke to God saying." 'One of my congregants pointed out that this is one of the few cases where Moses speaks to God and not the other way around, the way the Torah notes hundreds of other times throughout. Ironically, Moshe speaks out on the eve of his retirement from leadership!'

Verse 16: "Let the Lord, God of the spirits of all flesh, set a man upon the congregation." Rashi: "*Ribono Shel Olam*! It is well known before you the mindset of each and every one, and they are not like each other. Pick for them a leader who can be patient with each and every one according to their mindset." (Note that the same terminology is used when Moshe despairs and prays to God for guidance during the Korach rebellion. The issue there, according to the commentaries, is also that of Moshe not knowing how to deal with the diversity and conflicting demands of those he led.)

Verse 17: "Who will go out with them and come in with them, who will lead them out and bring them in, so that the congregation of the Lord will not be like a flock without a shepherd?" Rashi suggests a military theme here, both as analogy and also as reality, since the military campaign to conquer the Promised Land was imminent. "Not like the non-Jewish Kings who sit in their homes and send their soldiers to war, but rather as I fought with Sihon and Og . . . going out at the head and coming in at the head."

This idea still applies today. The officers' motto of *Tzahal*, the Israel Defense Forces, is *Aharai!* ("After me!") and the officers truly lead. That is why Israel has one of the highest officers' casualty rates among Western countries.

Verse 18: "And God said to Moshe, take for yourself Joshua Bin Nun, a man in whom there is spirit [*ruach*], and place your hand upon him." Rashi: "Just like you asked, someone who can walk according to the *ruach* of each one."

In other words, a leader has to have patience, as well as courage. A leader has to be able to listen and be tolerant. A leader has to inspire and be ahead of the group, but not so far ahead that they lose sight of each other. And a leader has to have spirit. Joshua was the one with these qualities, thus he was the choice.

Halvai our leaders would fit this framework!

David Sofian

It happens that your very question was anticipated by *Midrash Bamidbar Rabbah* in chapter 21:14. This section begins by noting that since Moses is about to die, he raises the subject of who shall lead the congregation of Israel with God (*Bamidbar* 27:15). He does this right after the interlude with the daughters of *Tselophchad*.

The midrash does not think the association of these two subjects is just a coincidence. Rather, *Bamidbar Rabbah* wants us to know that the subject of inherited leadership is being hinted at by this juxtaposition. Moses is said to have raised with God the point that if these daughters inherit, his sons should certainly inherit as well. This means that Moses' sons should succeed him as leader. God answers in a very interesting way. Moses is told that his sons sat idly by and did not sufficiently study the Torah.

On the other hand, Joshua rose early and stayed late taking care of the needs of the meeting place. Joshua would arrange benches and even spread out the necessary mats. God says that Joshua served Moses with all his strength and so is worthy also to serve Israel as leader.

Then, based on this passage, the answer to your question is clear enough. Leadership of the Israelites is not based on heredity, but on merit. And merit, in this case, means that Joshua put in the time and effort and demonstrated the necessary worth in terms of what matters to God. Joshua served Moses and the community well and so served God well, therefore he deserved to become leader.

However, there is another passage from the rabbinic tradition that casts some doubt on this clear answer from the midrash. It comes from BT *Temurah* 16a. In this passage, Rabbi Judah reports in the name of Rab about what happened when Moses was about to depart this life for the Garden of Eden. Moses asks Joshua if there are any matters of law that remain doubtful and require clarification. Joshua responds by pointing out that Moses himself had written in the book of *Shmot* 33:11 that his servant Joshua the son of Nun departed not out of the Tabernacle.

Joshua is answering Moses somewhat curtly by indicating that he had never left Moses and so, therefore, didn't have any questions. In other words, he is tersely telling Moses that he, Joshua, is adequately prepared, because he had put in all that time assisting and standing by Moses. Except for the shortness of his answer, so far this squares with the midrashic passage I've already described. But now our talmudic passage takes an interesting turn.

As soon as Joshua makes his remark, we are told that Moses became weak from it—that is, he took offense at it. And then we learn that Joshua promptly forgot 300 laws and became doubtful over another 700. So was Joshua adequately prepared or not? Did he merit being leader or not?

This part of the passage clearly is giving us the answer that, as it turned out, Joshua was not adequately prepared. Moses' leadership derived not only from God choosing him, but most importantly because he was the repository of law. In other words, Moses was the consummate rabbi, hence the way he is referred to in the tradition, *Moshe Rabbenu* (Moses, our Rabbi). BT *Temurah* is telling us that Joshua lacked respect for Moses at the crucial moment of transition, which resulted in his lacking the necessary knowledge to merit leadership.

I don't think we should be surprised to find these seemingly conflicting rabbinic passages. First of all, disagreement and debate is at the very heart of classical rabbinic discussion. However, also in a very important way, both passages are making the same point. In *Bamidbar Rabbah*, Joshua deserves leadership because he is like Moses. The rabbis anchored their own authority and leadership in their knowledge of Torah, written and oral.

Moses, as the vessel of Torah, would be their ideal model. On the other hand, the *Tanakh* tells us Joshua's leadership was based in knowledge of war, not of Torah, hence the passage from *Temurah* questioning his knowledge base.

The *Temurah* passage makes this even clearer in its continuation. We are told that the Israelites became so frustrated with Joshua over his forgotten learning and doubt that they were ready to kill him. Seeing this, God tells

Joshua that since the Torah is no longer in heaven, God cannot tell him everything he needs to know. So instead God instructs Joshua to distract the people by focusing their attention on war.

This part of the passage makes it seem as if the physical conquest of the land came about only because Joshua lacked Moses' knowledge of Torah, instead of as part of God's original plan. This intimation may be only a further reflection of the view that Israelite (Jewish) leadership should be based only on Torah knowledge, and not on other factors like inheritance (as the priesthood was) physical strength, or military prowess. It also may be a reflection of the historical experiences during rabbinic times of what happened when the Jews went to war against Rome. Whatever the case, I find this last piece of the passage fascinating.

What interests me about it is that it caused me to frame our question about the nature of leaders and leadership in a much more general way. There is an issue here not only about specific qualifications for leadership. There is also the question of how much the situation influences the choice of leader versus how much the choice of leader influences the situation.

Using Joshua as the case in point, was Joshua the leader because he had the qualities necessary to lead the Israelites at that time, or was it that certain circumstances followed because Joshua was chosen to be the leader? Was he chosen for his abilities, or was it that once he was chosen, his particular abilities determined the ensuing events?

It seems to me that, in its own way, the midrashic passage answers this question by saying that the situation was pre-eminent and influenced the choice of Joshua as leader, and, that the Talmudic passage in its own way is saying Joshua's choice was pre-eminent and influenced the events to follow.

Matot: Numbers 30:2–32:42

Prophetical Reading
Jeremiah 1–2:3

Overview of Torah Portion

The laws of making and breaking vows are listed. God commands the Children of Israel to avenge themselves against the Midianites, who had enticed the Hebrews with licentious idolatry at Shittim. The tribes of Reuven and Gad petition Moses to settle in the captured land of Jazer, prime grazing territory outside of the Promised Land.

Key Verses

"And the children of Reuven and the children of Gad had a very great amount of cattle, and when they saw the land of Jazer and the land of Gilead, that, behold, the place was a place of cattle . . . [they] spoke to Moses . . . saying . . . 'If we have found favor in your sight, let this land be given to your servants for a possession, do not bring us over the Jordan. . . .' And Moses said to them . . . 'If every armed man of you will pass over the Jordan before the Lord until He has driven out His enemies from before Him . . . this land shall be yours for a possession'" (Numbers 32:1–22).

Discussion Question

CANAAN, SITE UNSEEN: Moses, after rebuking the tribes of Reuven and Gad for seemingly failing to cast their lots with the rest of the Children of Israel, agrees to let them settle outside the land of Canaan, on the other side of the Jordan. They ask for the territory, and Moses accedes, before any of them have even seen the Promised Land. Was their request impetuous? Why did

Moses not at least ask that they inspect their designated territory in Canaan before opting for land elsewhere? Is the Torah condoning the making of crucial decisions without having all available information?

Shammai Engelmayer

There is nothing here about validating impetuous decisions and, indeed, there was nothing impetuous about the request. These people had spent the last forty years in the desert. It had become their home. It was their way of life, and they enjoyed it. On the other side of the Jordan, there was a land supposedly flowing with milk and honey, but only if they worked hard at it. What difference did it make to these two and a half tribes where they worked hard to see their milk and honey flow?

The issue was never whether the request was impetuous. Rather, it was whether these tribes were trying to shirk their responsibilities to the remaining tribes. From their response to Moshe's initial outburst, the answer is "no." That made their request okay in the eyes of Moshe and, ultimately, in God's eyes, as well.

The real question we need to ask—and answer—is why the request was okay in the eyes of God. He had made a big deal about freeing Israel from bondage so that it could occupy "the land." He had tied His covenant and its statutory requirements to continued peaceful existence in "the land." And yet, on the eve of Israel's crossing over the Jordan, He approves a request that will keep more than one-fifth of the tribes out of "the land."

What is God trying to tell us? Surely it is not that impetuosity is bad. Not only is there no impetuosity here, but if there was, then the lesson is that acting impetuously and without all the facts is not a problem. After all, these people get their way.

No, what we are being told has nothing to do with rash decisions. It has everything to do with certain realities, some of which Israel is aware and some of which only God understands at this point.

One reality has to do with strategic needs. Yehoshua wisely insists on following through on Moshe's conquer-and-destroy campaign for Canaan. He wants as much of the land as possible conquered before Israel's inheritance is parceled out to it piece by piece. Otherwise, as each parcel is taken, those who eventually would settle there would lose all interest in continuing the fight. Sooner rather than later, Israel will have too few soldiers to continue the conquest of Canaan.

Instead, Yehoshua sets up a permanent "home camp" on the west bank of the Jordan, near Jericho. To that camp, Israel will return after each campaign. No one will get as much as a quarter of a *dunam* of land until everyone can get land.

Before the camp is Canaan—a hostile conglomeration of nations determined to hang on to what they believe is theirs. Behind the camp is the Jordan, a narrow river that separates Canaan from the mountain redoubts of other enemies, some already defeated and waiting for their revenge, others skillfully avoided by Israel for now. Inside the camp, there are many scores of thousands of soldiers ready to do battle. There are also many scores of thousands of wives anxiously awaiting the outcome of each contact with the enemy. And there are many more scores of thousands of children. There are also the elderly, the infirm, and the squeamish. The priests and Levites are all there, too, thousands of them.

Has Yehoshua put the entire nation at risk—smack in the middle of its enemies? How will he protect them from assaults from the Canaanites before them, and the Edomites, Moabites, and all the others lurking behind them? How will he keep these people supplied with food, clothing, and other basic needs, as well as with war materiel?

Obviously, Yehoshua (and Moshe before him) would not have left Israel so vulnerable to either a direct or indirect attack by severed supply lines.

And that brings us back to the two-and-a-half tribes: If they had not asked for permission to settle on the east side of the Jordan, Moshe would have had to order someone to settle there. Only with a permanent presence on the east side of the Jordan, covering the supply lines and serving as a buffer against the enemies in the rear, could Israel have been able to follow through on the conquest of Canaan.

Moshe and Yehoshua also understood that this buffer zone was needed for the long-term, as well. Israel posed a threat to the peoples of the region in two ways. First, militarily: With each success Israel grew stronger and bolder. As the number of nations in the region dwindled following each Israelite campaign, those remaining would have to fear that their days were numbered unless Israel could be stopped. Second, religiously: With each Israelite success, the cults of Ba'al and his pantheon were placed further in jeopardy. The livelihoods of the priests of these false gods and the kings who ostensibly ruled in their name were at risk. The core beliefs of the peoples of the region were faced with a challenge they could not overcome. Only by defeating Israel could the God of Israel be defeated and the Ba'al gods be triumphant.

For as long as Israel lived in the land and prospered, Moshe and Yehoshua knew, its enemies would be lying in wait. They also knew that external alliances (such as the Davidic ties to Tyre) could not be relied on with surety. Only a viable Israelite presence outside the land could secure the Israelite presence inside the land. In other words, a viable Israel depends, in part, on an equally viable *diaspora*.

That is a reality of which Israel surely was aware. It is not beyond possibility that the two and one-half tribes even made such a case to Moshe; the Torah, in such case, does not record it, because it is of no interest to its purpose.

There is a reality, however, of which Israel could not be aware—a future reality. Entering the land and conquering it meant, to them, keeping the land in perpetuity. There was no way that they would consider, at this point, the possibility that God would keep His promise to throw them out of the land if they violated the Covenant.

Why should they believe God? He has been warning them of such dire consequences since the beginning and yet has never carried them out. One violation after another went unpunished. Sure, a few thousand died here, a few thousand died there—but they were still alive as a people and were still preparing to take possession of God's promised land, with His help. No, these people would have not entertained the possibility of impermanence.

God, however, knew the stay was likely to be temporary (unless the people chose a different path, one of holiness and dedication to God and His Covenant). That meant the day would come when Israel was no longer in the land. It would need to survive outside the land and God needed to let them know how they would survive.

Specifically, they would have to recreate their religion. The sacrificial cult was valid only inside the land and, at that, only in one specific place in the land at any one time. That specific place eventually also became a permanent place—the Temple Mount in Jerusalem. This limitation was deliberate, since God wanted to wean Israel from this throwback to paganism in any case.

Had God not allowed the two and one-half tribes to settle outside the land, such a recreation—essential to achieving the faith God had always intended for Israel—could have been thwarted. There would have been those who would have argued that, just as before Israel was in the land it could sacrifice outside the land, so after Israel left the land it could sacrifice outside it. God needed to make the point clearly and decisively: The River Jordan is the dividing line. Those Israelites living beyond the river on the east side may not perform sacrificial rituals. Their service to God would have to take a different form.

This point is brought home at the end of the conquest when the two and one-half tribes build an altar on the west bank of the Jordan, meaning inside the land. Pinchas heads an army to punish the heretics, only to learn that the altar was meant to be symbolic.

The message, however, is clear. If, on the proper side of the Jordan, meaning inside the land itself, it is still heresy to sacrifice to God except at the place He designates from time to time, how much more so is it heresy on the other side of the Jordan, outside the land? And, lest anyone should argue that this applies only to those who live within the borders of the land, these people did not, and yet they were still considered heretics until their explanation was heard.

So not just Moshe, but God, too, would have had to order the creation of a *diaspora* community on the east side of the Jordan, albeit for different reasons. That is why God allows Moshe to accede to the request.

That leaves us with one problem: Despite the fact that this played into the hands of Moshe and God, the request itself could be regarded as an insult to both—particularly to God. This land they were headed to was supposed to be the greatest piece of real estate since Eden. And it came with a guarantee of divine protection. And yet these two and one-half tribes rejected it without ever even setting foot inside it.

The rejection also meant rejecting the trappings of the Israelite religion as it was then practiced, since the sacrificial cult was only possible inside Israel. This was yet another slap in the face of God.

Yet God said it was okay; no problem. Obviously, then, it must not have been a problem, meaning that what we think we see is not what actually is.

And therein is another lesson to be learned. There is more than one "right way" to be faithful to God. What is right for one person may not be right for the other. God understands that and He accepts it. So long as a person adheres to the basics—observance of the non-sacrificial mitzvot—God will accept that person's love and loyalty. On the other hand, observance of the sacrificial mitzvot without observance of the others is worthless; as the prophets will declare to Israel time and again, God never made ritual a substitute for deeds, only a supplement to them.

Joseph Ozarowski

Your question concerns one of my favorite chapters in the Torah—the request by the two and one-half tribes to remain on the far side of the Jordan River in order to raise cattle. The two and one-half tribes originally wanted to stay on the East Bank of the Jordan for material reasons. After all, cattle makes for a prosperous livelihood. Moshe arranges a settlement. The chapter is filled with diplomatic nuances, negotiation, discussion, and what seems to be a happy ending. I highly recommend two fine essays to the reader interested in further exploring this chapter: "The Reubenites and the Gaddites—What Was Wrong with Their Claim" (Jacobson 1977,

Nechama Leibowitz, "Mammon or Eretz Yisrael" in *Studies in the Weekly Torah Portion (Numbers)*. Jerusalem: WZO, 1980).

In regard to your question, we came up with several simple but important answers. It occurred to me that Moshe may not have been able to do more than he did. He was old, his period of leadership was to end, and he was about to die. While he may not have been happy with this deal (and indeed he at first criticizes the request), he was in no position to stop it. He certainly could not demand that they see the Land first, given the fact that he himself was not to see the Land. How could he make a condition that he could in no way enforce? All he could do was shape the deal, demand that they lead the fight for Eretz Yisrael, put their children's needs before their cattle's needs, and soften the materialism that may have affected their request.

However, I soon realized this answer sells Moshe short. To the very end, he was able to lead, inspire, and guide as the remainder of the *sidra* shows. There had to be more.

Perhaps Moshe realized that giving them the land they wanted on the east bank of the Jordan would expand the land opportunities for the other nine and one-half tribes. This would have made everyone happy. After all, the Land was not divvied up yet; this did not happen until after this chapter. So, in answer to your final point, Moshe had all the necessary information available to him at that point. And he had to make a decision.

One of my regulars pointed out during our *shiur* that Moshe must have realized that for the conquest of Eretz Yisrael to be successful, our people's rear flank had to be protected. It was in the best strategic interest of the Jewish people to have a fortified Jewish area of settlement on the far side of the Jordan. After all, especially following the Ba'al Pe'or incident in the past two readings, a protected, built up set of rear communities would be helpful as the Jews pushed forward into the Promised Land.

I realized, in the end, that the deal provided Moshe with a means of doing exactly what your question suggests. The condition of requiring the warriors to go as *halutzim* (the Torah's term) in the battle for the Promised Land really did give them a chance to see the Land on the other side of the Jordan. Maybe, in this subtle way, Moshe did insure that they would see what they were giving up and eventually tell their families about it!

However, history, filled with all sorts of ironies, can be a great teacher. As Jacobson, quoting the midrash, points out, when the Assyrians invaded from the Northeast 1,000 years later, these two and one-half tribes were the first to be exiled and lost. In the long run, even with the sanction of Moshe, they did not gain anything.

David Sofian

In answer to your question to *parshat Balak*, I referred to a midrash that contrasted specific Israelites and non-Israelites in order to demonstrate why God favored the Israelites. The midrash often makes such comparisons. Here I would like to begin with that same kind of midrash, only this time it shows Israelites and non-Israelites to be similar. Unfortunately, the similarity is a negative one.

In *Midrash Bamidbar Rabbah* 22:7, we learn that there are three great gifts in the world—wisdom, strength, and wealth. The midrash wants us to understand that if the gift came from the Holy One, possessing any one of them can be the same as attaining everything. If not, the gift ultimately fails the one who has it.

To demonstrate this point, the passage gives us several examples of given Israelites and non-Israelites whose possession of one of the gifts ultimately failed. Ahitophel in Israel and Bilaam among the nations possessed wisdom. Samson in Israel and Goliath among the nations had strength. Korah in Israel and Haman among the nations were favored with wealth.

Yet, all ultimately were destroyed. The relevance of this midrash to our current parshah enters here. We are to see that the children of Gad and Reuben are a similar case. They were rich in that they possessed large numbers of cattle, but it is also clear that their gift was not from God, because they chose to settle outside the land of Israel and to separate themselves from their people. We know that their gift availed them not, since they were the first of all the tribes to go into exile, as 1 Chronicles 5:26 intimates.

This midrash begins to point us toward an answer to your question. In the midrash, the Reubenites and Gadites are being grouped with Ahitophel, Samson, and Korah. It is this association that is the point. Just as all three of these men rebelled against God's authority—Ahitophel against God's anointed one, David; Samson against the special status of the Nazir; and Korah against God's instrument, Moses—so too these tribes are rebelling against God's authority.

This rebellion is hinted at in their very approach to Moses. They fail to mention God at all. Their only concern is with the fitness of land of Jazer for cattle. In Ahitophel's defection, God saw to it that his advice to Absalom was not followed, and Ahitophel hanged himself.

Samson's undisciplined life comes to an end blinded, praying for vengeance instead of repentance. Korah's revolt ended up with him being swallowed by the earth. All meet unfavorable ends without returning from the path of rebellion. So if the rebellion of the Reubenites and Gadites is the same, the association means there was no hope of changing their attitude.

In paragraph 9 of the same chapter from *Bamidbar Rabbah*, the case against them is deepened. Ecclesiastes 10:2 says, "A wise man's understanding is at his right hand; but a fool's understanding is at his left." Working from this verse, the midrash teaches us that the wise man here refers to Moses and the fool refers to the Reubenites and Gadites. What makes them the fool is that they subordinated the more important to the less important. How so? They cherished their wealth more than human beings. We know this because they say to Moses in *Bamidbar* 32:16, "we will build sheepfolds here for our cattle, and cities for our little ones." They are putting the protection of their cattle before the care of their children.

After the Gadites and Reubenites offer to arm themselves, go before the Children of Israel, and bring them to their places in the land, Moses nevertheless calls them on their confused values. This is seen in the way Moses agrees to their offer. In 32:24, he tells them to build cities for your little ones, and then he says build folds for your sheep.

Now we can see that not only was Reubenite and Gadite wealth not a gift from God, and not only were they effectively rebelling against God, but their values were so confused that they came to care more for their cattle than even for their own children. Seen this way, is it any wonder that Moses contented himself with gaining the agreement he did?

I think there is something else worth thinking about that grows from this discussion. It is significant that this episode happens near the end of Moses' life, after he had dealt with Israel's stubbornness and rebellion over and over again. By this point, Moses has had considerable experience with Israelite defiance. In the earlier cases, defiance was met with uncompromising confrontation.

Maybe at this point Moses was remembering the aftermath of the golden calf, the outcome of the twelve spies, and the consequences of Korah's challenge. Perhaps that bitter experience had brought him to the point, nearing the end of his life, where he was more ready to accept these tribes as they were instead of as they should be. Maybe by this point Moses had been worn down and weakened, or maybe he had grown from his massive experience and become wiser in such matters. I tend to favor the latter view.

The tribes in question certainly should have at least inspected their designated territory in Canaan before making the request they did. But at this stage of his life, Moses knows that he can only move them so far. So he accomplishes what can be accomplished. God did not become angry and leave them in the wilderness, as Moses feared, and the children of Gad and Reuben lead the advance into Canaan.

Consequently, I do not think the Torah is condoning the making of crucial decisions without having all available information. I think the Reubenites and Gadites were not going to be convinced to change their view. Their choice could have led to disaster, but due to Moses' handling of the situation, disaster was averted and the best outcome available attained.

Masei: Numbers 33:1–36:13

Prophetical Reading
Jeremiah 2:4–28, 3:4, 4:1–2

Overview of Torah Portion

The Hebrews' journey through the wilderness, from Egypt to the banks of the Jordan, are recounted. God commands the people, when they enter the Promised Land, to drive out the inhabitants, destroy their idols, and establish 48 cities for the Levites—including six cities of refuge for persons who accidentally commit manslaughter. God gives the boundaries of the Holy Land and adds some laws of inheritance.

Key Verses

"And the Lord spoke to Moses . . . saying . . . 'When you cross over the Jordan into the Land of Canaan, you shall drive out all of the inhabitants of the land from before you and destroy all their carved stones and destroy all their molten images and demolish all their high places. . . . But if you do not drive out the inhabitants of the land from before you, those that you let remain of them shall be as thorns in your eyes. . . . And it shall come to pass that as I thought to do to them, I will do to you'" (Numbers 33:50–56).

Discussion Question

A GOLDEN RULE: Expel the idolatrous inhabitants of Canaan, God warns, or you will suffer the fate there—expulsion is implied—that I had reserved for them. Is that why the Children of Israel are supposed to obey God—not because certain behavior is correct, but as a means to escape punishment? It is a fundamental question of man's relationship to God: Do we keep the *mitzvot* out of love of the Creator or fear of punishment? If we believe that the ultimate reward and punishment take place in the world to come, why emphasize this temporal punishment?

Shammai Engelmayer

Let us deal with the final thought of the question first: The Torah does not know from "the world to come." Whether such a "world" exists is totally irrelevant to the Torah. Indeed, the whole concept is only about 2,000 years old. It does not make its first appearance until around the first century B.C.E. It is telling that the strict constructionists of the period, the Temple-based Zadokites (the Sadducees), would have nothing to do with the concept.

The Torah is of this world, exclusively. It is a code of behavior and practice for this world. It assumes that, at death, life ends both physically and spiritually. The Psalmist (115:17) put it best in a phrase familiar to us from the *Hallel*: "The dead cannot praise the Lord, nor any who go down into the silence [of the grave]."

In the biblical world, dead is dead and buried. With Yechezkel (Ezekiel) and Yishayahu (Isaiah), we begin to find allusions to the possibility of *resurrection*, but nothing is said about an afterlife.

And for good reason: We do not perform righteous acts or fulfill ritual obligations for the purpose of reward, or out of fear of punishment. Rather, we do them because they are the proper things to do. Said Ben Azzai (*Mishna Avot* 4:2), the "reward for a good deed is a good deed and the wages of sin is sin."

The fact is, the "wicked sprout like grass . . . all evildoers blossom" (Psalms 92:8). We trust in God and His justice to even things out; how is beyond our ability to understand.

Let us, then, turn to this world and the concept of divine reward and punishment as it occurs in the Torah. Actually, there is no such concept in the Torah—for the individual, that is. When God threatens to shut up the rains in the skies, for example, He is threatening a national punishment for national sins. When, as He does in this passage, He threatens Israel with ouster from the land, He means all of Israel and not any single individual.

Individual punishment is in the Torah, but it is meted out by an earthly court following a trial, the procedures of which are heavily weighted on behalf of the defendant in order to avoid the possibility of error. Thus, for example, as the rabbis of blessed memory interpreted the laws, if twenty witnesses, say, line up on the side of the prosecution and a mere two defense witnesses rebut that evidence (or even just one credible and valid witness), all of the testimony is excluded. This does not even approach Divine justice; when God judges, He has no need of testimony or witnesses.

Of course, it is possible to conclude that when God speaks globally, He implies the individual, as well.

Clearly, however, there is a danger in believing in such a system of personal reward and punishment. Indeed, it is given as the reason for the apostasy of Elisha ben Avihu, the teacher of Rabbi Meir, although there is no agreement on the specific event. One talmudic tradition (JT Hagigah 2:1) has him witnessing a dog dragging around the tongue of a scholar who was tortured to death by the Romans. Seeing this, Elisha exclaimed: "Is this the Torah and is this its reward?"

The closing verses of BT Hullin 142a contain a variation of that tradition, but earlier in the discussion, it presents another tradition.

Although the Torah several times expresses the notion that one must obey the law generally in order to "live long in the land" that God gave to Israel, only two commandments in the Torah specifically include long life as the reward. One is honoring parents (Exodus 20:12 and Deuteronomy 5:16); the other is chasing a mother bird away from its nest before taking its young, in order not to grieve the mother (Deuteronomy 22:6-7).

Thus it was that Elisha (known more often in the Talmud as *acher*, meaning "other") watched as a youth heeded his father's wishes (and the Torah's command) and climbed up to a nest to chase the mother bird away before taking its children. As the mother flew away, the youth plummeted to the ground and promptly died a painful death. For Elisha, so this tradition goes, the incident caused him to lose his faith. This led the rabbis to declare as doctrine that "there is no reward in this world for the fulfillment of *mitzvot*."

On the other hand, the rabbis were as troubled as Elisha by the notion that the good die young and the wicked prosper. It is this that caused them to consider seriously the possibility of a world to come. It was the only way for them to deal with the problem.

Having said all that, let us now look at the specific threat posed in this parshah, for it is instructive both as to the nature of God's "rewards" and "punishments," and to the one possible category of divine "punishment" that is indeed personal, namely *karet*.

What is it that God is saying here? "Drive out the Canaanites, or I will drive you out, instead."

Now, what does He mean? Essentially, God warns Israel that unless it roots out the pagan influences all around it, those pagan influences will seduce the people into apostasy. They will no longer be Israelites, because they will no longer believe in Israel's God. "Israel" will be gone from the land and only the "pagans" will survive.

In other words, God is not warning of a punishment He will mete out, but one that the people will impose on themselves. This is also what God means when He warns Israel that He will keep the land from producing its bounty. This is just a rhetorical restatement of the same "punishment."

As already noted in my answer to the question in *parshat Bechukotai*, the land of Israel is merely an *achuzah* (a holding) for the people of Israel; it is not their permanent possession. Yet it is Israel alone that determines the length of its stay in the land.

Ironically, as also noted in my answer there, just as Israel's fate is tied to the land, the land's fate is tied to Israel. The land cannot flourish without the people; so God said and so history proves. Yet the people can still be in the land for it to suffer the pangs of separation. If Israel does not *act* like Israel, Israel is *not* Israel. God does not have to lift a finger; Israel will do it all by itself. (See my answer to the question in *parshat Chukat* for an elaboration of this theme.)

The punishment of *karet* is similar. God "cuts off" a person from His people only when that person has cut himself off. There are two main categories of crimes for which *karet* is decreed: profaning the sacred (i.e., using anointing oil as a body lotion or eating sacrificial meat while in an impure state) and behaving in a way radically unsuited to an Israelite (i.e., engaging in incestuous relations or acting in a heinous manner to another person). One also suffers *karet* for failing to observe Pesach and also, specifically, for eating leavened bread during the festival, as well as for eating on Yom Kippur. Both are essential to the character of an Israelite, representing the justification for the Covenant on the one hand and an Israelite's unique connection to God on the other.

Finally, *karet* is also the punishment for those who eat the blood of animals or who arbitrarily kill animals for food without attaching to it the veneer of the sacred. The blood is life, according to the Torah. Killing animals is taking life, something that is reluctantly permitted by divine dispensation, but only under the most stringent guidelines. In this way, an Israelite must always stop to consider that he is ending a life for his personal pleasure.

These are the crimes for which *karet* is the punishment. As you can see, they involve trashing God by profaning that which is used for His service, the gratuitous murder of an animal He created, and trashing the character of His kingdom of priests by committing an abominable act of some kind. A person who commits any of these crimes separates him- or herself from Israel and from God. That person will be "cut off" in the sense that his or her behavior, as noted in my answer in *parshat Chukat*, will be carried on by children, then grandchildren, and so on.

To sum up, then, we do not perform *mitzvot* because of a Divine reward, and we do not suffer Divine punishment for non-performance. We do what is right because it is right, and for no other reason. And, when God warns of the "punishments" He will inflict on Israel, it is just His way of saying that Israel will punish itself. If a world to come exists, it is neither relevant to the performing of *mitzvot*, nor should we make it a consideration.

Why, then, does the Torah tell us to "fear" God? This "fear" is unlike the "fear" discussed by the rabbis. It is not an emotion; it is not dread or apprehension. Rather, the word is closer in meaning to reverence or devotion. To fear God in the biblical idiom is to revere Him, to serve Him with a full and open heart.

Joseph Ozarowski

While this particular verse offers a temporal punishment for our actions, there is no question that *Hashem*'s preferred motive for our behavior is love. After this *sidra* comes the Book of Deuteronomy, which is replete with Moshe's references to serving God out of love. The best known one is from the Shema (Deuteronomy 6:5): "And you shall love the Lord your God with all your heart, with all your souls and with all your strength. . . ." But God, recognizing that we are but human, knows that doing things altruistically may not always be an effective way of guaranteeing a holy life. In addition, the Torah, being a guide to life, teaches us that there are consequences to our actions.

Sometimes, these are not the consequences we would prefer, but they are inevitable results of our actions. So in many places, the Torah speaks of doing *mitzvot* out of *yir'ah*, often translated as "fear of God" but more probably "reverence of God" or "awe of God." This is a realistic balance to acting exclusively out of love, because sometimes, love without guidance, guidelines, discipline, and structure simply does not work. People who love each other sometimes hurt each other in ways which are not acceptable. Hence the need for other motivating factors.

The issue of the conquest of Eretz Yisrael is one good example of this. This question here is not one of nationalism or territorialism. Rather, as both the text (vs. 52) specifies and the commentaries embellish (see Rashi and Ramban), the issue is one of eradicating idolatry in order to establish a holy and model society. With classic *avoda zara* (idolatry), there really is no middle ground. The Torah makes quite clear in many other places that by giving idolatry any kind of a foothold, our own place in the Land is at risk. The incident at Ba'al Pe'or, which in the Torah's chronology just occurred, is the perfect example of this danger. Thus God's remarks to Moshe about the elimination of *avoda zara* are especially trenchant.

But as Kli Yakar points out, the best way to accomplish this difficult task is by positive means, which is why in the midst of this difficult commandment, the Torah inserts another *V'hitnahaltem et ha-aretz* . . . ("and you shall inherit (or settle) the Land . . ."). The best way to accomplish the above-mentioned goals is through positive means. Nevertheless, the Torah still includes the warning that if these goals are not reached, we risk being victims.

Sometimes, in order to fulfill a worthy goal, we are faced with difficult choices, some of which we would prefer not to have to make, as they may have unpleasant aspects. But, in order to complete what we set out to do, we are bound to gird ourselves and move on, knowing both the positive results if we accomplish what we seek and the negative consequences if do not reach our desired end. As Rashi comments on verse 51, "When you cross the Jordan (it will be) on dry land (like the Red Sea), on the condition that you cross. And if not, the water will come and drown you. . . ."

It is worth noting that according to the Ramban, these verses are a primary source of the mitzvah of *yishuv Eretz Yisrael* (settling the Land of Israel), which of course is the biblical/halakhic/historical basis of modern Zionism. I will let the reader or student draw his or her own conclusions connecting modern Zionism and Israel to the issues raised in my responses to the questions regarding doing *mitzvot* out of love or out of fear of punishment, as well as the issues of the consequences of our actions.

David Sofian

I think you have put your finger on a fundamental question about proper religious motivation for human behavior. Jewishly we would ask it in terms of *mitzvot*, as you did. Which is it? Do we observe them because we are motivated by our love of God, or are we motivated by hope for eventual reward and/or fear of punishment? Within the tradition, both sides are represented.

In chapter 1 of *Pirke Avot*, Mishnah 3, there is the famous passage attributed to Antigonus of Sokho. He tells us not to be like servants who serve their master for the sake of receiving a reward or prize, but rather to be like servants who serve their master without regard to receiving a reward or prize. He concludes his statement there with the admonition, let the fear of heaven be upon you. Antigonus of Sokho is making it very clear that we should keep the *mitzvot* simply because they are God's *mitzvot*, because we are filled with awe for our Creator, not because we hope to gain something. Respect for God should be the motivator of our behavior, not reward or punishment.

Pirke Avot gives us the other point of view, as well. In the very first Mishnah in chapter 2, Rabbi Judah the Prince teaches that we should be as heedful of a light *mitzvah* as of a weighty one, for no one knows the reward for any given *mitzvah*. He concludes his statement by cautioning us to consider three things that will keep us from falling into the hands of transgression: namely, that there is an eye that sees and an ear that hears above you, and all your deeds are being written down.

In other words, not only is there a reward for every precept and a punishment for every transgression, but Judah is implying that by watching, listening, and recording all of our actions, God is preparing for the final judgement. So beware! Knowing that there is reward and punishment is the motivator of our behavior.

I am often asked this question in a different way. I am asked it in terms of belief in the world to come. As a congregational rabbi, in classes and elsewhere, people ask theological questions about the reality of evil. They may be struggling with the *Shoah*, or they may personally be facing illness, tragedy, or setback. If the situation allows and an in depth discussion is possible, I point out that these questions have always faced humankind.

The biblical Book of Job raises them in a most powerful way, and much of what the rabbis of our tradition taught was about coming to terms with the destruction of the Temple. As part of this discussion, I bring up the rabbinic material dealing with the world to come and try to show how the rabbis used this concept to respond to the question of how we can believe in God's justice in a world where righteous people suffer, and wicked people prosper.

It is in the course of such discussions that I am often asked whether or not I, as a modern liberal rabbi, believe in the world to come. Essentially, I am being asked, do I believe in reward and punishment, and is that the motivation of Jewish behavior?

My answer is that I am uncertain, but for me, that is not the crucial question. How so? Since I experience the commanding presence of God, even if I cannot explain in a complete way why there is evil in God's Creation, the real issue for me as a liberal Jew is first determining as best I can what God demands and then observing those commandments.

If we are following God's commandments, it turns out that there is the life of the world to come, and we deserve to receive it, wonderful. Yet, if it turns out that there is nothing after death, that doesn't change the necessity of our following God's commandments.

In other words, I think Antigonus got it right. There may be an accounting going on, and there may not be. There may be a prize at the end, or there may not be. But as Jews in covenantal relationship with God, it is the experience of that relationship that should be our focus and motivation.

D'varim/Deuteronomy

D'varim:
Deuteronomy 1:1–3:22

Prophetical Reading
Isaiah 1:1–27

Overview of Torah Portion

Approaching the end of his life and the end of his mission as leader of the Hebrews, before they enter the Promised Land, Moses delivers his final exhortation to them on the banks of the Jordan. He recounts their travels and travails through the wilderness—including their sins and battles.

Key Verses

"And the Lord said . . . 'All the men who have seen My glory and My signs that I performed in Egypt and in the wilderness . . . and did not listen to My voice, they shall not see the land that I swore to their fathers and none of those who despised Me shall see it'" (Numbers 14:20–23).

"And the Lord heard the voice of your words, and was angered, and swore, saying, 'Not one man of this evil generation shall see the good land that I swore to give to your fathers—except for Caleb, son of Jephuneh; he shall see it'" (Deuteronomy 1:34–36).

Discussion Question

A VISION OF HOLINESS: When God promises the land of Canaan to the patriarchs as an inheritance for them and their descendants, it is as a place to be conquered, settled, and inhabited—not as an object to be viewed. But when the Hebrews' lack of faith after the spies' report about Canaan draws God's anger, He vows that that generation will not live to see the Promised Land.

Why this emphasis on sight? Does the Torah literally mean "sight?" Elsewhere, the Torah states that the erring Children of Israel will not enter Canaan, but it seems superfluous to mention the mere seeing of it. Is denying the Hebrews a view of the Holy Land also considered punishment? If so, why did God make an exception for Moses—who was punished for striking the rock and was not allowed to lead the people across the Jordan—and show him Canaan from atop Mt. Nebo before he died?

Shammai Engelmayer

As is so often the case, there is a simple answer and a more complicated one. The simple answer is that this is nothing more than rhetoric, and familiar rhetoric, at that. How often have we read, or heard (or used?), the phrase "he will never live to see the day" and similar comments? In the simple sense, this is no more than another version of this common expression.

Yet the simple answer is not fully satisfying. The Torah, after all, does not merely "say" things for effect; there often is a purpose to its choice of language. That certainly seems to be the case here.

God's justice, we are told, is measure for measure; "an eye for an eye," if you will. That is how it works out here. For the Israel of the Exodus, "seeing" was its biggest problem. As noted in my answer to *parshat P'kudei*'s question:

> "When they [the Israelites] saw Moshe do his parlor tricks for them, they believed in God; but when they saw their work increased, they stopped believing. When they saw that the plagues brought about their freedom, they believed; when they saw the Egyptians coming after them, they stopped believing. When they saw the waters part and the attacking army destroyed, they believed; when they saw the heat of the sun and the dearth of water, they stopped believing."

In other words, where God was concerned, they did not believe what they saw, only what they saw last.

"Seeing is believing" also brought about the terrible sin of the golden calf. This people refused to accept the notion of a God that is unseen and without form. It insisted on "seeing" Him at all times in the physical sense, and then created a representation of Him in the form of a calf to accomplish this. That led God to the conclusion that Israel was too primitive to accept a religious structure devoid of pagan influences, thus bringing about the creation of the sacrificial cult.

This was not something God would easily forgive. He knew that, under the best of circumstances, it would take many generations to cleanse Israel of that more primitive form of worship, and that Israel was not known for creating "the best of circumstances." And yet, until Israel could separate itself from its pagan trappings, it could not truly be God's spiritual messenger to the world, which is the whole point of its existence.

Because the Israel of the Exodus refused to see beyond what its eyes could behold, it was denied the right to "see" the fulfillment of the Exodus drama—from the House of Bondage to the Land of Promise.

Moshe, on the other hand, believed not only what he saw (God's great powers, His infinite mercy and justice, etc.), but also what he could not see (God Himself). For this, he was not denied the right to see the land before his death. He could not enter, but he could see it from afar.

Joseph Ozarowski

The only commentary I could find that dealt with the issue of sight and the entry to the Promised Land was the one written by Rabbi Hayim ben Attar, an eighteenth century Italian/Jerusalem commentator, whose commentary, ironically enough, is called the *Or Hahayim*, literally "the Light of Life." While he does not put his comments in our references together as a systematic commentary, he does interpret sight in three very different ways. This may suggest that there are different kinds of sight.

In our *sidra*, *Or Hahayim* understands sight in its basic textual sense, that those who followed the spies would not live to see the land. Caleb (and, by implication, Joshua (see vs. 38)), who separated himself from the evil inclinations of the spies and followed after God, would live to see the Land and also inherit it.

In the earlier reference to sight, back in Numbers 14:22–3, where God promises to punish the spies and the Jews who followed them by not "seeing the land," *Or Hahayim* suggests a different meaning to the word. The root for the word "see," *ro-eh*, is the same Hebrew root for the word "worthy," *ra-oo-ee*.

Thus, where God appears to use the concept of not seeing the land as a means of stated punishment, God really means they are not worthy of coming to the Promised Land. Rather than being a punishment, it can be seen as a statement of fact that the people are simply not worthy to enter Israel. Within this idea, it is worth noting that the spies were the ones who actually did see the Land in its physical sense but were still not worthy to see it in a more permanent way.

There is a third reference to seeing in Numbers 27:13, where *Hashem* tells Moshe that he will see the Land without physically entering it. Moshe would not accompany his people, but he would instead view the Land in sort of a Divine Omnimax presentation. There, *Or Hahayim* offers yet a third interpretation of seeing, that of a hidden mystical sight in a way that "the natural eye is unable to see with the light of the sun . . . that the light of life would light up for him [Moshe]." (This is a clever wordplay because, as we noted earlier, the very name of this commentary is *Or Hahayim*, "the Light of Life!") So there is a deeper kind of sight, one perceived by the inner mind, heart, and soul that the eye cannot see. This is what Moshe was privileged to have.

Light and life are indeed intimately connected and can be perceived at different levels. May we be worthy to have all three: The Or Hahayim of basic life in the physical sense, that we live to see our goals and dreams; that we are *re-oo-yim* (that we are seen as worthy of those goals); and that God blesses us with the hidden *Or Hahayim*, the inner light of spiritual life, as well.

David Sofian

When first reading the verses you featured from the *parshah*, it seemed to me that the meaning of the word in question, "see," is nothing more than a way of emphasizing God's decision not to let that generation enter the Land of Israel. Reading it in either the *Bamidbar* or *D'varim* context, I heard it saying, "not only will you not enter it, but you are not going even to see it!"

Nevertheless, given the rabbis' approach that none of the words of Torah are superfluous or haphazardly chosen, I looked to see if there wasn't the possibility of something deeper to be found in this word choice.

In *Midrash Kohelet Rabbah* 10:1, there is a discussion of the manna God fed the Israelites in the wilderness. Within the discussion, cucumbers and their appearance are used as a metaphor to illuminate the nature of experiencing the manna. We hear it was like God setting before our ancestors two cucumbers, one whole and the other broken.

When asked how much each was worth, the Israelites responded the whole one was worth twice the broken one. God then asks them why there is a difference in value, since eventually each will be broken into pieces. They responded that the broken one is not like the whole one because there is not only enjoyment in the taste, but also in the appearance. So, extrapolating from this passage, the denial of seeing the Land did have specific meaning.

The Torah is not just emphasizing God's determination not to let them enter. It is telling us that the particular enjoyment of seeing the land was denied them as an additional punishment.

The continuation of the same passage furthers the point. Rabbi Eleazar, in the name of Rabbi Yose ben Zimra, relates that three things are said about the inside of the fig: It is good to eat, it is fair to behold, and it increases wisdom. Again we see that just the sight of something as simple as a fig, its appearance, is an enjoyment of significance. Similarly, this passage wants us to believe that Isaac was emphasizing the enjoyment brought by the sight of food when he told Esau to make him a savory dish.

The midrash proposes that in this interlude, Isaac was actually suggesting that he used to enjoy the sight of the food, but now that his eyes had grown dim, he could only enjoy its smell. And just for good measure, the passage adds that Solomon also recognized the power of sight. The midrash teaches that when Solomon said, "when goods increase, they are increased that eat them" (Ecclesiastes 5:10), he meant that just the sight of abundant food relieves hunger.

After reflection, to me the possible meaning of "seeing" that is most significant is seeing in the sense of knowing or experiencing. When God tells them that they will not see the good land, its stress is that they will not have firsthand knowledge or experience of that good land.

The passages enumerating the value the rabbis placed on knowing and experiencing the land are almost without end. A few examples are in order. Working from part of Isaiah 42:5, "and the spirit to them that walk therein," BT *Ketubot* 111a tells us that just the experience of walking four cubits in the Land of Israel assures one entry into the world to come. On that same page of the Babylonian Talmud, this time using part of Isaiah 33:24, "the people that dwelleth therein has its iniquity lifted," Rabbi Eleazar teaches that anyone who makes his home in the Land of Israel lives uncorrupted by sin.

And in BT *Sotah* 14a, Rabbi Simlai explains why Moses longed to enter the Land of Israel. Rabbi Simlai teaches that we shouldn't think that Moses needed to eat the land's fruit or be sated with its bounty. Rather, Moses' deep desire stemmed from his knowledge that many precepts given to Israel could only be fulfilled in the land. The heightened experience of fulfilling those mitzvot is what Moses craved.

Now, then, it is clear that the denial of even seeing the land is notable. Moreover, we can also understand the importance of God making an exception for Moses. This was indeed a meaningful kindness. Moses was never able to experience living in the land, but at least he was allowed the enjoyment of looking out and seeing it.

Va'etchanan:
Deuteronomy 3:23–7:11

*Prophetical Reading
Isaiah 40:1–26*

Overview of Torah Portion

Moses continues his review of the journey in the wilderness and repeats the necessity of keeping each commandment. He designates cities of refuge for someone who accidentally commits manslaughter, repeats the Ten Commandments, and introduces the *mitzvot* of *mezuzah* and *tefillin*.

Key Verses

"**B**ehold, I have taught you statutes and ordinances, as the Lord my God commanded me, to do thus in the midst of the land into which you are going to possess. Observe and do them, because this is your wisdom and your understanding in the eyes of the people, that when they hear all these statutes, they shall say, 'Certainly this great nation is wise and understanding.' And what great people have statutes and ordinances as righteous as all this Torah that I place before you today?" (Deuteronomy 4:5–8).

Discussion Question

WHO GETS THE CREDIT? The Children of Israel didn't give the world the Torah's laws and commandments—so why should they get the credit? God did the work; should He not receive the honor? God initiates, the Hebrews simply obey. Why does God think that the Hebrews' observance of the Torah will raise their status in the opinion of the other nations? Has history—Jews' interaction among the nations—proven God's contention to be true?

Shammai Engelmayer

Let us be clear about what the Torah represents. It is not the "law book" of the Jewish people. Rather, it is the source text for the laws.

As I have noted before in this work, God gave Israel very few "laws." For the most part, He provided only chapter headings. He left it to Israel to write the chapters themselves; to fill in the blanks, as it were. Here is an example from this week's parshah:

> Observe the Shabbat day to keep it holy, as the Lord your God has commanded you. Six days shall you labor and do all your work, but on the seventh day it is a Shabbat onto the Lord, your God, you shall do no manner of work—you, your son and your daughter, and your male and female slave, your ox and your she-donkey, or any of your cattle, and the stranger within your gates.

That is the commandment. Now here are a few of the problems that need to be dealt with before it can be followed:

1. What is a "day"? When does it begin and when does it end? This question is not as foolish as it sounds. Beginning with Genesis 1, we know the order of the day, for the text states, "It was evening, it was morning, the first day," and so forth, meaning that the "day" actually begins in the evening. Evening, however, begins somewhere between the time the sun begins to set and the time the stars begin to appear. Just where it begins within this period is not precisely known. Thus, a legal definition for "day" is essential in order to properly fulfill this commandment.

2. How does one "observe" a day? Similarly, from the original version in Exodus 20:8, what actually is required to "remember" a day? This leads to another question: Are there different requirements for observing and remembering, or does fulfilling the one imperative also fulfill the other? If there are differences between observing and remembering, does observing take precedence, seeing that the term is more often used in the Torah regarding Shabbat than is remembering?

3. What does it mean to "keep [a day] holy"? If one prays, eats, studies, and sleeps on this day, does this meet the test (especially since

these are activities one may do on any other day, as well)? What is "holy" in this sense?

4. What is the definition of "work"? Is it an activity requiring a minimum amount of physical exertion, or does merely flicking a switch or pushing a button (which require hardly any expenditure of physical energy) qualify? Can work be mental (i.e., although one may not do actual work, one thinks about work on Shabbat, especially if one's job requires him or her to use the head, not the hands)?

5. If one must do "all his or her work" in six days and "no manner of work" on the seventh, does this preclude doing any work whatsoever on Shabbat? Some specific examples: Can a Shabbat-observant hotel employ a kitchen and dining room staff on Shabbat? Can a pulpit rabbi, whose "work" is being a pulpit rabbi, lead the congregation on Shabbat? Can a physician care for patients on Shabbat? Is it permissible to indirectly ask a non-Jew to turn on your lights on Shabbat?

6. How is "slave" defined—any slave, or just an Israelite slave?

7. Does "stranger within your gates" refer to a resident alien, or someone who just dropped into town for a brief visit?

8. How does one define "stranger"? Can it be someone who is known? Is it an Israelite, a non-Israelite, or both?

These are just the tip of the iceberg for this commandment—and each answer raises other questions that need to be answered, as well. The Torah supplies none of the answers. God told Israel what it needed to do; He left it to Israel to construct the legislation by which to achieve the goal.

Interestingly, the one set of laws in the Torah that is more detailed than any others involves the sacrificial cult. It is as if God is saying, "I will set all these out for you in detail, so you will have no reason to embellish them in any way, or to extend them in any way beyond the narrow limits I will set." The fact is, the more meat put on the bones, the more limited those bones become. Perhaps this was yet another signal from God that the sacrificial cult was only a temporary route to holiness and, He had no intention of leaving Israel any leeway to perpetuate it.

In any case, when it comes to most of the laws of the Torah, it is by filling in the blanks that Israel demonstrates its wisdom and understanding.

That brings us to the second part of the question: Why, in filling in the blanks, should Israel's stature rise among the peoples of the world?

In essence, what is the point of the laws for which God supplied the chapter headings? The rabbis of blessed memory, who studied every letter of every word in the Torah, boiled it down to one commandment: "You shall love your neighbor as yourself." That, they concluded, was the essence of the Torah's "laws." All else, as Hillel said, was commentary.

Consider our example of Shabbat. What is the essence of the law? It is not simply that a person cannot work on Shabbat. Rather, it is that every living creature, man or beast (and even field, as the Torah also insists), gets time off to regenerate, to smell the roses, and to honor the Creator of all that is. "Slave" is made a relative term here, not an absolute. Unlike any other "slave master" in the world (such as those in the pre-Civil War South), the Israelite does not have total control over the bodies of his slaves and no control whatever over their souls. Never mind that "you cannot treat a human being like an animal," a noted western concept, you cannot even treat an animal like an animal; it, too, gets one day off in seven.

What a remarkable legal code this is. We will read later that, during a war, you may not destroy the fruit-bearing tree of your enemy. That leaves out such brutal tactics as scorched-earth. It also makes it impossible to ever drop a nuclear bomb of any kind. In addition, it also serves as the basis for rules against wasting fossil fuels and, by further extension, anything of use to humanity. What other people have such laws?

And sooner or later, God is saying here, those "other people" will take notice of the humanity inherent in the Torah's code. They will see how Israel interprets the code and puts it into force. If Israel, by filling in the blanks, fills them in the manner God intended that it should, then its stature surely will rise among the nations.

Finally, the question wonders whether history shows any evidence that God's contention regarding Israel's stature has come true. The answer is yes and no.

Yes: The fact that two other religio-legal systems derive from it is one proof. Imitation, after all, is supposed to be the sincerest form of flattery. Another proof, of a negative sort, comes from recent history. Israel's incursion into Lebanon in the early 1980s and its handling of the *intifada* (the uprising of Arab residents in territories administered by Israel) later in that decade both came under heavy criticism from the world, precisely because Israel did not seem to live up to the moral and ethical standards the world came to expect of "Jews."

And no: When it comes to the Jews, the world picks and chooses what it wants to see. So, while it sees the moral and ethical imperatives of Judaism, it turns a blind eye to other laws, such as the right of self-defense.

More importantly, the world has not yet come around to wanting to emulate these laws. In the last half-century or so, we have seen wholesale slaughter become the norm—from the Holocaust, to the Cambodian massacres, to the Bosnian atrocities.

We have developed weapons that can destroy cities, and improved them so that they can destroy the entire planet and, perhaps, wreak havoc on the universe at the same time (who really knows what effect a global nuclear war would have outside the gravitational pull of the earth, or on its rotation?).

We have more poor people in the world today than ever before and we seem increasingly less inclined to do anything about it (most disturbingly, especially here in the United States). "Love your neighbor as yourself" is something only religious fanatics need worry about, as far as the world is concerned; it does not apply to anyone else.

In that sense, God's prediction still awaits fulfillment. The world holds the Jew to a higher standard when, in fact, imitation is the recognition that is required.

Joseph Ozarowski

Who should get the credit for the wisdom of the Torah in the eyes of the nations? During our Shabbat afternoon *shiur*, one of my erstwhile discussants pointed out that when a song becomes popular, people recognize it through the singer, rather than the songwriter. So why should the Jewish people not get the credit? "It is a good *moshul* (analogy)," I responded. But after a little reflection, I also said that when a movie wins an Oscar for "Best Picture," the actors, producer, director, and all the other partners go up to receive the award! (And it is enjoyable as long as everyone does not make a speech!)

An important tenet of Jewish thought, found especially in the works of Rabbi Joseph Soloveitchik of blessed memory, is that we are *Hashem*'s partners. When we study *Hashem*'s Torah, when we keep *Hashem*'s *mitzvot*, when we live our lives in a Jewishly-defined way, we become partners with the Almighty in the process of bringing the Divine down to Earth. And as a result of this process, we have Divine wisdom to share with the rest of society. There is much the Torah can teach a world so filled with pain and loneliness. This is probably what Moshe intended to say in his words. If all this is so, why shouldn't the partners not get at least some of the credit?

These verses strongly suggest what some thinkers have written—that we are a people only by virtue of the Torah. This means that while we are a people, we are also a religion in the sense that faith, worship, religious practice, and study all have the goal of bringing God and Godliness into the world. Although in the immediate sense, all Jews, whether observant or not, are part of the Jewish people by virtue of birth and identity, it is exclusively the Torah that offers a long-term basis for Jewish identity.

This mode of thought in modern times has been adopted by Rabbi

Samson Rafael Hirsch and more recent rabbinic leaders in the *hareidi* (so-called right-wing or ultra) Orthodox community. Secular nationalist Jews would have trouble with this idea, for it does not leave room for a Jewish nationhood divorced from religious practice. But other thinkers, such as Israel's first chief rabbi, Rav Avraham Yitzhak Kook, saw a specific sanctity to *Kneset Yisrael*, the Jewish people, even if divorced from the Torah.

In terms of the last question, it certainly seems that the *pshat*, the plain meaning of these verses, is that observance will raise our status among the nations. This thought is echoed in other places in the Torah. For example, in Deuteronomy 28:10, Moshe says, "And all the nations of the earth will see the Name of God is called upon you, and they will be in awe of you." The Talmud (BT *Berakhot* 6a) interprets this to refer to the *tefillin she-be-rosh*, the head *tefillin*.

The implication is that if we proudly keep the *mitzvot*, symbolized by the head *tefillin*, we will gain the respect of the nations around us. But Rabbi Levi Yitzchak of Berdichev (eighteenth century Poland/Ukraine Chasidic leader) pointed out that the Talmud used the term *tefillin she-be-rosh*, literally "*tefillin* in the head." This means that if we want to gain the respect of the world, we must internalize the messages of the Torah through pride in being Jewish in our families, homes, jobs, and lives. We should not be afraid to be openly Jewish, but rather do so in a positive and straightforward way.

Is this true sociologically? Another congregant pointed out that this is certainly the case in the United States today. After all, the latest statistics suggest that 70 to 80 percent of non-Jews would not be unhappy if their children married Jews. This proves that we are respected and accepted. True, I responded, but the fact that we would allow such a phenomenon to occur—that the majority of Jews would consider marrying non-Jews—goes against the intent of the Torah that we should be proud and open Jews in practice; in spirit; and in our homes, families, and jobs.

We cannot retain our distinctiveness if this occurs. Putting aside the statistics though, I think it is true that in this country, we do gain the respect of those around us best by being loyal and sincere in our Jewish practice. By remaining true to the Torah's system of religious, ethical, and social *mitzvot*, we stand to gain the honor of those around us.

Has this worked for us historically? Certainly not a lot of the time. For large chunks of our past history, maybe for most of it, we have been derided and persecuted for our reluctance to give up our religious identity. And there were times when giving up our uniqueness helped individual Jews remain alive, but not as Jews. Our historic relationship with organized

Christianity, and to a lesser extent Islam, illustrates this. And, as classical Judaism teaches, if we cannot remain alive as Jews, why bother with life?

The Holocaust revealed a different story regarding this point. The Nazis and their allies did not care whether we were religious, secular, practicing, or Jews totally outside the religious and/or national community. We were persecuted and murdered for what we were, not for what we did or believed. Our open pride and distinctiveness, or lack thereof, did not matter to the enemy.

Yet in the end, our Torah and our people have still tenaciously survived all the assaults on our religious practice and our peoplehood. What offers us the best chance for survival in the future—religious identity or national identity? This is one of the burning issues facing us today. If Torah and Jewish life are indeed a partnership between God and our Chosen People, as Rabbi Soloveitchik has taught, then I think the best bet for both Jewish survival and influencing the world for good lies in a broad combination of religion and spirituality, as defined by Jewish religious practice, Torah study, and *halakhah* on one hand, and Jewish nationalism and peoplehood on the other.

For Israel as a Jewish state and homeland, as well as for those of us still here in *galut*, the diaspora, this is, in my humble opinion, our best and most effective definition of *Yiddishkeit*.

David Sofian

God is the main character of the entire Torah. Everything could have been related in terms of God's actions. However, the Torah would not have us understand our relationship with God that way. As I indicated in my comment to *parashat Shelach Lecha*, God in the Bible cares and even becomes frustrated because of that caring.

In the Torah, we read about God's anger and how it can be overcome. We read about how God loves and has plans for humankind. In this image of God, God is intimately involved with creation, with human beings, and with us. God is involved with the world in the Torah.

The notion of covenant, *brit*, that evolves from God as portrayed in the Torah is central to this discussion. We learn that God is concerned with creating a certain kind of social order on earth. We learn that as the other party to the covenant, our duty is to transform the world of everyday human activity.

As we learn from the Judaism of the prophets, God's priority for us is to be involved with the fate of the widow, the orphan, the oppressed, and the weakest in our midsts. Judaism means that, as partners in the covenant, we must be constantly asking what God demands of us now. As I said in my comment to *parshat Beshalach*, we cannot overlook that contemporary Jews and the modern movements they belong to honestly and sincerely differ on their understanding of exactly what God demands of us today. I like to believe that these differences are *l'shem shamayim*, and that as long as they are *l'shem shamayim*, they each represent an authentic Jewish expression.

Yet, notwithstanding these differences, as serious religious Jews, we all can agree that to be a member of the covenanted community is to stand in partnership with God endeavoring to create the world God commands us to create. The *mitzvot*, the commandments, however much we may differ on the specifics of how we understand them, then, are the way this is brought about.

Stating all this, let me respond directly to your question. The Jewish story is not only God's story. It is the story of the relationship between God and the Jewish people. It is the story of God's need for the Jewish people to work to transform the world as a result of its relationship with God. This means that as the Jewish people, we have a responsibility to actually do things that improve God's creation. And a significant way we should do that is by serving as an example, by being an *or la'goyim*, a light to the nations.

That is why Deuteronomy tells us that Israel's heeding of God's statutes and ordinances draws the attention of the nations. The hope is that the world is further transformed by their following Israel's lead.

Your final question is very difficult to answer. Certainly in untold ways the Jewish people's interaction among the nations has proven to be a positive force in the transformation of the world. The expansion of the monotheistic idea stems from that interaction. The notion of Shabbat, of a day of rest and prayer, a day of non-manipulation of nature so as to strengthen our spiritual bond with God, is another example of a practice that has improved the world.

It is through the Jewish people that the world came to see the God who cares about the weak and enslaved, the God who redeems and liberates.

Yet, on the other hand, the entire biblical story is replete with Israelite failure to trust God and observe God's commands. I think we must earnestly ponder today if we are losing sight of our mission as God's people to serve as an example and be a light to the nations. Are we abdicating our role as God's partners in order to be just like all other peoples?

Assuming now that we are serious about our historic task, we should return to the motivating question that has always stood at the heart of the Jewish enterprise. How are we to be that example today? What is the meaning of being God's partner and striving to transform the world today?

There is a favorite story in the midrash that gives us a good example of how. It tells us that there is nothing really new or elusive about our role. It tells us that what is necessary is to find the strength to actualize the ideals of our tradition as taught by Micah: it has been told you what is good and what God commands, to do justly, love kindness, and walk humbly with God.

D'varim Rabbah 3:3 tells us the story of what happened when Rabbi Shimon ben Shetah purchased a donkey from an Ishmaelite. Afterward, his disciples found that hanging from the animal's neck was a jewel. They turned to him and exclaimed the verse from Proverbs 10:22, "Master, the blessing of God makes one rich." However, Shimon ben Shetah responded that he had only purchased a donkey and not the precious stone. So he went and returned the jewel to the Ishmaelite, who then forever after was known to say, "blessed is the God of Shimon ben Shetah."

Being an example means real Jews actualizing the life God commands, and by doing that, we fulfill our role as God's partners, helping God transform the world.

Ekev:
Deuteronomy 7:12–11:25

Prophetical Reading
Isaiah 49:14–51:3

Overview of Torah Portion

Reviewing some of the events that took place during the Hebrews' wandering in the desert, Moses reassures them that God will bring them safely into Canaan if they keep the commandments. If you disobey, Moses warns, you will be exiled from the Promised Land. Idolatrous statues are to be burned, and their precious metals are not to be brought into a Jewish home. Someone who eats and is satisfied should thank God for the food. The commandments of *tefillin* and *mezuzah* are reprised.

Key Verses

"And you shall remember all the way that the Lord your God has led you these forty years in the desert, that He might afflict you, to test you, to know what was in your heart, if you would keep His commandments or not" (Deuteronomy 8:2).

Discussion Question

Who remembers "all the way" that the Children of Israel were led in the desert for forty years? It is a new generation—the ex-slaves who came out of Egypt have died, many of these people on the bank of the Jordan are young, born midway through the desert sojourn. They cannot remember "all the way," since they did not experience it. Can the command be for generations who read this verse millennia later? The Torah skips over the Hebrews' middle 38 years in the desert, earlier describing the year after the Exodus, and resuming the narrative with the year before the entry into Canaan; the barest details are provided about the interim period. We cannot remember "all the way" either.

Why does God give this seemingly illogical command? How can we—how could they?—observe it? Do we have to know "all" the details?

Shammai Engelmayer

The question presupposes a narrow meaning for the word "way." Yet what a wonderfully flexible word it is; a noun, it can mean different things at different times, to wit (*The American Heritage Dictionary*) [p. 2021]:

> 1. A. A road, path, or highway affording passage from one place to another. B. An opening affording passage: This door is the only way into the attic. 2. A. Space to proceed: cleared the way for the parade. B. Opportunity to advance: opened the way to peace. 3. A course that is or may be used in going from one place to another: tried to find the shortest way home. 4. Progress or travel along a certain route or in a specific direction: on his way north. 5. A course of conduct or action: tried to take the easy way out.

Which "way" is meant here? (The Hebrew word *derekh* is just as fraught with meanings.)

The key is in the word *kol*, meaning "all." The word is superfluous to the meaning. The sentence could have simply read, "And you shall remember the way the Lord your God led you these forty years." So why is "all" there? To tell us that we must consider every form of "way" in remembering the desert sojourn.

Thus, "A road, path, or highway affording passage from one place to another" refers to the actual route. We do not need to remember the specifics of every way station. We need to know only the general route, because it is here that the significance of the route can be found: God took us out of Egypt and brought us to Canaan by way of Mount Sinai. In other words, the physical "way" to the Land of Promise for us depends on participation in revelation and acceptance of Torah. We "remember" the way by remaining true to the Torah revealed to us at Sinai.

"An opening affording passage" is obvious: Before Israel arrived at Sinai, it had to cross the *Yam Suf*. To do that, God had to divide the waters for us. At the same time, He delivered us from the Egyptians by closing the waters upon them. Again, this is not something anyone had to be there to remember. It is memorialized in song (the Song of the Sea, a part of the Torah and, now, a daily part of the liturgy), and recalled in various psalms and other biblical writings. There is no chance of our forgetting. (Note that I did not translate *Yam Suf*. See my commentary for *Beshalach* for a discussion of the reasons for this.)

"Space to proceed": There were many different peoples populating the desert route Israel took. Most likely, they would have been none too happy about seeing several hundred thousand people coming their way. Elsewhere in the desert, if the Exodus took place at the end of the reign of Mernephtah (as I believe it did), the desert was filled both with Egyptian soldiers manning outposts and hordes of invaders coming down from Canaan and Lebanon. That Israel could traverse this desert with so few nasty encounters is truly a miracle.

There is also the question of the physical space needed. Even if more than 600,000 people huddled together on a line of march, it would still be an enormous sight involving a large expanse of desert. Marching, however, is not all these people did. They made camp at night and, for long stretches, even set up temporary residences, such as at Kadesh. No matter how close the tents were, when Israel was encamped, it would require far more space than when the people marched.

There also is "space" in the sense of room to breathe. People need their "space." This people was cramped together for forty years. They were always on top of each other. Yet, somehow, they were able to move from "peoplehood" to "nationhood" in this period. Rather than becoming so fed up with their neighbors, they grew closer together, allowing them to put aside petty rivalries for the general good (a far cry from what would be the case once they were all settled in the land). That Israel could find such "space" in the cramped line of march is only due to God's beneficent intervention.

Whatever space Israel needed to get from point A to point B, and however you define the word "space," Israel had it because God gave it to Israel. Again, we do not need to recall the specifics; it is sufficient that we remember it at all.

"Opportunity to advance." Here we have such roadblocks as the golden calf, the rebellions against Moshe and God, even the apostasy at Ba'al Pe'or. These were roadblocks God had to overcome in order to allow Israel to continue on its journey. Each time, Israel showed itself unworthy of what God was doing for it. He had to get beyond the disbelief of the people and their testing of Him. He did—and Israel got to Canaan.

"Opportunity to advance" also means giving Israel the wherewithal to survive the journey—food, water, clothing, and shelter. This was no small band of Bedouin able to survive on the sparse pickings of the desert. There were hundreds of thousands of people who needed to be cared for and the desert, by its nature, is not normally known for an abundance of life-sustaining resources. Desert oases also are not equipped to handle that many people for too long.

Yet, for forty years, Israel ate and drank; it had clothes to protect its bodies from the sun and sandals to protect its feet from the desert heat; it had food and drink to sustain itself. Here, the "way" God led Israel was to provide for its needs, as the very next two verses of this parshah state explicitly.

"A course that is or may be used in going from one place to another": There were many routes Israel could have taken. That it took the route that was least problematic again is a "way" God led it through the desert. In this vein, too, God showed the "way" by a pillar of cloud by day and a pillar of fire by night.

"Progress or travel along a certain route or in a specific direction": This is clear. The progress was not simply slowed after the spies report was accepted by the people; it was halted. It could have been stopped altogether, but God "led the way" again by allowing the second generation to continue the journey.

"A course of conduct or action" relates to the previous definition. The "way" God leads here is in not letting Israel off the hook. It stood before Sinai and accepted God's employment contract to be His kingdom of priests. Try as they did to break its deal, God forgave the people their iniquities and kept them as His treasured people. Mercy and compassion are God's "way." Also, as the God of history, nothing will deflect Him from the course He has set for the world—a course that depends on Israel living up to its bargain. Whatever it takes, God will do; that, too, is His "way."

There are many more definitions, but the point is made. We must look at "way" in all its forms. We do not need to know the exact route. We just need to remember that Israel moved from Egypt to Canaan, and that the journey was no less miraculous than the events that immediately preceded it.

As for the missing thirty-eight years, we know something significant about them: Israel survived them, and even thrived during them. Thirty-eight years is a long time for so huge a group to survive in the desert. They did, but only because God led the "way."

Remember that, the Torah says, and you will never lose your "way."

Joseph Ozarowski

Christian, secular, and non-Traditional Jewish biblical critics have often used the fact that the literary style of Deuteronomy differs from the rest of the Torah as proof for its non-Mosaic authorship. Rabbi David Hoffman (biblical and halakhic scholar and late head of Berlin's pre-Holocaust Hildesheimer Yeshiva), in his commentary on the Torah, suggested that the reason for Deuteronomy's difference in style was Moshe's purpose in writing Deuteronomy. Here, he was playing not only the role of historian and lawgiver, but also of educator.

This explains not only the stylistic differences, but also why Moshe seems to change some of the details of the history he recalls. Compare, for example, his version of the spy episode in Deuteronomy 1 with the actual account in Numbers 13 and 14; also compare his version of the golden calf story in chapter 9 of this *sidra* with the original in Exodus 32-33. Here, Moshe's purpose was to instruct, inspire, and leave a lasting impression of the Israelites' desert trek on "the next generation." They did not see these events as did their parents, only as children. So Moshe teaches them the eternal and abiding lessons that are to guide them after he is gone from the scene.

Within this context we can understand why Moshe tells them to "Remember all the way that the Lord you God has led you these forty years in the desert. . . ." Some of the classic commentaries (Ramban S'forno) associate this with the immediate textual context of the manna and the people's survival in the desert; God wants them to remember how they were fed, clothed, and sustained by Divine Providence over the forty years.

This may be part of a larger lesson. Following Rabbi Hoffman's approach, Moshe may be giving them a discourse in history, not for history's sake, but for the lessons to be learned from the desert experience. Moshe is not telling them to remember "all the details" of the desert trip but *kol haderekh*, "all the way," what they learned from the way. The details may be part of this, but the message is the key. The memories of the trip are now fuzzy, since "the next generation" started while they were still children. Some were not even born yet! But they needed to remember "all the way" in order to comprehend where they are today.

This is quite similar today to our rabbis and teachers telling us to "remember the Holocaust," or "remember the birth of Israel." Understanding these watershed events of the last generation is important in itself, but perhaps more important in helping us to comprehend how we got to where we are today, and to where we are going in the future on our trek through

Jewish history. In this sense, Moshe is speaking to us, as well. We also need to "remember all the way that the Lord our God has led us these years. . . ."

David Sofian

Your discussion question assumes that the words "all the way" in the instruction must refer either to remembering the entire distance travelled through the wilderness of Sinai, or to remembering the whole time spent there. Rather than looking at it this way, I think this is about identifying with the essential formative experiences of the Jewish people. If this is correct, this generation of our ancestors needed to remember because that is necessary to the covenantal relationship.

Let me refer back to the book of *Shmot*, in particular to *parashat Beshalach*, to make my point. There, the problem in the way of accomplishing this genuine partnership was the people's slave mentality, the mentality of a people who had been shaped and formed by their long experience in Egypt.

You asked why all the miracles weren't enough to secure the people's faith and why they were not enough to secure their sense of being God's partners. My point, then, was that real faith, real partnership with God, cannot be established through the experience of miracles alone. Such partnership requires true religious character, and true religious character is built on the way we experience the regular or even ordinary aspects of routine life. As I said then, solid faith is constructed on a whole pattern of living, not on momentary experiences, no matter how dramatic.

The issue continues in our current parshah, namely, how to ensure the Jewish people's confidence that they are God's partners and that the covenant is real. However, now a new, yet inevitable, obstacle arises for the first time. Recognizing that the entirety of the story from Joseph on shows us God's intent to build the relationship with the Jewish people on the formative experiences of the Exodus through Sinai, the new problem is what to do about a people who did not undergo these essential experiences themselves. As you point out, they were too young to remember for themselves, or they were not even born yet.

Indeed, for certain this issue was soon to arise anyway. If it wasn't this generation that faced it, then it would have been the next. Every generation of Jews since has had to wrestle with it. How do we who were not there experience these crucial events? The verse is pointing us in the right direction by teaching us that each individual can become part of the collective memory; that by identifying with the formative story, it is as if each individual is part of it and remembers it.

Judaism accomplishes this kind of "remembering" in the *Pesach Seder* with the careful combination of study of the sacred story, use of symbols, and ritual experience. Everything we do that night is designed to help us experience the Exodus individually by tying ourselves into our collective memory. The *Haggadah* is filled with midrash, allowing us to study the story through the eyes of the rabbis.

We don't merely read the story as any episode in history, but we dwell upon it, plumbing its depths as the foundation of our people's existence. We eat symbolic foods, each imbued with some aspect of our people's collective memory, which by activating our personal senses help us identify individually. It is not enough to hear what happened to us as a group in some academic way; we need to stretch to experience it as individuals. We recline, dip, recite, or sing all with the intent of making sure we "remember," that is identify as best we can with this crucial formative experience.

Indeed, one cannot be Jewish without this kind of memory. So, then, in answer to your question, the command was both for that generation and for the generations who read this verse millennia later.

R'eih:
Deuteronomy 11:26–16:17

Prophetical Reading
Isaiah 54:11–55:5

Overview of Torah Portion

In an extended warning against being influenced in Canaan by idolatry, Moses states that the blessing and the curse will be placed on individual mountains in the Promised Land. He offers details about *kashrut* and about bringing sacrifices. A false prophet is to be killed. Moses repeats the commandments to support the needy and observe the pilgrimage holidays.

Key Verses

"If your brother, the son of your mother, or your son, or your daughter, or the wife of your bosom, or your friend who is as your soul, entices you in secret, saying, 'Let us go and serve other gods' that you or your fathers did not know . . . you shall not consent to him nor listen to him, your eye shall not pity him, you shall not spare or conceal him. Rather, you shall surely kill him; your hand shall be the first upon him to put him to death, and afterwards the hand of all the people" (Deuteronomy 13:7–10).

Discussion Question

ZEALOTS FOR GOD: Created in God's image, we are supposed to be Godlike; mercy is one of God's paramount traits. What is merciful about this zealous killing of an idolator? Not only are we commanded to kill the sinner, but also to show no pity. What do we—and the other nations, who are supposed to judge God by our behavior—learn from this commandment? What about this particular sin merits such uncompromising condemnation?

Shammai Engelmayer

This is not as difficult a question as it may seem. What is difficult is the time in which the question is asked. The problem with modern man is that he or she tends to look at things from his or her perspective. Thus, for example, the whole idea of sacrifice is repugnant when seen through twentieth century eyes. No matter how often we re-read the next parshah, *Shoftim*, we cannot avoid a feeling of revulsion when we come across the requirement to break the neck of a poor little heifer because a person or persons unknown committed a murder in the neighborhood.

We view things in the ancient world through eyes that have seen men walk on the moon. We judge actions in the ancient world by the standards of the modern one, yet it is neither fair nor helpful to do so. The world that was and the world that is are too far separated for that.

None of us today live amidst the paganism encountered by the Israelites in Canaan. For most of us, our neighbors are Christians or Moslems, who both believe in the same God as we, albeit in different frameworks. While Buddhism does not profess belief in this God, it does proffer a mode of belief consistent with Him—namely, the so-called Eightfold Path of right thinking, right seeing, right speaking, right acting, right living, right effort, right mindfulness, and right meditation. (There are portions of Buddhist thought that seem to mirror kabbalistic doctrine, as well.)

The paganism of Canaan is unknown to us. Thus, we have no way of judging God's demand for the death of he or she who would lead us to pagan beliefs. However, we know many of the elements of those beliefs and, therefore, it is possible to see a logic in the demand. (We are aided in this understanding by modern proclivities, which will be discussed further on.)

Canaanite religion was agricultural-based. This means that fertility rites were central features of worship. These rites included the performance of various sexual acts, including the impregnating of the *kedoshim*, or the sacred prostitutes of the pagan temples. There is also evidence of male prostitutes in those temples, although it is unclear what their purpose was and who they were meant to serve, men or women.

Compare this with Israelite religious practices, which sought to moderate sexual behavior, at least to the extent that it sought to limit sexual liaisons to people in some way committed to each other (i.e., spouse, concubine, betrothed) and to regulate the time such liaisons could take place (namely, never when the woman is impure because of her menstrual cycle, and thus probably less inclined to want physical intimacy). Clearly, the "free love" theme of the pagan cults could be quite seductive to "repressed" Israelites. (Actually, *halakhah* is very liberal in the latitude it allows legitimate intimate relationships.)

It is for this reason that so much care is taken to impose modesty on the dress and actions of the Israelite priesthood. For example, one of the first laws God issues after the revelation on Sinai is, "Do not ascend my altar on steps, so that your nakedness will not be exposed on it" (Exodus 20:23). That is a far cry from, say, the practice in Sumer, where the priests conducted the cultic rituals in the nude.

Other pagan rites were simply abominable in God's eyes, such as human sacrifice. We do not know how often it was practiced, or why, but the physical evidence uncovered by archaeologists confirm the biblical references that the practice existed, and that it was not uncommon. For a God who declared the unnecessary killing of an animal to be akin to murder, killing human beings is intolerable.

The Torah places a heavy emphasis on not marking up one's body precisely because some pagan practices insisted on it—such as men emasculating themselves in order to better serve the goddess Anath. (How this fits in to a "fertility" cult is beyond me, by the way.)

Above all, I believe, God could not tolerate the pantheon of pagan deities because of what they represented—a way for the malefactor to disassociate him- or herself from wrongdoing. Did your wife commit adultery? No, Astarte made her do it. Did your son kill your neighbor? No, it was Mot's hand that guided his. And so on.

God wants people to take responsibility for their actions. We have no one to blame but ourselves for what we do. As long as the pagan cults continue to exist, they offer freedom from guilt along with free love. Thus, they deflect people from ever doing *teshuvah*. What need is there to repent if it was not your fault? What need is there to ever improve yourself? Some god or other will only get in your way. In many ways, this is far more seductive than paganism's sexual license.

How can God not take such an uncompromising stand? Israel, after all, is in its infancy. It is still more accustomed to the pagan world than to God's. Because Israel is unable to fully break free from paganism, God is forced into a compromise. He creates the sacrificial cult, both as a temporary substitute and as a halfway measure to ease His people into a higher form of worship. He knows how strong paganism's pull is on His people. How can He do anything else but to demand that an Israelite who seeks to draw others into pagan belief be killed?

Today, 3,500 years later, we cannot understand how dangerous paganism was, because it no longer exists.

Or does it? The gods are gone, but we have provided substitutes. Indiscriminate sex between consenting adults is condoned by society in general; if that has diminished somewhat in the last decade, it is not due to a moral shift but a mortal fear. No one commits crimes anymore. Some deficit disorder is at fault, or a social condition, or the aftereffects of a medication. A defendant in Florida some years ago actually argued that his actions were the result of a sugar overload. Another argued that his hand was possessed and, thus, he was not responsible for what it did. Colin Ferguson, the man who committed the Long Island Railroad murders, tried to present evidence that he was the hapless victim of a mind-control machine.

From the moment God called to Adam and Chava as they hid in the Garden, the Creator of all things has been trying to get us to take responsibility for what we do. Anything less is paganism, no matter how it is clothed. And, as we can see day after day in our newspapers and on our news programs, that kind of paganism can lead to the disintegration of society.

Is it so hard to understand why so destructive a force must be dealt with in a manner that befits the crime?

Joseph Ozarowski

We might say that the major purpose of the Torah is to implant Godliness and the heavenly Spirit into the world through a practical set of laws, observances, and ethics. Anything which frustrates this process would be defined as evil by the Torah's moral standards. Thus, idolatry negates the core of the Torah's plan for humankind.

One of the worst forms of this is when a Jew not only worships idols, but entices others to do so. This is why the *maysit u'maydiah* (the seducer of others into idolatry) is considered so severe a criminal. Not only is he or she violating the Torah's most basic commandment, but deliberately involving others as well. As Rashi expresses it:

> "This is a great disgrace for you, for even the other [idolatrous] nations do not put aside what their parents passed on to them, but this one says to you, 'Forsake what your parents passed on to you.'"

Thus, involving others in evil is considered a sin of the greatest magnitude. One can have no pity on the *maysit u'maydiah*.

However, Hertz (1960) in his commentary (p. 807) points out that there is no recorded instance of punishment for the seducer. So why is this law on the books? Ramban and Rashi emphasize the fact the one cannot be silent if one knows the evil of this seducer. Perhaps, then, this law is included to teach a moral lesson that one cannot be silent in the face of evil.

The Holocaust was the greatest idolatry of this generation, for it glorified death and the defeat of the God of Israel via the extermination of our people. The guilt of the world in the Holocaust is illustrated by its silence in the face of this monstrous evil. So much of the world was either taken in by the Nazis or silent in its reaction.

The Torah teaches us that when anti-God, anti-humanity evil rears its ugly face, when others seduce generally moral people into abandoning morality, then we cannot be silent. Rather, we must speak out and act.

David Sofian

As you point out by your choice of discussion questions, there is a continuation of theme from this parshah to the next one of *Shoftim*. Your question here is a prelude to the one there. Given this continuity, my remarks to these parshot should be read together. Let me focus here on your key verses from Deuteronomy 13:7–10 and the command to kill the one enticing others to idolatry, even if he or she is a member of one's own family.

When reading these verses from Deuteronomy, I was struck by the mentioning of these family members. It seems to me it would be difficult enough to execute the command on a stranger. How much the more so on one as close as a sibling, child, or spouse. What makes idolatry so significant that even the mere suggestion of it prompts such an extreme course? Why does the need to obliterate it override both divine and human mercy?

Clearly, the absolute uncompromising nature of the command shows us just how opposed the Torah is to any form of idolatry from any individual. However, in particular it is opposed to an enticer.

Tractate *Yoma* 5:11 of the *Tosefta* tells us that anyone who causes others to sin does not have the power to repent. Why is this individual denied the opportunity to repent? It explains that this is the case so that such a person's students would not descend to *Sheol* while he or she inherits the world to come. The rabbinic belief in the efficacy of repentance is not in question here. The efficacy of repentance is part of the bedrock of rabbinic values.

The *Tosefta* wants us to see that since repentance is effective, it would not be fair to allow one who causes others to sin to repent. Otherwise, his sin could be expiated while those led astray by him, his victims, remain responsible. The point for us here is that as a general rule, God's mercy is overridden in the case of one who entices another to sin.

The Torah is making the same point but emphasizing how much worse the case is if the person who entices you in secret to idolatrous ways is a member of your own family. Who has a greater chance of success than someone so close? Therefore, the Torah leaves the matter in no uncertain terms. Idolatry, especially if it begins with secret urgings whispered within the confines of one's family, is not to be tolerated. To tolerate idolatry in any form, in any amount, from anyone undermines the entire Jewish enterprise.

Shoftim:
Deuteronomy 16:18–21:9

Prophetical Reading
Isaiah 51:12–52:12

Overview of Torah Portion

Moses instructs the Hebrews to appoint a system of judges and police officers, cleanse the nation of idolators, and bring difficult legal decisions to the central religious court in the location that God has chosen—Jerusalem. The conditions for establishing a monarchy and for determining the veracity of a prophet are explained. Details are given for setting up cities of refuge for someone who accidentally kills another person. Moses tells the conditions for military exemption, seizing a city in battle, and accepting responsibility when a person is found slain and the killer's identity is not known.

Key Verses

"If your brother . . . or your son, or your daughter, or the wife of your bosom, or your friend . . . entices you in secret, saying, 'Let us go and serve other gods' that you or your fathers did not know . . . you shall not consent to him nor listen to him, your eye shall not pity him, you shall not spare or conceal him. Rather, you shall surely kill him" (Deuteronomy 13:7–10).

"If there is found in your midst . . . a man or a woman who does that which is evil in the eyes of the Lord your God . . . and has gone and served other gods and bowed to them—to the sun or to the moon or to any of the hosts of heaven that I have not commanded—and it is told to you and you hear it and you investigate well, and behold, it is true and certain that this abominable matter is done in Israel, you shall bring that man or that woman . . . to your gates and you shall stone them with stones, that they die" (Deuteronomy 17:2–5).

Discussion Question

BEHIND CLOSED DOORS: The Torah has already established the severity of proselytizing idolatry—someone who leads another person to worship false gods is deserving of the death penalty. But why an equally strong— and irrevocable—punishment for someone who commits the act in secret, alone, in his or her own home? Is there no concept of invasion of privacy? Who suffers if someone does a banned act, even as serious as idol worship, in secret?

Shammai Engelmayer

The theme we began in *parshat R'eih* continues this week. The focus shifts, however. Now, the idolater works in secret, behind closed doors, enticing no one. Yet the severity of the punishment remains; we stone the person to death. We can understand the punishment for the enticer, but not for the secret worshiper.

Again, however, our problem is our twentieth century minds. "Worship," to us, means prayer and, if properly understood by us, it also means deeds of lovingkindness and justice consistent with God's will. Thus it is that this week's parshah actually begins with the admonition *tsedek tsedek tirdof*, translated as "justice justice shall you pursue." It is not enough to pray to God and say you love Him; you have to prove it by the way you live your life. (More about this below.)

Worship, however, was vastly different in those days. People did not pray, as we understand the term; they burned incense and sacrificed living creatures (including, at times, people). To live as your pagan deity wants you to live also could mean acting in ways that are inconsistent with the Torah.

There is no way this could be done in "secret." The smells of the incense or the sacrifices are giveaways. And, if you are loyal to this alleged god, so are your actions.

The cited verse from *Shoftim* makes that clear when it states, "and it is told to you and you hear it and you investigate it well"; this would not be possible if secrecy was truly possible. The person involved may think he or she is putting one over on everyone else, but that is not the case.

And that is the point. There will always be people who know what is going on. If the idolater prospers, they may conclude that it is this alien deity who is providing his or her prosperity. After all, in the superstitious, pseudo-pagan belief system of early Israel, that is a reasonable assumption. So the secret worshiper is also a secret enticer.

That makes this person all the more dangerous. He or she is not making any effort to win over anyone with false promises of a rosier future. Rather, he or she is demonstrating the beneficence of the pagan god by living a life that appears to be blessed. That makes the pagan belief system all the more desirable to those who know what is going on behind the closed doors. They will want in on the action.

There are other dangers, however. At the very least, the pseudo-pagan belief system of early Israel requires that God take revenge on those of Israel who would not believe in Him and go off seeking other gods (as well as on the strangers living among Israel who choose to flaunt Israel's laws). If the not-so-secret worshiper of alien gods goes along from year to year unharmed (in this case, he or she does not have to be any more prosperous than the next person), then God is diminished in the eyes of all those who know the secret. Obviously, they would maintain, God is not powerful enough to penetrate the protective shield the alien god has placed around his or her adherent.

And so, the punishment is the same for both the enticer and the secret worshiper. The evil must be rooted out at all costs, because it is a cancer that will grow and, eventually, afflict the whole community. Perhaps they will not all turn to idol worship, but they will turn from the worship of the One True God.

Actually, it is precisely this that Moshe and God sought to avoid before the golden calf incident. As I have noted in other sections, there is a danger in believing that God sits atop the universe ready to hurl lightning bolts at the sinner and pennies from heaven at the faithful. There is a danger in believing that God can be bought by pleasing odors and fatted calves.

God cannot even be bought by wearing *tefillin*, keeping kosher, and *davening* all day long. He demands *tsedek tsedek tirdof*. We need to understand what these three words mean. The first thing we have to do is define the phrase, which means we have to define each word in the phrase.

The word *tirdof* is easy; it is a verb meaning "to pursue." Defining *tsedek* is a little more difficult. It is a word with many meanings, including "righteousness," "justice," "truth," "purity," and "sincerity." In a verse in the next parshah, *tsedek* means "honest," as in honest weight and measure.

To that definition, the Talmud adds yet another—"to be liberal with," specifically, "to be liberal with what is your own and give it to [the poor person] by adding overweight and overmeasure."

From *tsedek*, we also derive such meanings as "kindness," "virtue," and "piety." A *tsadik*, for example, is not a saint in the Christian sense, just a normal person whose very being is defined by one or more qualities associated with a definition of *tsedek*.

Then there is the word with which we are all so familiar—*tsedakah*. It means "righteousness," "purity," "equity," and "to be liberal with." But, despite its common translation, it does not mean "charity." The English word "charity" comes from a Latin word, *caritas*, which means "from the heart." It implies a voluntary gift proffered when you are moved by your heart, your good nature, or your emotions to make such a gift. We have no such thing in Judaism. *Tsedakah*, the feminine form of *tsedek*, has nothing whatsoever to do with the heart. It is obligatory on those who have, because it is the God-given right of those who have not.

Tsedakah is a purifying act that should be engaged in liberally, because it is righteous and equitable. All things come from God, and He decides how it is to be divided. There is nothing voluntary about it.

These are a lot of definitions to choose from. Which definition is the right one for this phrase?

To answer that, we have to look at the phrase again. There is something strange about it. We are dealing here with three words, when all we needed were two. *Tsedek tirdof*, pursue *tsedek*—that is all the Torah needed to say. Yet it did not. It threw in an extra *tsedek*.

It did that to tell us that *tsedek* in this context may not be defined narrowly. The double use of the word here demands that all the definitions of *tsedek* be used. Justice that is not righteous, equitable, kind, virtuous, pure, and pious is not *tsedek*.

Tsedek tsedek tirdof, justice justice shall you pursue—righteousness righteousness shall you pursue . . . equity equity shall you pursue—choose the definition you prefer, they are all correct because, in *tsedek*, in truth, each individual definition of the word implies all the other definitions.

More importantly, the double use of the word here defines *tsedek* wherever it appears in a legalistic framework. *Tsedek* always requires all of its definitions.

Take the example of *tsedek* meaning "to be liberal with." The verse from which this definition derives is, "You must have a complete and honest weight and a complete and honest measure."

The word here for "honest," as I noted, is *tsedek*, but there are more common choices that would have been quite appropriate for the sentence—words such as *tamim*, *tahor*, *emet*, and *ne'eman*. These are all words that instantly evoke honesty and truthfulness, tinged with the weight of sacred trust. Instead of these words, however, the text uses *tsedek*, because in this context *tsedek* means a weight and a measure that go beyond strict honesty; these weights and measures must also be just, equitable, righteous, kind and, yes, even liberal when circumstances require it.

The fact that the Torah chose *tsedek* over the more precise words means that the Torah wants all of the definitions of *tsedek* to be included in the terms "honest weight" and "honest measure." It is never *tsedek* to shortchange someone; but *tsedek* at times requires that you add to the weight or the measure (i.e., charge a person for a pound of some food, but give that person a pound and a half).

This begs the question: What is the point? There is nothing new here; we already know that the underlying principle of the Torah is based on these qualities. We have to be honest? We know that. We have to be just? We know that. We have to be kind, equitable, and virtuous? We know that. So, again, what is the point?

That is where *tirdof* comes in. It is the kicker. It is not enough to live a life of *tsedek tsedek*. This commandment is not fulfilled passively. It must be pursued.

If injustice exists in your community or in your world, it is not enough to say, "It's not my problem; I lead a good life, a virtuous life. I don't have to get involved with other people's *tsoris*. I have enough of my own." You do have to get involved. You are commanded to *tirdof*, to pursue, *tsedek tsedek*. So you have to get involved in Bosnia, in the Sudan, in Appalachia, in the inner cities of America, and in the development towns of Israel. You have to get involved in your community, your neighborhood, your workplace, and your synagogue.

The Torah makes a big deal about environmental protection. Later on in this *sidrah*, the Torah asks, "Is a tree a man that you should make war on it?" To *tirdof* means to get involved in protecting the environment.

God created all living beings and gave them all a place on earth. Where is the *tsedek* in our forcing species into extinction? To *tirdof*, then, means to concern yourself with wildlife preservation and animal rights.

This is not political and social liberalism that is meant here. There is a big difference. Yes, the Torah says, "You shall not subvert the rights of the needy in their disputes," but only after it warns against showing "deference to a poor man in his dispute."

In other words, you cannot just go off blindly to "do good." You have to be sure that the good you do is *tsedek*, with all that implies. Doing good is not just doing something that makes you feel good. *The good you do actually has to do good.*

Why must we live lives of *tsedek tsedek*—and have to *tirdof* such lives and to pursue them? Why? Because we are the Chosen People.

What a misunderstood term that is. It does not mean that we were chosen to be better than anyone else, more blessed than anyone else, or greater than anyone else. It simply means that God chose us for a specific task: We are to be His kingdom of priests, His holy nation. We are to be "a light unto the nations"; to demonstrate by the way we live our lives how lives should be lived.

They must be lives of *tsedek tsedek*, pure, ethical behavior for its own sake, not for the sake of reward or out of fear of punishment. That is why we cannot be passive in the way we live our lives. That is why we must *tirdof*.

And that is what makes these three words so vital; so dominating of *halakhah*. *Tsedek tsedek tirdof* is not just a phrase; it is the sum and substance of the entire Torah. If all that was written on the Torah scrolls in that ark were just these three words, we would still have the entire Torah, and we would still have our mission.

To truly love God means to do God's work on earth, period. God does not expect to be patted on the back for His works, and neither should you.

Joseph Ozarowski

The previous question and its subsequent answer dealt with the severity and contemporary relevance of idolatry. The context concerned those who entice others to worship idols. I do not think we have to repeat the points raised. We will, however, address the issues of privacy raised in your question.

There does not seem to be any indication that the idolatry referred to in our verses is private. On the contrary, as the *Or Hahayim* reminds us, there are distinct conditions mandatory if capital punishment is to be carried out. These include *edim*—actual eyewitnesses to the act, and *hatra-ah*—official warnings. These conditions apply to this crime, as well as others, and would indicate that the crime is a repeated one and a witnessed one. If these two conditions are fulfilled, then the idolatry would be far from private. It had to be witnessed by others prepared to testify to that effect, and it had to have been committed more than once.

In fact, rabbinic literature (see both BT and JT tractate *Sanhedrin*, in several places; and the *Sifri* in extensive references) uses these passages as one of the primary sources for Jewish law regarding witnesses and the taking of testimony. Unlike American law, which places great emphasis on the arguments of the attorneys in convincing the jury (like the O. J. trial!), *halakhah* requires absolute proof of guilt before any punishment is carried out. As the *Sifri* says,

> "You shall bring that man" (17:5)—"that man" and not an *anoos* (one who was forced to worship idols); "that man" and not a *shogeg* (one who did so mistakenly); "that man" and not a *mut'eh* (one who was misguided or lost).

The idolatry had to be committed freely, knowingly, and willingly, and in front of others, for their testimony to be effective.

The verses following yours are revealing. They specify that the hand of the witnesses must be the first to throw the stones. This is like saying that if you are going to implicate someone, you had better be prepared and willing to throw the electric chair switch or put the noose on the criminal's neck. How many of us would be willing to do this? As far as protecting people from conniving and dishonest witnesses, the Torah has a number of built-in safeguard laws regarding false witnesses; these verses happen to be among the sources (see BT *Makkot* 6a).

Obviously, someone who worships idols in the total privacy of his or her home may not be culpable in front of a *Beth Din* (a rabbinic court) because of the lack of testimony. This does not take away from the severity of his or her sin. It does mean, though, that their punishment would be in the hands of heaven. The perpetrators of these "private crimes" are certainly hurting themselves and their relationship with God and Torah by even privately worshiping idols. And there is always a danger that this idolatry will spread beyond the confines of the seclusion. But it would not condemn them before a *Beth Din*.

David Sofian

You are, of course, correct. Many times before, indeed in the last parshah, in no uncertain terms, the Torah has expressed its attitude towards idolatry in favor of ensuring the worship of God only. Israelite loyalty to God is key within the covenantal idea virtually from the moment God calls to Abraham in *B'reishit* 12.

Furthermore, it is not the Torah alone that expands on this theme. The prophets primarily directed their passion against idolatry and against the immorality that went with it. In Kings, each king is often judged by his participation, or lack thereof, in the worship of idols. Indeed, this is the overarching theme of the *Tanakh*. Therefore, it is not surprising that in this parshah we find the strong statements against idolatrous practices that we do.

This attitude was continued by the rabbis. Accepting idolatry is equivalent to repudiating the whole of the Torah and everything else that flows from it. Three examples of all those possible will suffice to make the point. *Sifre* to *D'varim* 54 tells us that anyone who recognizes idols denies the entire Torah, and anyone who denies idols recognizes the entire Torah.

BT *Berakhot* 12b prohibits even thinking about idolatrous worship. And we learn in tractate BT *Avodah Zarah* 12a that when in the presence of an idol, a Jew is forbidden even to bend down to remove a thorn stuck in one's foot or to pick up coins, lest it appear that he was bowing down to the idol.

It is the prevalence of this theme that teaches us just how difficult the task of driving idolatry from Israel was. Operating from the assumption that there is no need to frequently condemn a practice not taking place, the vehemence and regularity of the condemnations tell us just how common the practice was. The uprooting of polytheistic worship, of idolatry, was indeed so difficult that the biblical text repeatedly warns against it in the strongest terms.

Idolatry was so antithetical and threatening to the Israelite enterprise, and so attractive to Israelites, that even acts committed in secret could not be overlooked. Secret conversations and urgings would have been seen as the thin edge of the wedge leading to the undermining of Israel's entire relationship with God.

In *parshat Emor*, you asked about the penalty of stoning for someone who dishonors God's name. I indicated there that the denial of God's authority destroyed the very foundation of Judaism. The same applies here. When it comes to the primary reason for Israel's existence, the worship of God and God alone, there is no issue of privacy. It simply never arises. It is at the heart of who we are as a people to testify publicly to the reality of God alone.

This is why the *Shema* has become so central to Jewish expression. Virtually every Jew has memorized this Deuteronomic verse from the *Siddur*—*shema yisrael adonai elhoheynu, adonai ehad*; "Listen Israel, the Eternal One is our God, the Eternal One alone."

Ki Tetze:
Deuteronomy 21:10–25:19

Prophetical Reading
Isaiah 54:1–10

Overview of Torah Portion

Moses explains the provisions for dealing with a beautiful woman who is captured in battle, for leaving one's estate to the firstborn children of a beloved and unbeloved wife, and for disciplining a rebellious son. A list of several moral rules are given, including the responsibilities for returning someone's lost property, and various prohibited combinations are listed. Moses gives the laws in the cases where a man accuses his wife of not being a virgin at the time of marriage, where a man rapes a woman, where he divorces her, and where he dies before she has borne a son.

Key Verses

"**Y**ou shall not deliver to his master an escaped slave . . . he shall dwell with you in your midst, in the place that he will choose, in one of your gates where it is good for him" (Deuteronomy 23:16–17).

Discussion Question

A SLAVE'S CHOICE: The Torah prescribes liberal laws for a slave owner's treatment of a slave—the slave is to be accorded the same (if not more) dignity as the owner. But why does such behavior extend to a runaway slave? Can a fugitive can determine his new venue "in the place that he will choose"? What is the responsibility of a heretofore stranger in acceding to

351

the request of a such a needy individual? The Torah curiously uses the exact language in this case—"in the place that He will choose"—as in describing God's eventual selection of Jerusalem as the location for His holy Temple. Is this similarity a mere coincidence? Does the Torah imply a commonality between the Creator and a powerless slave?

Shammai Engelmayer

I want to start with the notion that the phrase "in the place that He will choose" refers to Jerusalem's eventual selection as the site for a permanent sanctuary. The phrase means exactly what it says: Israel has a portable sanctuary, and where it is to be set down from time to time is God's decision exclusively.

In no way is God going to allow this fractious, contentious people to turn the Tabernacle into a political football. Every tribe will want the honor of the *Mishkan* in its midst. Wars could be fought over it. Only if God alone makes the decision could such debacles be avoided.

This is a particular peeve of mine. This phrase, and the insistence that it is a prophetic clue to the holiness of Jerusalem, has been pounced on by biblical critics as proof that Moshe had nothing to do with writing the Torah and that, indeed, the Torah was an afterthought, written after the Temple was already standing (if not after it had been destroyed by the Babylonians).

The text does not support such a claim. Many times throughout the Torah, God commands that a particular sacrifice be performed "in perpetuity" before the portable sanctuary, or within it. Why, if God already had Jerusalem in mind as a permanent home, did He have to play games? Why should we assume that God, when He says "in perpetuity" in connection with the *Mishkan*, really means, "only until I get a permanent home"? Why can we not just take God at His word?

Having said that, let me proceed to the question—the relevance of the runaway slave law and the use of a phrase otherwise associated with God Himself.

Immediately we run into a problem. There are two kinds of slaves in the Torah—the Israelite slave and the non-Israelite slave. The rules are different for each. Most of all, the Israelite slave is treated, in most cases, either as a household member or as hired help. The slave's period of servitude never extends beyond six years, unless the slave chooses to stay. When the slave departs, the slave owner must make a liberal financial settlement with him. (Yes, him. Her, the female Israelite slave, must either become the slave owner's wife, or be immediately set free.)

The alien slave, on the other hand, has fewer rights. True, he or she cannot be ill-treated, but they are slaves for life, they are inheritable property, and so forth. In no way can it be argued that the alien slave is "accorded the same (if not more) dignity as the owner."

Now, here is the problem. Based on wording in Deuteronomy 23:17, it is presumed that the slave being discussed here is an alien slave who has run away from his alien master. Verse 17 would seem to make no sense if the slave was an Israelite and the master was an Israelite, because the slave would therefore already be living "in your midst." He also would most likely choose to live within "his gates," in such case (i.e., in his own home, among his own family and tribe or community), rather than "your gates," since there is nothing his former master can do about it. (Kidnaping an Israelite in order to enslave him is punishable by death.) And, presuming that he has his own family property to run to, his family is more likely to have redeemed him from slavery than to wait for him to escape.

The most common situation postulated for this commandment is that the slave runs away during wartime, seeking safe haven in the Israelite encampment. He is to be protected and, if he so desires, brought back to Israel and given a place of his own. In no way may he be mistreated or taken into slavery by an Israelite. (The Italian commentator, Rabbi Ovadiah S'forno, offers an alternative route to this conclusion. He notes that this commandment comes immediately after commandments regarding an Israelite war camp, and is thus related to those.)

Thus, *Targum Onkelos* has no trouble rewriting these two verses at the same time as he is translating them into Aramaic. He actually adds the word *am'min*, meaning "of the nations," to verse 16. In this, he has the authority of the sainted rabbis of the talmudic age, who also saw this commandment as being about an alien slave of an alien slave owner (see BT *Gittin* 45a). That there is wording here similar to wording usually reserved for God is, in such case, of no consequence.

On the other hand, the text itself does not suggest what kind of slave is being discussed here. And it could be that the rabbis of blessed memory and the commentators all missed an important point by seeing the wrong slave in the commandment—a point the questioner did not miss.

If, indeed, this commandment refers to the Israelite slave, or even to all slaves, it is a virtual death knell to slavery in Israel. Any slave who wants out merely has to knock on the door of the house across the road. In this case, the similar wording would be deliberate: A signal that God abhors the idea that Israel would ever enslave anyone. Because He will not change human nature, God accepts that people, out of greed or for whatever reason, will enslave others. Because He does not want them to do so, He creates laws that, in the end, make the practice too difficult and highly uneconomical.

This is not an isolated instance of such a manipulative approach by God. At the end of this week's parshah, for example, God commands us to "remember" what Amalek did to us while at the same time insisting that we "blot out the memory of Amalek." He ends the command by saying, "Do not forget."

On the surface, this is a commandment to commit genocide, but the opposite is true. God recognizes that there is always going to be an enemy so vicious, so cruel, and so undeserving of life that we will want to destroy him. Rather than stop us, which He knows He cannot do, He crafts a commandment that implodes on itself. If we fulfill one-half of the commandment, to remember, we have failed to utterly blot out Amalek's memory. If we succeed in fulfilling that half of the commandment, then we cannot fulfill the half requiring us to remember. The paradox forces us to stop and think about what we are about to do and, hopefully, cools us down before we go too far. In other words, this is not a command to commit genocide. It is a device to prevent it.

Thus it may be here, too. God will thwart slavery by allowing slavery—but under His rules. Starting at the revelation at Sinai, God began to unveil the laws of Israelite slavery. You want to make your brother your slave? Fine, but treat him kindly. Give him off every Shabbat and on *chagim* (the festivals). He can own property and make his own profits, enough even to buy his freedom. You cannot treat him poorly or burden him with excessive rules and regulations.

To hurt him is to free him; to kill him is to commit murder. His children are his, not yours, but you must care for and feed his family while he is with you. At the end of the sixth year, he is free to leave, and you have to give him a liberal financial settlement.

That kind of "slavery" is almost meaningless. It becomes virtually impossible if you add the provision that an Israelite slave can run away from his master and be automatically entitled to his freedom and the full protection of the community.

By using words so reminiscent of those used in connection with God, He is saying that the human being, having been created in His image, can also choose where his name shall be called, meaning whether he chooses to be enslaved or to seek shelter, and that whatever choice he makes is also the choice God makes.

Which version of this commandment is the correct one—the rabbis' or the questioner's? Both, it would seem to me. The rabbis of blessed memory are correct in a practical sense when they see in these verses the alien slave of an alien master. Any other interpretation, as noted, would have made slavery impossible in Israel. (Even with the laws as the rabbis interpreted them, the "Judeans" were made fun of by their Roman conquerors for the benevolent way they treated their slaves.)

The questioner, meanwhile, is correct in a theological sense in seeing in this verse the slave, period. God never intended that human beings be enslaved. As long as people insist on keeping slaves, God insists on fair, equitable, and just treatment. Sooner or later, God knows, the world will see the truth about these laws and cast aside slavery forever.

Joseph Ozarowski

The question of slavery in the Torah is an important one. One might ask why the Torah even permitted slavery altogether. It could be that, like the Rambam's explanation of sacrifices, this was a way for *Hashem* to wean our people away from a practice that was common for so many generations.

Notwithstanding this, there is no question that the Torah's definition of servitude was quite different from slavery as it has been practiced in the Western world and elsewhere. In our terms, the Torah allows the owner rights to the servant's employment, but not his being. The proof is in this passage, that if the servant chooses to escape, we are not allowed to return the individual to his previous master. In fact, *Hazal* (see *Sifri* and *Pesikta Zutrata*) understands the entire passage to offer major benefits to the servant:

> "He shall dwell with you," in the city itself. "In your midst," among you and not on the edge (not near the border of Israel—*Torah Temimah*). "The place that he shall choose" means a place where *parnasa* (sustenance—an ability to make a living) can be found. "In your gates" and not in Jerusalem. "In one of your gates" he should not be exiled from city to city. "Where it is good for him" from a poor dwelling to a nicer dwelling.

Compare this to our own American history; the horrifying scenes of slave capture and mutilation that we saw in "Roots" could have never happened under Torah law.

There might be a religious dimension to the escaped servant law. Many of the commentators assume this verse is talking about an escaped non-Jewish servant from outside of Israel seeking refuge in the Holy Land. We are bidden to accept this person in the possible (but not guaranteed) hope that the individual will elect to become a *ger toshav*, a partially Jewish resident of Israel with partial acceptance of the commandments. (According to some, this means formal acceptance of the Noahide laws. Thus, worshiping God and forsaking idolatry is part of the picture, as well.)

The *Sifri*'s "in your gates, and not in Jerusalem," is difficult to explain, and even the *Torah Temimah* has trouble with it. He and the *Meshekh Hokhma* suggest that the Torah was reluctant to allow too many escaped slaves whose Jewishness was not complete into Jerusalem because they were more strict on *yichus* (Jewish family lineages) in Jerusalem, or perhaps because they wanted to keep a Jewish majority in Jerusalem. While these answers partly explain, they honestly do not fully satisfy me.

After all this is said, none of the commentaries that I could find came up with your linguistic connection between the escapee coming to "the place that he shall choose" and the exact same terminology regarding God's choice of Jerusalem and the Temple. This language regarding the Temple is used in quite a few places in Deuteronomy: 12:5 regarding the ridding of idolatry and offering sacrifices; 16:2, 6, and 15 regarding God's choice of Jerusalem as the place to appear for the Pilgrim Festivals of Pesach, *Shavuot*, and *Sukkot*; and 26:2 in conjunction with the bringing of *bikkurim* (the first fruits) to the Temple.

It would be lovely if we created a *drash* (a sermon), or *d'var Torah*, connecting *Hashem*'s choice of Jerusalem for the spot to rest the Holy Spirit and the escaped servant's choice of his or her own location to rest his or her weary spirit and possibly find his or her Creator, as well. After all, the escaped servant is also created in the image of God. Therefore, we are bidden to assist in so many ways. The only problem is with the exclusion of the escapee from Jerusalem itself. It just does not fit in. But then again, not all questions can be answered by itinerant rabbis who study Torah with esteemed reporters by fax.

David Sofian

The tradition suggests to us several responses to why such welcome was offered to a runaway slave. Ramban offers us a simple and practical answer by assuming that the runaway slave or escapee was arriving in a time of war. The knowledge this person would have of the enemy could be very important to the Israelites. Therefore, returning him would be foolish.

On a theological level, Ramban also points out that he should not be returned to idolators. How could Israel, dedicated to God and God alone, send a person who escaped into their midsts back to a life of idolatry?

In my response to *parashat D'varim*, I indicated the high value the Rabbis placed on knowing and experiencing the Land of Israel. This value is expressed again, this time in the context of accepting the escaped slave, when Rashi comments that even an Israelite's Canaanite slave who escapes from outside the Land of Israel into it is accepted.

How could someone who just arrived be made to leave the Land of Israel? Continuing his earlier point, Ramban adds that this is because, in other lands, *mitzvot* are not practiced.

Rambam adds a different twist to this discussion in *Sefer HaMitzvot*. While discussing the negative commandment (number 255) against wronging an escaped slave, he places him in a category with proselytes by explaining that neither can be wronged with speech. Rambam teaches us that this concern with wrongful speech applies to both the escaped slave and the proselyte because both are individuals who have accepted the Torah. They are embraced because, by accepting the Torah, they are righteous proselytes.

You ask if there is any special significance to the wording, "in a place that he will choose." Ramban is helpful here also. He tells us that we may no longer treat this individual as a slave. His freedom is confirmed by his right to choose where he will dwell. By emphasizing choosing, human freedom is being emphasized as the source of human dignity.

Looking back to the midrash on the beginning of *B'reishit*, we find Rabbi Tifdai in the name of Rabbi Aha teaching that the freedom to choose is at least part of the dignity of being created in God's image. Although this phrase, *b'tzelem Elohim*, "in the image of God" (*B'reishit* 1:27), evokes many profound interpretations, Rabbi Tifdai explains regarding it (*B'reishit Rabbah* 8:11) that God thought: "If I create him [the first human being] of celestial elements he will live and never die, and if I create him of terrestrial elements, he will die and not have life in the future world. Therefore, I will create him of the upper and the lower elements, so if he sins he will die, and if he does not sin, he will live." In other words, what makes us human, our creaturehood in God's image, is that the sinning or not sinning is ours to choose. Our freedom is the source of our dignity.

So if using the phrase, "in a place that he will choose," in both instances is more than coincidental, the Torah is associating the slave's right to choose, the slave's freedom, and the slave's dignity with God. What we should see is that the association here is not only about God and the powerless slave. Its instance here comes to reinforce what *B'reishit* already taught us. Every human being is created *b'tzelem Elohim* and is therefore endowed with infinite dignity.

Ki Tavo:
Deuteronomy 26:1–29:8

Prophetical Reading
Isaiah 60:1–22

Overview of Torah Portion

Moses explains the procedures for bringing the first fruits of a crop to the priests in Jerusalem. The Hebrews are instructed to write the commandments on plaster stones when they cross the Jordan, and to build an altar on Mount Ebal. The blessings for obeying God and the curses for disobeying Him are listed.

Key Verses

"And it will come to pass that if you do not listen to the voice of the Lord your God, to keep, to do all His commandments and His statutes that I command today, all of these curses shall come upon you. . . . just as the Lord rejoiced over you to do good for you and to multiply you, so the Lord shall rejoice over you to cause you to perish and to destroy you" (Deuteronomy 28:15, 63).

Discussion Question

REJOICING IN HEAVEN: Will God rejoice in His people's suffering? A long list of wrenching curses is given for the bound-to-stray Children of Israel. God's anthropomorphic tears would make sense here. Why does the Torah say God will rejoice? What does rejoicing mean in this context? How is this a guide for our behavior—or for other nations—in reacting when misfortune strikes?

Shammai Engelmayer

Oh, how easy it would be to say, "wrong; that is not what the text says." This, in fact, is what the rabbis of blessed memory insist in BT *Megillah* 10b: "Rabbi Eleazar replied: He Himself does not rejoice, but He causes others to rejoice. This is also evident in the text, which uses [the word] *yasis* and does not use *yasus*."

Yasis is in the *hiphil* construct of the verb *sus*, meaning it is a causative construct. Thus, the verb implies causing someone else to perform the action. The fact that *yasis* was used here, therefore, means that the phrase in question should read, "He will cause others to rejoice."

Looked at it this way (and Rashi, for one, does look at it this way), there is no difficulty here and the question is moot. As the Babylonian Talmud notes in BT *Megillah*, just as God held back the ministering angels from rejoicing when Egypt's army was drowning in the *Yam Suf*, so God never rejoices when people are suffering, even when that suffering is justified. Surely, then, God would not rejoice over the suffering of His beloved Israel. That would be the easy way out, but Torah study, as we have noted at other times, rarely allows for such simple solutions.

While it is true that *yasis* is the *hiphil* form of the verb *sus*, it is also both the simple and the *hiphil* form of the verb *sis*. *Sus* and *sis* are identical in meaning (mainly because the letters *vav* and *yod* were interchangeable in the very earliest, pre-biblical days of the Hebrew language). While Rabbi Eleazar was correct about *yasus* and *yasis*, he was probably wrong about *sus* versus *sis*; it is *sis* that is the intended root, not *sus*. That means that the translation is as it appears in the question posed for this week.

How can we be so certain of which root is being used by the biblical writer? Words from the *sus/sis* root appear fewer than thirty times in the entire *Tanakh*. In each instance, the text surrounding the word makes it virtually impossible to use anything but *sis* as the root. Outside of the current verse, *yasis* itself appears four more times. In Isaiah 62:5, the verse translates as, "God will rejoice over you." In Zephaniah 3:17, the translation is, "He will rejoice over you in gladness." The translation for Psalms 19:6 is, "and rejoices like a hero [eager] to run his course." Finally, Job 39:21 reads, "and rejoices in his strength."

That this, then, would be the only appearance of *yasis* as the *hiphil* of *sus*, rather than the *kal* (simple form) of *sis*, is an untenable position to take. It makes for a good homily, but it is not what the text says. Even the *Targum Onkelos* does not attempt to turn the *sis/yasis* into the *sus/yasis*.

That means we are forced to address the first part of the question posed this week: Why would God rejoice over Israel's suffering? He does not. That is not what the text is really saying.

Understand the entire section, please. This is hyperbole in the extreme. Moshe adopts the most colorful language his vocabulary allows to convey to Israel the price it most certainly will pay for turning its back on the Covenant and the God with whom that Covenant is made.

That this sentence is hyperbole is clear from the next sentence. Here, we are to be utterly destroyed. Yet in the next verse, that "destruction" takes the form of losing our homeland and being scattered among the nations, never to find permanent peace (presumably, from related texts, until such time as God decides that we are ready to return to our land). Just as God will not destroy us utterly, so He will not rejoice over our destruction.

So what will He do? The answer, according to many commentators, is that He will punish us for our evil ways (we are dealing here with collective punishment and collective evil), and rejoice over the opportunity we have to repent and be restored to our land. There is much truth in this view of the verse. I believe, however, that it is not complete.

God will rejoice because He will have been proven right. Israel's sins are the result of the pagan influences that permeate its primitive, sacrificial-based belief system, a belief system He initially did not endorse. If all the Israelite religion represents is a reformed paganism, then paganism eventually will win out.

The only way God can eliminate the paganism once and for all is for the people to falter, for Him to carry out His promised punishment of them, and for the belief system to be reformed to fit God's original intention. God limited the cult to presence in the land. Once outside the land, the people must either abandon God or find new ways of serving Him.

That, in fact, happened in the brief span of the Babylonian Exile—when the scribes rose to prominence (eventually to evolve into the class known as rabbis), Shabbat took on increased importance and the predecessor institutions of the synagogue and the yeshivah began to take shape. Once begun, that process could not be turned off, even by the building of a new Temple in Jerusalem. And when that Temple was destroyed, so much had changed in the belief system that the rabbis of the first and second centuries c.e. had little difficulty in winning acceptance for the reformation that was necessary for Judaism to survive the cataclysm.

So yes, God will rejoice (and very likely did, in His own non-anthropomorphic way) because the sins of Israel had provided the nation and their God with the opportunity to wipe the slate clean and start all over again.

What does this tell us about our own behavior vis-à-vis the suffering of those who give us grief? To be in God's image, in this case, meant that we may not rejoice in the pain suffered by anyone, friend or foe. What are these curses for, anyway? They are for the sins we have committed by the way we behave toward others.

We cannot, however, base our actions on this verse alone because, while we are in the image of God, we are not like God in any way. He alone knows when "curses" are really blessings in disguise. These punishments, as gross as they sound, when they are actually carried out, improve our lot, and do not diminish it. As history shows, with each successive "tragedy," we have emerged stronger than before. The First Temple's destruction planted the seeds of rabbinic Judaism. The Second Temple's end brought rabbinic Judaism to full flower and proved that we were here to stay. The Holocaust gave way to the rebirth of Israel and the return of its people to the land.

God can rejoice because He knows the truth behind the curses; we may not because we will rejoice only in the curses, not in the blessings that might lurk beneath their surface.

Only of one thing can we be certain: God alone knows whether yet another national tragedy awaits us in the future, but the progression of history makes it clear to us what lies ahead, with or without such a tragedy (and, God-willing, let it be without it): the *geula*, the Redemption. We have come so far, and we are so near. It will happen, sooner than we think and, perhaps, sooner than many of us may want. And when it does, it will be less difficult to envision God "rejoicing" at the *Shoah*—not because His people were reliving the curses yet again, but because it marked the beginning of the end to their suffering. May we all live to hear the call of the *Mashiach's shofar*, speedily and in our days.

Joseph Ozarowski

It is certainly possible to answer your question by just understanding God's rejoicing over our suffering as a poetic expression, a figure of speech. It could be that Moshe is simply trying to underscore the severity of our forsaking the Torah. But of course, are we ever satisfied with this type of simple answer? Of course not!

Many of the classic commentaries—Rashi, *Tosafot Da'at Zekenim*, and Ibn Ezra—follow the rabbinic explanation from BT *Megillah* 10a, which suggests that the Hebrew in the text for rejoice, *yasis*, grammatically refers to causing our enemies joy over our suffering, not Divine joy for our traumas. They explain *yasis* as a verb that requires an object (in Hebrew grammar, a *poal yotzeh*).

The object here would be our enemies. It is theologically untenable, they say, for God to rejoice over our troubles. If *Hashem* would be the One rejoicing, the Hebrew would have read *yasus* (which is a *poal omeid*, a free-standing verb). The *Torah Temimah* and the *Avi Ezer* super-commentary on Ibn Ezra defend and explain this approach.

This answer is good homiletic *drash* (sermonics) and theologically quite sound, for it lets God off the hook and assumes that *Hashem* does not really feel happy when our people are suffering. But in spite of the arguments of the commentators, we might still wonder if it is grammatically sound. The term *yasus* is nowhere found in all of Scripture. But the term *yasis* is—in fact, it is in the *Haftarah* for the next reading taken from Isaiah 62. There, (62:5) we are told, "As a groom rejoices over a bride, so will your God rejoice over you." In fact, this is the source for the lovely verse in Friday night's *L'kha Dodi* prayer, "Your God will rejoice over you, as a groom rejoices over a bride." The same Hebrew term, *yasis*, is used in both places to describe God's joy without any object other than Israel. And none of the commentaries understand it any other way. So the *drash*, the homiletical approach, may not match the *pshat*, the basic meaning of the words in context.

One of my congregants who endured personal tragedy in his life, suggested a different answer to your question. Suffering is not always a punishment but often a *tikun*—a Divine means of correction, or a learning experience for the sufferer. For the individual sufferer, the challenge may be in trying to find the meaning and purpose of suffering. Assuming the ultimate goal of the suffering is a noble one, then it can be seen as a goal worthy of joy, for its ultimate end is good.

David Sofian

Rashi has a clever way of dealing with the question you raise. He makes the difficulty disappear by focusing on a quirk in Hebrew verb structures. What if the phrase, "the Eternal will rejoice over you," (*yaseis*) could be translated differently? It turns out that this intransitive verb form *yaseis* is the very same when it is transitive (when it is in third person, masculine, singular, future *hiphil*). If you read it that way, it then translates, "the Eternal shall cause rejoicing over you. . . ."

After making this move, Rashi tells us the object of the verb is Israel's enemies. Of course, the fact that there isn't an object for the verb in the actual sentence correctly leads us to the original translation. Yet, the forms are the same, so Rashi can solve the problem the way he does. Reading it

Rashi's way, it is as if God rejoices in doing good for Israel but stands to the side when Israel's enemies have cause to rejoice.

As Rashi saw an opportunity in a verb form to circumvent the problem, it might be possible to sidestep it by finding other hidden meanings embedded in the text. W. Gunther Plaut, in the Union of American Hebrew Congregation's *Torah Commentary* (1981), draws our attention to just such a meaning explained in a Chasidic *gematria* to the long list of curses found in chapter 28.

Gematria is a method that reveals hidden messages in the text by examining and manipulating the numerical value of the letters that make up Hebrew words. Words can be associated in totally unexpected ways using this technique, and through that association, new understandings arise. The one here begins by noting that there are 676 total letters in chapter 28's curses. Step two is the numerical value of the Hebrew word *ra-ot* (evil events) which is also 676.

The next stage is to recognize that the numerical value of the tetragrammaton (God's Name) is 26. The connection is that 26 times 26 equals 676. This equation is suggesting that even though the Torah repeatedly threatens with curses (*ra-ot*), God's Name (the tetragrammaton) resides within the very substance of those curses. The question of God's seeming harshness is dodged by concentrating on finding God's Presence even within the curses.

Instead of evading the difficulty, the other tack is to understand the verse by concentrating on its context within the book of *D'varim*. To begin with, Moses offers his farewell words to the Israelites. Moses has been through many difficulties with his people. He knows their weaknesses. He knows their deficiencies. Standing out in his mind must have been the building of the golden calf; Korah's, Dathan's, and Abiram's rebellion; the constant whining and complaining about food and water; the episode of the spies; and the Reubenites and Gadites desire not to accept their inheritance within the Promised Land.

Moses certainly had no trouble remembering how God had repeatedly become angry and threatened them. He wants to convince them to stay on the right path. He tells them of the blessings. But he also needs to word the curses in terms that will not fail to penetrate. Israelites, do not believe God's curses are mere threats. Israelites, do not rely on God's mercy to protect you. The threats will come about if you fail.

What better way to clarify this and accentuate this than with the hyperbole of saying God will delight in Israel's destruction, even as God delighted in making Israel prosperous and many?

Netzavim:
Deuteronomy 29:9–30:20

Prophetical Reading
Isaiah 61:10–63:9

Overview of Torah Portion

Moses reminds the Hebrews of their servitude in Egypt and their trek through the wilderness. He cautions them to avoid idol worship and not to disregard the heavenly curses. The land itself will suffer for the people's sins. If the people return to God, God will return them to the Holy Land and curse the enemies, Moses promises. He states that the Torah and its commandments are accessible to everyone and calls heaven and earth as witnesses.

Key Verses

"And it shall come to pass that when [an Israelite] hears the words of this curse and blesses himself in his heart, saying, 'I shall have peace, although I walk in the stubbornness of my heart . . .' the Lord will not be able to forgive him . . . and the foreigner that will come from a distant land will see the plague of that land and the sicknesses with which the Lord has made it sick. . . . and all the nations shall say, 'Why did the Lord do this to that land? What is the meaning of the heat of this great anger?' And they shall say, 'Because they forsook the covenant of the Lord, God of their fathers . . . and they went and served other gods and bowed to them. . . . the anger of the Lord was kindled in the land to bring upon them all the curse that is written in this book'" (Deuteronomy 29:18–21, 23–26).

Discussion Question

A SECOND OPINION: Who gives one nation the right to judge others? Obviously, God does. If Israel disobeys His commandments, the Gentile nations will point their fingers and attribute the curses to the Hebrews' sins. Why does the Torah state this? Why should we care what others think? For centuries, Christians and other groups have mocked the Jews' dispersions and persecutions, seeing a divine punishment for straying from God's path—or in the case of Christians, for "rejecting" the divinity of Jesus. How can we resent such judgments if the Torah declares them proper and inevitable?

Shammai Engelmayer

We should care what other nations think about us. That is the whole point of our existence as a people. We are God's kingdom of priests, His holy nation. We are the people He has chosen to live special lives, lives that are moral, ethical, righteous, and just.

We must live those lives separately and apart from everyone else. And we must incorporate into those lives rituals and practices designed to make us stand out as strange, different. That way, people will become curious about us and want to learn more about who we are and, more important, why we do what we do. Through learning about us, they also will learn how God wants humankind to behave. That is our "job description." That is the assignment we accepted from God at Mt. Sinai. In return for being His treasured nation, we agreed to put ourselves in a fish bowl.

The problem with calling attention to ourselves, however, is that the attention is not selective. We cannot say, "Look at us only when we do what God wants us to do. Don't look at us when we ignore His instructions."

Of course, no one likes to be singled out for doing wrong. That is the price you have to pay, however. I recall a news item recently that talked about the arrest of a 50-year-old man who for a long time had been spray painting sexually explicit pictures on public property. At the time of his arrest, the first thing he said was, "Please, don't tell my family." No one had to tell his family, however, since the news broadcasts were telling it to the whole world.

You especially have to pay the price if you present yourself as living by a higher standard than your actions indicate.

Should we be bothered by this? Should we care what other people think?

Of course. That is the whole point of living in God's fish bowl. The chiding and the deriding are embarrassments to us. They make us feel ashamed. They make us want to run and hide. Only, there is no place to run and hide in a fish bowl. If you do not want the embarrassment, if you do not want to feel the shame, then the only thing you can do is stick to the deal you made with God and do your "job" for Him as best you can.

On the other hand, we do not have to say "thank you" to people who turn us into objects of derision and mockery. We can resent their opinions because their behavior is no better than ours. In fact, all we are doing when we act inappropriately is what we have always done: We are trying to climb out of the fish bowl and be like everyone else. So, we can resent their judgment because it contains a double standard. They can behave this way, but we cannot.

The question this week adds another element, however: They chide us because we do not accept their beliefs. This is a different story entirely. We do not insist that they believe in our God, only in the code of conduct He has set forth for the world. And they have no right to insist that we believe what they believe. The question errs when it says that the Torah calls this "proper" and "inevitable" conduct. It is not—so long as we are being faithful to God and our agreement with Him.

It becomes proper conduct and it is inevitable only when we demonstrate that what we say we believe in is not what we actually believe in. We cannot say we believe in the God of Israel when, by our actions, we demonstrate a disdain for Him because we are ignoring His laws.

Then—and only then—do they have a right to chide us for not accepting their beliefs. After all, if our beliefs mean so little to us, and if we are so intent on being like everyone else, what is the difference to us what we are and in what we say we believe?

Clearly, it must matter to us because, despite our lapses, we do not march *en masse* into the camp of the "other." We still insist on clinging to our identities as Jews. Yes, the demographics show that many of us are doing so, but the majority retain their identity. It means something to them.

In the end, that is the real point here. The chiding and criticism we get from others demand that we make a choice. We say that we want to be like everyone else. We act like everyone else. But when pushed to the wall, we put on the brakes. We are not like everyone else, and we do not want to be.

That leaves us with only one question that each of us must answer individually and we must all answer collectively: What are we going to do about it? If we come up with the right answer, we will be back on God's path. The chiding and the mockery will have served their purpose.

Joseph Ozarowski

I think the use of the nations of the world asking these hard questions about the fate of the Jewish people may simply be a figure of speech, a dramatic means for Moshe to convey his message of consequences for our actions. I do not think we need be that concerned with the non-Jewish reaction to our troubles. The key question here is not so much, "What would the *goyim* say?" but rather, is the *Brit*, the Covenant between God and our people, still in force? And if it is, why all the suffering? Are our people being punished for sins? And, assuming we do sin and reap the negative results, is there a future for our people?

Rabbi Meir Simcha of Dvinsk, in his commentary *Meshekh Hokhmah*, suggests that up to the time Moshe uttered these words, the Jewish people could not be fully blamed for their sins. After all, they had been enslaved (both physically and spiritually) to the Egyptians for all those years. They would not have been able to survive in the desert without the miraculous help of *Hashem*. This is probably, according to the *Meshekh Hokhmah*, the meaning of the famous rabbinic comment (BT *Shabbat* 88) *Kafah aleihem har k'gigit*, that God held Mt. Sinai over our people's heads like a tub and told them, "if you accept the Torah, good, but if not, here will be your burial place."

Thus, they really had no choice but to accept the Torah and the Covenant at Sinai. When they reach the Promised Land, Moshe renews the covenant with them so that they may receive the gift of the Land. When they sin later in history, they are exiled from the Land and the gift, as it were, is taken away. But during this (Babylonian/Persian) Exile, for which these verses can be seen as prophecy, our people voluntarily renew the covenant. The end of the Book of Esther tells us following the miracle of Purim, *Kiymu v'kiblu*, "They fulfilled and they accepted."

While the immediate context of this refers to Purim itself, *Hazal* (BT *Shevuot* 39a and elsewhere in the Talmud) understand it to refer to the whole Torah in the sense of, "They fulfilled [the Torah] that which they had earlier accepted." So, as the *Meshekh Hokhmah* reminds us, now our own people, voluntarily and away from the Promised Land, renew the Covenant; it is still indeed in force.

In fact, the next chapter of our *sidra* (30:1–14), which follows this week's key verses, makes abundantly clear the possibility of *teshuvah*, repentance, return, and renewal of the Covenant. So in spite of the seeming implication that all is lost, and the non-Jewish world is making nasty comments about our fealty to the Covenant and the Divine consequences thereof, Moses' own words later show us the way to keep our relationship with God intact as well as to overturn the arguments of those outside our world who do not have our best interests at heart.

One of my congregants brilliantly pointed out that your question leaves out a key part of the phrasing in verse 21. The question about our persecution and dispersion as result of our actions is not only asked by the non-Jews, but also (and maybe primarily) by the *dor ha-aharon*, "the last generation, your children who will rise up after you. . . ." This shows, my erstwhile *baal-habos* suggested, that the Covenant has been and is still very much in force, because there is an implied promise that there will indeed be another generation in the far future who will be able to ask such questions. Could this generation, "the last generation," be us?

Maybe. I am not sure how I could apply these verses in chapters 29 and 30 to all the events our generations have witnessed in recent history. As a child of Holocaust survivors, I find it difficult to see how the *Shoah* is punishment for anything. I do not know why it happened and am at a great loss to philosophically explain the Holocaust. I prefer to live with my questions rather than diddle with theologically and emotionally unsatisfying *pilpul*. But, as a believing and observant Jew, I can still affirm the Covenant in force. The events of our own generation only reinforce this belief. Certainly the miracles of modern Israel, its wondrous survival through the battles of 1967 and 1973, and the blessed liberation of oppressed Jewry that we have witnessed with our own eyes are testimony to the fact the *Hashem*'s Covenant is still in effect after the tragedies of the 1930s and 1940s.

It is now our turn. Will we in America be able to respond and renew our side of the Covenant while we are away from the Promised Land? And by doing so, can we make our own contribution to the future of Torah, Judaism, and Jewry by insuring that there will be future generations who can look upon these passages and study them?

David Sofian

As I began thinking about your question, it occurred to me that this is not the first time the subject has arisen. At least twice before we have found that what the other nations might think or say has come up. And these were both critical situations indeed.

In *Shmot* 32, God reacts to the building of the golden calf by wanting to destroy the whole people of Israel. Moses is told that God intends to start over with him. God's reaction to the golden calf is to want to make Moses into a new Abraham. What bears on your question is how Moses responded. Moses begins his plea in defense of his people by speaking of the great power God used to redeem Israel from Egypt. Moses wants God to remember how the Exodus brought God and God's power to the attention of all others.

Already in his opening move, Moses is appealing to God's reputation among the nations. Then, for emphasis, Moses narrows his argument to the Egyptians who God specifically defeated. Moses argues the Egyptians will say it was for evil that God brought the Israelites out, only to kill them in the mountains and terminate them from the face of the earth. In other words, the boosting of God's prominence accomplished in the Exodus would be for naught.

Moses' appeal is to how God would be perceived in the world. Moses argues that the Israelites' idolatry would be forgotten, and only God's killing them in the wilderness would be retained. The argument works— God does not destroy the whole people. But why does it work? Was it simply that Moses successfully appealed to God's ego as it were?

This happens again in *Bamidbar* in the episode of the spies. At the end of the 40 days of scouting the land of Israel, the twelve spies return and report their findings. As we recall, ten are of the opinion that it would be too difficult to go in and convince the people they are right. Only Caleb and Joshua exhort the people not to be afraid, for God would be on their side.

Again, as was the case with the golden calf, God reacts by determining to strike them all down and to start over with Moses. How does Moses deal with the impending demise of his people this time? He must have felt that whatever worked once would work again, for he appeals to God's reputation a second time. Moses reasons that the Egyptians will hear of it and tell it to those living in the land. The pillars of cloud and fire make it clear to everyone that God is in the people's midst.

This means the nations will conclude that if God is indeed with them and they died in the wilderness, it must be because God was powerless to bring them into the land. In the case of the golden calf, the argument went that everyone knows your power but will misconstrue its use. Now Moses argues that God's power itself will be questioned.

And again the argument works, although not totally. God forgives but determines that none of the generation who had seen the signs performed in Egypt, except for Caleb and Joshua, would be brought into the land. Again, we need ask, why does this work?

So there is an obvious answer to your question. We should care what others think, because God cares what others think. Now let us turn to the question of why God would care in these examples. Why does Moses' appealing to God's reputation have the desired effect?

I believe the key is to focus on our purpose as a people in Covenant with

God. The Ashkenazi *Siddur*'s *Aleinu* prayer expresses this extremely well. The prayer begins by acknowledging God's sovereignty and establishing our people's role as God's servants. But then, in the second half of the prayer, we go on to say that our ultimate hope is the establishment of righteousness, even as humanity unites in its acknowledgement of God as the ruler of all the earth.

The prayer concludes with Zechariah's expression of the Messianic hope, "On that day the Eternal God shall be one and God's name shall be one." The goal is that all should be won over to God's service as expressed in the universal acknowledgement of God's name. The prayer implies that Israel's example as God's servants is the vehicle by which this message is brought to the world.

To return to your question and *parashat Netzavim*, to keep God's plan from being thwarted, it surely would be necessary for the Gentile nations to know that punishment of Israel results from Israelite sins. This being the case, is there any wonder that God cares how the world perceives God's concrete behavior within the covenantal relationship with Israel?

It turns out that Moses was not just a clever persuader appealing to God's ego, but he was persuasive because he understood that what matters to God is the ultimate unification of humanity in righteousness through the recognition of the unity of God.

Va'yelech:
Deuteronomy 31:1–30

Prophetical Reading
Hosea 14:2–10, Micah 7:18–20,
Joel 2:15–27

Overview of Torah Portion

Moses, in announcing that his reign as the Hebrews' leader is nearly over, cautions them to maintain their obedience to God. He writes a copy of the Torah and entrusts it to the priests. God tells Moses and Joshua that the Hebrews will stray after other gods, and He will hide His face from them.

Key Verses

"And the Lord said to Moses, 'Behold, you are about to sleep with your fathers. This people will rise up and stray after the foreign gods of the land whose midst they are entering. They will forsake Me and break My covenant that I made with them. And My anger will be kindled against them in that day and I will hide My face from them and they shall be devoured and many evils and troubles shall come upon them'" (Deuteronomy 31:16–17).

Discussion Question

God's timetable: Moses is about to die on Mt. Sinai. The Children of Israel are about to enter the Promised Land. But they are clearly not ready. So why does God let them cross the Jordan now? Is there a deadline? Why not keep them longer in the wilderness, until they are ready—and deserving—to go into Canaan and face its challenges? Do they deserve the inevitable curses God has promised if He has already determined that they are now not prepared for their new task? Should Moses, their leader, not protest that more time is needed?

Shammai Engelmayer

How much more time is needed—a week, a month, a year, an eternity? Sooner or later, Moshe must die. Sooner or later, these people must "grow up." Sooner or later, they must assume their rightful roles as the nation Israel. So it might as well be now. They have had their forty years of testing, proving, molding, and shaping. If they are not ready today, they will probably be no more ready tomorrow. It is time to let them cross over and hope for the best.

For one thing, God's reputation is on the line. If the people stay on the east bank of the Jordan, then the world can say the God of Israel is impotent, for He is afraid of going head to head, as it were, with the gods of the peoples of Canaan. Or they will say His promises are meaningless, for did He not promise Israel a land of its own, and here they are landless still?

For another thing, the only chance that this people will reform is in the Land. Unless they see that God keeps His word, they have no reason to follow Him. They only have Moshe's word that God did all those miracles forty years earlier. Their parents may have told them, too, but their parents also set terrible examples of how to be grateful to God for those miracles, leading to the suspicion that they were either lying or delusional.

They need to see these things for themselves. Then, perhaps, they might begin to shape up and get on with the job of being the Israel God intended.

Then again, perhaps God wants them to fail. After all, as long as they continue on their present path, even if they adhere to all the laws Moshe gave them, this will never be the Israel God had intended. He had sought an Israel devoted to prayer and good deeds. Since the golden calf episode, this is an Israel whose "religion" is nothing more than paganism adapted to the worship of the One True God. It had a sacrificial cult, magic incantations, supernatural rituals, and a primitive understanding of God and His nature. It is just possible, then, that God wanted this people to carry this part of its existence to one of its two logical conclusions: First, because of the severe restrictions He imposed on the cultic aspects of Israelite religious practices, they will begin to evolve a new religious format closer to that which God intended in the first place; or, second, their experiment with pseudo-paganism will lead them back to paganism and, thus, to the exile God had promised—where, in order to survive as a people, they would have no choice but to adopt the religious format originally intended by God. Either way, God wins. Israel will become Israel.

But that cannot happen while they remain outside the Land. On the east bank of the Jordan, they are, at best, in a holding pattern—and the longer they stay, the further they drift. Without incontrovertible proof of God's ability to deliver on His promise, that drifting will never lead them to a higher form of service to Him.

What difference is there between being exiled from the Land and never even being in the Land? Is the result not the same? No. The cultic restrictions—sacrifice at the front of the Tent of Meeting only, and only in the Land—do not fully apply until after the people cross over. Until then, the *Mishkan* remains the only place one can sacrifice, but it is not necessary to be in the Land. Thus, there is no reason to evolve alternatives. Before they can be outside the Land, they need to be in the Land.

And so, off they go, ready or not. God is ready—and that is all that matters. Everything else will fall into place, sooner or later.

Joseph Ozarowski

Upon asking the question, one of my Shabbat afternoon regulars immediately chimed in with, "Would they be readier at any other time?" I had to admit that this is the core of the basic answer. Moshe could not ask for more time; his time was up (in the words of *Hazal* on Deuteronomy 3, when Moshe protested his own inability to enter Israel, *Avra sha'ata*, "the time has passed.") They will never be more ready or more deserving than they are now. Forty years in the desert has been enough.

This does not mean that the people of Israel are perfect. Far from it. In fact, the whole point of our text is that there will be inevitable backsliding. People are only human. But look carefully at the next few verses (18–21) where Moshe is told *Kitvu lakhem et hashira hazot*, "Write for yourselves this song. . . ." From here, the *halakhah* derives a mitzvah (the final one in the Torah) for every Jew to write, or at least participate in the writing of, a *Sefer Torah*. This will serve as an *eid*, a witness, when it seems that the *Brit*, the Covenant, has been broken. When this happens, the Torah that we actively write for ourselves (both physically and metaphorically) will insure our continuity. God so much as says this in verse 21, "I know their inclination"—I know what will ultimately happen, that they will at times forsake Me. Still, the Torah serves as witness to our eternal relationship with God.

This is not the only time we have such a situation. God's covenant was broken in the time of Noah. God decides to start again with Noah and his family. There is no guarantee that after the flood things will be all that perfect. Still, God is willing to say that this is the best we will get. *Hashem* says, I will give you my Covenant and the tools to make the world work. There will be backsliding, but it is up to you, the seed of humanity, to make it work. Just as with our people in the desert, we have a period of forty (the Flood). It seems that forty in the Torah is a the symbol of isolation, preparation, and growth. After these periods, we have to begin and then continue on our own.

It is no accident that this *sidra* always falls out close to Rosh Hashanah— either just before or just after. The themes of the Covenant and also of *teshuvah*, repentance and return, which keeps the Covenant functioning, follow the idea that we have prepared all we can. We have to take the tools God has given to us, do the best we can with them, and continually try to improve. There will always be backsliding and consequences, but *Hashem* still loves us. We always have the possibility of return and repentance with the Torah as our witness, just as *Hashem* promised Moshe.

David Sofian

One way to answer your question is to assume that the passage must have been written after the fact. That is, the passage is not a prediction but a description of what had actually already occurred back to the time of the transition from Moses' leadership to Joshua's. Then, the passage would reflect the reality of the Israelites' rebellion rather than anticipate it.

In fact, this may be how the text came to be as it is and therefore a way to resolve the difficulty. However, using this approach would tend to cut off the possibility of additional meaning being drawn from the text as a result of the difficulty. Traditionally, difficulties like the one you raise serve as an opportunity to explore the text further. This continual exploration is what makes the text live with meaning.

The question you raise from these key verses is not the only time we have wondered about the conflict between God's knowledge of the future and human choice. As I pointed out in my response to your question to *parashat Shelach Lecha*, medieval philosophers struggled with this same problem. How can God's omniscience and human freedom be reconciled? Earlier in the book of *Shmot*, we wondered at how God could harden Pharaoh's heart, thereby predetermining Pharaoh's responses, and yet hold Pharaoh responsible for those responses. Where was Pharaoh's freedom of choice?

When we looked at this issue in *parshat Bo*, we saw that the tradition also wrestled with it. There, given that this problem is not resolvable, the narrative was read so that a positive moral lesson could be derived from it. Here in this case, we wonder how God can know of our ancestors' future infidelity and still have them cross into the Land of Israel. If God knows what they will do and even predicts what punishment will ensue, did they really have freedom of choice? As before, we can use this difficulty to look for a positive lesson derivable from it.

I think we can find such a positive lesson if we ask how we might have reacted if the text read as you suggested. Suppose the generation of the wilderness older than twenty when leaving Egypt had died, and God then told Moses the Israelites were still not ready to enter the Land and would be staying put. What might we have thought? I would have been drawn back to the story of the spies to see what God had said then. There, in *Bamidbar*, after their response to the spies' report, God had wanted to destroy the people and start over with Moses as the progenitor of a new people.

Moses refused the offer and succeeded in convincing God not to destroy them all. *Bamidbar* 14:20 tells us that God pardoned them as Moses asked. And then, after saying in verse 29 that no one 20 years and up would enter the land, God promises in verse 31 that their children would be allowed to enter. By the time of our current parshah, the punishment had been fulfilled.

Could God have done anything other than to let them proceed? If God had kept them in the wilderness would we not have wondered about God's commitment? Would we not have wondered about God's suspension of the original promise?

This, then, is what is at stake by God not changing the timing of the people's entry into the Land, even though they may not have been ready.

Israel must be able to rely on God and on God's commitments. Israel itself may be unable or unwilling to keep its commitments. And indeed, over and over again, we have seen that this is the case. So much of the biblical tradition would have been unnecessary if Israel had been able to keep its commitments. BT *Nedarim* 22b teaches us that only the first five books and the Book of Joshua would have been necessary from the whole of the Hebrew Bible, had Israel not sinned.

However, as evidenced by the case you raise, Torah emphasizes that God's promises are genuine and that God's commitments can be relied on. Indeed, by God not leaving them in the wilderness, this text stresses that such confidence and faith were to be the bedrock of Israel's very existence.

Ha'azinu:
Deuteronomy 32:1–52

Prophetical Reading
2 Samuel 22:1–51

Overview of Torah Portion

Moses, following God's commands, reads to the Jewish nation his final rebuke in the form of a song. Having done that, he ascends Mount Nebo, where he will view the Promised Land and die.

Key Verses

"And the Lord said to Moses, 'Behold, you are about to sleep with your fathers. This people will rise up and stray after the foreign gods of the land whose midst they are entering. They will forsake Me and break My covenant that I made with them. And My anger shall be kindled against them on that day and I will hide my face from them. . . . Now write for yourselves this song and teach it [to] the Children of Israel, place it in their mouths, that this song shall be a witness to Me for the children of Israel . . . this song shall testify before them as a witness'" (Deuteronomy 31:16–21).

"Is corruption His? No; His children's is the blemish; a generation crooked and perverse . . . a forward generation . . . in whom there is no faithfulness" (Deuteronomy 32:5, 20).

Discussion Question

DAMNING TESTIMONY: Since Israel will undoubtedly stray, God gives Moses a song that will testify for it—one translation renders the song as testifying against Israel—in the future. The song condemns the Hebrews throughout, listing all sorts of shortcomings and possible punishments. This will save them? This is their defense? How does a recitation of one's sins appease a judge? Why not offer the good deeds that the Hebrews performed?

Shammai Engelmayer

When Israel is punished for its abandonment of God, what will its response be? "Excuse me, Lord, but are You not forgetting all these good things we have done in Your Name? Are You not forgetting all the righteous individuals who have served You faithfully, even if the nation as a whole has failed You? Remember *Avraham*'s argument about ten righteous men in Sodom and Gomorrah. Surely, we have ten times ten righteous men ten times over? How can You destroy us, when You would have saved Sodom and Gomorrah?"

It is a good argument, but to God it is irrelevant. He will punish Israel when it crosses a line too far. How far out that line is depends on the good things and the righteous people, but it is still there to be crossed. If Israel crosses it (and God is certain that it will), it only means that the scales of Israel's deeds have become hopelessly out of balance; the weight of the bad has tipped its scale tray so far that its bottom rests securely on the table.

Israel, of course, will be angry at God at that time. It will respond by charging that He ignores the good. But to whom will it "respond"? Not to God, really, because He has already done what He felt needed to be done. Rather, Israel will put its case before the court of public opinion. It will downplay its bad deeds (which to the rest of the world may not look so bad, in any case) and exaggerate its good ones. It will seek to paint God as an evil deity, unworthy of love and trust.

What will God do? Will He descend from Heaven and testify on His own behalf?

Moshe and God both know what most people in the world at the time could not begin to grasp—that such anthropomorphic behavior on the part of God is never going to happen. God is not a physical being in any way we would define the term. He is composed of nothing, at least nothing we can begin to understand. He is not even matter and/or energy. There is not an atom's worth of anything in His being.

God exists outside all of that, apart from the "natural" world He created. And He is not going to stoop so low as to adopt a corporeal form just to defend Himself against Israel's lies.

Nevertheless, He is concerned about Israel's response to His judgment.

No, He does not care about the bad publicity, or whether anyone will believe it (He expects they will). What He is concerned with is that, once it makes its case, no matter how spurious, Israel itself will begin to believe it.

That is a serious problem, because the whole point of imposing judgment on Israel and carrying out the sentence is to bring about Israel's repentance and its eventual return to the service of God. If Israel itself believes God has acted cruelly, unjustly, and mercilessly, there is no chance of its ever returning to His service.

Yet, God in the last verse (32:43), makes clear (as the Ramban points out) that redemption is inevitable and there is no *quid pro quo* involved, no "you repent and then I will redeem you." God does not want to be put in the position of redeeming an unworthy people who, once redeemed, will continue with its evil ways. That misses the point of punishment.

And so God sets out the charge sheet in advance and insists that Israel rehearse it long before it crosses that line too far. "You do not like what I am doing to you? You do not think I am just, merciful, and righteous? Go back and look at that charge sheet again. Now, do not tell Me about what you have done that is right, honorable, and good. Tell Me about the charges and specifications in *Ha'azinu*. Show Me where you have not committed the infractions listed there. Show Me how I have misread your actions based on the charges and specifications in *Ha'azinu*. If you can honestly say you are not guilty of this one and that one, then you will have made your case against Me. But if you cannot—if, indeed, you know you have committed all these wrongs—then accept My judgment and repent your ways."

Why would such a "charge sheet" end with the assurance of redemption regardless of whether Israel did *teshuvah*? One must look more closely at the poem to understand. God, here, is setting out the history of Israel, but He is also revealing His uncompromising love for Israel.

Amid the harsh words, a tender streak keeps coming through. As much as God wants this poem to stand as witness to why He executed judgment against Israel, He also wants it to reflect that He never abandoned Israel and, in the end, will never abandon Israel. To be punished for its sins is not to be abandoned because of them. A parent who sends a child to his or her room is not abandoning the child. Sooner or later, the child will come to realize that the punishing parent still loves her or him and will seek to please the parent as a way of returning that love.

Thus, this is God's way of throwing Israel a life preserver. Without it, when punishment is finally executed, Israel will reread the charge sheet and accept its crimes against God—but it will not return to Him because He left them no hope. His judgment is uncompromising and final.

Not so, says God. "My punishment is malleable and temporary. It is only My love that is uncompromising and final."

God, of course, could not tie Israel's repentance to its redemption, because that would violate the nature of God's laws. Reward and punishment are national in scope, yet the national character is defined by the behavior of its individuals. The individual must do good for the sake of doing good, not for a reward.

For Israel to finally become what God intends it to be—His kingdom of priests, His emissary to the world, His flesh-and-blood instruction book to humankind on how to live worthy lives—each Israelite must individually accept God's burden for no other reason than that it is the right thing to do.

On the other hand, if each Israelite individually accepts God's burden in order to share in a national "reward"—redemption, a return to the land, the favor of the Lord—there can be no reward, for Israel has not done *teshuvah*. God's love is the lifeline. Sooner or later, the individual will feel the need to return that love.

This, however, creates another problem for God. The message this delivers could be seen as an indication that Israel is better than everyone else—superior in every way. That is the wrong message, too, because God is Creator of all things, and His love extends to all He has created. All are equal in God's eyes. God can insist that the killing of an animal for food is akin to the murder of a human being (see Leviticus 17:3) because, in His eyes, it is the same crime—an attack on His creation. (*Shechitah*, which we define as "ritual slaughter," is meant to remind Israel that the eating of meat was not God's intention at Creation but the result of Divine dispensation after the Great Flood, by which time it was apparent that humankind needed some outlet for its bloodlust.) Israel, therefore, cannot argue that it is better than another people. Yet, how else should Israel interpret the fact that God's love for it is immutable?

That is why there is another aspect to the poem God has Moshe read to Israel. There are three elements to be found here: God, Israel, and the rest of Creation (including the other nations, all plant and animal life, and the forces of nature). It is often difficult to figure out about whom God is talking at any point, and at times even whether He is the one doing the talking.

Clearly, this is deliberate. God is saying that the three are dependent and inseparable: God is the Creator, the world is what He created, and Israel is His link to Creation. Israel is unique because it is God's "personal portion," meaning that it is His to do with as He pleases. God created the world and then created people for that world—to care for it, nurture it, and continue creating it. On the other hand, God created Israel for Himself. That makes Israel subject to stricter rules and gives it a much narrower leeway for error (which is why the Avrahamic defense of Sodom cannot work for Israel). But it does not make Israel better than anyone else.

The notion that this poem is actually a defense that Israel can offer when God seeks to punish it is obviously wrong. Rather, *Ha'azinu* is meant as a defense against Israel's doing wrong. The poem sets it all out for Israel. Read it, understand it, and act on it—and what the poem says will happen will never happen. Ignore it, and the evils in the poem will become only too true.

But take heart, Israel; even those are only temporary.

Joseph Ozarowski

I do not believe that it is an accident that this *sidra* always comes out close to Yom Kippur, either just before in the form of *Shabbat Shuva*, the Sabbath of Repentance and Return, or just after. The lesson of both Yom Kippur and *Ha'azinu* is that recognizing one's shortcomings and knowing the consequences of one's actions is essential to the *teshuvah* (return) process. Though it seems that Moshe is "dissing" the Jewish people (to use a contemporary colloquialism), he is really teaching us a most important lesson.

In essence, honest confession of the truth, awareness of our failings, and knowledge of our frailties really are better than denial of our situation, turning everything into sweetness and light. When you stand in front of the judge, you usually get a better deal when you confess and admit your guilt while resolving to truly do better than you would by covering up. How much more so before the Divine judge, the Holy One, Blessed Be He!

That is why so much of Yom Kippur is spent confessing one's sins, and even sins one did not do. (The latter is because we are part of the aggregate known as the Jewish People, *Klal Yisrael*, and each of us somewhere along the way is guilty of these misdeeds. The confessional is in the plural; by sharing each other's sins and burdens, we lighten the communal load and insure that *Hashem* will forgive us both as a group and individually.)

The *Dubner Maggid* (Rabbi Yakov Kranz, eighteenth century Lithuania) tells two wonderful stories to explain why we seem to emphasize the negative when coming before *Hashem*. The Yom Kippur pre-confessional prayer *Ki anu amekha* begins by listing the various positive aspects of our relationship with God, "For we are Your people and You our God. . . . we Your sheep and You our shepherd. . . . we Your vineyard and You our keeper. . . ." However, it ends on a negative note, "We are insolent but You are gracious. . . . we are obstinate but you are long-suffering. . . ."

The *Maggid* tells of a seller of wooden spoons who at first tries to peddle his wares in the wealthier part of town. There are very few customers for wooden spoons in this neighborhood, so he is forced to sell his meager goods in the poorer section of town. But at least here he gets a response. At this time of year, we realize how frail and meager our spiritual resources are. But rather than cover up our situation, we admit that all we have are wooden spoons. Yet, God guarantees us the desired response.

The *Maggid*'s second story is about the last line of *Avinu Malkeinu*. After a whole litany of requests to the Almighty, we then ask *Hashem* to answer us through pure kindness and *tzedakah*, though we have no deeds we can present. The *Maggid* compares this to a person who comes into a store with a long shopping list and goes through every item on the list with the storekeeper. When it is time to pay, the shopper meekly and softly asks for credit because there is nothing with which to pay. So, too, we have our needs for which we ask *Hashem*. But we have no payment and must meekly admit this. Yet in spite of this, we are assured that *Hashem* will answer us and bless us.

Judaism, especially at the season of *Ha'azinu* and Yom Kippur, teaches us that in order to be forgiven, we have to confront the reality of our situation, our shortcomings and consequences of our actions, and honestly but humbly face God. This will indeed be our defence and salvation.

David Sofian

Let me begin to respond to your question by drawing our attention once again to two other instances when the unfaithfulness of the people led God to decide to destroy Israel. First was the incident of the building of the golden calf. The other was the people's refusal to enter the Land of Israel after the return of the spies. In each of these cases, God became so angry with the Israelites' behavior that God wanted to destroy them all and start over with Moses.

However, also in each case, Moses convinced God not to do so by appealing to how God's reputation would be affected by destroying them. Although God does punish the people in each case, thanks to Moses' intercession, the covenantal relationship is nevertheless maintained.

A similar thing, with one very important difference, is happening in our current parshah, *D'varim* 32. We hear about the people's failure and ingratitude as in the other two cases. Verse 16 tells us that they would incense God with alien things and would vex God with abominations. And we hear about the terrible punishment that will ensue also as in the other two cases. Verse 23 tells us that God will sweep misfortunes on them and use up God's arrows on them.

However, that is not all we hear. Before reading this, we are reminded of the formation of this very special relationship. We are reminded that Israel is God's people. We first hear in verses 10–13 about God's lovingkindness toward them and how they were borne on eagle's wings from the desolation of the wilderness to a land of butter, wheat, and wine. And then, the important difference I mention is found when the song does not stop with the telling of their punishment but continues to express God's mercy regarding them, and how in deviating from the path of strict justice God will bring them back.

Verse 36 tells us how God will relent after judging the people. The important difference is that in this case there will be no Moses to prompt God to nullify the decree.

You ask how this song saves or defends. I don't think it does except in the sense that it gives hope. In *Shmot* and *Bamidbar*, Moses' pivotal role is emphasized. If Moses had not interceded, the ruin of the people would have proceeded. In this song, Moses is not the intercessor. Hearing it witnesses to the people that even when they sin and Moses is no longer there to intercede on their behalf, God alone eventually will stop the devastation of the people.

The song tells us this when God makes Moses' argument for him. In verse 27, we hear how for fear that Israel's enemies will misjudge and believe they brought about their own fall, God relents. The people know that Moses is about to die. Indeed, the end of the parshah tells us of God's command to Moses to ascend the heights of Abarim to Mount Nebo.

This moment of losing Moses had to be terrifying for the Israelites. How comforting and hope conferring to have first heard that even after Moses is gone, God's mercy will ultimately prevail over God's judgment of their sin, and they will be spared.

V'zot Ha'beracha:
Deuteronomy 33:1–34:12

Prophetical Reading
Joshua 1:1–18

Overview of Torah Portion

Moses, on his last day, gives his blessings to the Tribes of Israel. He ascends Mount Nebo, is shown the Holy Land by God, and breathes his last breath at age 120. The Hebrews mourn him for a month. Joshua succeeds him as the nation's leader.

Key Verses

"This is the blessing with which Moses, the man of God, blessed the Children of Israel before his death . . . 'Let Reuven live and not die. . . . And this for Judah. . . . And of Levi, he said . . .'" (Deuteronomy 33:1–8).

Discussion Question

TRIBAL BLESSINGS: When the patriarch Jacob blessed Reuven, Judah, and the rest, they were his children, individual people standing at the foot of his deathbed. By the time Moses offered his blessings with his last breaths, Jacob's sons' descendants had grown into tribes, each with tens of thousands of people. If Moses could not bless each person individually, why not a blessing for the whole group—or by some other categorization? Why did Moses continue to bless the Children of Israel as tribes—literally as the children of Jacob? How much did tribal genealogy continue to determine the members' traits? Are the people's fates predestined by virtue of birth in a particular tribe? Are these blessings still in effect today, 2,000 years after the Second Temple was destroyed and the identity of most tribes was lost?

Shammai Engelmayer

Moshe blessed tribes individually because the Israel he had led for forty years was a federation of tribes. Indeed, the land they were about to begin occupying had just been tentatively divided along tribal lines.

Remember that Israel had come down to Egypt as a family. In the long period that followed, the families each grew into larger units, namely clans and tribes. Unless and until they were all settled in their own land and forced to think and act on a national scale, they would remain "Levites," "Reubenites," and "Ephraimites"; they would also be "Israelites," but tribal interests would always be of greater concern.

And, indeed, this is how they would stay until King David and his successor, Shelomo (Solomon), begin the process of redividing the land along administrative lines, thus effectively forcing individual tribes to "merge" for the sake of common interests.

The reality is that it was not "ten tribes" that broke away after Shelomo's death as much as it was the rest of Israel breaking away from what was perceived as the tyranny of the Yehudahites (a tyranny Rechavam foolishly pledged to intensify). By then, the tribal divisions had blurred considerably.

In Yehudah, they were virtually non-existent by then. The tribe of Shimon, for all practical purposes, no longer existed, having been absorbed into Yehudah (which is why it really did not break away with the others, despite its being included in the "ten tribes" tradition; it disappeared long before Israel did). The same is true of those that stayed with Yehudah, namely Binyamin, and the half-tribe of Menashe.

Unity was not yet the case in Moshe's day. So determined were the people to maintain their individual tribal identities that, when Moshe agreed to change the laws of inheritance in the matter of the daughters of Tselophchad, he was then forced to amend that change to accommodate tribal concerns.

As the question notes, Ya'akov blessed his sons, but actually, he blessed tribes, too. His "blessings," which were not all positive, reached beyond his sons to the future (see Genesis 49). Examining these blessings is instructive in understanding what these were and what they were not: The blessings were expressions of hope for the future or warnings of what would happen unless the object of the "blessing" reformed his/its ways. They were not prophecies.

Thus, Zevulun, says Ya'akov, "shall dwell on the seashore . . . And his flank shall rest on Sidon," yet the allotted territory the tribe receives is inland. The closest it gets to "the seashore" is at a point on its southwestern border that is six-and-a-half miles due east of the Mediterranean; most of its western border is 14 miles from the sea. As for Sidon sitting on its flank, the Lebanese city is located 39 miles north of Zevulun's northern border.

With the possible exception of Shimshon (Samson), who was no paradigm of either morality or leadership, Dan offers no leaders to Israel, yet "Dan shall judge his people," Ya'akov says. Indeed, Devorah will chide the tribe for its lack of military participation against the Canaanites. Such a lack certainly offers no hint of leadership.

In his "blessings," Ya'akov curses Shimon and Levi, "for when angry they slay men, and when pleased they maim oxen. Cursed be their anger so fierce, and their wrath so relentless. I will divide them in Ya'akov, scatter them in Israel."

Levi was, in fact, scattered throughout Israel, but only because it was given the role of religious functionary; a Levite, from the family of Aharon, served as *Kohen Gadol* in the Jerusalem Temple. This can hardly be seen as fulfillment of Ya'akov's curse or punishment for bad behavior, even if the non-priestly Levites had a tough time making ends meet.

As for Shimon, although its territory was placed within that of Yehudah, and it was eventually absorbed by it, it was a contiguous territory, never scattered. Only if one believes that Shimon was not absorbed by Yehudah, but that the entire tribe picked itself up, abandoned its own territory, and moved to breakaway Israel to join Yaravom's revolt, there to find homes wherever individual tribal members could, can anyone say this "blessing" was ever fulfilled—and not even the Bible suggests that Shimon did so.

Ya'akov says that Yoseph would assume national leadership, at least in the near term. Yet it is from the cursed Levi, not Yoseph, that national leadership emerges in the persons of Moshe and Aharon. Indeed, the Yoseph tribes are insignificant until Yehoshua, an Ephraimite, assumes command, and then they pass back into insignificance upon his death. It re-emerges again only when Yaravom of Ephraim rebels and divides the country in two. Because of this, the prophet Hoshea refers pejoratively to the breakaway Israel as "Ephraim" throughout his book.

Of course, this could be seen as reflective of the blessing, in that "Ephraim" is symbolic of the non-Yehudahite kings of Israel. However, considering that the revolt was clearly against God's wishes and led to total disaster, this could hardly be considered a blessing given to a favorite son.

Yehudah, on the other hand, eventually does take command of Israel, but it would reign "forever," according to Ya'akov, and that too did not happen. Not only was Yehudah rejected by most of Israel when the kingdom divided, but once the First Temple fell, Yehudah never again rose to that kind of power. During the Second Temple period, Levites of the Aharonid dynasty were the actual power, and some even occupied the throne (i.e., the Chasmoneans).

With the fall of the Second Temple in 70 C.E., the rabbis of blessed memory took center stage and, for all practical purposes, which tribe any rabbi belonged to was totally irrelevant (although it was used as the basis of authority for both the *nasi* [president] in Judea and the Babylonian exilarchate). Whether Yehudah rises to prominence again will depend on who the *Mashiach* is—and, tradition aside, we will not know the answer until the *Mashiach* does come, hopefully soon.

The fate of Yehudah is most relevant when considering Moshe's blessings. No matter how you read the part relating to Yehudah, you cannot make a serious case for it reflecting that tribe's leadership. Very clearly, the Yehudah referred to here is isolated and apart from his brothers. Moshe already saw in Yehudah the seeds for separatism. Its territory was large and choice in many ways. It would seek to establish itself independently of its brethren (which is what happened to a large degree). Moshe hoped for a restoration and reconciliation. This did occur, when David was named king of both Yehudah and Yisrael, but it did not last long, because first Shelomo and then his son Rechavam literally spat in the face of Israel.

Blessings are not prophecy in the Bible. Moshe's blessings, like Ya'akov's, are musings about possibilities based upon current information, not future knowledge. The only reality they reflect is the reality of the moment, not of tomorrow.

As to whether the fates of people are predetermined by the tribes to which they belong, they are not, with the obvious exception of tribal interest. If the economy of a tribe is based on shipping, for example, tribal members are likely to be involved in shipping or a support industry. If the land you are in cannot grow wine grapes, you are not likely to become a grower of vineyards.

The gene pool of each tribe was Ya'akov's gene pool, not the individual tribal founders, because there was considerable intermarriage between tribes. That this was true even in Moshe's day also would seem to be confirmed by the daughters of the Tselophchad incident; if tribal intermarriage was infrequent or unknown, the tribal elders would not have been so concerned about losing tribal land.

Finally, the question of whether the blessings of Moshe are still in force is obviously moot. They never were in force. And even if they had been for a time, "let Reuven live and not die" is sufficient to declare the blessings no longer operative, since Reuven is dead and buried.

Moshe was our greatest teacher and our greatest prophet. Not everything he said in his life was meant to teach us anything and not every prediction he made was the result of divine prophecy. Moshe was flesh and blood. He had a mind of his own and he exercised it often (perhaps once too often, given God's refusal to let him enter the land).

He loved his people, and he worried about their future. Reuven suffered great losses because of the revolt of Datan and Aviram. The tribe is already beginning to disappear even before entering Canaan; Moshe prays for it to survive. Yehudah is already becoming haughty and independent; Moshe prays that it wises up and remembers that it is part of a greater unit than a mere tribe.

In other words, Moshe's blessings are hopes and desires, not prophecy. To insist that they are prophecy is to diminish Moshe's stature as a prophet, and that is not fair to the "father" of all true prophets.

Joseph Ozarowski

What I am about to share with you was developed by my *shiur* (study group), which included congregants, family members, and our guests from Yeshiva University and Stern College. We discussed these questions on *Simchat Torah* afternoon, to the extent that we were not too tired from the dancing or too drunk from the liquor. Thus, this is a group response and a fitting conclusion to both the High Holiday season and a year of exciting journeys into the weekly *sidra* via your faxed questions.

There are several questions in your paragraph; let us deal with the simple ones first. First: in 31:1, the Torah says, "And Moses went. . . ." Where did he go? Moses, according to many commentaries, really went to bless each person individually (see *Kli Yakar*, Ramban, Ibn Ezra, and S'forno on this).

Second: Moses also blessed the group as a whole after the tribal blessings (33:28–29): "And Israel will dwell in safety . . . in a land of grain and wine. . . . Happy are you, O Israel, who is like you, a people saved by the Lord . . . ?"

Third: as far as other categorizations, at that time in the desert, there simply was no other categorization. The people of Israel were now for forty years well organized by tribe, so why not blessings by tribe, as well?

The two main questions here relate to the connection of Moses' blessings to Jacob's blessings, and what all these tell us today. Of course, people's individual fates are not determined by tribal genealogy. But a basic theme of rabbinic thought is *Ma'aseh avot siman labanim*, "the Ancestors' doings are a sign (or guidepost) for their children." There were certain qualities that each tribe had. Jacob alluded to them in his blessings, though his tone was rather negative at times. Moses, editor and transmitter of the Torah, certainly knew Jacob's blessings well; he used the framework of tribal qualities to bless Jacob's descendants in a more positive way.

However, we decided that there must be a deeper connection between Moses and Jacob. In fact, Moses hints at this in his introduction to the blessings (33:4): "Torah tziva lanu Moshe, morasha kehilat Ya'akov," "The Torah commanded to us by Moshe is a heritage of the community of Jacob." (And we often sing this song a lot on Simchat Torah!) Moses' blessings, his death, and the Jewish people's entry in the Land of Israel mark the end of a cycle begun by Jacob and his deathbed blessings.

Upon Jacob's death, the sons began to grow from families into tribes. They were subsequently enslaved, suffering greatly. They were freed and redeemed by God, taken across the Red Sea, given the Torah, and turned into a people. And now, with the blessings, the circle has been completed.

This is not the only level of connection. The arrangement of the tribes in the desert, which was taking place for the last time in history to receive Moses' blessings, was based in the arrangement around Jacob's death bed and the arrangement around his casket. (See *Midrash Bamidbar Rabba* 2:8. When Moshe doubts the success of the desert encampments in the second year after the Exodus, God responds, "They already have an image, a previous plan from Jacob. . . .") Jacob says goodbye to his family for the last time with this arrangement. Now Moses says goodbye to the assembled tribes, "his extended family," knowing that this will be the last time in history the entire Jewish family will be together with this ordering.

After this point, they will be on their own and disperse all over the Promised Land. A thousand years later, they will be dispersed by forced exile throughout the Middle East; years after that, all over the world. Only in our generation have we seen the dispersed exiles coming back together again in the Land of Israel. We can view this development as a precursor to the coming of the Messiah, speedily and in our days, that will bring our extended family back together again and once more close the circle.

Is there an important message in the idea of tribal blessings for us? Ten out of the tribes were for all purposes lost after the Assyrian destruction of the North of Israel about 2,700 years ago. The rest lost their tribal ancestry after the Babylonian destruction of the First Temple 2,500 years ago. In essence, most of us (with the exception of *Kohanim*, priests and Levites) do not know our tribal ancestry. So, until the dispersed and lost tribes are found and reunited by the Messiah, the actual blessings will have to remain metaphoric for us.

But Moses' blessings, based on Jacob's, remind us that there can be blessing in diversity. We are all so different from each other. We all have strengths (as Moses pointed out) and weaknesses (as Jacob pointed out). Yet, we are all part of *Klal Yisrael*, the corporate body of the Jewish people. We need to look at the blessings we can each share with our people. We also need to find each others' blessings because we need each other.

If we can accomplish these things, then Moses' blessings can still be in effect today. And maybe this is the inner meaning of why we end the major holiday season by dancing with the Torahs and reading Moses' blessings.

David Sofian

Midrash B'reishit Rabbah 100:12 applies to your question. Referring to Jacob, *B'reishit* 49:28 tells us that "their father" addressed the sons as the tribes of Israel. The midrash wonders why this verse says "their father" instead of "Jacob." *B'reishit Rabbah* answers by indicating that "father" here is a hint, pointing to another man, a father of Israel, who will bless Israel. This other "father" is Moses in our current parshah.

The midrash specifically teaches that Moses commences where Jacob left off. I take this to mean the coherence of the Torah's narrative is being emphasized. We are to see that there is but one continuous story, regardless of its various stages. Using this midrash as a basis, Moses' blessing of the tribes as tribes represents the narrative's continuity.

As a liberal rabbi, I accept the premise of biblical criticism, that the Torah was not written as a single piece but came about over time from varying sources. However, we must also recognize that the Torah we now have *is* the Torah. God is to be found in the text as we have it. This is the significant lesson the above midrash focuses on. Recognizing this coherence is essential.

This said, I think you concluded too quickly that Moses didn't bless the entire group, the whole people. After all, does the parshah not begin with Moses referring to the entirety of the people? As Ramban tells us, chapter 33:4 means that the Torah is a permanent possession of Israel, passed on from generation to generation.

What greater statement of blessing could there have been, then, to the people as a whole, or for that matter to us now, than to exclaim they had been gifted with the possession of Torah? Clearly, Moses begins his blessing addressing the people as a whole and then moves to express the continuity described above by speaking to each tribe.

Moses' address to the entire people can also be seen in verse 26 when he speaks to Jeshurun, a collective name. This continues in verses 27–29. Moses concludes his words to Israel, as a group, by displaying his feelings of love and praise for them in reminding them that God is their refuge, and that they are people delivered by God, who continues to protect them from their enemies.

You also ask whether the notion of tribes and tribal traits continues for us today. I think the answer must be absolutely not. Above, I maintained that the Torah must be studied as a coherent document. Even so, we must also see the historical development and progress of the Jewish people and of Judaism. The Jewish people and Judaism have grown and matured. We have long outgrown any meaningful notion of tribes. This is an aspect of our past that remains in our past. That is as it should be.

And with that, we say, *Chazak, chazak, v'nitchazek,* and let us return to the beginning.

About the Authors

Shammai Engelmayer is rabbi of the Conservative Lake Hopatcong Jewish Community Center in Hopatcong, New Jersey, and teaches Judaica in adult education programs. He has spent much of his life as a journalist, including serving as executive editor of *The Jewish Week*. His writings garnered him several awards, including three from the American Jewish Press Association and the Washington Journalism Center's Thomas L. Stokes Award for National Reporting. In addition to his rabbinic and teaching duties, he is currently the news editor of the *New Jersey News* (formerly the *MetroWest Jewish News*), and is the author of seven nonfiction books. He is married, has three children and six grandchildren, and lives in Teaneck, New Jersey.

Joseph S. Ozarowski studied at Yeshivat Sha'alvim in Israel, received his rabbinic ordination from Hebrew Theological College, Skokie, Illinois, and his doctorate from Lancaster Theological Seminary, Lancaster, Pennsylvania. He is the author of *To Walk in God's Ways—Jewish Pastoral Perspectives on Illness and Bereavement* as well as numerous articles. Rabbi Ozarowski has served pulpits in Pennsylvania, California, and the Midwest and currently is rabbi of the Elmont Jewish Center in Elmont, New York. He is a national officer of the Rabbinical Council of America and serves as rabbinic consultant to the National Center for Jewish Healing. He lives in Long Island, New York with his wife, Ashira, and their children, Eli, Shalom, Chani, and Ralph.

David M. Sofian is the spiritual leader of Emanuel Congregation of Chicago, Illinois. He received his education from the University of Missouri, Columbia and Hebrew Union College–Jewish Institute of Religion, Cincinnati. He is the preparer of several booklets of teachers' materials for Ktav Books. Rabbi Sofian currently serves on the Chair of the Admissions Committee of the Central Conference of American Rabbis. He resides in the Chicago area with his wife, Dr. Simone L. Sofian, and their children, Joshua, Nehama, and Aaron.

About the Editor

Steve Lipman, a staff reporter for *The Jewish Week*, is the author of *Laughter in Hell: The Use of Humor During the Holocaust*. He graduated from the State University of New York at Buffalo and received his master's degree from Ball State University. He was awarded fellowships from both the National Journalism Center and the John McCloy Foundation. Mr. Lipman has contributed stories to several publications, including *The New York Times* and *Newsday*. He has been a frequent student at Ohr Somayach Yeshiva in Monsey, New York.